SAT Math: Master Guide to Hard Problems Volume 1

Number Theory __ Algebra __ Functions __ Complex Math __ and More

Subject Reviews... 800+ Problems...
Detailed Solutions... Explained Like a Tutor

By Dr. C. Hamilton

Copyright © 2019 by Dr. C. Hamilton

All rights reserved. No part of the book may be reproduced, stored in a retrieval system, transmitted in any form or by any means, electronic, mechanical, photocopying, recording, or otherwise, except as may be expressly permitted by the applicable copyright statutes or in writing by the author.

ISBN: 9781080599806

Contents

Introduction for Volumes 1 & 2 1
Subjects Covered 2
Chapter Organization 2
Plans of Study 4
To The Instructor 5
Nature of the Test 6

Chapter 1 Multiples, Factors, Fractions, and Remainders 9
Don't Show Up Without Knowing… 10
Quick Review and Definitions 11
SAT Archetypes 17
      Remainder Analysis 17
      Divisibility and Least Common Multiples 18
      Arithmetic Operations on Units Digits 19
      Factors of a Product of Primes 20
      Factors of Algebraic Expressions 21
      Prime Factor Analysis of a Number 22
Practice Problems 23
Practice Problem Hints 27
Practice Problem Solutions 29

Chapter 2 Number Theory and Integers 35
Don't Show Up Without Knowing… 36
Quick Review and Definitions 37
SAT Archetypes 41
      Algebraic Equations With Integer Variables 41
      Integer Inequalities 42
      One Integer Equation With Two Unknowns 43
      Range of Integers Satisfying Algebraic Inequalities 44
      Algebraic Expressions With Even and Odd Integers 45

Algebraic Expressions Constrained to Integer Values 46
  Counting Equally-Spaced Integers Within An Interval 47
  Distributing Objects into Groups of Different Sizes 48
  Linear Combinations of Two Different Size Sets 49
  Integer Equations Involving Roots and Powers 50
Practice Problems 53
Practice Problem Hints 59
Practice Problem Solutions 61

Chapter 3 Digit Manipulations 69
Don't Show Up Without Knowing.. 70
Quick Review and Definitions 70
SAT Archetypes... 71
  Integer Decomposition into Powers-Of-Ten.. 71
  Transposition of Digits: AB ↔ BA 72
  One Number With Mystery Digits 73
  Two Numbers With Mystery Digits 74
  How Many Integers Satisfy Digit Constraints 75
  Properties of Units Digits 76
Practice Problems 77
Practice Problem Hints 80
Practice Problem Solutions 81

Chapter 4 Percent Calculations 85
Don't Show Up Without Knowing.. 86
Quick Review and Definitions 87
SAT Archetypes... 89
  Percent of One Kind in a Set of Two Kinds 89
  Algebraic Relationships Involving Percents and Ratios 90
  Calculating an Unknown Percent With Two Constraints 91
  Percent Increase and Subsequent Decrease 92
  Sales Commissions Expressed Algebraically 93
  Markup Required for a Certain Profit 94

Compound Interest 95
Interest Compounded Quarterly 96
Practice Problems 97
Practice Problem Hints 102
Practice Problem Solutions 103

Chapter 5 Ratios, Shares, and Totals 107

Quick Review and Definitions 108
SAT Archetypes 111
A Ratio Determines the Possible Totals 111
Share of Expenses Among Several Persons 112
Unknown Ratio, Given Two Combined Sets 113
Ratios, When Objects Are Added or Taken Away 114
Exact Total, Given Ratios and the Number of One Kind 115
Determine Number of Members of Two Combined Sets 116
Practice Problems 117
Practice Problem Hints 121
Practice Problem Solutions 123

Chapter 6 Average, Median, and Mode 129

Don't Show Up Without Knowing… 130
Quick Review and Definitions 131
SAT Archetypes 133
Expressing Averages in Terms of Other Averages 133
Properties of a Sequence, Given the Median 134
Properties of an Arithmetic Sequence, Given the Average 134
Median and Average of a Set That Changes 135
Mode and Average, Given Ratios Among Members 136
Combined Averages of Two Different Sets 137
Extreme Values Possible, Given The Average 138
Practice Problems 141
Practice Problem Hints 147
Practice Problem Solutions 149

Chapter 7 Rates and Dimensional Analysis 155

Don't Show Up Without Knowing 156

Quick Review and Definitions 157

SAT Archetypes 161

    Final Distance, Given Two Perpendicular Trajectories 161

    Algebraic Expression of Average Speed 162

    Algebraic Expression of the Average of Speeds 163

    Rate Calculation Requiring Unit Conversions 164

    Round Trip Travel Time At Multiple Speeds 165

    Labor Performed by People Working at Different Rates 166

    Project Duration Based on a Compound Rate 167

Practice Problems 169

Practice Problem Hints 177

Practice Problem Solutions 179

Chapter 8 Sequences 187

Don't Show Up Without Knowing 188

Quick Review and Definitions 189

SAT Archetypes 193

    Sequence Transforms 193

    Arithmetic Sequences: Symmetry About Zero 194

    Algebraic Relationships Between Sequence Terms 195

    Finding The nth Term in a Repetitive Sequence 196

    Properties of Sequences, Given Averages 197

    Deriving Relationships Between Sequence Terms 198

    Properties of a Sequence, Given the Formula 199

    Sums of Arithmetic Sequences 200

    Arithmetic Sequences: Find a Term, Given Other Terms 201

    Inferring the Formula of a Sequence From a Few Terms 202

    Calculating Terms in a Recursive Sequence 203

    Odd / Even Properties Of Arithmetic Sequences 204

Practice Problems 205

Practice Problem Hints 213

Practice Problem Solutions 215

Chapter 9 Inequalities, Absolute Values, and Extreme Values 221

Don't Show Up Without Knowing… 222

Quick Review and Definitions 223

SAT Archetypes 225

    Number Lines With Confusing Scales 225

    Greatest or Least Algebraic Expression 226

    Ranking Algebraic Expressions, Given Inequalities 227

    Algebraic Inequalities Involving Absolute Values 228

    Real-World Inequalities 229

Practice Problems 231

Practice Problem Hints 233

Practice Problem Solutions 235

Chapter 10 Exponents 237

Don't Show Up Without Knowing… 238

Quick Review and Definitions 239

SAT Archetypes 241

    Factoring Exponential Expressions 241

    Evaluating Complicated Exponential Expressions 242

    Determining an Exponential Model 243

    Signs In Exponential Expressions 244

    Inequalities Involving Exponential Expressions 245

    Expressing Equations in a Common Base 246

    Compound Interest 247

    Identifying a Mathematical Model that Fits Data 248

Practice Problems 249

Practice Problem Hints 255

Practice Problem Solutions 257

Chapter 11 Algebra and Real-World Problems.........................265

- Don't Show Up Without Knowing.. 266
- Quick Review and Definitions 267
- SAT Archetypes... 277
  - Translating Verbal Algebra Into Symbolic Math...277
  - Word Problems: Confusing Additions and Subtractions 278
  - Direct Algebraic Substitution 279
  - Brute-Force Algebraic Isolation 280
  - Raising Both Sides by the Inverse Power..281
  - Algebraic Common Denominators...282
  - Inverse Proportionality 283
  - Direct Proportionality, With Two Unknowns...284
  - Dividing One Variable by Another to Solve for the Ratio 285
  - Algebraic Relationships: Simpler Than They Look 286
  - Joint Variation 287
  - Combined Variation...288
  - Calculating $x^2 - y^2$ from $(x + y)$ and $(x - y)$ 289
  - Relationship Between $x^2 - y^2$, and the Average of x and y 290
  - Equating Coefficients of the Same Powers of x..291
  - Quadratic Equations with Change of Variables 292
  - Quadratic Equations Solved with Quadratic Formula 293
  - Polynomial Division (1)..294
  - Polynomial Division (2)..295
  - Polynomial Factoring (1) 296
  - Polynomial Factoring (2) 297
  - Higher Order Polynomials 298
  - Solving Cubic Equations 299
  - Quadratic Inequalities 300
  - Simultaneous Equations with Absolute Values: Unmixed.................................302
  - Inequalities Involving Absolute Values and Exponents.....................................303
- Practice Problems 305
- Practice Problem Hints 317
- Practice Problem Solutions... 321

Chapter 12 Simultaneous Equations 333

Don't Show Up Without Knowing… 334

Quick Review and Definitions 335

SAT Archetypes 341

      Direct Substitution 341

      Interpreting Verbal Simultaneous Equations 342

      Real World Simultaneous Equations 343

      Base Cost And Rate From Two Data Points 344

      Purchase of Two Types With Different Unit Costs (1) 345

      Purchase of Two Types With Different Unit Costs (2) 346

      Subsets With Two Different Sizes 347

      Purchase of Two Types With Different Unit Costs (3) 348

      Changing Ratios That Define Simultaneous Equations 350

      Two Equations With Three Variables (1) 351

      Two Equations With Three Variables (2) 352

      Two Equations With Three Variables (3) 353

      Simultaneous Equations Involving Absolute Values 354

      Simultaneous Equations With One Inequality 355

      Simultaneous Equations With Two Inequalities (1) 356

      Simultaneous Equations With Two Inequalities (2) 357

      Simultaneous Equations Involving Quadratics 358

      Simultaneous Equations with No Solution 359

Practice Problems 361

Practice Problem Hints 367

Practice Problem Solutions 369

Chapter 13 Functions 379

Don't Show Up Without Knowing… 380

Quick Review and Definitions 380

SAT Archetypes 393

      Determining the Vertex of a Quadratic Function 393

      Putting a Quadratic Function in Vertex Form 394

Vertex Form in Real World Scenarios 395
Greatest Integer Function..396
Range of a Function, Given the Domain..397
Exponential Function..398
Algebraic Expressions of Function Values 399
Finding The Zeroes Of A Quadratic Function 400
Determining A Function From Data 401
Absolute Value Functions...402
Functions of Two Variables: Special Constraints................................403
Equations With Symbolic Functions of Two Variables 404
Symbolic If-Then Functions..405
Quadratic Missile Trajectory: Simultaneous Equations......................406
Substitution of Variables 407
Functions of Functions 408

Practice Problems 409
Practice Problem Hints 415
Practice Problem Solutions... 417

Chapter 14 Transforms and Symmetry 423

Don't Show Up Without Knowing... 424
Quick Review and Definitions... 425
SAT Archetypes 427
Properties of a Function of a Function (1) 427
Properties of a Function of a Function (2) 428
Transformation of Variables: Evaluating Functions............................429
Linear Transforms..430
Transformation of Variables: Algebraic Expressions 431
Recognizing Transforms: Shifting and Flipping 432
Recognizing Transforms: Shifting, Flipping, Scaling.........................434
Reflection About a line of Symmetry 436

Practice Problems 439
Practice Problem Hints 442
Practice Problem Solutions 443

Chapter 15 Logic and Venn Diagrams 445

Don't Show Up Without Knowing… 446

Quick Review and Definitions 446

SAT Archetypes 451

    Shared Attributes Analysis with Venn Diagrams 451

    Venn Diagrams Filled With Some/None Attributes 452

    Logical Negation 454

    Confusing If-Then Relationships 455

Practice Problems 457

Practice Problem Hints 459

Practice Problem Solutions 461

Chapter 16 Complex Arithmetic and Algebra 465

Don't Show Up Without Knowing… 466

Quick Review and Definitions 467

SAT Archetypes 469

    Complex Addition 469

    Complex Multiplication 470

    Complex Division 471

    Complex Factoring 473

    Complex Simultaneous Equations 474

Practice Problems 475

Practice Problem Hints 477

Practice Problem Solutions 479

Chapter 17 Science, Engineering, and Business Problems 481

SAT Archetypes 483

    Kinetic Energy 483

    The Effects of Thermal Insulation 484

    Population Flows 485

    Geothermal Gradient 487

    Comparison of Different Cost Plans 488

- Cost Ratio of Ingredients to Final Products 489
- Splitting Costs Among People 490
- Changing Cost Per Person With More People 491
- Translating Limits into Absolute Value Expressions 492
- Duration of Travel, Given Change of Time Zones 493
- Exponential Behavior 494
- The Leaky Fluid Pump 495

Practice Problems 497
Practice Problem Hints 500
Practice Problem Solutions 501

Introduction

for Volumes 1 & 2

The goal of *SAT Math: Master Guide to Hard Problems* is to help good students get a top math score on the SAT. It is an exhaustive guide to the most difficult problems found on the test. This two-volume set is based on a thorough analysis of SAT specifications, published tests, prep books, websites, and the author's years of experience tutoring SAT students. It includes all subject areas and distills the scope of questions into archetypes of the most challenging math problems.

There are over 300 such archetypes covering every problem solving technique a student will need to score an 800. The framework of this guide is anchored on these archetypes. They form a basis set of problems designed to minimize the virtual distance between them and any math problem a student might encounter on the SAT.

Subject reviews are included <u>along with over 500 additional practice problems</u> that reinforce, fill in, and expand the areas covered by the archetypes. Practice problems do not simply recast the archetypes – almost all are unique variants. Some are very different from, and more difficult than, their corresponding archetypes. A few practice problems, identified by the signifier *CHALLENGE*, are more intricate or abstruse than similar problems on the SAT. However, these are great practice for the warrior class and require only the same basket of problem solving techniques needed for the test.

Over 800 problems are fully explored in these two volumes. They are very challenging for most students and would frequently be missed by those scoring less than 600 on the math section. Every problem includes a hint and a clear, detailed solution presented as a tutor might teach it from a white board.

This huge collection allows students and instructors to easily focus on shaky subjects.

<u>Unique to this set are the hundreds of alternate solutions</u> that illustrate shortcuts and clever methods that are less obvious, but save valuable time if employed. Their purpose is to impart creative intuition and insight into the many paths a solution may take.

With easy questions filtered out, volumes 1 and 2 contain enough hard problems for about 50 different SAT tests.

Introduction

Subjects Covered

Volume I

Multiples Factors Remainders	Rates / Dimensional Analysis	Functions
Number Theory and Integers	Sequences	Transforms and Symmetry
Digit Manipulation	Inequalities	Logic and Venn Diagrams
Percent Calculations	Exponents	Complex Algebra
Ratios Shares and Totals	Algebra / Real World Problems	Science/Engineering Problems
Average Median and Mode	Simultaneous Equations	Data Analysis

Volume II

Line Segments and Points	Angular Speed and Period	Permutations Combinations
Angles and Triangles	Rectangular Solids	Probability Theory
Rectangles and Triangles	Cylinders Prisms Spheres	Analyzing Geometric Figures
Polygons	Pyramids Cones	Basic Trigonometry
Circles and Sectors	Data Analysis and Flowcharts	Combinatorics Full Review
Circles and Polygons	Intersecting Graphs, Functions	Probability Full Review

Chapter Organization

Each chapter is organized into the following sections:

Don't Show Up Without Knowing

This section lists basic concepts and how-to skill sets that you should be familiar with on the day of the test.

Quick Review and Definitions

This section provides a concise review of the terms and concepts used to solve problems you'll see on the test. Simpler example problems are included here.

SAT Archetypes

The SAT Archetypes are presented in the following format:

The Question is written in the style of the SAT. Multiple choice and student response, or grid-in style questions, are included. The abbreviation SR indicates student response; on the SAT these questions require a numerical answer to be written in on the answer grid. In this book, students will just write their answers out – no grid or bubble forms are provided.

The SAT has two math sections: one that does not allow calculators and the other section that does allow calculators. Problems that allow calculators in this book will be indicated by 🖩 , while those forbidding calculators will be indicated by 🚫. Problems in this book are not organized by calculator permission, but rather by optimal subject order.

How do I start? is a section providing a boost into the problem when the path to the solution is obscure. More than a hint, this section gives a gentle push, often outlining the darkest parts of the problem that must be illuminated before the solution path is clear.

Solutions are very detailed. They are written to teach and to secure the lesson in memory. Solution steps are completely disclosed as if a teacher were at the white board.

Alternate solutions provide valuable second (and sometimes third and fourth) perspectives into the problems. Typically, the first solution presents the most straightforward, methodical path. Alternate solutions usually apply shortcuts and deeper relationships that help build mathematical savvy. Understood together, they impart an intuitive sense of the creative leaps often useful and occasionally required on the test.

The Take-Away section summarizes the central lessons of the archetype.

Practice Problems

Practice problems reinforce and expand on material covered in the archetypes. The most difficult problems in each chapter will often be found here.

Practice Problem Hints

Short hints to every practice problem are provided to get you started if you're stuck.

Practice Problem Solutions

Complete solutions to every practice problem are located at the end of each chapter. Many practice problems, just like the archetypes, come with alternate solutions that illuminate their several methods of approach.

Introduction

Plans of Study

Additional Resources

SAT Math: Master Guide to Hard Problems should be used in conjunction with official, retired SAT tests found in *The Official SAT Study Guide*. Practice using the retired tests will give you experience with their overall structure and time limits, as well as familiarity with question formats and the official bubble and grid forms. In addition to that book, there are lots of other SAT prep books, such as Kaplan and Princeton, that include good simulations of SAT tests. The website www.khanacademy.org/sat is also recommended as an instructional resource, although most content on that site is relatively easy for advanced students. The present volumes focus on the subjects and techniques necessary to attack the most aggressive math questions found on the test. Diligent study with several sources is suggested to optimize your score.

Master Guide: The Concentration Plan

There are so many hard problems in this collection that there are plenty in each subject area. Just need help with algebra, simultaneous equations, and probability? There are three chapters devoted to those topics, with subject reviews and 144 hard problems. Don't bother with complex math and triangles, for example, if you know those cold. You've only got so much time to prepare. But this note of warning: it will be necessary to see around corners to answer some questions, even in your star subjects. Spend all the time you can. Especially with algebra. The score you save may be your own.

Master Guide: The 16 Hour Plan

16 hours is the absolute bare-bones time commitment necessary to get through both volumes if you wish an overview of all subjects. Unless you are ignoring chapters and material in which you are already proficient, you'll only have time to:

- Skim the "Don't Show Up Without" and "Quick Review and Definitions" sections
- Attempt every archetype
- Quickly read the solutions and "The Take-Away" sections for the archetypes

This plan gives you about 3 minutes per archetype, which includes reading the question and solution(s). That isn't much time. There won't be time for you to profit from the additional practice problems at the end of each chapter. But it's much better than nothing.

Master Guide: The 48 Hour Plan

48 hours will allow enough time for you to thoroughly read the review material in both volumes and work all the archetypes and practice problems. You'll have time to:

- Read the "Don't Show Up Without" and "Quick Review and Definitions" sections
- Attempt every archetype
- Read the solution(s) and "The Take-Away" sections
- Attempt all the practice problems

This plan gives you almost 4 minutes per problem attempted. Still, that's a fast burn.

To the Student

- Consider reading each problem twice , underlining data and the question asked.
- All problems should be attempted first before reading the solutions.
- The alternate solutions often contain the most valuable tips for the test.
- Consult How-To-Start and Hint sections as needed - don't just read the solutions!
- Examine the choices – sometimes the only possible answer is easily determined.
- Equations and inequalities that restrict variables are referred to as *constraints*.

To The Instructor

- Evaluate each student carefully. The SAT Score Report is not very detailed.
- Algebra is everywhere and weighs more heavily in the test than any other subject.
- Some practice problems are excellent examples - they could have been archetypes.
- Homework should be assigned and given high priority. Review it with the student.
- The problems in each chapter are not necessarily organized by increasing difficulty.
- Most problems are devised and solved in ways that will not require a calculator.
- Session time division: 1/4 lecture, 1/2 student problem solving, 1/4 problem reviews.

Introduction

Nature of the Test

The Ugly Truth

Of course, the SAT tests a broad range of subjects taught in U.S. high schools: essay writing (optional), vocabulary, grammar, reading comprehension, etc., and math. The math sections cover number theory, algebra, geometry, combinatorics, probability, data analysis, complex numbers, trigonometry, and other subjects in between. However, beyond the dry subjects, there are other faculties and talents that are tested on the SAT.

Speed

Except for take-home tests, every test you've taken in your life has had some time limit. The 10-minute pop quiz and the 2-hour final exam are typically designed so that every student who knows the material will be able to complete the test.

This is not the case with the SAT. The no-calculator math section allows 25 minutes to complete 20 questions. The calculator section allows 55 minutes to complete 38 questions. This gives students an average of ~83 seconds per question. The sections are arranged in ascending order of difficulty – the easy ones will take less time than average. Harder problems may not only take more steps to complete, but may (in the words of Shakespeare) puzzle the will, forcing many students to make several unsuccessful attempts before a solution is found, further eroding the remaining time.

Gaining speed in solving math problems can be achieved in several ways. First, practice with a stopwatch and/or timer: it will force you to hurry before the bomb goes off, so to speak. If you know that a timer chime will chime soon, you'll tend move fast and think fast. This is a skill that can be trained and improved through practice.

Second, test taking speed and concentration can be improved by increasing what might be referred to as *cerebral velocity*. As you approach each math problem, the right pieces of the puzzle have to click into place before a solution path is apparent. The rate at which a problem is solved depends on the rate at which potential solution pieces are fetched, discarded, selected, and placed to form a path. While this rate varies from person to person, problem to problem, and from good days to bad days, your cerebral velocity *can* be revved up at will. By mindfully psyching yourself up into a quicker mental state, your mental processes will flow more rapidly. Take a pause prior to beginning each section of the test to calm down, focus, and start the train of your mind down the tracks, slow at first, and then faster and faster in your imagination. By engaging the figurative wheels in your head with increasing speed, at the end of that pause you will be better able to begin each section and problem at cruise speed.

Third, by practicing with problems in this book and tests in *The Official SAT Study Guide*, you will become better able to ignore mental distractions and gain a state of natural flow. Unless you come from Planet X, some hard questions will naturally cause you to slam on the brakes at first. Our minds tend to panic in these situations. Mother can't help you here. A state of panic will cause you to momentarily lose focus and energy. Somewhere between your brain and the printed page is a path to the answer. If you concentrate, cut out extraneous feelings, and zone-in on the universe of the problem, more of your mind will be efficiently employed. Train yourself to identify those mental states you should avoid and those states leading to greater concentration and flow. Watch and learn from yourself.

Reading Comprehension in Math Problems

Yup. In the math sections too. Some questions present long paragraphs of background information. A few problems could be more clearly written, but are not – perhaps on purpose. Therefore, don't hack every math problem at blinding speed. This is another reason to focus on the problem. Lots of problems are missed because students misinterpret data, assume the problem is asking for a different unknown, or stop at some important intermediate result in the calculation and choose that as the answer.

As a simple example of the latter, consider the isosceles triangle below:

If $y = 120$, and $y \neq 3x$, what is $3x$? Since the sum of the interior angles equals 180 (and since this is an isosceles triangle), the governing equation must be $180 = 120 + 3x + 3x$. Simplifying, $60 = 6x$, and so $10 = x$. Quite a few students will blow it here and choose 10 as the answer. But the question asked for the value of $\underline{3x}$, so the answer is 30. Take care.

Math questions can sometimes be purposefully confusing. Speed your mind up to a rapid, but controlled flow. You may find it helpful to read the question twice: once for an overview and a second time to underline critical data and the desired unknown value or expression.

Why Would They *Do* That?

The SAT tests academic prowess. These aren't just subject tests. The College Board provides those as well. The subject tests are primarily designed to test knowledge in their respective fields. The SAT does this too, but it also provides a profile of the student's ability to accurately answer questions under fire. We've discussed the need for speed and reading accuracy. However, what makes a really hard SAT math problem difficult is that every path to its solution is obscure. Some problems, and you'll encounter many of them in this guide, can only be solved by applying conventional math in unconventional ways.

Introduction

The Curve

The SAT is designed to have a wide variance about the average score. Moreover, the scope of the test is limited. There are no questions involving higher math. If they didn't pack 58 math problems into 80 minutes, the test would skew top-heavy – there would be too many high scorers. Consider yourself lucky in this respect: the original SAT given in 1926 had 315 questions and a 90 minute time limit. That's 17 seconds per question!

What the Best Colleges Look For

One might smile and say that the best colleges look for the best students who will grow into successful adults and become generous alumni. They certainly *are* looking for the most successful students – students who will be able to take full advantage of the academic and social environment provided by the school. Great students also enrich each other – and the faculty. But of central concern to undergraduate administrators is the reputation of the school, expressed and promoted most directly by its graduates. A university claiming to be selective in admissions could hardly be given high regard if its graduates go on to lead lives of low achievement.

If a school wants successful graduates, it had better use measures that predict future success. Entrance exams aren't the only metrics, of course. Grades, essays, extra-curricular activities, and alumni recommendations count too. However, an SAT score can provide direct insight into a person's ability to *process* – to perform without error under novel, stressful conditions. Complex business endeavors and software releases can infamously fail from what seem like tiny oversights. An attorney who overlooks a strategically place comma that significantly alters the client's intention may be on the hook for any loss. Astronauts in the early space program were subjected to countless tests verifying their ability to think, to follow instructions, to understand garbled transmissions, and to process unexpected situations – all while hungry, thirsty, sleep deprived, and spinning out of control in a spacecraft simulator.

You did well? Step *this* way.

The Big BUT Show

"*Aaand* folks, over *here* we have the Ga-*raaate* Pyramid. Age-old, massive testament – the veritable image of Society's hierarchy. Just *look* up there. Note the very few blocks near the top. *Why so few?* Solid geometry, Junior. They measure the Earth up there. Indeed, yes. Now folks, imagine yourselves *at* that *very top*, looking out over the horizon. Picture it. The commanding height, the balmy breeze. Big BUT: as far as you can see, there are no guarantees."

Click. Now what? You're a teenager. Go to a good school. Grab everything it has to offer. It'll improve your view, your story, your clout, and your chance at a sweet, long ride.

Chapter 1

Multiples, Factors, Fractions, and Remainders

At first glance the concepts in this chapter might seem trivial. *Trivial*, by the way, derives from the Latin noun *trivium,* "the place where the three roads meet," a sublime, even mystical description that conjures the image of a venerable, prosperous nexus of ancient peoples, cultures, and commerce. Yet such places would inevitably attract beggars and other undesirables, who would squat, mess, panhandle, rob, and generally ruin the neighborhood for the neighbors who came before. The word devolved into a disparaging insult. Much later still, as a droll joke by upperclassmen, *trivium* became the name for the set of three basic courses given to first year students at medieval European universities – to the lowly blow-ins, so to speak. Freshmen. From the sublime to the ridiculous.

It's been years since multiples, factors, fractions, and remainders were covered in depth for most of you, and the SAT will occasionally select questions that require the use of these concepts in unconventional ways for their solutions.

There are 6 archetypes of difficult questions on the SAT that center on these subjects. In this chapter you will refresh the concepts, learn the archetypes, and practice 19 additional problems.

Multiples, Factors, Fractions, Remainders   Chapter 1

Don't Show Up Without Knowing...

These Concepts

- Multiple
- Least Common Multiple
- Remainder
- Factor

- Greatest Common Factor
- Prime Numbers less than 100
- Prime Factors of a number
- Rational and Irrational Numbers

These Relationships

- $\frac{N}{D}$, with remainder R, means that k•D + R = N (where N, D, k, and R are integers).

- $\frac{N}{D}$ has a cyclic pattern of remainders for increasing N and fixed D.

- A^B results in a cyclic pattern of the units digit as B increases.

How To...

- Calculate and use the least common multiple
- Calculate and use the greatest common factor
- Calculate the prime factors of a number
- Calculate remainders using a calculator
- Use the cyclic properties of remainders to solve problems
- Manipulate fractions: simplify, invert, convert to decimal, etc.

Chapter 1 Multiples, Factors, Fractions, Remainders

Quick Review and Definitions

The SAT frequently uses integer values in the math sections because many problems and their answers can be readily expressed in terms of integers. This sometimes enables in-your-head math for those inclined to do so.

Multiples

An integer multiple of x is n•x, where n is an integer. For example, multiples of 2.5 include 0, 2.5, 5, ... and also -2.5, -5, ... This concept also applies to algebraic expressions. For example, 2x+6 is a multiple of x+3 because 2x+6 = 2(x+3). In this chapter, we will use the terms "multiple" and "integer multiple" interchangeably.

Remainders

The remainder is the integer left over after division when one integer does not evenly divide into another integer. This is 3rd grade math, but constant use of calculators may obscure such properties and how they can be used. For example, 11 divided by 3 yields 3, with a remainder of 2. There are two *thirds* left over. The complete division is $3\frac{2}{3}$.

Remainder Analysis

In the above example, "11 divided by 3 yields 3, with a remainder of 2," can be algebraically expressed as 3•3 + 2 = 11. In general, d•m + R = n, where the numerator is n, the denominator is d, the number of times d can go into n is m, and the remainder is R. This decomposition equation representing integer division may be necessary when solving some remainder problems.

Remainders may be manually calculated using your calculator. As an example, what is the remainder of 1023 divided by 24? The division by calculator yields 42.625. Subtract the integer part of the answer, 42, yielding .625. Multiplying this by the divisor yields 24 • .625 = 15. This is the remainder.

Some calculators, such as the TI-84 plus, have a remainder function.

The remainder must always be less than the divisor.

Multiples, Factors, Fractions, Remainders   Chapter 1

If n and d are integers, and d divides evenly into n, then d also divides evenly into m•n, where m is a nonzero integer.

Likewise, if each term in a sum has no remainder when divided by the same divisor, then the sum will have no remainder when divided by that same divisor.

Imagine fixing the value of the denominator and letting the value of the numerator increase sequentially. In doing so, the remainder cycles through a repetitive sequence of values. For example, if the denominator is 3, the value of the remainder will cycle through a sequence of numbers as the numerator increases. 3 divided into 10, 11, 12, 13, 14… yields remainders of 1, 2, 0, 1, 2…. Again, the remainder is always less than the divisor.

If a number is divided by 10, the remainder is equal to the units digit of the number.

If a number is divided by 9, the remainder will be the repeating decimal digits resulting from the division. For example, 121/9 = 13.4444…, and therefore the remainder is 4.

Factors

If $\frac{n}{d}$ is an integer (no remainder), then d is a factor of n. For example, the factors of -4 are -4, -2, -1, 1, 2, and 4. On the SAT, factors will most often refer to the *positive* factors.

On the SAT, the term *divisible by* implies a remainder of zero after division, also called *evenly divisible*. If a is divisible by b, then b is a factor of a; a = n•b, where n is an integer.

If integers a and b have a common factor of c, then c will be a factor of a+b and a-b.

If a number m has factors a, b, and c, then the number n•m, where n is an integer, will have factors a, b, and c, *and* n•a, n•b, and n•c (and more if n is not prime). For example, 15 has factors 1,3,5,15, and so 2•15 = 30 will have factors 1,3,5,15, *and* 2,6,10, and 30.

Greatest Common Factor

Greatest common factoring is useful in simplifying algebraic equations. The greatest common factor (GCF) of two or more integers can often be found by hand: list the factors of each number, find those in common to all the integers, then find the greatest of those. Example: find the GCF of 18 and 30. The factors of 18 are 1, 2, 3, 6, 9, and 18. The factors of 30 are 1, 2, 5, 6, 15, and 30. The GCF of 18 and 30 is 6.

There is also a method of calculating the GCF that employs prime factorization (see below). First, find all the prime factors of each integer. Then find all the prime factors these integers have in common. The GCF is the product of these common prime factors.

In the example above, the prime factors of 18 are 2, 3, and 3. The prime factors of 30 are 2, 3, and 5. The common primes are 2 and 3, and the GCF equals their product, 6.

Consider the expression (24x + 36y + 48z). The coefficients are all multiples of their greatest common factor, 12. The factor of 12 can be pulled out of the parenthesis to yield the equivalent factored expression 12•(2x + 3x + 4z).

GCF can be used to factor variables out of expressions. For example, (xy + x^2) = x(y + x).

Least Common Multiple

Consider two numbers, 18 and 30. The multiples of 18 and 30 are sometimes identical – these are the common multiples. For example, multiples of 18 are 36, 54, 72, 90, 108…, and multiples of 30 are 60, 90, 120… The least common multiple (LCM) is 90.

There is a method to calculate the LCM of two numbers. First, find the GCF of the two numbers (see above). Divide the first number by this GCF, then multiply this by the second number. This product is the LCM. For example, the GCF of 18 and 30 is 6. Divide 18 by 6 gives 3. Multiply 3 by 30 gives 90, the LCM of 18 and 30.

One important feature of a least common multiple is divisibility. In the above example, *only* multiples of 90 will be evenly divisible by both 18 and 30. The LCM of a set of denominators can be used to form the least, or lowest, common denominator.

Fractions and Decimal Numbers

The SAT (and this book) assumes you are at ease with the following operations:

- Arithmetic operations with fractions (adding, multiplying, inverting, exponents, etc.)

- Finding the least common denominator among a set of fractions using LCM

- Expressing a mixed number, for example, $4\frac{2}{3}$, as an improper fraction, $\frac{14}{3}$

- Reducing fractions to the lowest terms ($\frac{3}{15} = \frac{1}{5}$)

- Simplifying fraction expressions, for example, $\frac{2}{3} / \frac{6}{16}$ = 32/18 = 16/9

- Converting fractions to their decimal number equivalents. For example, $\frac{7}{8}$ = .875.

- Converting decimal numbers to their fraction equivalents. For example, .6 = 3/5.

Multiples, Factors, Fractions, Remainders — Chapter 1

Converting Decimals to Fractions with a Calculator

Many graphing calculators have a fraction function that enables conversion from a number in decimal format to a fraction. Occasionally, in multiple choice problems, the answer choices will all be fractions, but the answer you calculate may be in decimal form. It may be quicker to use your calculator (if allowed) to convert from decimal to fraction if the answer is not a common fraction.

Many answer choices in this book are purposefully written as fractions instead of decimal representations should students wish to solve problems without a calculator.

Rational Numbers

A rational number is a number that can be expressed as the ratio of two integers, $\frac{n}{d}$. In decimal form, such numbers may be represented with either a finite number of digits (1/4 = .25), or an infinite sequence of repeating digits (5/11 = .45454…). Irrational numbers cannot be represented as the ratio of two integers. The properties of rational and irrational numbers aren't on the test, but the concepts help to bring order to integer math.

Prime Numbers

Prime numbers are integers greater than 1 that can only be divided evenly by themselves and 1. In other words, a prime has no factors other than 1 and itself. The SAT may have one or two questions for which recognizing and working with prime numbers is essential.

Since there is no formula or pattern for prime numbers, problems involving prime numbers usually rely on trial-and-error solution methods.

The only even prime is 2.

It'd be wise to memorize, or be able to recognize on sight, all prime numbers up to 109:

2	3	5	7	13	17	19
23	29	31	37	41	43	47
53	59	61	67	71	73	79
83	89	97	101	103	107	109

Chapter 1												Multiples, Factors, Fractions, Remainders

Prime Factorization

Prime factorization of an integer results in a set of prime factors for that integer: when these factors are multiplied together the result is the original number. 18 has the prime factors 2, 3, and 3. The prime factor decomposition of 18 yields 2 • 3 • 3 = 18.

There is an algorithm (mathematical method) for determining the set of prime factors for any positive integer. Start dividing the number as shown below by the smallest prime number, 2, and continue until 2 will not divide evenly. Repeat with 3, and then larger primes as needed: 5, 7, 11, …

Example: find the prime factors of 6552 by prime factorization. The following table represents the outcome of sequential divisions by increasing primes as described above. Prime factorization of 6552 gives the set 2,2,2,3,3,7,and 13. That is, $6522 = 2^3 \cdot 3^2 \cdot 7^1 \cdot 13^1$. As seen below, 6552/2 = 3276, 3276/2 = 1638, 1638/2 = 819, 819/3 = 273, …

6552

Divide By	Result
2	3276
2	1638
2	819
3	273
3	91
7	13
13	1

Number of Factors

The total number of factors of an integer has a formula that might be useful. First, perform prime factor analysis. Add one to each exponent of the prime factors. Then multiply these terms to give the number of factors. In the example above, $6522 = 2^3 \cdot 3^2 \cdot 7^1 \cdot 13^1$. Adding one to each exponent and multiplying gives (3+1)(2+1)(2)(2) = 48 factors of 6522.

It is *highly* unlikely that finding the number of factors of such a large number will be needed on the SAT. Yet, this simple method of calculating the number of factors may be used to verify quick hand calculations for even small numbers.

Example: how many factors does 65 have? The prime factors are 5 and 13. So their exponents are 1 and 1, respectively. Adding one to each exponent and multiplying these yields 2 • 2 = 4 factors of 65. It's true: the factors of 65 are 1, 5, 13, and 65.

Multiples, Factors, Fractions, Remainders   Chapter 1

Divisibility Patterns

The SAT may rarely test students' ability to discern the divisibility properties of a number. While knowing such patterns may not be necessary to solve a problem, this knowledge can sometimes help eliminate answer choices quickly. You know most of these already:

- Divisible by 2   Even (last digit is 0,2,4,6, or 8).
- Divisible by 3   Sum of all digits is divisible by 3
- Divisible by 4   Last two digits together divisible by 4 (e.g., *16* in 11*16*)
- Divisible by 5   Last digit is 0 or 5.
- Divisible by 6   Divisible by both 2 and 3
- Divisible by 8   Last three digits divisible by 8 (e.g., *072* in 7*072*)
- Divisible by 9   Sum of all digits is divisible by 9
- Divisible by 10   Last digit is 0

Cyclic Patterns of Increasing Powers

Consider integers a and b, and the value a^b. The units digit of a^b depends only on b and the *units* digit of a. The patterns shown below show the cyclic pattern of the units digits of a^b for different units digits of a, as b increases according to the sequence b = 1,2,3,…

If the units digit of a is 1, then the units digit of a^b = *1*, 1, …
If the units digit of a is 2, then the units digit of a^b = *2,4,8,6*, 2,4, …
If the units digit of a is 3, then the units digit of a^b = *3,9,7,1*, 3,9, …
If the units digit of a is 4, then the units digit of a^b = *4,6,4 ,6*, …
If the units digit of a is 5, then the units digit of a^b = *5*, 5, …
If the units digit of a is 6, then the units digit of a^b = *6*, 6, …
If the units digit of a is 7, then the units digit of a^b = *7,9,3,1*, 7,9, …
If the units digit of a is 8, then the units digit of a^b = *8,4,2,6*, 8,4, …
If the units digit of a is 9, then the units digit of a^b = *9,1*, 9,1, …

Don't memorize: they are easily reproduced as needed. Just remember the units digits of a^b holds to a pattern. Note that there are no more than 4 numbers in any pattern and that any number ending in 1, 5, or 6, raised to any integer, will end in 1, 5, or 6, respectively.

Chapter 1   Multiples, Factors, Fractions, Remainders

SAT Archetypes

Remainder Analysis

When 21 is divided by a positive integer, the remainder is 5. For how many different integers is this true?

SR

How do I start?

First, the remainder is always smaller than the divisor, so we're only looking for divisors greater than 5. Since 21 and 5 are pretty small numbers, brute force is one possible (but lengthy) path. Try thinking of numbers that, when divided into 21, yield a remainder of 5.

Solution

This is covered in the review section. From the definition of remainder, for integers d (the set of numbers we seek) and m, it must be true that d•m + 5 = 21, where d is the divisor. Therefore, (1) d•m = 16. Since the remainder is 5, the divisor must be greater than 5, or (2) d>5. The only pairs (d,m) that satisfy (1) and (2) are (16,1), and (8,2). There are 2 numbers, 16 and 8, that satisfy the criterion.

Alternate Solution

You could bang away on the calculator trial-and-error, or realize that 21-16 = 5, so 16 is one of the desired divisors. Since 16 = 8•2, 8 will go into 21 twice with 5 remaining.

Alternate solution II

One other approach this problem is to brute force the calculation, testing each possible divisor. But what if the dividend were 120 instead of 21? That would be an impossibly long path to the solution. If you ever encounter a problem, and it looks like it would take too long to manually search through possible answers, you're haven't seen the shortcut.

Answer 2

The Take-Away

Remainder problems can often be analyzed using remainder decomposition: d•m + R =n, where R is the remainder of n/d, and m is the largest integer number of times d can go into n. Also, the remainder is always less than the divisor.

17

Divisibility and Least Common Multiples

If m is an integer such that 700 ≤ m ≤ 800, and m can be evenly divided by 3, 6, and 15, what is one possible value of m?

SR

How do I start?

You shouldn't force your way out of this by guessing numbers in the given range - the numbers are too big. However, any number that is divisible by all of the members of a set of integers must be divisible by the least common multiple (LCM) of that set.

Solution

First, any number that can be evenly divided by 6 and 15 can also be evenly divided by 3. We can ignore 3 in our analysis. 6 and 15 are small numbers, so the LCM is easily found by listing the multiples of each. The multiples of 6 are 12, 18, 24, 30… and the multiples of 15 are 30, 45…, the LCM is 30. Because the least common multiple of 6 and 15 is 30, *only* numbers that are multiples of 30 will be divisible by both 6 and 15 (and of course, 3). We must then search for multiples of 30 between 700 and 800, inclusive, using a calculator or head-math. The only such numbers in this interval are 720, 750, and 780.

Alternate Solution

If you forget the LCM approach, you could solve this with a smart brute-force method. Take one of the big numbers. Divide 700 by 15: the answer is 46.666… Not an integer, but the next integer, 47, multiplied by 15 equals 705. So 705 is divisible by 15. Is 705 divisible by 6? Impossible - 705 is odd and 6 is even. What is the next number divisible by 15 in the interval of interest? That would be 705 + 15 = 720. Is this divisible by 6? Yes, 720/6 = 120. So 730 is divisible by 30. Of course, 720 is also divisible by 3. So 720 is divisible by 3, 6, and 15.

Answer 720, 750, or 780

The Take-Away

The set of numbers that is divisible by the set of integers a, b, and c will be divisible by the LCM of a, b, and c.

Chapter 1   Multiples, Factors, Fractions, Remainders

Arithmetic Operations on Units Digits

If $11^x = y$, where x is a positive integer, what is the remainder when y is divided by 10?

SR

How do I start?

When in doubt, try a few values of 11^x and divide by 10.

Solution

This problem can be solved by trial and error. Try a few small values of x and divide 11^x by 10. When x = 1, 2, and 3, y = 11, 121, and 1331, respectively. After dividing by 10, all of these values have a remainder of 1. Did we really need to test three values of x? See alternate solution II below.

Alternate Solution

All powers of 11 have units digits of 1. When a number is divided by 10, the remainder is equal to the units digit. Therefore, the remainder is 1.

Alternate Solution II

The problem only mentions one remainder. Whatever it is, it is the same for all x. $11^1/10$ has a remainder of 1. You can infer that the remainder is 1 for any value of x.

Answer 1

The Take-Away

Learn some of the details of the cyclic properties of the units digits of integers in the review section. They might (rarely) come in handy. Any number ending in 1, 5, or 6, raised to any integer power, will have a units digit of 1, 5, or 6, respectively.

Factors of a Product of Primes

Let k, l, m, and n be four different prime numbers, and let p be the product of all four. How many factors greater than zero, including 1 and p, does p have?

SR

How do I start?

Ugh. Analyze the problem one chunk at a time, and write the problem in clear, mathematical language. Thus, p = k•l•m•n, where k, l, m, and n are all primes. Primes don't have any factors other than 1 and themselves. A factor, of course, is any number that divides evenly into another. So, only those four primes and combinations of those primes (and 1) can be factors of p.

Solution

Since p = k•l•m•n and k, l, m, and n are all prime, the only factors, other than 1, will be the primes and combination-products of those primes. The single factors will be k, l, m, and n, or 4 factors. The double factors will be k•l, k•m, k•n, l•m, l•n, and m•n, or 6 factors. The triple factors will be k•l•m, k•l•n, k•m•n, and l•m•n, or 4 factors. Finally, k•l•m•n = p is a factor, as well as 1. Counting every combination, there are 4+6+4+1+1 = 16 factors.

Alternate Solution

The number p is the product of four different primes, k, l, m, and n. So p = k•l•m•n. Each term in the product has an exponent of 1. From the formula discussed in the review above, add 1 to each of these exponents and then multiply these together: 2•2•2•2 = 16 factors.

Alternate Solution II

The sum of all possible combinations of n distinct things (see volume 2) is 2^n: $2^4 = 16$.

Answer 16

The Take-Away

Factors of a product, for example a•b•c•..., include a, b, c ..., as well as the products of all possible combinations of these factors.

Chapter 1   Multiples, Factors, Fractions, Remainders

Factors of Algebraic Expressions

If a and b are integers greater than 3 and a is a factor of both b + 7 and b - 2, which of the following values could be a value of a?

(A) 4
(B) 5
(C) 6
(D) 9

How do I start?

This is a pretty hard one. Ignore the fact that a and b must be greater than 3 for now; such constraints are usually either a technicality (like avoiding division by zero) or a constraint on the possible answers (e.g., you can't enter a negative number). What is really important here is that a is a factor of both b+7 and b-2. As a result, there must be an integer number of a's between b-2 and b+7. Therefore, a must be a factor of their difference: (b+7) - (b-2) = 9.

Solution

Since a is a factor of b+7 and b-2, a must be a factor of the difference, 9. That is, whatever values b+7 and b-2 are, the difference between them, 9, must be a multiple of a. Therefore, a must be ±1, ±3 or ±9, and since a is greater than 3, a must 9. The answer is choice (D).

Alternate Solution

If a is a factor of b+7, then (1) n·a = b+7, where n is an integer. If a is also a factor of b-2, then (2) m·a = b-2, where m is another integer. Subtracting (2) from (1), (n-m)·a = 9. Therefore, a must be a factor of 9. The only integer values of a that solve this equation are a = ±1, ±3, and ±9, and only a = 9 in listed among the choices.

Answer D

The Take-Away

A number that is a factor to two numbers or expressions (in this problem, b+7 and b-2) is also a factor of their sum or difference.

Multiples, Factors, Fractions, Remainders   Chapter 1

Prime Factor Analysis of a Number

How many prime factors, multiplied together, give the product 5544?

SR

How do I start?

This one is pretty direct – if you know how to perform prime factor analysis. You need to find *how many* prime factors there are; you'll have to calculate them all and count them. Use the method outlined in the review section.

Solution

From the discussion in the review section,

	5544
2	2772
2	1386
2	693
3	231
3	77
7	11
11	1

$5544 = 2 \cdot 2 \cdot 2 \cdot 3 \cdot 3 \cdot 7 \cdot 11 = 2^3 \cdot 3^2 \cdot 7^1 \cdot 11^1$. There are $3+2+1+1 = 7$ prime factors.

Had the question been how many *different* prime factors, the answer would have been 4.

Had the question been how many factors, the answer would have been (see the review in this chapter) $4 \cdot 3 \cdot 2 \cdot 2 = 48$.

Answer 7

The Take-Away

Problems involving factors (especially prime factors) often require prime factorization. On the SAT, this problem would probably involve a smaller number than 5544. Even better!

Chapter 1   Multiples, Factors, Fractions, Remainders

Practice Problems

1. How many different pairs of prime numbers, when added together, sum to 31?

    (A) 0
    (B) 1
    (C) 2
    (D) 3

2. How many different sets of three integers can form the product 110, if each integer is greater than 1?

    (A) 0
    (B) 1
    (C) 2
    (D) 3

3. If a and b are integers greater than 3, and if a is a factor of b+3 and b-2, which of the following values could be a value of b?

    (A) 3
    (B) 4
    (C) 5
    (D) 12

4. For all positive integers, x, let $\boxed{x}$ be defined as the product of all the even factors of 4x. For example, $\boxed{3}$ = 2•4•6•12 = 576. What is the value of $\boxed{7}$?

    SR

Multiples, Factors, Fractions, Remainders   Chapter 1

5. If x is divisible by 5 and y is divisible by 7, which of the following must always be divisible by 35?

   I. 5x + 7y
   II. 7x + 5y
   III. 3xy

   (A) I only
   (B) III only
   (C) I and III
   (D) II and III

6. **CHALLENGE** Let n be an integer between 41 and 51, inclusive, having only two different prime factors. How many different values may n take?

   (A) 4
   (B) 5
   (C) 6
   (D) 7

7. Let a and b be positive integers, and let the operation R(a,b) be defined as the remainder when a is divided by b. If 3<x<20 and R(x,11) = 3, what is the value of x?

   SR

8. When n (a positive integer) is divided by 6, the remainder is 3. If 16n is divided by 12, what is the remainder?

   SR

9. Let the operator ◎ be defined such that a◎b equals the remainder when a is divided by b for all positive integers a > b. If 31 ◎ b = 8, what is the only possible value of b?

   SR

24

Chapter 1 Multiples, Factors, Fractions, Remainders

10. The quotient 34 ÷ n has a remainder of 3. How many integer values of n satisfy this condition?

(A) 0
(B) 1
(C) 4
(D) 5

11. How many integers between 100 and 199 can be evenly divided by all three of the following numbers: 2, 3, and 8?

SR

12. If 5^a, where a is a positive integer greater than 1, is divided by 9, which of the following numbers can never be the remainder?

(A) 2
(B) 4
(C) 6
(D) 7

13. CHALLENGE The function u(m), for any positive integer m, is defined as follows. First, consider the set of all m^p, with all integer powers p≥1. The function u(m) is then the number of all possible <u>different</u> units digits present in this set. For example, u(2) = 4; i.e., 2 raised to any integer power will result in numbers having 4 different units digits: 2, 4, 6, or 8. Which of the following numbers do not result in u(n) equal to 4?

(A) 33
(B) 37
(C) 1243
(D) 646

14. The quotient 45 ÷ n has a remainder of 3. How many different integer values of n satisfy this condition?

SR

Multiples, Factors, Fractions, Remainders   Chapter 1

15. Lytetia is building a model spaceship from miniature parts and she must cut a linear length of PVC tubing exactly 5/16 of an inch in length from one of several tubes in stock. Which choice of tube listed below would result in minimum leftover length?

(A) 9/32 inch
(B) 3/10 inch
(C) 3/8 inch
(D) 2/5 inch

16. m is a positive integer, and (2^{512}•m + 6) and (2^{512}•m - q) are both divisible by 5. Which of the following is a possible value of q?

(A) 24
(B) 25
(C) 28
(D) 30

17. Let x, a, and b be positive integers where a < b < 27. If (x+a) and (x+b) have the same remainder when divided by 8, what is the maximum value of b - a?

18. Let x be an integer that when divided by 48 has a remainder of 32. If it is currently midnight as shown on a 24-hour clock, what time will this clock show x hours later?

19. If x and y are real, xy ≠ 0, and x > y, which of the following conditions must be true?

(A) $y^2 < x^2$
(B) $\dfrac{1}{x} > \dfrac{1}{y}$
(C) $x^3 > y^3$
(D) $\dfrac{1}{y} > \dfrac{1}{xy}$

Chapter 1 Multiples, Factors, Fractions, Remainders

Practice Problem Hints

1. List the prime numbers that could contribute to pairs that add to 31.

2. Start with prime factorization, then see what triples may result.

3. Since a is a factor of b+3 and b-2, a must also be a factor of the positive difference.

4. Multiply 7 by 4 and find all the <u>even</u> factors.

5. Represent x and y as 5m and 7n, respectively, where m and n are integers, and then test each choice.

6. This problem requires one to manually search the numbers between 41 and 51, inclusive, for the requirements stated.

7. Think carefully, or rewrite this mess so that it is clear what is being asked. What integer between 3 and 20 has a remainder of 3 when divided by 11?

8. From the definition of remainders, n = 6m + 3, where n and m are integers. Multiply this equation by 16 and then divide by 12.

9. Remainder analysis: 31 = n•b + 8, where n and b are integers, and b is the answer.

10. 34 = a•n + 3, where a and n are integers. How many values of n are possible?

11. Such an integer must be a multiple of the least common multiple of 2, 3, and 8.

12. Use your calculator to calculate successively higher powers of 5, divide by 9, and take note of the pattern of remainders.

13. Only the units digits will effect u(n). Test each answer choice to find u(n) ≠ 4. Or use your knowledge of the cyclic pattern units digits.

14. 45 = a•n + 3, where a and n are integers.

15. Use your calculator!

16. If both terms are divisible by 5, their sum and difference are too.

Multiples, Factors, Fractions, Remainders   Chapter 1

17. Two numbers, each divided by a third number, can only have the same remainder when their difference is a multiple of the third number.

18. Try the smallest number of hours, x, with a remainder of 32 after dividing by 48. Note that 48 is a multiple of 24.

19. Examine each choice at various values of x and y. Let each be positive, negative, magnitude greater than 1, and magnitude less than 1.

Chapter 1　　　　　　　　　　　　　　　　　　　Multiples, Factors, Fractions, Remainders

Practice Problem Solutions

1. Answer B

   You should be familiar with the prime numbers less than 100. List, or think of primes from 2 to 29 and search for pairs adding to 31. The primes are: 2 3 5 7 11 13 17 19 23 and 29. Only the sum 2 + 29 = 31 employs a pair of primes that sum to 31.

   Alternate solution: We're summing integers. Because it is odd, 31 must be the sum of an even integer and an odd integer. The only even prime is 2, and since 29 is also prime, we can only form 2 + 29 = 31. Smart.

2. Answer B

   This is best approached through prime factorization. 110/2 = 55. 55/5 = 11. So the prime factors of 110 are 2, 5, and 11. Had there been only one or two prime factors there could be no 3-factor product. Had there been more than three prime factors, then prime factors could be combined in various ways to give 3-factor products. As it is, with only three prime factors, there is only one 3-factor product: 2•5•11 = 110.

3. Answer D

   First, since b must be >3, choice (A) can be discarded. Since a is a factor of b+3 and b-2, a must also be a factor of the positive difference. And since the difference, 5, is prime, a must be 1 or 5, and since a is greater than 3, a must 5. Therefore, b is an integer such that b-2 and b+3 are both divisible by 5. Look through the choices and find values of b such that b-2 and b+3 are multiples of 5. Choice (D): b = 12 is the only choice among those listed satisfying these conditions: b - 2 = 10 and b + 3 = 15

4. Answer 3136

   Since 7•4 = 28, and the even factors of 28 are 2, 4, 14, and 28, $\boxed{7}$ = 2•4•14•28 = 3136.

5. Answer D

   Represent x and y as integers 5m and 7n, respectively, and test each expression. Expression (I) equates to 25m + 49n. If m = n = 1, this expression is not divisible by 35. Expression (II) equates to 35m + 35n = 35(m+n). Since (m+n) is an integer, (II) is always divisible by 35. Expression (III) equates to 3•(5•m)•(7•n) = 3•35•m•n and is therefore always divisible by 35. (II) and (III) satisfy the conditions in the problem.

Multiples, Factors, Fractions, Remainders   Chapter 1

6. Answer B

Now, n must be between 41 and 51, inclusive, and must have only two <u>different</u> primes as factors. Use prime factor analysis, if needed, on all possible values of n to determine their prime factors. Then count the values of n that have exactly two different prime factors.

41 is prime	47 is prime
42 different prime factors: 2, 3, 7	**48 different prime factors: 2, 2, 2, 2, 3**
43 is prime	49 different prime factors: 7, 7
44 different prime factors: 2, 2, 11	**50 different prime factors: 2, 5, 5**
45 different prime factors: 3, 3, 5	51 is prime
46 different prime factors: 2, 2, 3	

44, 45, 46, 48, and 50 satisfy the requirements. There are 5 such integers.

7. Answer 14

This problem is made more difficult by the confusing values and words chosen. What integer, x, *between* 3 and 20 has a remainder of 3 when divided by 11? The domain of x is 4, 5, ..., 19. From the constraints in the problem and the definition of remainders, x = 11m + 3, where m is an integer. Considering the domain of x, m could only equal 1. Therefore, x = 11•1 + 3 = 14.

Alternate Solution: Head-math: only 14/11 has a remainder of 3 in the domain of x.

8. Answer 0

When n is divided by 6, the remainder is 3. Using remainder analysis (see the review in this chapter) and the data in the problem, we know that that (1) n = 6m + 3, where m is an integer. We are asked to find the remainder when 16n is divided by 12. Multiplying equation (1) by 16 yields (2) 16n = 96m + 48. What is the remainder when (2) is divided by 12? Examine the right side of (2). *Both* terms are divisible by 12. In other words, there are an integer multiple of 12's as a result of dividing 16n by 12. So 12 will *always* divide into 16n = 96m + 48 evenly, for all integer values of m, with no remainder. The remainder is zero.

9. Answer 23

8 is the remainder after 31 is divide by b. Using remainder analysis, 31 = m•b + 8, where m is an integer. Therefore, 23 = m•b. Since 23 is a prime number, b must be 1 or 23. But there would be no remainder if b were 1. So b must equal 23.

Chapter 1   Multiples, Factors, Fractions, Remainders

10. Answer B

The numerator is 34. You can toss choice (A): how could there be zero possible divisions resulting in a remainder of 3? The question implies that 34 = a•n + 3, where a and n are integers, and 3 is the remainder. So a•n = 31, and only two pairs of numbers satisfy this equation: (a=1, n=31), and (a=31, n=1). Since dividing by 1 will never result in a remainder, only one value of a, 31, satisfies the conditions stated in the problem.

11. Answer 4

Because the least common multiple of 2, 3, and 8 is 24, only numbers that are multiples of 24 can be evenly divided by 2, 3, and 24. We must search for multiples of 24 between 100 and 199, using a calculator. The only such numbers in this interval are 120, 144, 168, and 192. There are four such numbers.

12. Answer C

Remainder decomposition, 5^a = 9n + R, where R is the remainder, seems of little use here. We're looking for a pattern in the sequence of possible remainders, and which of the choices never occurs in the pattern. Use your calculator to calculate successively higher powers of 5, divide by 9, and take note of the remainders. Doing so, you'll find this sequence of remainders: **7, 8, 4, 2, 1, 5,** 7, 8, ... So the pattern that repeats itself is 7, 8, 4, 2, 1, 5, ..., and therefore 6 will never be a remainder. Necessary brute-force.

13. Answer D

u(2) = 4 because 2^p can have units digits of only 2^1 = 2, 2^2 = 4, 2^3 = 8, and 2^4 = 1<u>6</u>, ... for any positive integer value of p. Note that when 2^4 = 1<u>6</u> is multiplied by 2, the result is 3<u>2</u>, thereafter starting the cycle of units digits 2, 4, 8, 6, ... again, ad infinitum. Each of the numbers in the problem choices must be tested to find one such that u(m) ≠ 4. For (A), take the units digit, 3, to successively higher powers: **3, 9, 27, 81,** 243, ...etc., where we highlight the pattern comprising the only 4 different units digits. Continuing through the other choices, (D) results in 6, 36, 216, etc., meaning that u(6) = 1. All other choices result in u(m) = 4.

Alternate Solution: Any number ending in 1, 5, or 6, raised to any integer power, will end in only 1, 5, or 6, respectively. Any number ending in 1, 5, or 6 would have failed the u(n) = 4 requirement. While this is a *CHALLENGE* question requiring acute reading comprehension, this was really not too difficult.

Multiples, Factors, Fractions, Remainders   Chapter 1

14. Answer 5

From reasoning similar to problem 10, 45 = 3 + a•n, or 42 = a•n. 42 is evenly divisible by 2, 3, 6, 7, 14, 21, and 42. However, the divisor, n, must be greater than the remainder, 3. Thus only n = 6, 7, 14, 21, and 42 satisfy the constraints in the problem, and there are thus 5 such values.

15. Answer C

Sure, this is not higher math. But some students might start by finding the least common denominator to all 5 fractions listed in the question - a massive time waste. This is a calculator question - just convert all 5 fractions to decimal and compare values. The desired length is 5/16 = .313. Going down the list of choices, (A) 9/32 = .281, (B) 3/10 = .3, (C) 3/8 = .375, and (D) 2/5 = .4. Some good students will pick the *closest* choice - but remember, there has to be enough tubing out of which .313 can be cut - any length less that this won't work. Therefore, (A) and (B) can be discarded, and (C) is the shortest piece of those listed that is greater than .313.

16. Answer A

This problem is designed to crack pencil points in frustration. But it's actually easy once you read beyond the huge numbers. If (2^{512}•m + 6) and (2^{512}•m - q) are both divisible by 5, then their difference must also be divisible by 5. Subtracting the second term from the first: 6 + q must be divisible by 5. Of the listed possible choices of q, only q = 24 gives rise to a sum, 6 + 24 = 30, that is divisible by 5.

17. Answer 16

We're given the domains: (1) a < b < 27. We're looking for the *largest* value of b-a, given that both have the same remainder after division by 8. If two numbers have the same remainder when divided by 8, then their positive difference will be divisible by 8. Try some examples to convince yourself: if a = 9 and b = 17, both have a remainder of 1 when divided by 8. Their positive difference is 8. Next, if a = 9 and b = 25 both have a remainder of 1 when divided by 8 and *their* positive difference is 16. It looks like if (x+a) and (x+b) have the same remainder when divided by 8, their positive difference, b - a, is divisible by 8. In other words, their positive difference must be a multiple of 8: 8, 16, 24... We've already seen values of a and b giving rise to a difference of 16. Can we find values of a and b in domain (1) with a positive difference of 24 and the same remainder after division by 8. No. The least value of a would be 8 (having a remainder of zero). But 8 + 24 is out of domain (1). It appears that the largest value of b - a under the stated conditions is 16. Yup. VERY hard.

18. Answer 8

A 24-hour clock will cycle every 24 hours. If x divided by 48 has a remainder of 32, one possible value of x would be 48 + 32 = 80 hours. If it's now midnight, what time is it 80 hours from now? Divide by 24: 80/24 = $3\frac{1}{3}$ days. Exactly 3 days from now it is midnight. Advancing $\frac{1}{3}$ day = 8 hours means that the time displayed on a 24-hour clock is 8. As a check, the next value of x with a remainder of 32 when divided by 48 would be 2•48 + 32 = 128. Divide by 24: 128/24 = $5\frac{1}{3}$ days. So we still have $\frac{1}{3}$ day beyond midnight. No matter how many times x is divided by 48 (a multiple of 24), the remainder must be 32, which can be decomposed as 32 = 24 + 8. So all possible values of x hours display 8 on a 24-hour clock.

19. Answer C

We know that (1) x > y, and that neither one can equal zero (xy ≠ 0). (2) Either could be positive or negative, and (3) either one could have a magnitude less than 1. So care must be taken when evaluating the inequalities among the choices. Find representative cases of (2) and (3) to break the truth of each choice, if possible.

Test (A): $y^2 < x^2$. We know x^2 and y^2 are always positive. If y = -3 and x = 1/2, inequality (1) is satisfied, but $y^2 < x^2$ is false. So (A) is not always true.

Test (B): $\frac{1}{x} > \frac{1}{y}$ is always false. By inverting the quotients and reversing the inequality, (B) becomes x < y, which is clearly false given that x must be greater than y.

Test (C): $x^3 > y^3$. Carefully. If x and y are both positive and x>y, then $x^3 > y^3$ is *always* true. But what about cases where x, y, or both are negative? If x is positive and y is negative, x^3 will be positive and y^3 will be negative, regardless of the magnitudes of x and y. So $x^3 > y^3$ is always true in this case. But we must consider cases where x < 0 carefully. Here are 3 representative scenarios covering the possible magnitudes of x and y: (4) x = -1/4, y = -1/2, (5) x = -1/4, y = -2, and (6) x = -2, y = -3. Notice that in each case, x > y. Plugging (4) into $x^3 > y^3$, -1/64 > -1/8. ✓ Plugging (5) into $x^3 > y^3$, -1/64 > -8. ✓ Plugging (6) into $x^3 > y^3$, -8 > -27. ✓ So choice (C) is always true.

Just to check, examine choice (D). If $\frac{1}{y} > \frac{1}{xy}$, then inverting the quotients and reversing the inequality, (7) y < xy. Dividing both sides by y (remember xy ≠ 0), (7) becomes 1 < x, which is not always true (x could be 1/2).

Only choice (C) is always true.

Alternate Solution: Taking the square roots of (A), $\pm y < \pm x$. This is clearly not always true: you could pick a negative value on the right and positive value on the left. Inverting each side of (B) and reversing the inequality results in $x < y$. Not always true. From (C), consider the cube roots of $x^3 > y^3$. We can ignore any complex roots. If we take the cube roots of both sides, we get $x > y$. True, by definition. As a check, if $x > 0$ and $y < 0$, then $x > y$. If both x and y are less than zero, then y must be more negative than x, and thus $x > y$. Inverting (D) and reversing the inequality, $y < xy$. Dividing both sides by y (which is allowed since neither x nor y equals 0), $1 < x$. This is not necessarily true. Only (C) is always true.

This problem foreshadows things to come. We will deal with inequalities in great detail in Chapter 9.

Chapter 2

Number Theory and Integers

The word *integer* came to English directly from the Latin adjective meaning "whole or complete." Parsed, *in-*, meaning "not," and *teger*, from the root *tangere*, "to touch," *integer* literally means "untouched." That's a beautiful thought.

"God created the integers," wrote mathematician Leopold Kronecker, "all the rest is the work of Man."

Number theory and integer math problems on the SAT involve properties of integers that you may not have thought about in some time. First, algebraic equations involving variables restricted to integer values often require a brute-force hunt among likely solutions rather than straightforward algebraic methods. Second, the even & odd properties of integer variables affect the even & odd properties of algebraic expressions in which they take part. Accounting for the even & odd properties of expressions with several variables can be confusing. Third, some real-world word-problem scenarios involve combining sets of different sizes. The resulting linear combinations are constrained in size, depending on the sizes of the component sets. Finally, the properties of prime numbers may be something you have ignored lately.

In total, the 10 archetypes of difficult integer math problems found on the SAT are presented in this chapter. The concepts necessary to solve these problems are reviewed, and 26 additional problems for practice (and greater scope) are included.

Don't Show Up Without Knowing...

These Concepts

- The squares of 2 through 16
- The cubes of 2 through 6
- The properties of adding and subtracting even and odd numbers
- The properties of multiplying, dividing and exponentiating even and odd numbers

How To...

- Algebraically express the number of integers in a given interval
- Determine the possible linear combinations of different size sets

Chapter 2   Number Theory and Integers

Quick Review and Definitions

Memorize The Squares Of Integers 2 Through 16

The SAT is loaded with perfect squares and cubes as a way to save savvy students time on problems. For example, a perfect square in a problem suggests that a square root might be involved. A solution might require the Pythagorean formula. Memorizing the following list of perfect squares might not only save time but help you see how to develop a solution.

2	4	10	100	25	625
3	9	11	121	20	400
4	16	12	144	30	900
5	25	13	169	40	1600
6	36	14	196	50	2500
7	49	15	225	…	…
8	64	16	256	90	8100
9	81				

Memorize The Cubes Of Integers 2 Through 6

2	8
3	27
4	64
5	125
6	216

Recognizing $8^3 = 512$ might come in handy, in addition to those listed above.

Note that the lists above also give you the square roots and cube roots of perfect squares and perfect cubes. Cubes and cube roots will sometimes arise in geometry problems involving 3-D figures such as cubes and spheres.

Shaving even a few seconds off a question on the test could give you extra time to complete one more question. The SAT is scored in 10 point increments. Any little extra time might make a significant improvement to your score.

Properties Of Even And Odd Integers

- If m is an integer, then 2m is always an even integer.
- If m is an integer, then 2m±1 is always an odd integer.
- Don't forget that even and odd integers can be negative.
- Zero is an even number!
- If a and b are integers, then if a - b is odd, then a + b is odd.
- If a and b are integers, then if a - b is even, then a + b is even.

Counting Integers Between Two Numbers

- The number of integers *between* any pair a and b is b - a - 1.

  0**1234567**8   Number of integers = 8 - 0 - 1 = 7

- The number of <u>odd</u> integers *between* a and b when <u>both are even</u> is (b-a)/2

  0**1**23**4**56**7**8   Odd integers = (8-0)/2 = 4

- The number of <u>even</u> integers *between* a and b with <u>both are odd</u> is (b-a)/2

  1**2**34**5**67   Even integers = (7-1)/2 = 3

- <u>In all other cases</u> the number of 2-spaced integers *between* two integers is (b-a-1)/2

  0**1**23**4**56**7**89   Odd integers = (9-0-1)/2 = 4

  01**2**34**5**67**8**9   Even integers = (9-0-1)/2 = 4

Note that the above rules do <u>not</u> include the two numbers that define the intervals.

Rules For Operations on Even and Odd Numbers

You should memorize the following rules and properties for operations involving even and odd integers. Letting e represent a number that is even and o a number that is odd, the following must be true:

(even)±(even) = (even)
(odd)±(odd) = (even)
(even)±(odd) = (odd)
(even)•(even) = (even)
(odd)•(odd) = (odd)

(even)•(odd) = (even)
$(even)^n$ = (even)
$(odd)^n$ = (odd)
(even)/(odd) is never an odd integer
(odd)/(even) is never *any* integer

- The product of any set of even integers is even.
- The product of any set of odd integers is odd.
- If *any* member of the product set (of integers) is even, their product is even.

Big Hints in Expressions Involving Powers and Roots

In algebraic equations that use powers and roots, the expressions within can sometimes provide a hint at a possible solution. For example, if $x^3y = 27\sqrt{z}$, since 27 is a perfect cube ($3^3 = 27$), you might try $x = 3$ and $z = y^2$ as a possible solution.

Linear Combinations of Sets

Example: Pens are sold in either a 3-pack or 5-pack of pens. As a result, you can't buy just *any* number of pens. You are restricted to integer multiples of 3-packs and 5-packs. In general, if you buy m 3-packs and n 5-packs, where m ≥ 0 and n ≥ 0, you get 3m + 5n pens. You are restricted to these linear combinations of pen-packs; with varying values of m and n, you are restricted to the purchase of 3, 5, 6, 8, 9, ... pens.

Sum of 1/n + 1/m + ... Can Never Equal An Integer

Any sum of the type 1/n + 1/m ..., where the denominators are all *different* positive integers, can never equal an integer (unless there are an infinite number of terms). Of course, more general sums of rational fractions can be integers: 1/3 + 5/3 = 2.

Notes

Chapter 2　　　　　　　　　　　　　　　　　　　　　Number Theory and Integers

SAT Archetypes

Algebraic Equations With Integer Variables

If n and m are integers, $n^3 = 64$, and $2m^2 = 72$, which of the following equations could be true?

　　I. $n = 4$
　　II. $m + n = -2$
　　III. $m - n = 2$

(A) I only
(B) I and II only
(C) I and III only
(D) I, II and III

Where do I start?

These equations seem pretty simple. Even though they involve integers, the variables aren't mixed. We can solve for n and m via algebra. Don't forget the negative roots.

Solution

The equations should be further simplified to yield solutions. n is the cube root of 64, which has only one real value, n = 4. So, I is true. Solving the equation for m, $m^2 = 36$, so m can be +6 or -6. Test (II): if m = -6, then m + n = -6 + 4 = -2, so II can be true. Test (III): If m = 6, then m + n = 6 - 4 = 2, so III can also be true.

Answer D

The Take-Away

Sometimes algebraic methods may be employed with integer equations. As a rule, if equations involve a *mix* of more than one integer variable, you'll often have to perform a brute-force search to determine the solution. But in this problem the equations in the problem are unmixed - they involve single variables - and you were able to employ standard algebraic techniques to develop solutions. And never forget negative roots!

Number Theory and Integers   Chapter 2

Integer Inequalities

If m is an integer, let n = m + 2/m. If m > 0, which of the following expressions is always true?

      I.   n is an integer
      II.   m ≠ n
      III. $m^2 < nm$

(A) I only
(B) II only
(C) III only
(D) II and III only

How do I start?

Problems involving integers and conditions like "always true" are seldom designed for you to prove rigorously. Quickly come up with a short set of examples employing small integers that seem likely to test the conditions stated.

Solution

For most problems involving integers, one shortcut may be to examine a few test cases. Choose the first few values of m > 0. So, (1) n = m + 2/m. Test (I): When m = 1, n = 3, when m = 2, n = 3, when m = 3, n = 3 2/3. So n is not always an integer, and (I) is not always true. Test (II): We can see from equation (1) that because m>0, 2/m>0, and thus n is always greater than m, so (II) is always true. From (1), test (III): nm = m(m + 2/m) = m^2 + 2, which is always greater than m^2. So (III) is always true.

Answer D

The Take-Away

For many integer math problems, the *only* way to proceed is trial-and-error, or brute-force, testing each of the choices and cases given. In this problem our only practical option to test the truth of case (I) is to search for values of n and m that break or establish the truth of the propositions listed in the choices. Whenever practical, use small integers to test the truth of equations.

One Integer Equation With Two Unknowns

If x and y are nonnegative integers, and 2x + 4y = 20, how many possible values may y take?

SR

How do I start?

We have one equation and two unknowns, x and y. For unrestricted values, there are an infinite number of pairs (x,y) that solve this single equation. However, since x and y must be nonnegative integers, there is an additional constraint on the solution set. The only approach here is a brute-force search for values of x and y that satisfy the equation. Since the coefficient of y is larger than the coefficient of x, the set of possible values of y will be smaller than that of x. Since 2x + 4y = 20, y can only take the values 0 through 5.

Solution

Since x and y are integers, just test increasing values of y that can solve the above equation and count the number of corresponding values of x that solve the equation. You could also test increasing values of x instead, but that would require more tests.

y=0 x=10
y=1 x=8
y=2 x=6
y=3 x=4
y=4 x=2
y=5 x=0

There are 6 values. Note that there are no odd values of x in the solution set.

Alternate solution

Simplify the equation: divide each side of the equation by 2, giving x + 2y = 10. Since 10 is even, and since 2y is even, *x must also be even*. This further reduces the (x,y) solution space and may even allow you to do this in your head if time is critical.

Answer 6

The Take-Away

Simplifying expressions or equations in a problem can reduce the domain of possible variables that must be tested. Don't ignore even & odd properties – they may allow you to significantly reduce the solution space that you must manually search through.

Number Theory and Integers   Chapter 2

Range of Integers Satisfying Algebraic Inequalities

Let A be the set of positive integers between 1 and 20, inclusive. Let B be the set of positive integers between 1 and 10, inclusive. If a is a member of set A, and b is a member of set B, what is the largest value of c = a + b, such that c and a•b are both members of A?

SR

How do I start?

We need the *largest* value of c = a + b. Carefully analyze what is known (the intervals and membership assignments) and what is being asked. We know 1≤a≤20, 1≤b≤10. To meet the constraints, it must be true that 1≤a•b≤20 and 1≤a+b≤20. Search and destroy.

Solution

Examine those pairs (a,b) where a•b ≤ 20, and look for the pair for which a+b is maximum and also a member of A, i.e., (1≤a+b≤20). You might start with the maximum product, 20. Try the middle values: a•b = 5•4 = 20. But the sum a+b is only 9. Likewise, 10•2 = 20, but their sum is only 12. At the extreme, a•b = 20•1 = 20, but their sum = 21, and is not in A.

The next largest product pair toward this extreme would be the product a•b = 19•1 = 19, and *their* sum = 20. a = 19 and b = 1 satisfy the conditions 1≤a•b≤20 and 1≤a+b≤20. So the largest value of c = a+b is 20.

Alternate solution

Of course you could start with pairs of numbers that *sum* to 20, 19,... and examine the product of those numbers. However, there are *many* pairs that sum to 20, and each must be checked to see if the product is in A: e.g., 10 + 10 = 20, but 10•10 = 100. A long search would eventually yield the pair 19 + 1 = 20 and 19•1 = 19, both results belonging to set A.

Answer 20

The Take-Away

You'll sometimes need to examine the extremes (and middle) of a given domain interval to determine the basic characteristics, contours, and extremities of an expression. One additional take-away fact: the sum of two positive integers is always less than the product (unless one of the integers is 1, or both are 2). That was why it was wise to start by maximizing the product here, instead of the sum.

Chapter 2 — Number Theory and Integers

Algebraic Expressions With Even and Odd Integers

Let a, b, and c be positive integers. If a+b is even and $(a+b)^2 + (a+c)$ is even, which of the following must be true?

A. ab is even
B. a is odd
C. a is even
D. If c is odd, then a is odd.

How do I start?

Clearly, you're going to need the rules for operations on even and odd integers. Read the review if you don't. You know that a+b is even, and you are given another expression involving a+b that is also even. Analyze that expression to determine what other even & odd properties must be true. Hint: if x is even, then x^2 is even.

Solution

If a+b is even, then $(a+b)^2$ is even. So, in the second expression, (even) + (a+c) = (even). Rearranging, (a+c) = (even) - (even). Since (even) - (even) is always even, (a+c) must be even. This occurs whenever both a and c are even, or both a and c are odd. This later property corresponds to choice (D).

Answer D

The Take-Away

You must know the rules for adding, subtracting, multiplying, dividing, and exponentiating even and odd numbers. Also - as we saw above, compound expressions can sometimes be parsed and analyzed using even & odd properties.

Number Theory and Integers   Chapter 2

Algebraic Expressions Constrained to Integer Values

If $\dfrac{(7-x)}{4}$ is an integer, then x must always be

(A) a multiple of 4
(B) odd
(C) even
(D) positive

How do I start?

In other words, $\dfrac{(7-x)}{4}$ = n, where n is an integer. This equation can be rearranged to solve for x. The properties of x can thereafter be revealed.

Solution

From the data given, (1) 7 - x = 4n, where n is an integer. Rearranging, (2) x = 7 - 4n. So x is not a multiple of 4, and it could be positive or negative, eliminating (A), and (D). Since x is the difference between an odd integer (7) and even integer (4n), x *must* be odd. So (B).

Alternate Solution

Since 4n is even, the left side of (1) must be even. 7 is odd. Only an odd number subtracted or added to an odd number can result in an even number. x must be odd.

Alternate Solution II

Do a brute-force hunt. If n = 0, x is 7. This is odd and positive, and is not a multiple of 4. This eliminates (A) and (C). If n = 1, x = 3: still odd and positive. But if n = 2, then x must be -1, which is odd, but negative. Toss (D). The only possible correct answer is (B).

Answer B

The Take-Away

The even & odd characteristics of a variable integer will depend on the even & odd characteristics of the several terms in a compound expression for that variable.

Chapter 2 Number Theory and Integers

Counting Equally-Spaced Integers Within An Interval

Let n be an odd integer greater than 4. How many odd integers are greater than 4 and less than n?

(A) n - 4
(B) n - 5
(C) (n-3)/2 +1
(D) (n-5)/2

How do I start?

Probably the fastest solution is to test odd integers n = 5, 7, ... and see which choice gives the correct count of odd integers for every value of n. When n = 7, all choices are broken except (D). However, let's derive the formula here. It's straightforward. You'll have to infer the formula by first manually counting the number of odd integers between 4 and n starting with n = 5. The pattern, i.e., formula we come up with will be one of the choices.

Solution

We must count the number of odd integers starting with 5. Look for a pattern by testing a few examples. If n is 5, there are zero odd integers that fit the criterion. If n is 7, then only one, 5, is greater than 4 and less than 7. With similar reasoning if n is 9, there are two odd integers. If n is 11, there are 3 odd integers in the interval. The number of even or odd integers in an interval typically includes a term that is divided by two, and we see that here: as n increases by 2, the number of odd integers increases by 1. We can infer the pattern: for n = 5, 7, 9, and 11, the # of odd integers between 4 and n equals (n-5)/2.

Alternate Solution

While there are formulas that will help you to calculate this in general, the SAT does not require such knowledge. However, we know from the review section in this chapter that the number of odd integers between a and b, where a is even and b is odd, is (b-a-1)/2. Here, a = 4 and b = n: the count is (n-4-1)/2= (n-5)/2.

Answer D

The Take-Away

You may have to infer patterns or relationships by using a few examples. But in this problem, testing the first couple of values let us toss all choices but (D).

Number Theory and Integers   Chapter 2

Distributing Objects into Groups of Different Sizes

A company leases a 7-story building. The office layout of each of the 7 floors is the same, and the employees are identically distributed among the 7 floors. Each identical floor layout is divided into several office areas: all areas have 8 employees <u>except</u> for one area that only has 5 employees. The company then moves to a large, one-story building designed with office areas that can hold 14 employees, and all offices are filled completely except one area has fewer than 14 employees. From among the following choices, how many employees does this area have?

(A) 7
(B) 8
(C) 9
(D) 10

How do I start?

Because, in the old building, the employees are *identically distributed* among 7 floors, the total number of employees is a multiple of 7. Also, the number of employees on each floor is a multiple of 8, with 5 leftover. Letting T be the total employees, $T = 7(8n+5) = 56n + 35$.

Solution

The number of employees on *each* of the 7 floors is a multiple of 8, with 5 leftover. Letting T be the total employees, and n an integer, $T = 7(8n+5) = 56n + 35$. After the move, all T employees are split up into 14-employee office areas. So, how many groups of 14 employees are there in $T = 56n + 35$ people? Dividing this equation by 14, we see that the first term is evenly divisible: 56n people, for any value of n, may be evenly divided into 14-person areas. The second term, 35, can be split into two 14 person areas (28), with a remainder of 7 left over. So this remaining office area will only have 7 employees.

Alternate Solution

The number of employees must be divisible by 7 (the employees are evenly divided among the 7 floors). If they move into 14 person office areas, they must either fit evenly into those areas (no remainder), or there will be a remainder of 7 people. (A) must be it.

Alternate Solution II

What if, in addition to 7, zero had been an answer choice - i.e., the leftover office was empty? If there is no remainder, the number of employees is a multiple of 14, which is even. But the number of employees, $T = 56n + 35$, must be odd. As a result, there must be 7, not zero people left over in the last office area.

Chapter 2   Number Theory and Integers

Alternate Solution III

(1) T = 56n + 35 = 14•(4n) + 35. But, (2) T = 14•m + x, where m is the number of 14-person offices and x is the number of leftover persons (correct choice). Equating (1) and (2) and rearranging, 35 - x = 14•(m-4n). So 35 - x must be divisible by 14. Answer (A).

Answer A

The Take-Away

When analyzing two different divisions of objects, take care to take into account common factors in the two divisions. In this case 7 is a factor of 14, and accounting for the remainder was easier as a result. Check out the first alternate solution. Even though there were several approaches to the answer, this one was hard.

Linear Combinations of Two Different Size Sets

Nails come in boxes of 6 or 7 pounds. Buyers may purchase combinations of both kinds of boxes. Which of the following weights of nails would it not be possible to purchase?

(A) 26
(B) 27
(C) 29
(D) 33

How do I start?

So buyers could purchase 6, or 7, or 12, or 13, or 14, ... lbs of nails. They may buy any linear combination of sets of 6 lbs. and 7 lbs. In general, the weight of the nails could be (1) 6m+7n pounds, where m and n are non-negative integers. The choices represent weights of nails. Test various values of m and n to see which choice is cannot happen.

Solution

It is only necessary to check all the choices to see which one cannot fit the 6m+7n formula. One good method is to choose increasing values of one variable, say n (because it multiplies the largest number, 7), and then search for values of m such that 6m+7n is a choice. So 7n can equal 0, 7, 14, 21,.... For example, we find that if n = 2 and m = 2, the sum is 14 + 12 = 26lbs; likewise, if n = 3 and m = 1, we get 21 + 6 = 27lbs. Similarly, 21 + 12 = 33 is a solution. We can stop here. All choices but (C) have been accounted for.

Number Theory and Integers — Chapter 2

Alternate solution

Check the even & odd characteristics of each choice to reduce the domain of possible solutions. The weight must be 6m+7n. 6m is always even. If the weight represented in the choice is even, then 7n must be even, and hence n is even. If the choice is odd, then n must be odd. For example, to test 26, we only need to consider n=2 (because n=4, 6, and 8 result in numbers greater than 26). The answer can be discovered with fewer steps using even / odd analysis.

Answer C

The Take-Away

If an object always comes in sets of m members, then you must select an integer number of sets, or n•m members, where n is the integer. If the object can come in two set sizes (as above), then you can select a linear combinations of sets - an integer number of one set size and an integer number of the other size set. Often you must use brute-force search methods to find the answer. Consider an even & odd analysis to hasten a solution.

Even & odd analysis in equations involving integers can be a powerful tool and is sometimes a *necessary* step in the development of a solution to math.

Integer Equations Involving Roots and Powers

Let $x^3 y = 8\sqrt{64}$, where x and y are both integers greater than zero. Which of the following values could equal y/x?

(A) 1
(B) 2
(C) $2\sqrt{2}$
(D) 4

How do I start?

Don't cross your eyes. In general, there would be an infinite number of solutions (x,y) that satisfy the equation, but here x and y are restricted: both must be positive integers. And we only need *one* value of y/x. Maybe a search? You only need to match reasonable values of x and y against the ratio choices. Also, note that both 8 and 64 are powers of 2. Hmmm.

Chapter 2 — Number Theory and Integers

Solution

Choice (C) is irrational - it can't result from any ratio of integers. So toss (C). We aren't out to prove all the possible values x and y make take, we just have to find a pair whose ratio, y/x, equals one of the answers. The answer choices are small, so that's good. Because 8 is a perfect cube, the equation suggests that perhaps x^3 = 8, in which case x = 2. That would force y = $\sqrt{64}$ = 8, resulting in y/x = 8/2 = 4. That fits choice (D).

Alternate solution

Simplify the equation. Since $\sqrt{64}$ = 8, (1) $x^3 y$ = 64. Rearranging this, (2) y = $64/x^3$. Now x^3 is a perfect cube and can only have the values 1, 8, 27, 64, 125 ... Moreover, y must be a positive integer. In light of this and equation (2), x^3 must be 1, 8, or 64. These correspond to x = 1, 2, of 4, respectively. Using these values of x in (2) y can only be 64, 8, or 1, respectively. Their respective ratios, y/x, are 64/1 = 64, 8/2 = 4, and 1/4. Of these, only y/x = 4 is one of the choices.

Answer D

The Take-Away

When presented with multi-variable, or compound, expressions in equations involving integers (like the above), look first to see if there are analogous parts on each side of the equation. Sometimes simple pair-wise equalities might fit the context of the problem.

Actually, if x and y were *any real* numbers in the above problem, and you were asked to come up with *one* value of x/y, 4 would suffice as an answer.

Notes

Chapter 2   Number Theory and Integers

Practice Problems

1. Let a and b be integers such that $a = b + \frac{2}{b} - \frac{2}{b^2}$. Which of the following could be a value of a?

      I.   1
      II.   -3
      III.   -5

(A) I only
(B) II only
(C) III only
(D) I and III only

2. Let $a^2\sqrt{b} = 16\sqrt{22}$ where a and b are both integers greater than zero. Which of the following values could equal ab?

(A) 22
(B) 38
(C) 88
(D) 256

3. Let $a^3 b^{\frac{1}{3}} = 64\sqrt{16}$ where a and b are both integers greater than zero. Which of the following values could equal $\sqrt{ab}$?

(A) 12
(B) 16
(C) 88
(D) 256

53

4. Let $x^3 y = 4^{\frac{3}{2}} \sqrt{64}$, where x and y are both integers greater than zero. Which of the following values could equal y/x?

   (A) 1
   (B) 2
   (C) $2\sqrt{2}$
   (D) 4

5. *Challenge* Let A be the set of positive integers between 1 and 15 (inclusive). Let B be the set of positive integers between 1 and 10 (inclusive). If a is a member of set A, and b is a member of set B, what is the largest value of a•b such that a•b is a member of A, and a+2b is a member of B?

   SR

6. Let m and n satisfy the inequality 3m + 2n < 12

   For how many ordered pairs of positive integers, m and n, is the above inequality satisfied?

   SR

7. What is the smallest integer m such that m > 0 and 12m is the cube of another integer?

   SR

8. Let A equal the sum of even integers between 3 and 30. Let B equal the sum of odd integers from 9 to 35 (inclusive). What is the value of B - A?

   (A) 37
   (B) 65
   (C) 75
   (D) 100

Chapter 2 — Number Theory and Integers

9. If $\dfrac{x^2 y^3}{2} = 80y^2$, $y \neq 0$, and x is a positive integer less than 5, which of the following values may y have?

   (A) {2, 4, 16, 32}
   (B) {10, $\dfrac{160}{9}$, 40, 160}
   (C) {2, 4, 40, 160}
   (D) {2, $\dfrac{160}{9}$, 16, 40, 160}

10. If $\sqrt{ab} = 25a$ and a is a positive integer, what values can b take?

    (A) {-5, 5}
    (B) {-5, 0, 5}
    (C) n•5, where n is a positive integer
    (D) n•625, where n is a positive integer

11. If x and y are integers, where -10<x<10, 0≤y<5, and 2x + 4y = 21, how many possible values can y take?

    SR

12. Commercial cookie mix comes in boxes of 3 pounds or 5 pounds. Cookies must be made in batches using 7 pounds of mix. We have to make several batches with this condition: after baking the cookies, no boxes of mix can be left over. What is the minimum number of boxes that must be purchased in order to have no boxes left over after the batches are made?

    SR

55

13. If a and b are integers such that a > b > 0, $a^2 - b^2 \le 10$, and a + b > 8, what is the value of a?

   (A) 3
   (B) 4
   (C) 5
   (D) 6

14. Let a, b, and c be positive integers. If a - b is odd and $(a + b)^2 + a - c$ is even, which of the following must be true?

   (A) ab is odd
   (B) a is odd
   (C) a is even
   (D) If c is odd, then a is even.

15. If $\frac{(8-x)}{3}$ is an odd integer, then x must always be

   (A) an integer multiple of $\frac{3}{8}$
   (B) an integer multiple of $\frac{8}{3}$
   (C) odd
   (D) not an integer

16. Let n be any integer greater than zero. Which of the expressions below must be an integer divisible by 3 that is twice the value of an odd integer?

   (A) 3n
   (B) 3(n-1)
   (C) 3(2n+1)
   (D) 12n - 6

56

17. Assuming n is an integer, which of the expressions below can never be even?

    I. $5n^2 - 4n + 1$
    II. $n^5 - n^2 + 1$
    III. $n^3 + n^4$

(A) I only
(B) II only
(C) III only
(D) I and II only

18. If m is an odd integer, which of the following expressions will always be the product of two integers that are odd.

(A) $m^2 - m - 2$
(B) $m^2 - 4$
(C) $m^2 + m - 2$
(D) $m^2 + 7m + 6$

19. Let n be an even, non-negative integer. How many odd integers are greater than -2 and less than n?

(A) n - 2
(B) n - 1
(C) n/2 - 1
(D) n/2 + 1

20. Let x, y, and z be consecutive integers such that 0<x<y<z. If the units digit of the product of x and z is 9, what is the units digit of y?

21. If the sum of 5 consecutive even integers is 120, what is the greatest of these?

22. If the sum of 8 consecutive odd numbers is 96, what is least of these?

Number Theory and Integers Chapter 2

23. If a and b are positive integers and 2b = a + 1, which of the following must be true?

  I. a is even
  II. a is odd
  III. $\frac{1}{b} + \frac{a}{b}$ is an integer

  (A) I only
  (B) II only
  (C) I and III only
  (D) II and III only

24. If x divided by 10 has a remainder of 9, what is the remainder if x + 2 is divided by 5?

25. If a and b are integers greater than 1, and b•(a - 4b) = 7, what is the value of a?

26. a and b are non-consecutive integers, both of which are positive. L is a prime number greater than 5. If $a^2 - b^2$ = 5L, what is the value of L as a function of b?

  (A) b + 5
  (B) 2b + 5
  (C) $b^2 + a^2 - 5$
  (D) $b^2 - 1$

58

Chapter 2   Number Theory and Integers

Practice Problem Hints

1. The right hand side must be an integer, where b is an integer. Don't forget negative values of b.

2. The big clue here is *could.* Try $a^2 = 16$.

3. The big clue here is *could.* Try $a^3 = 64$.

4. The big clue here is *could.* Try $x^3 = 4^{3/2}$

5. Start at 15 and examine successively smaller products of pairs (a,b) such that a•b ≤ 15. Look for a pair in which a+2b is less or equal to 10.

6. Choose progressively larger values of m, and for each, enumerate values of n that satisfy the condition.

7. Manually search through the first few perfect cubes to see which is a multiple of 12.

8. B is the sum of odd integers 9 + 11 + …35. Watch out for the term "inclusive."

9. Simplify the equation and plug in allowable values of x. Note that y doesn't have to be an integer.

10. Square both sides of the equation.

11. Examine the even & odd characteristics of both sides of the equation.

12. The number of boxes must weigh (in pounds) an integer multiple of 7. Test 7, 14, …

13. $a^2 - b^2 = (a+b)(a-b)$, (a+b) ≥ 9, and a>b.

14. If x is even, then x^2 is even. Integer c could be even or odd.

15. Form the equation implied in the problem, and solve for x. (Odd)•(odd) is always odd.

16. Develop an expression for an odd integer based on n, then an expression that is twice this odd value, then an expression that will force this to be divisible by 3. But there is a shortcut!

17. Examine the three expressions first with n odd and then n even to see the resulting even & odd characteristics. Use the even & odd rules you should have memorized. Remember, products of odd numbers are always odd.

18. Factor the quadratic expressions into products of linear terms. For example, $m^2 - m - 2$ = (m-2)(m+1). Both factors must be odd in the correct choice. Shortcut: think about the even & odd rules and how they read on the facts given in the question.

19. So n = 0, 2, 4, ... Examine a few test cases with small even n to discover the pattern. You are counting the number of odd numbers greater than -2 and less than n. Don't forget odd numbers less than zero that satisfy the criteria.

20. Write the digits 1 through 21. Examine the order of unit digits. Examine how the product of units digits described in the question constrains the choice of y.

21. The sum of a set of n numbers is n times their average. What is the average of these 5 numbers? The average is the middle number. Note: all the numbers are even.

22. Find the average of these 8 numbers. Distribute the 8 odd numbers about this average.

23. Examine even & odd characteristics. Divide the equation given in the question by b.

24. Which numbers divided by 10 will always have a remainder of 9? Add 2 to those.

25. 7 is prime. One of the factors must be 1 and the other 7.

26. $a^2 - b^2 = (a+b)(a-b)$. Consider the properties of prime numbers.

Chapter 2   Number Theory and Integers

Practice Problem Solutions

1. Answer D

   Clearly, b cannot be 0 because a would then be undefined, and likewise |b| cannot be greater than 1 because a must be an integer. There is no integer b other than ±1 that results in $b + \frac{2}{b} - \frac{2}{b^2}$ being an integer. If b = 1, then a = 1, and if b = -1, then a = -5. So (I) and (III) are correct.

2. Answer C

   We aren't out to prove all possible values that a and b make take, we just have to find a pair whose product equals one of the choices. The equation suggests that $a^2 = 16$, in which case a = 4. That would force b = 22 and the product a•b = 88. That is choice (C).

3. Answer B

   We aren't out to prove all possible values that a and b make take, we just have to find a pair whose product equals one of the choices. The equation suggests that $a^3 = 64$, in which case a = 4. That would force $b^{\frac{1}{3}} = 4$, making b = 4^3 = 64. The product a•b = 4•64 = 256. Therefore, $\sqrt{ab}$ = 16.

4. Answer D

   The equation suggests that perhaps $x^3 = 4^{\frac{3}{2}}$, or by squaring both sides, $x^6 = 4^3$. Simplifying, $(x^2)^3 = 4^3$, so $x^2 = 4$, and therefore x = 2 (since x must be >0). If so, then that would force y = $\sqrt{64}$ = 8, resulting in y/x = 8/2 = 4. This is choice (D).

   Alternate Solution: More directly, if we start with $x^3 = 4^{\frac{3}{2}}$, but take the cube root of each side, we arrive at x = $4^{1/2}$ = 2. This then forces y = $\sqrt{64}$ = 8, resulting in y/x = 8/2 = 4.

   Alternate Solution: If we first choose y = $\sqrt{64}$ = 8, then we must choose $x^3 = 4^{\frac{3}{2}}$ = $(\sqrt{4})^3 = 2^3$. So $x^3 = 2^3$. Therefore, x = 2.

Number Theory and Integers Chapter 2

5. Answer 12

We must maximize a•b such that a•b≤15 and a+2b≤10. Since the maximum a•b could take is 15, examine pairs of (a,b) that fit that criterion. Such (a,b) pairs would be (1,15), (3,5), (5,3), and (15,1). However, (1,15) has b>10, so that pair cannot be considered. Of the remaining three (a,b) pairs, (3,5) yields a+2b = 13; (5,3) yields a+2b = 11; and (15,1) yields a+2b = 17. In each case, a+2b is greater than 10. So try a•b = 14. Pairs satisfying this are (1,14), (2,7), (7,2), and (14,1). In all cases a+2b is greater than 10. (1,13) and (13,1) won't work either. Try a•b=12. Pairs satisfying this condition are (1,12), (2,6), (3,4), (4,3), (6,2), and (12,1). Out of this set, (4,3) and (6,2) both result in a+2b = 10, which satisfies the second condition. The maximum value of a•b satisfying both conditions is a•b=12.

Alternate Solution: a+2b≤10 probably means we should seek pairs (a,b) where b<a. (5,3), (15,1), (7,2), (14,1), and (13,1) all fail a+2b≤10. But (4,3) and (6,2) satisfy the criterion a+2b≤10. The maximum value of a•b satisfying both conditions is a•b=12.

6. Answer 7

Enumerate the possible combinations of m and n that satisfy the condition stated in the problem. Vary the value of m: the 3m term means there'll be fewer m's to test.

m	then n can be
1	1,2,3,4
2	1,2
3	1

There are 7 such pairs.

7. Answer 18

If 12m is a perfect cube, look for perfect cubes that are divisible by 12. A manual search is best. Start testing from 3^3... onwards with a calculator, and you will find that 6^3 = 216 is the smallest cube divisible by 12. So 12m = 216, and therefore m = 18.

Alternate Solution: If 12m is a perfect cube (note 12 is *not* a perfect cube), we might be able to factor 12 and m together into the form of a twin-cube, $n^3•p^3$, where n and p are integers. That is, (1) 12m = $n^3•p^3$. 12 can be prime factored into 12 = 2•2•3. Using this, (1) becomes (2) $(3•2^2)m = n^3•p^3$. We need extra powers: of 2 on 3 and 1 on 2. If we let m = $3^2•2^1$ = 18, (2) becomes $(3•2^2)•3^2•2^1 = 3^3•2^3 = n^3•p^3$. So m = $3^2•2^1$ = 18. This math-y solution is not so direct as the simple search for perfect cubes above.

62

Chapter 2   Number Theory and Integers

8. **Answer D**

    Read carefully! The sum of even integers *between* 3 and 30 = (1) 4+6+...28 = 208. The sum of odd integers from 9 to 35, inclusive, = (2) 9+11+...35 = 308. So the answer is 308 - 208 = 100. But that solution takes a long time to enter on a calculator.

    Alternate Solution: You could also solve this by using the fact that there is a difference of 5 between each of the first 13 pairs of members of set (2) and set (1) above, with 35 in (2) not having a pair partner. Therefore, the difference is 5•13 + 35 = 100.

    Alternate Solution II: you will review in chapter 8 that the sum of a sequence of n evenly spaced numbers is the median (or average) times n. There are 13 numbers in the first sequence and their median is (4+28)/2 = 16. The sequence sum therefore equals A = 13•16 = 208. The second sequence of 14 terms yields a median of (9+35)/2 = 22 and a sum of B = 14•22 = 308. The difference is B-A = 100.

9. **Answer B**

    Because y ≠ 0, we can divide by y to simplify the equation given: x^2y = 160. We are told that x can only take on values 1, 2, 3, and 4. So x^2 can only have values 1, 4, 9, and 16. Rearranging to solve for y, y = $160/x^2$. Plug the allowed values of x^2 into this equation: y can only take on values of 160, 40, 160/9, and 10.

10. **Answer D**

    Squaring each side of the equation yields ab = $625a^2$, or b = 625a. So b is an integer that is an integer multiple of 625, or b = n•625, where n is a positive integer.

11. **Answer 0**

    A lengthy brute-force search for x and y will produce zero solutions. Here's why:

    Alternate Solution: The equation may be factored as 2(x + 2y) = 21. If x and y are integers, the expression on the left is always even, while the right side is odd. There are no solutions to the equation. There are zero values of y that solve the equation.

    Alternate Solution II: 2(x + 2y) = 21, or x + 2y = 10.5. With integers? Impossible!

12. **Answer 4**

    Possible total weights of the mix can be expressed 3m + 5n, where m and n are nonnegative integers. We are told that this weight must be used to make batches that use 7 pounds of mix, with none left over. The weight must be an integer multiple of 7. Therefore, 3m + 5n = 7p, where p is some integer. Since the coefficients are all prime numbers, it isn't possible to factor or simplify this equation. You have to look manually at possible solutions, testing values of m, n, and p. 7p is a multiple of 7: the number of pounds must be one of 7, 14, 21, 28... Since no combination of m and n can result in 7 pounds, check if some combination of boxes can equal 14 pounds. A few trials will reveal that m = 3 and n = 1 will result in 3•3 + 5•1 = 14. No other combination results in 14 pounds. The minimum number of boxes is 3+1 = 4.

13. Answer C

$a^2 - b^2 \leq 10$. But $= a^2 - b^2 = (a+b)(a-b)$. So (1) $(a+b)(a-b) \leq 10$. Now, $(a+b) > 8$, or more clearly, (2) $(a+b) \geq 9$. In light of (2), we see from (1) either $(a-b) = 0$ or $(a-b) = 1$. But a > b, so (a-b) cannot equal 0. Therefore, (3) (a-b) = 1. Therefore (1) becomes (4) $(a+b) \leq 10$. Thus, in light of (2), (5) (a+b) is either 9 or 10. But from (3), b = a - 1. Plug this into (5): 2a - 1 = 9 or 10. Either a = 5 or a = 5.5. Integer a must be 5.

Alternate Solution: Brute force a search through all values of a and b, blowing time.

14. Answer D

If a-b is odd, a+b is also odd, and so $(a+b)^2$ must be odd. Since $(a+b)^2 + (a-c)$ is even and $(a+b)^2$ is odd, (a-c) must also be odd. Note that integer c could be even or odd. Because (a-c) is odd, if c is even, a must be odd; if c is odd, a must be even. Looks like (D) is the answer. But check the others: the product of one odd and one even number is always even. Therefore, (A) isn't true. (B) and (C) are clearly not true because c is undetermined. (D) is the only expression that must be true.

15. Answer B

Simplify and solve for x. Remember, (odd)•(odd) is always odd. From the data given, (1) $\frac{(8-x)}{3}$ = n, where n is an odd integer. Rearranging (1), (2) x = 8 - 3n. Since we are given that n is odd, and 3 is odd, 3n is odd. Since 8 is even, from (2) we have a generalized equation x = (even) - (odd). Now even - odd is always odd: x must be odd.

16. Answer D

The odd positive integers are given by the formula 2n-1, where n is any integer. Twice these odd integers would then be 4n-2. Numbers like this that are divisible by three must have the formula 3(4n-2) = 12n - 6.

Chapter 2 Number Theory and Integers

Alternate Solution: A number that is divisible by 3 will have 3 as a factor. The answer must be divisible by 3. All choices are divisible by 3, including (D): 12n - 6 = 3(4n-2). Also, the expression must be twice the value of an odd integer, so the expression must be 3•(an expression that is twice the value of an odd integer). (A), (B), and (C) do not satisfy this criterion. By elimination, (D) must be the correct answer. To prove this, notice that (D) can be rearranged as 3(4n-2). The expression 4n-2 can be further factored as 2(2n-1). Since 2n-1 is guaranteed to be odd, 2•(2n-1) is indeed twice the value of an odd integer.

Alternate Solution II: Twice any integer must be even. Only (D) is always even. Next!

17. Answer B

Useful even & odd properties: The product of any set of all-even integers is even. The product of any set of all-odd integers is odd. If any <u>one</u> member of a product-set is even, the product is even. The sum or difference of two odd integers or two even integers is even. The sum or difference of an odd and an even integer is odd. Whew. Given these ideas, let's see what happens when n is even and then when n is odd.

First test (I), (II), and (III) when n is even. Both (I) and (II) are (even) - (even) +1, which is always odd. Test (III) when n is even: (III) is (even) + (even), which is always even. Now test when n is odd. (I) is (odd) - (even) + 1, which is always even; (II) is (odd) - (odd) + 1, which is always odd; (III) is always even because (odd) + (odd) = (even).

Only (II) can never be even.

18. Answer B

One could certainly test several odd values of m by plugging them into the 4 expressions. But we can prove this. Each of these quadratic expressions can be easily factored into a form (m+a)(m+b), where a and b are integers. The correct answer choice will be odd•odd. Therefore, (m+a) and (m+b) must both be odd. Since m is odd, a and b must both be even since the sum of an odd and an even integer is always odd. Factoring the choices gives these results: (A) (m-2)(m+1); (B) (m+2)(m-2), (C) (m+2)(m-1); (D) (m+6)(m+1). If m is odd, only (B) will be odd•odd. All other choices are odd•even.

Alternate Solution: Easier still. If the answer must be the product of two odd integers, then the answer must always be odd. Simply analyze the 4 choices (mentally plugging in "odd" as a substitute to m) to determine (using odd/even rules) whether or not the expression is odd: without numbers! (A) is odd - odd - even = even. (B) is odd - even = odd. (C) is odd + odd - even = even. (D) is odd + odd + even = even. Only (B) is odd.

Number Theory and Integers	Chapter 2

19. Answer D

We must count the number of odd integers between -2 and n. Don't forget -1; thereafter, include all odd integers between 0 and n. Look for a pattern by testing a few examples. If n is 4: -1, 1, 3, or three odd integers. If n is 6: -1, 1, 3, 5, or four odd integers. With similar reasoning if n is 8, there are 5 odd integers. We now can infer the pattern: the number of odd integers between -2 and n equals n/2 + 1.

Alternate Solution: If you recall the formula for this scenario given in the chapter review, the number of odd integers between two even integers, m and n, is (n - m)/2. In this question, m = -2. So the number of odd integers between -2 and n (when n is even) is, according to the formula, (n + 2)/2 = n/2 + 1.

Alternate Solution II: n = 0 is allowed in the interval definition. When n = 0 every choice is negative except choice (D). The number of integers is negative? Impossible!

20. Answer 0

Algebra is not the way to go here. One way to proceed might be to write the first several integers that include all possible units digits and find a pattern. Here's a list:

1 2 3 4 5 6 7 8 9 10 11 12 13 14 15 16 17 18 19 20 21 ...

Hmmm. Pick any three sequential units digits: x,y,z. The question states that the product of the units digits of x and z must equal 9. There are only three ways a product of two units digits can equal 9: (1,9), (3,3), and (9,1). But all 3 digits must be *sequential*. No consecutive units digits (1,y,9) exist. Likewise, no consecutive units digits (3,y,3) exist. The only possible sequence of units digits is (9,y,1). This pattern fits (9,10,11), or (19,20,21), or (29,30,31)... etc. In every case the units digit of the integer between x and z must be zero: 10, 20, 30... So the units digit of y is 0.

21. Answer 28

There are 5 consecutive even numbers, so the middle number must be the average of these (see chapter 6). Their average is 120/5 = 24. Therefore, the numbers in question are 20, 22, <u>24</u>, 26, and 28. The largest is 28. More on this in chapter 6.

Alternate Solution: The five consecutive even integers must sum to 120. Therefore, they must be clustered around 120/5 = 24. In fact, since they are consecutive-even, and there are 5 of them, 24 must be the center number with the two largest numbers to its right. 20, 22, *24*, 26, <u>28</u>. So 28 is the largest number.

66

22. Answer 5

There are 8 consecutive odd numbers that sum to 96. The average of these numbers is 12 (not one of the 8 odd numbers). There will be 4 odd numbers less and 4 odd numbers greater than the average, 12. The 8 consecutive odd numbers summing to 96 are 5, 7, 9, 11, and then 13, 15, 17, and 19. The least of these is 5.

Alternate Solution: The 8 consecutive odd numbers must cluster around 96/8 = 12. By symmetry, there must be 4 odd numbers less than 12 and 4 odd numbers above 12. They are 5, 7, 9, 11, 13, 15, 17, 19. The least of these is 5.

23. Answer D

The only constraints on a and b are that they are positive integers. Both a and b could be even or odd. We know (1) 2b = a + 1, so obviously 2b is always even. Let's go through each of the possibilities (I, II, III) in turn. In choice (I), a is even. From (1) if a were even, a+1 would be odd. So (1) becomes even = odd. Obviously, (I) is not true. Now we know that a must be odd, and (II) must be true. (III) looks scary. Maybe we could use (1) to somehow say something about the expression $\frac{1}{b} + \frac{a}{b}$. Dividing (1) by b, we obtain 2 = (1+a)/b = $\frac{1}{b} + \frac{a}{b}$. So, $\frac{1}{b} + \frac{a}{b}$ *always* equals 2, which is an integer. So both (I) and (III) are always true.

24. Answer 1

Which numbers divided by 10 have a remainder of 9? 19, 29, 39, ... Any one of these, when added to 2 will give a number ending in 1, such as 21, 31, 41, ... Those numbers will always have a remainder of 1 when divided by 5.

25. Answer 29

We have integers a and b, both greater than 1, constrained by the equation (1) b•(a-4b) = 7. Notice that 7, a prime number, is the product of two integer factors, b and (a-4b). Given the property of primes, one of these terms must be 7 and the other term 1. Some students will solve (1) too quickly using b = 1 and a = 11. However, we are given that *both* a and b are greater than 1. Since b is a factor by itself in (1), it must be true that b = 7. Therefore, the second factor in (1) must equal 1. Thus, (2) a - 4b = 1. Plugging b = 7 into (2), we get a - 28 = 1. Thus, a = 29.

Number Theory and Integers   Chapter 2

26. Answer B

If $a^2 - b^2 = 5L$, this might be a time to try the ol' "$a^2 - b^2 = (a+b)(a-b)$," especially since the right side of the equation involves primes. Thus, $(a+b)(a-b) = 5L$. Remember, both a and b are positive *non-consecutive* integers. Thus, (a-b) cannot equal 1. Since both 5 and L are prime, one factor in parenthesis on the left must be 5 and the other term L. Either (1) (a+b) = 5 and (a-b) = L, or (2) (a-b) = 5 and (a+b) = L. Since L is greater than 5, and (a+b) is greater than (a-b), (a+b) must be L, and therefore (a-b) must be 5, and thus simultaneous equations (2) are correct. We can use (2) to solve for b in terms of L. Subtracting the first equation in (2) from the second: 2b = L - 5. Solving for L in terms of b: L = 2b + 5. This one is tricky hard.

Chapter 3

Digit Manipulations

Fun for some and brain poison for others, digit manipulation problems are rarely on the SAT in the last few years. Digit puzzle problems usually represent integers as unknown digits, like ABCD, or M1N6. Relationships among these digits or relationships to another integer determine, or constrain, the possible values of these digits: essentially a they are simultaneous equations and inequalities.

Powers-of-ten decomposition is introduced as an analytic technique.

Other problems discussed in this chapter ask you to determine the *number* of integers that satisfy a given set of relationships between their digits, or other criteria.

These problems are <u>very</u> <u>rare</u> on the SAT, but they are within the scope of the test. The concepts involved, 6 archetypical problems, and an additional 10 practice problems can be found below.

Digit Manipulations — Chapter 3

Don't Show Up Without Knowing…

How To…

- Decompose a number into powers-of-ten
- Solve digit manipulation problems involving one number
- Solve digit manipulation problems involving two numbers
- Determine the set of possible digits or integers, given various constraints

Quick Review and Definitions

Digit Constraints

Consider a 3-digit integer, ABC, where A, B, and C are the hundreds, tens, and units digits, respectively. The values of B and C may take 0, 1, 2, 3, 4, 5, 6, 7, 8, 9. However, A is restricted to 1, 2, 3, 4, 5, 6, 7, 8, 9. This will be true of the leftmost digit of any integer.

On SAT questions further digit constraints may be defined within questions. For example, if the digits of ABC are constrained by the equality (1) $A = B + 2C$, then C is restricted by the value of A since $1 \leq A \leq 9$. The maximum value of A is 9. What is the maximum possible value of C? C must be less than 5, otherwise A will be greater than 9. The maximum value of C is 4.

Powers-Of-Ten Decomposition

A 3 digit number, ABC, where A, B, and C represent the hundreds, tens, and units digits, respectively, can be decomposed into powers-of-ten such that $ABC = 100 \cdot A + 10 \cdot B + C$. This is an important relationship used to solve some mystery digit problems.

Chapter 3 Digit Manipulations

SAT Archetypes

Integer Decomposition into Powers-Of-Ten

How many two-digit numbers exist such that the product of the tens and units digits equals the number?

(A) 0
(B) 1
(C) 2
(D) more than 2

How do I start?

This one looks difficult to guess or quickly test manually. But remember: if A is the ten's digit and B is the unit's digit, then the number AB may be decomposed into powers-of-ten such that AB = 10A + B, which we are told equals A•B.

Solution

It would take a long time to go through every two-digit number and count those satisfying the condition in the problem. Instead, set up an algebraic equation representing the conditions to see if a solution even exists. If the two-digit number is AB, the value of the number will equal 10A + B. According to the conditions in the problem, this must also equal A•B. So if a solution exists, 10A + B = A•B. We may rearrange this equation to get (1) A(10 - B) = -B. Because A is the tens digit, A>0, and since $0 \le B \le 9$, it is also true that the second term in the product, 10 - B > 0. Therefore, the product on the left hand side of (1) is composed of two positive factors. The left side is *greater* than zero. Since $0 \le B \le 9$, the right side of (1) is never greater than zero. Equation (1) is never true, and therefore there are *no* values of A and B that satisfy the conditions given in the problem.

Alternate Solution

Can the product of the digits *ever* equal the number, or is the product always less than the number? A few examples of maximum possible products might allow you to infer a rule. 1•9 < 19; 2•9 < 29; 3•9 < 39; 4•9 < 49;...; 9•9 < 99. One *might* safely guess that in every possible pair of two digit integers, the product of the digits is less than the digit itself.

Answer A

Digit Manipulations   Chapter 3

The Take-Away

Equalities that involve digits and the numbers they compose can sometimes be analyzed effectively using powers-of-ten decomposition. Of course, this type of decomposition is also possible for integers with even more than two digits. Plus, as seen in the alternate solution, a manual search and inference is an option if the algebraic route is dark to you.

Transposition of Digits: AB ↔ BA

Let a two-digit number, m, be signified by AB, where the tens digit of m is A, and the units digit of m is B. Another number, n, is similarly signified by BA. If n - m = 27 and A + B = 9, what is the value of n?

(A) 36
(B) 45
(C) 63
(D) 72

How do I start?

You could either start by analyzing the digits using the AB = 10A + B powers-of-ten decomposition, or brute-forcing the solution, knowing that the universe of numbers AB, where A+B = 9, is fairly small.

Solution

We know m = AB = 10A + B and n = BA = 10B + A. We know that (1) n - m = 27. Substituting the above expressions in (1), n - m = (10B + A) - (10A - B) = 9B - 9A = 27. Dividing both sides by 9, we get (2) B - A = 3. We are given that (3) A + B = 9. Adding (2) and (3) gives 2B = 12. Solving for B gives B = 6. Plugging this value for B into (2) gives A= 3. Since n is signified by BA, n = 63. Schweet.

Alternate Solution

Since A+B = 9, n = BA can only be from the set {90, 81, 72, 63, 54, 45, 36, 27, 18}. Moreover, since BA - AB = 27, BA is greater than AB: BA must then belong to the subset {90, 81, 72, 63, 54}. AB belongs to (45, 36, 27, 19}. A brute-force search through these numbers to find where n - m = BA - AB = 27 will reveal that 63 - 36 = 27. So n = BA = 63.

Answer C

Chapter 3 — Digit Manipulations

The Take-Away

Problems involving two-digit transposition, AB ↔ BA, can be analyzed using powers-of-ten decomposition or a brute-force search as well if the solution space is small. This was a confusing problem, and both solution methods required time and thought.

One Number With Mystery Digits

DCBA is a four-digit integer where digits D, C, B, and A are the thousands, hundreds, tens, and units digits, respectively. These digits satisfy the following rules:

1. D = A+B+C
2. C = B+1
3. A = C-5

What is the four digit number?

SR

How do I start?

The 3 simultaneous equations above are also constrained by the digits' domains. Examine the rules to discover the most restrictive constraint. For example, from (3), C must be greater than 4 if A is to be nonnegative. Use such rules successively to further narrow the allowed intervals of the digits until the digits have all been determined.

Solution

A, B, and C belong to the set {0...9}, whereas D belongs to the set {1...9}. Examine the rules to discover the min and max values of the digits. For example, from equation (3), C must belong to {5...9}, otherwise A would be less than zero. As a result, from (2), B must belong to {4...8}, otherwise C might be less than 5 or greater than 9. So the minimum of C is 5 and the minimum of B is 4. Now, consider rule (1). D can't be greater than 9, and since the minimum of B+C is 9, we see A must be 0 and therefore D=9. C and B must be their minimums: A=5 and B=4. So A=0, B=4, C=5, and D=9. DCBA = 9540.

Answer 9540

The Take-Away

In digit manipulation problems, look at the rules or other constraints given in the problem, and use them in conjunction with the limited domains of the digits (which are themselves a type of constraint) to answer the question.

Digit Manipulations   Chapter 3

Two Numbers With Mystery Digits

A, B, and C are digits from the set of integers {0...9}. Let 6A4 and 6B6 represent two three digit numbers. If 6A4 + 6B6 = 1C00, what are the possible values of C?

(A) 2
(B) {2,3}
(C) 3
(D) {2,3,4}

How do I start?

Before tackling the equation, determine the greatest and least possible values of 6A4, 6B6, and then the greatest and least and least possible values of their sum. What constraints will these have on the possible values of C, the hundreds digit of the sum? Continue by analyzing further constraints from the equation 6A4 + 6B6 = 1C00.

Solution

The greatest possible sum occurs if A and B are both 9. In this case 6A4 + 6B6 = 694 + 696 = 1390. Likewise, the least possible sum would be 604 + 605 = 1210. The sum must therefore be in the set (1) {1210...1390}. Using just this analysis, C, the hundreds digit of the sum, could only be 2 or 3. We can toss out choice (D). Furthermore, from the equation in the problem, the tens digit of 1C00 must be zero. The smallest number in set (1) above with a tens digit of zero is 1300. So, the sum must be in the set {1300...1390}. Only C=3 is represented in this set and the answer is (C). In fact, since the tens and units digits are both known to be zero, we know that the mystery sum 1C00 is 1300.

Alternate Solution

Since the units digits sum to 10, there is a carry digit, and so 1+A+B must equal 10 because the tens digit of 1C00 is also zero. Therefore, there is a carry digit over to the hundreds digit: 1+6+6 = 13 = 1C. So C must equal 3.

Answer C

The Take-Away

In a (rare) mystery digit problem involving two numbers, you'll often have to sequentially refine the intervals of possible digits and numbers. Analyze the problem by determining minimum and maximum possible values given the conditions set forth in the problem.

Chapter 3 Digit Manipulations

How Many Integers Satisfy Digit Constraints

Let n be a positive 3-digit integer such that n<400. If the sum of the hundreds digit and the tens digit equals the square of the units digit, how many different values of n satisfy this condition?

(A) 7
(B) 8
(C) 9
(D) more than 9

How do I start?

The sum of the hundreds and tens digits must be a perfect square: 1, 4, 9, 16, ... But also notice that the hundreds digit is 1, 2, or 3. This will constrain the values that the tens and units digits can take.

Solution

Since n is 399 or less, the hundreds digit has a maximum of 3 and the tens digit has a maximum of 9. (1) Their sum must be less than or equal to 12. But the sum of the hundreds and tens digits must also be the square of an integer: 1, 4, 9, 16, ... Thus, from (1), we know (2) the sum of the hundreds and tens digits can only be 1, 4, or 9. So the units digit must be the square root of those sums: therefore, (3) the units digit can only be 1, 2, or 3. It is only necessary to brute-force enumerate all 3-digit numbers less than 400 satisfying conditions (2) and (3). Start with the 100's and work up to the 300's.

101:	1 + 0 = 1, the square of 1	(sum of hundreds and tens, square of units)
132:	1 + 3 = 4, the square of 2	(sum of hundreds and tens, square of units)
183:	1 + 8 = 9, the square of 3	(sum of hundreds and tens, square of units)
222	2 + 2 = 4, the square of 2	(sum of hundreds and tens, square of units)
273	2 + 7 = 9, the square of 3	(sum of hundreds and tens, square of units)
312	3 + 1 = 4, the square of 2	(sum of hundreds and tens, square of units)
363	3 + 6 = 9, the square of 3	(sum of hundreds and tens, square of units)

Answer A

The Take-Away

Always look behind the conditions given in a problem to discover relationships possibly more pertinent to the solution. For example, in this problem, the fact that the number is less than 400 means that the hundreds digit is 1, 2, or 3. The units digit must be a perfect square, which will then further constrain the values of the other digits.

Digit Manipulations

Properties of Units Digits

Let m be a positive integer such that the units digit of m equals the units digit of m^2. Which of the following integers could be m?

(A) 13122
(B) 27648
(C) 18457
(D) 52596

How do I start?

In this problem we're told that the units digit of the correct choice must be equal the units digit of the correct choice squared. If you aren't sure what units digits fit this criterion, manually go through the choices. But you really only have to test the units digits.

Solution

Remember third grade: when squaring a number (manually), you start with the product of the units digits. The only digits that produce the same units digit upon squaring are 1, 5, and 6: $1^2 = \underline{1}$, $5^2 = 2\underline{5}$, and $6^2 = 3\underline{6}$. Only choice (D) has one of these, 6, as a units digit.

Alternate Solution

You could slog through all five choices, square them and see which retained the same units digit as well, but the problem is designed to destroy time if this method is used.

Answer D

The Take-Away

When an integer is raised to some power, the resulting units digit will equal the units digit of the original units digit raised to that power. For example, $69^2 = 476\underline{1}$ and $9^2 = 8\underline{1}$. Only units digits 1, 5, and 6 generate the same units digit upon squaring (or raised to any positive integer power.). Also, remember that for *any* units digit, successive higher powers result in a repeating pattern of resulting units digits. The above integers can be squared by a calculator. But what if they had been larger numbers that when squared caused the calculator to be out of range?

Chapter 3 Digit Manipulations

Practice Problems

1. A, B, and C are digits ranging from 0 to 9, and 5A4 and 5B6 represent two three digit numbers. If 5A4 + 5B6 = 1C00, then what are the only possible values of C?

   (A) 0
   (B) {0,1}
   (C) 1
   (D) 9

2. A and B are different digits between 1 and 9, inclusive. If AA and AB represent two different two digit numbers, which of the following numbers can never divide evenly (i.e., with no remainder) into AA + AB?

   (A) 2
   (B) 3
   (C) 5
   (D) 11

3. How many two-digit numbers, AB, where A is the tens digit, and B is the units digit, have a value equal to $(A + B)^2$?

   (A) 0
   (B) 1
   (C) 2
   (D) 3

4. A positive two-digit number, AB, where A and B are the tens and units digits, respectively, has a remainder of 3 when divided by 7. When AB is added to BA (where the digits have been reversed), the result is 99. What is the value of AB?

   SR

77

Digit Manipulations   Chapter 3

5. Set A consists of all integers between 100 and 199, inclusive, that have exactly two digits equal to 1. A subset of A comprises those numbers that are also divisible by 6. What fraction of the members of A are also in the subset?

    (A) 0

    (B) $\dfrac{1}{18}$

    (C) $\dfrac{2}{19}$

    (D) $\dfrac{1}{9}$

6. In the equation below, A, B, C, and D are the digits of three integers as shown. What is the value of the three digit sum, CD8?

$$\begin{array}{r} AB \\ +BA \\ \hline CD8 \end{array}$$

SR

7. Let A and B represent digits between 0 and 9, inclusive. The following four-digit number and three-digit number are added such that the sum follows the form given below. What is the value of B?

$$\begin{array}{r} 1\,1\,A\,5 \\ +\,3\,B\,2 \\ \hline 1\,5\,6\,A \end{array}$$

SR

Chapter 3　　　　　　　　　　　　　　　　　　　　Digit Manipulations

8. Let A, B, C, and D represent the digits of two 3-digit integers, where D ≠ B. They are added such that the sum follows the form given below. What is the value of ABC?

$$\begin{array}{r} A\,D\,D \\ +\,A\,B\,C \\ \hline 1\,0\,1\,0 \end{array}$$

(A) 406
(B) 500
(C) 510
(D) 511

9. How many two-digit numbers have digits such that twice the product of their digits equals the number?

(A) 0
(B) 1
(C) 2
(D) 3

10. DCBA is a four-digit integer where D≠C≠B≠A. Digits D, C, B, and A are governed by the following rules:

1. D = A+2B+C
2. C = B+3
3. A = C−5

What is the four digit number?

SR

79

Digit Manipulations

Practice Problem Hints

1. Examine how the known digits must create a carry in the sum.

2. AA will always be evenly divisible by 11, regardless of the value of A.

3. Examine only those two-digit numbers that are perfect squares.

4. List all the two-digit numbers AB and BA that sum to 99.

5. Enumerate those numbers with two 1's as digits. Find those that are divisible by 6. Some problems are just a slog.

6. Examine the sums of the digits and the constraints on their possible values. C must equal 1. Is there a carry digit? What does that mean?

7. The hundreds digits tell that there must be a carry from the tens.

8. Examine the hundreds digits first.

9. If A is the ten's digit, and B is the unit's digit, then $10A + B = 2 \cdot A \cdot B$.

10. Examine the rules to discover the minimum or maximum values of the digits. For example, from (3), C must be ≥ 5. Use these types of rules successively to further narrow the choices.

Chapter 3   Digit Manipulations

Practice Problem Solutions

1. Answer C

   (1) 5A4 + 5B6 = 1C00. The largest sum possible is 594 + 596 = 1190, so C must be less than 2. The smallest possible sum would be 504 + 505 = 1010. In this case, C = 0. Hmmm. Start over. From (1), 4 + 6 = 10, so there must be a carry from the units digits into the tens. Since the tens digit on the right side of (1) is zero, A+B plus the carry must equal 10. Therefore, there will also be a carry into the hundreds digit: 5+5+1 = 11, and so the value of C must be 1.

   Alternate Solution: the units sum to 10, carry 1. Therefore the ten's (plus the carry) sum to 10, carry 1. The hundreds (plus the carry) sum to 11. Final sum = 1100.

2. Answer D

   The trick to solving this problem is to notice that AA is always evenly divisible by 11, regardless of the value of A. Since AA is different from AB, B is not equal to A, and no two-digit integer of the form AB will be evenly divisible by 11. What about (AA+AB)/11? Since AA/11 is an integer, but AB/11 is not, (AA+AB)/11 is not an integer. Thus, when AA + AB is divided by 11, there will always be a remainder.

3. Answer B

   Since AB must equal $(A+B)^2$, only values of AB that are perfect squares are possible. Only 6 two-digit integers are perfect squares: 16, 25, 36, 49, 64, and 81. Only one number, 81, satisfies the conditions set forth in the problem: $(8+1)^2$ = 81.

4. Answer 45

   List those pairs AB and BA that sum to 99 (this will require some thought at first): (18,81), (27,72), (36,63), (45,54). One of those numbers will have a remainder when divided by 7. A calculator slog through the list finds 45/7 = 6 with a remainder of 3.

   List the multiples of 7, then add 3. E.g., 7+3 = 10, 14+3 = 17, etc. Look for a candidate that satisfies the digit-reversed and sum requirement: 10, 17, 24, 31, 38, 45 (aha!), 52, 59, 66, 73, 80, 87, 94. So only one value of AB, 45, added to its digit reverse, BA =54, will sum to 99.

Digit Manipulations   Chapter 3

Alternate Solution: We can employ powers-of-ten analysis: (10A+B) + (10B+A) = 99. So 11(A+B) = 99, or (1) A + B = 9. Now list numbers AB satisfying (1): 18, 27, 36, 45, 54, 63, 72, 81. Then test each number by dividing by 7, looking for the one that has a remainder of 3. If careful, this is head math. Only 45 satisfies this constraint.

5. Answer B

One way to solve this problem is to list the members of the set quickly and perform the requested division with a calculator or in your head. Set A, having two 1's, is {101, 110, 112, 113, 114, 115, 116, 117, 118, 119, 121, 131, 141, 151, 161, 171, 181, 191}, which has 18 elements. A number that is divisible by 6 must be even and also divisible by 3. If the sum of the digits of a number is divisible by 3, then that number is divisible by 3. A quick search through the set above reveals that 114 and 141 are the only numbers in this list that are divisible by 3. Since 141 is odd, it is not divisible by 6. There is only one member of the subset that is divisible by 6. The fraction of the first set that is also divisible by 6 is therefore 1/18.

Alternate Solution: Start by saving only the even numbers out of the 18 total. These are 110, 112, 114, 116, and 118. Of these, only 114 is divisible by 3.

6. Answer 198

AB + BA = CD8. The largest sum of any two-digit numbers is 198, which means that C = 1. Moreover, there must be a carry digit from the tens addition. Either A+B is 10 or more, or A+B is 9 + a carry from the units. Thus, (1) A+B ≥ 9. Looking at the units digits, either A+B = 8, or A+B = 18. But from (1), A+B ≥ 9, so A+B = 18. There is only one pair of digits that could possibly sum to 18: A = B = 9. Check by plugging these values in: the mystery sum is 99 + 99 = 198, which does have the required form, CD8.

Alternate Solution: 10A+B + 10B+A = 11(A+B) = CD8. The multiples of 11 that have units digit 8 are 88, 198, 308 ... But 1 ≤ C ≤ 2. Therefore, CD8 = 198.

7. Answer 9

11A5 + 3B2 = 156A. From the units digits, A = 5+2 = 7. Look at the hundreds digits. 3 + 1 ≠ 5. There *must be a carry digit from the tens* into the hundreds: 1 + 3 + carry = 5. Examining the tens digits, A+B = 7+B must equal 16, not 6, Therefore, B = 9.

8. Answer C

ADD + ABC = 1010. Examine the hundreds digits first. Since there is a carry into the thousands, the only way for A+A (plus any carry) to equal 10 is if A = 5 and for there to be *no* carry digit from the tens digits. Thus, the tens: either D+B = 1, or D+B = 0 (but there is a carry digit from the units), resulting in the tens digit equaling 1. However,

Chapter 3   Digit Manipulations

D+B cannot equal 0 because D cannot equal B. So D+B = 1, and therefore there is no carry digit from the units. Thus, examining the units digits, D+C must equal 0. So both D = 0 and C = 0, and therefore, since D+B = 1, B = 1. ABC = 510.

9. **Answer B**

It would *way* too long to go through every two-digit number and count those numbers having digits such that twice the product of the digits equals the number. Instead, use powers-of-ten decomposition to set up an algebraic equation representing the conditions, and see if a solution even exists.

If the two-digit number is AB, the value of the number equals 10A + B, which according to the conditions must equal 2AB. A, of course, never equals zero.

10A + B = 2•A•B, and after rearrangement, A(10-2B) = -B. Solving for A in terms of B, (1) A = B/(2B-10). B must be a digit ≥6 (otherwise A would be negative or undefined), and digit A must also belong to {1…9}. Using (1), test all values of B ≥6. If B = 6, then A = 3. All larger values of B result in non-integer values of A. So A = 3, B = 6, AB = 36. There is only one two-digit number satisfying the given constraint.

Alternate Solution: 2AB = 10A + B. Rearranging, (2B-10) = B/A. Since 2B-10 is even, B/A must even. If B/A = even, then B = A•even. And so B must also be even. The only integers AB with digits A and B where both B is even and B/A is even are 12, 14, 24, 36, 28, 48. Only AB = 36 satisfies the criterion of twice the product of the digits equaling the number.

Alternate Solution II: From (1) above, A = B/(2B-10), so B must be a digit ≥6. Moreover, A must be an integer. Test B = 6,7,8 and 9 in (1) and see which value of B results in an integer value of A. Only B = 6 results in integer A = 3. So AB = 36.

10. **Answer 9520**
    D≠C≠B≠A and

    1. D = A+2B+C
    2. C = B+3
    3. A = C-5

What is DCBA? Examine the rules to discover the allowed intervals of the digits. From (3), C must be: {5…9}, otherwise A would be less than zero. Using this information in (2), B must be: {2…6}, otherwise, C would be out of range. D = A+2B+C, and cannot be >9. Since the minimum of C is 5, and the minimum value of 2B is 4, from (1), the value of D is A + 4 + 5. Since A < 10, A must equal 0. So D = 0 + 4 + 5 = 9. We have discovered all the digits: DCBA = 9520.

Notes

Chapter 4

Percent Calculations

We define *percent:* "for every hundred." People have been counting on their ten fingers for as long as they have counted. *You* might even do that on a couple of questions. So groups of ten seem natural enough. The magic of *ten* groups of ten – who knows? The ancients were often numerologically superstitious. And their rulers, who had to manage the needs and capabilities of thousands, probably found it easier to think in groups of a hundred. If the king were to ask, "How many out of a hundred men can see to throw a spear?" the answer, 12%, goes down much faster than a ratio of jumbo numbers. Percentages can simplify the world in base 10.

SAT tests may include a difficult problem involving intricate uses of, and conversions between, percents, fractions, ratios, and percent increases and decreases. Multiple relationships may be involved among problem elements, requiring a careful accounting of percent changes or other quantities. Sequential operations of percent changes such as compound interest or inflation are sometimes featured in problems on the test.

In all there are 7 archetypes of difficult percent problems on the SAT that test the student's ability to organize mathematical constraints and practical scenarios into sequences of mathematical operations. In this chapter you will review the concepts, the archetypes, and practice 17 additional problems in this area.

Don't Show Up Without Knowing…

These Concepts

Fraction	Discount
Percent	Commission
Decimal	Compound Interest
Ratio	Markup

How To…

- Convert between percents, fractions, decimals, and ratios
- Calculate percent increase and percent decrease
- Calculate a sequence of percent increases and percent decreases
- Calculate compound interest
- Calculate sales commissions
- Calculate sales markups
- Calculate sales discounts

Chapter 4 — Percent Calculations

Quick Review and Definitions

Percents ⇔ Fractions ⇔ Decimal ⇔ Ratios

The SAT assumes you know how to convert between percents, fractions, decimal notation, and ratios.

For example, 70% ⇔ 70/100 ⇔ .70 ⇔ Ratio of 70:100.

Percent Increase, Decrease, Discount, Markup

Don't be confused by the percent of a value and the percent increase of a value. For example, 200% of $100 is $200. A 200% increase of $100 is $300. In general:

- Increasing y by x% equals y•(1 + x/100), or y•(100 + x)/100

- If x<100, increasing by x% is the same as multiplying by "1.x," or "1.0x," if x is less than 10 and greater than 1. For example, an increase of 45% is the same as multiplying 1.45. An increase of 8% is the same as multiplying by 1.08.

- Decreasing y by x% equals y•(1 - x/100), or y•(100 - x)/100. Note: 0 ≤ x ≤ 100, *always*.

- Decreasing by x% is the same as multiplying by "1 - .x," or "1 - .0x," if x is less than 10 and greater than 1. E.g., a decrease of 45% is the same as multiplying by 1 - .45 = .55. A decrease of 8% is the same as multiplying by 1 - .08 = .92.

- A discount of x% off a price is the same as decreasing the price by x%.

- A markup of x% is the same as increasing the price by x%.

- x% of y = y% of x. For example, 25% of 40 = 10. 40% of 25 = .4•25 = 10.

Percent Change Between Two Values

If a value changes from x to y, the percent change is defined as 100(y - x)/x. The original number, x, goes on the bottom. Example: if last year's income was $1000, and this year's income is $1500 ($500 more than last year), then the percent change from last year to this year is 100(1500 - 1000)/1000 % = 50%. Now suppose that *next year's* income will be $1000 ($500 less than this year's income). The percent change between this year and next year is 100(1000 - 1500)/1500 % ~ -33.33%. The magnitudes of the percent changes are *not* the same. Yet first we gained $500 over $1000 and later we lost $500 from $1500.

Sequences of Percent Increase and Percent Decrease

Some problems may involve taking a value or variable and applying a *sequence* of percent increases and/or decreases. For example, a bank balance has an initial value of $900. If 40% is withdrawn, and then later a deposit is made equal to 50% of the remaining balance, what is the balance after that deposit? First apply the 40% decrease. The balance after the decrease equals 900 • .6 = 540. After this, the balance is increased by 50%, so the final balance = 540 • 1.5 = 810.

Compound Interest

Compound interest describes a sequence of identical percent increases applied to some initial value in an account. The interest may be compounded yearly or at other intervals. There is a formula to calculate the final value in an account when interest is compounded over a given period of time. A compound interest of x% compounded *yearly* for y years on an original balance of D dollars gives a final balance of $D \cdot (1+x/100)^y$ dollars. For example, if the original principle is D = $100, and the bank gives 2% interest, compounded yearly, then after y = 5 years the account would be worth $100 \cdot (1+2/100)^5$ = $110.41 (approximately). In general, if interest is compounded n times per year over y years at x% interest *per year*, the final balance would be $D \cdot (1+x/(n \cdot 100))^{ny}$. Memorize this.

Solving for a Ratio or Product of Variables

Some problems boil down to one equation with two variables. If the variable terms are isolated on each side of the equation, and if the exponents on the variables are ±1, then the equation can be rearranged to isolate either x/y or xy. For example, if 2x = 4/y, then xy = 2. As another example, if 6x = 2y, then x/y = 1/3.

The Order of Operations May Matter

Note that while x% of y = y% of x, increasing by x% and then decreasing by y% is <u>not</u> the same as decreasing by x% and then increasing by y%. Example: increasing $100 by 50% yields $150. Decreasing $150 by 50% yields $75.

Chapter 4 — Percent Calculations

SAT Archetypes

Percent of One Kind in a Set of Two Kinds

There are 100 more freshmen than sophomores attending a certain 2 year college. If there are x sophomores, then what percent of those attending are sophomores, in terms of x?

(A) $\dfrac{x}{100 + 2x}\%$

(B) $\dfrac{x}{100 + x}\%$

(C) $\dfrac{50x}{100 - x}\%$

(D) $\dfrac{100x}{100 + 2x}\%$

How do I start?

Write down what you know. If there are x sophomores, then the number of freshmen, f, will be 100 more than x, or f = x + 100. To get the percent of total students that are sophomores, you'll need the total number of students in terms of x.

Solution

Let T equal the total number of students = number of freshmen + number of sophomores. Let the number of freshmen be f and the number of sophomores be x. From the data in the problem, the number of freshmen equals f = x + 100. So T = f + x = (x + 100) + x = 100 + 2x. The ratio of sophomores to the total is x/(100+2x), and the *percent* of sophomores is 100x/(100+2x) %.

Answer D

The Take-Away

This x/(N + 2x) type of fraction in 2-component mixtures where there are N more of one type than x of the other is pretty common. This construction, with 2x in the denominator, should pop into your mind when confronted with such 2-component mixtures. Also - if a problem asks for an answer as a percent of some quantity, calculating the ratio or fraction first is often the most direct approach. But don't forget to convert back to percent.

Percent Calculations   Chapter 4

Algebraic Relationships Involving Percents and Ratios

If a + 2b equals 250 percent of 6b, and b ≠ 0, what is the value of $\frac{a}{b}$?

SR

How do I start?

First, convert 250 percent to decimal format, as 2.5. Then a + 2b = 2.5 • 6b = 15b. This equation may be rearranged to solve for a in terms of b.

Solution

250% of 6b is 2.5 • 6b = 15b. Therefore, given the info in the problem, a + 2b = 15b. Isolating a, a = 13b. Dividing both sides by b produces the desired ratio: a/b = 13.

Alternate Solution

This same problem might have been written in terms of ratios: if the ratio of a + 2b to 6b is 2.5:1, what is the value of $\frac{a}{b}$? Therefore, $\frac{a+2b}{6b} = \frac{2.5}{1}$. Multiplying both sides by 6b, we obtain a + 2b = 15b. Isolating a, a = 13b. The desired ratio is a/b = 13.

Answer 13

The Take-Away

SAT problems often combine percent conversions with algebra or other confusing transformations. Also – some students will mistakenly take 250% of b instead of 6b. Another common mistake is calculating a 250% *increase* in 6b. Read carefully.

Chapter 4 Percent Calculations

Calculating an Unknown Percent With Two Constraints

If decreasing 20 by x percent is the same as increasing 5 by x percent, what is the value of x?

(A) 50
(B) 55
(C) 60
(D) 65

How do I start?

Translate the verbiage into math. For example, decreasing 20 by x percent is the same as multiplying it by (1 - x/100). Set the two "same as" expressions equal to each other and solve for x.

Solution

Set up an equation using the words of the problem. Decreasing 20 by x percent is the same as multiplying 20 by (1 - x/100). Increasing 5 by x percent is the same as multiplying 5 by (1 + x/100). We are told that these two expressions are equal to each other, or 20•(1 - x/100) = 5•(1 + x/100). Multiplying both sides by 100 and expanding gives us 2000 - 20x = 500 + 5x. Isolating x, 1500 = 25x, or x = 60.

Answer C

The Take-Away

An equation that relates an unknown percent increase to an unknown percent decrease allows one to solve for the unknown percentage. Of course, you might encounter a similar problem, where the percent is known, but an amount is unknown. For example, if decreasing x by 20% is the same as increasing 10 by 100%, what is x? This is easier. Increasing 10 by 100% is 20. So the implied equation is 1.2 • x = 20. Dividing both sides by 1.2 yields x = 16.666...

Percent Calculations   Chapter 4

Percent Increase and Subsequent Decrease

A house went on sale for x dollars in March. The price was increased by <u>a</u> percent in April. However, the house didn't sell, so in May the owners lowered the April price by <u>2a</u> percent. If the May price was y dollars, what is y/x in terms of <u>a</u>?

(A) $\dfrac{5000-100a-a^2}{10{,}000}$

(B) $\dfrac{5000+100a-a^2}{10{,}000}$

(C) $\dfrac{5000+200a-a^2}{10{,}000}$

(D) $\dfrac{10{,}000-100a-2a^2}{10{,}000}$

How do I start?

First, algebraically express the April price after increasing x dollars by <u>a</u> percent. Then take that expression and apply a decrease of <u>2a</u> percent for the May price = y. A recipe!

Solution

Raising x by <u>a</u> percent yields x•(100+a)/100. To get y, decrease this expression by <u>2a</u> percent by multiplying by (100-2a)/100. After doing so, y = x•(100+a)/100 • (100-2a)/100 = x•(10,000 - 100a - 2a²)/10,000. Rearranging, y/x = (10,000 - 100a - 2a²)/10,000.

Alternate Solution

Because we desire the ratio of y to x, you could just set the price of the house, x, to 1 dollar. The ratio will remain the same and you don't have to carry the x throughout the algebra. But in this case little time would be saved.

Answer D

The Take-Away

Situations involving serial applications of percent changes must be performed in the sequence stated. Remember, increasing by x% and then decreasing by y% is not the same as decreasing by x% and then increasing by y%.

Chapter 4 — Percent Calculations

Sales Commissions Expressed Algebraically

Jayla is hired by a car dealership to sell cars. She is paid solely with sales commissions on each car she sells. Her commission is p percent of the final price of a car, minus $200 for each car sold to cover dealership overhead (rent, taxes, administrative costs, etc.). Which of the following expressions represents her commission, in dollars, on 3 cars, each of which sold for $29000?

(A) $\dfrac{29{,}000p - 200}{100}$

(B) 870p - 600

(C) 29,000p - 200

(D) 87,000 - 600

How do I start?

Translate carefully. The comma before "minus" indicates that the subtraction takes place *after* the percent operation. You take p percent of the price and *then* subtract $200 for each car sold. By definition, p percent of 29000 equals p•29000/100.

Solution

For each car sold, Jayla's commission will be (p percent of $29,000) - $200. Since p percent of 29,000 is 29,000•p/100 = 290p, her commission for each car is 290p - 200. Her total commission on selling 3 cars is 3•(290p - 200) = 870p - 600.

Answer B

The Take-Away

Develop a formula for commission based on a careful reading of the verbal terms of the commission, and don't forget to take into account multiple sales or other adjustments described in the problem. Punctuation can occasionally determine the meaning of a math problem.

Markup Required for a Certain Profit

20 identical cars just arrived at a car dealership. They pay a wholesale cost for each car and then sell it at a higher, retail price to generate a profit. If the dealership needs to make a combined $80,000 profit on these 20 cars, and it sells each of them for the same price, it will have to sell each car for $64,000. What must be the markup (the percent increase over the wholesale cost) for each car?

SR

How do I start?

In order to calculate the markup, we'll need to calculate the wholesale cost of each car. The profit *per car* needs to be $80,000/20 = $4000.

Solution

Retail price = Wholesale cost + profit. The *profit per car* needs to be $80,000/20 = $4000. If each car has to generate $4000 profit, then the wholesale cost for each car is $64,000 - $4000 = $60,000. A markup of x% will raise the cost from $60,000 (the wholesale cost) to $64000 (the retail cost). A markup of x% = (100+x)/100 percent. Applying an x% markup to $60,000 (the wholesale cost of each car) results in a retail price of $60,000 • (100+x)/100 percent, which we are told must equal $64,000. In equation form, $60,000 • (100+x)/100 percent = $64,000. After a little algebra, we can isolate x: x = -100 + 64,000•100/60,000 = 6.666... The percent increase over the wholesale cost, i.e., the markup, is 6.666... percent, or 6 2/3 percent.

Answer 6.67 or 20/3

The Take-Away

Markup is the same as "the percent increase applied to the wholesale cost." Markup and commission problems may require additional analyses to determine the values on which these operations are performed. Here, we had to determine what the wholesale cost was before calculating the markup.

Chapter 4 — Percent Calculations

Compound Interest

One style of above-ground pool costs $5000 this year, but is increasing at a rate of 10% per year. An employee knows that if he stays with the company 4 more years, he can get a 20% discount on the cost of the pool. To the nearest dollar, how much would a pool cost the employee 4 years from now?

(A) 5856
(B) 5922
(C) 6466
(D) 6498

How do I start?

This isn't a compound interest problem per se, but if you know the formula for compound interest, here is your moment. Otherwise, calculate the price of the pool after the first, second, third, and forth years. Then apply the discount.

Solution

Next year the pool will cost 10% more than this year = 5000 • 1.1 = 5500. In two years, the cost will be 5500 • 1.1 = 6050. In three years, the pool will cost 6050 • 1.1 = 6655. In four years, the pool will cost 6655 • 1.1 = 7320.5 dollars. After four years the employee gets a 20% discount, so his cost will be 7320.5 • .8 = 5856.4 dollars. To the nearest dollar, his cost will be $5856.

Alternate solution

You should memorize (if you haven't already) the formula for compound interest. Of course, compound interest is analogous to any sequential application of identical percent changes. A 10% increase is equivalent to multiplying by 1.1. After four years, the cost will be $5000 \cdot (1.1)^4 = 7320.5$ dollars. Thereafter, take the 20% discount, equivalent to multiplying by .8. The final cost is 7320.5 • .8 = 5856.4 dollars. To the nearest dollar, his cost will be $5856.

Answer A

The Take-Away

Sequential applications of identical percent changes is analogous to compound interest. Whenever possible, save time by using the compound interest formula.

Percent Calculations • Chapter 4

Interest Compounded Quarterly

A bank has a type of savings account that pays interest compounded quarterly (every 3 months). To compute the amount of money after y years in the account since an initial deposit of D dollars, they use the formula $D(1 + i/400)^{4y}$, where i is the annual percentage interest rate. Which of the following is the expression for the additional money earned at 2% interest compared to 1% interest (both compounded quarterly) after 18 months?

(A) $D(1.005)^6 - D(1.0025)^6$
(B) $D(1 + 2/400)^6 - D(1 + 1/400)^3$
(C) $D(1.0025)^{18} + D(1.00125)^{18}$
(D) $D(1 + 2/400)^{18} - D(1 + 1/400)^{18}$

How do I start?

This is just a complicated problem in understanding the data given and formulating the difference between two exponential expressions. 18 months is 1.5 years.

Solution

Just plug in the numbers given into the formula. After 18 months (1.5 years), the money earned at 2% annual interest would be $D(1 + 2/400)^{4 \cdot 1.5}$, or $D(1.005)^6$. Likewise, the money earned at 1% annual interest would be $D(1 + 1/400)^{4 \cdot 1.5}$, or $D(1.0025)^6$. The additional money earned at 2% over 1% would be $D(1.005)^6 - D(1.0025)^6$.

Alternate Solution

The answer will be the difference between two terms, both of which *must* have an exponent of 4y = 4 • 1.5 = 6. Only choice (A) meets this requirement.

Answer A

The Take-Away

A complication sometimes thrown into compound interest problems is compounding intervals other than 1 year, even though the interest rate is given in annual terms. Also - be careful to keep the units of time intervals straight in such problems. Check out the alternate solution. They keep handing you shortcuts. If only you will take them.

Chapter 4   Percent Calculations

Practice Problems

1. If a + 1.5b equals 150 percent of 6b, what is the value of $\frac{a}{b}$?

   SR

2. If decreasing 20 by x percent is the same as increasing x by 40 percent, what is the value of x?

   (A) 10
   (B) 12.5
   (C) 50
   (D) 60

3. The sum of a pair of real numbers, a + b, is 120 percent of b. What is the ratio of the sum to their difference, a - b?

   (A) $\frac{1}{2}$
   (B) $\frac{3}{4}$
   (C) $-\frac{3}{2}$
   (D) 2

4. The sum of two nonnegative numbers is 250 percent of one of the two numbers. What is the ratio of this sum to the positive difference between the two numbers?

   (A) $\frac{1}{2}$
   (B) 2
   (C) 4
   (D) 5

Percent Calculations   Chapter 4

5. The numerator of a fraction is diminished by 20% and its denominator is increased by 140%. If the new fraction equals $\frac{1}{5}$, what was the original fraction?

   (A) $\frac{1}{28}$

   (B) $\frac{3}{20}$

   (C) $\frac{7}{20}$

   (D) $\frac{3}{5}$

6. If y is 40 percent less than x and x is 40 percent greater than 300, what is the value of x - y?

   SR

7. If $x \neq 0$ and y is 40 percent less than x and x^2 is 40 percent greater than y, what is the value of 10y - x?

   SR

8. Vicente gets p percent of the negotiated price of every yacht he sells, plus a $1000 bonus. Which of the following is his take, in dollars, on 2 yachts that sold for $850,000 each?

   (A) 850000p/200 + 2000
   (B) 850p + 2000
   (C) 34,000p +2000
   (D) 17,000p + 2000

Chapter 4	Percent Calculations

9. A golf foursome pooled their funds and tipped their four caddies a total of $200 to carry clubs and advise them during a round of golf at a resort in Thailand. If this sum was 25 percent of the other fees the foursome paid to the resort to play golf, and each player paid the same, what did each player pay to play golf that day, including his portion of the caddie tip?

(A) 175
(B) 200
(C) 250
(D) 275

10. An electric motor scooter sells for $8400, reflecting a 20% markup over dealer cost (i.e. the sales price is 20% more than the dealer's cost). As a benefit, employees of the dealership can purchase one of these motor scooters at 5% off dealer cost. How much are employees charged for such a sale?

(A) 6650
(B) 7000
(C) 7250
(D) 7424

11. *CHALLENGE* Jack has 25 percent deducted from his gross pay for income taxes every year. Insurance contributions are also deducted as a percentage of his gross pay. Last year, he had 5 percent of his gross pay deducted for insurance, but this year he doubled the percentage deduction for insurance. His gross pay was raised by 8 percent this year compared to last year. What is the ratio of this year's net income after taxes and deductions to last year's gross pay before taxes and deductions?

(A) .7
(B) .702
(C) 1.06
(D) 1.12

12. The share price of a company's stock is constantly changing on the stock market. The P/E ratio of a company's stock is the price of one share of company stock divided by the company's reported annual earnings per share (EPS). For example, if the price of one share is $100 and the earnings per share is $10, then the P/E ratio is 10. But the P/E ratio can change. When either the price or earnings per share change (or both), the P/E can change. When this year's EPS was announced, the company revealed it had declined by 10% from last year. The stock price almost immediately thereafter dropped by 25 %. What was the percent change in the P/E ratio after the announcement?

(A) $-16\frac{2}{3}$
(B) -15
(C) -7
(D) $-7\frac{1}{2}$

13. An investor loses 50 percent of the value of his investments in a bad year. He hopes they will gain enough value to recoup his losses over the next 2 years by compounding yearly his gains with the same percentage each year. To recoup his loss, which of the values below will most nearly equal the required yearly percent increase?

(A) 38
(B) 41.4
(C) 44.5
(D) 46.7

14. The school cafeteria uses canned juice concentrate mixed with water to make juice. Once emptied, the can may be used as a measuring device. Each can of concentrate contains 15% high fructose corn syrup (HFC) by volume. Of the following expressions, which represents the percent volume of HFC syrup in a mixture of x cans of concentrate and y cans of water?

(A) 7.5x / (x+y)
(B) .15x / (.15x+y)
(C) 15x /y
(D) 15x / (x+y)

15. There are 100 fewer freshmen than twice the number of sophomores attending a certain 2 year college. If there are x sophomores, then what percent of those attending are sophomores, in terms of x?

(A) $\dfrac{100x}{(3x-100)}$

(B) $\dfrac{20x}{(x-20)}$

(C) $\dfrac{100x}{(2x-200)}$

(D) $\dfrac{50}{(3x-200)}$

16. There are 100 fewer freshmen than twice the number of sophomores attending a certain 2 year college. If there are 300 freshmen, then what percent of those attending are sophomores?

(A) 20
(B) 25
(C) $33\dfrac{1}{3}$
(D) 40

17.

	Number of Students	Members of Athletic Club
7th Graders	300	250
8th Graders	275	210

The data above shows the total number of 7th and 8th grade students in a certain middle school along with data showing the number of students belonging to the athletic club in each grade. During a recent week, 60 percent of all students attended the club. If official club attendance is measured by the following formula,

$$\dfrac{\text{Number of Students Attending Club}}{\text{Number of Members}},$$

what was the official attendance measured for that week?

SR

Percent Calculations   Chapter 4

Practice Problem Hints

1. 150% of 6b is 1.5 • 6b = 9b.

2. Translate, set the two expressions equal to each other and solve for x.

3. a + b = 1.2b.

4. Let a + b = 2.5b, where b must be the smaller of the two numbers.

5. For numerator a and denominator b, a(1-.2) / b(1+1.4) = 1/5.

6. Calculate x first, then y.

7. Express each relationship in equation form: two equations, two unknowns.

8. He sells *two* yachts. p percent of x equals p•x/100.

9. The problem asks for the amount paid by each player: resort fees plus caddy tip.

10. Calculate dealer cost first, and then calculate employee cost.

11. Let m equal last year's gross income. Calculate this year's net income in terms of m, including all increases, taxes, and deductions.

12. Calculate this year's earnings in terms of last year's earnings. Calculate the post-announcement stock price in terms of the pre-announcement price.

13. If his account increases x percent each year for 2 years, he will have $(1 + x/100)^2$ times as much as he started with.

14. Juice is made in the ratio of (x cans concentrate): (y cans water). But concentrate is only 15% HFC. Calculate the percentage of x cans in the total, and then take 15% of that.

15. Express the total number of students in terms of sophomores.

16. Express the total number of students in terms of freshmen.

17. Calculate the number of students attending the club that week, using the given percentage.

Chapter 4 — Percent Calculations

Practice Problem Solutions

1. Answer 7.5

   150% of 6b is 1.5 • 6b = 9b, and therefore a + 1.5b = 9b. Solving for a, a = 7.5b, so a/b = 7.5.

2. Answer B

   Set up the equation using the words of the problem. Decreasing 20 by x percent is the same as multiplying 20 by (100-x)/100. Increasing x by 40 percent is the same as multiplying x by (100+40)/100 = 1.4x. Equating these expressions gives us 20•(100-x)/100 = 1.4x. Rearranging this equation produces 2000 - 20x = 140x. 160x = 2000, or x = 12.5.

3. Answer C

   From the problem, a + b = 1.2b. So a = .2b. The difference a - b = -.8b. And the ratio of the sum to the difference is 1.2b/(-.8b) = -1.5 or -3/2.

   Alternate Solution: The sum, a + b = 1.2b, So a = .2b. Thus, the difference a - b = -.8b. The ratio of sum/difference must be negative. Only choice (C) is a possible solution.

4. Answer D

   Let the two numbers be designated a and b. Since a + b is 2.5 times one of those numbers, *that* number must be the smaller of a or b. In general, we can let b be the smaller number. From the problem, a + b = 2.5b. So a = 1.5b. The positive difference is always the larger minus the smaller number: a - b = .5b. The ratio of the sum to the positive difference is 2.5b/.5b = 5.

5. Answer D

   Let the original fraction be a/b. From the problem, a(1-.2) / b(1+1.4) = 1/5. Simplifying, .8a/2.4b = 1/5, or a/b = 1/5 • 2.4 /.8 =.6 = 3/5. Don't forget the fraction function on your calculator, although you don't need it here, do you?

Percent Calculations   Chapter 4

6. Answer 168

Since x is 40 percent more than 300, x = 1.4 • 300 = 420. Since y is 40 percent less than x, y = 420•(1-.4) = 420 • .6 = 252. The difference, x - y = 420 - 252 = 168.

7. Answer 4.2

We need the value of 10y - x, so we need to solve for both x and y. If y is 40 percent less than x, then (1) y = .6x. If x^2 is 40 percent greater than y, then (2) x^2 = 1.4y. We have two equations with two unknowns. Substitute the expression (1) for y in terms of x into (2) and solve for x. Thus, x^2 = 1.4(.6x) = .84x. Isolating x gives x = .84. Then, from plugging this value of x into (1), y = .6 • .84 = .504. We now have values for both y and x. So 10y = 5.04, and 10y - x = 5.04 - .84 = 4.2.

8. Answer D

For each yacht sold, Vicente will get (p percent of $850,000) + $1000. Since p percent of 850,000 is 850,000•p/100 = 8500p, his total take is 2•(8500p + 1000) = 17,000p + 2000.

Alternate Solution: He sells 2 yachts for a total of 1,700,000. Because the $1000 bonuses are shown as separate terms in each of the choices, the final expression must have a "17" somewhere to account for the price of the 2 yachts. Only choice (D) presents such an expression.

9. Answer C

Let x be the total amount all four players together paid the golf course in other fees to the resort. If 200 is 25 percent of x, then 200 = .25 • x. Solving for x, x = 800, the total resort fees paid by the foursome. The total paid by the foursome in resort fees plus tips was then 800 + 200 = 1000. Each player paid 1000/4 = 250.

Alternate Solution: 200 is each player's resort fee < (fee + tip). Answer is (C) or (D).

10. Answer A

Letting the dealer cost be D, if 8400 is 20% more than D, 8400 = 1.2•D. Solving this, D = 7000. The employee cost is 5% less than that = .95 • 7000 = 6650.

Chapter 4　　　　　　　　　　　　　　　　　　　　　　　　　　　　　　Percent Calculations

11. Answer B

Let last year's income before deductions = m. Since his gross income increased this year by 8 percent, this year's income *before* deductions = 1.08m. His tax deduction this year will be 25/100 • 1.08m = .27m. His insurance rate doubled: this year's insurance rate = .05 • 2 = .1. Using this new rate, insurance this year will cost him .1 • (current income) = .1 • 1.08m = .108m. So this year's net income after deductions and taxes = 1.08m - taxes - insurance = 1.08m - .27m - .108m = .702m.

The ratio of this year's income after all deductions to last year's gross pay equals .702m/m = .702.

12. Answer A

Let e1 = last year's earnings per share. From the data given, this year's earnings per share is 10% less, or e2 = .9e1. Let s1 = pre-announcement stock price. From the data given, the post-announcement stock price, s2, is 25% less than s1: s2 = .75s1. From the definition of P/E ratio, the pre-announcement ratio, P1, was s1/e1. The post-announcement ratio, P2 = s2/e2 = .75s1/.9e1 = .75/.9 • P1. The percent change in P/E ratio = 100•(P2 - P1)/P1 = 100 • (.75/.9 • P1 - P1)/P1 = 100 • (.75/.9 - 1) = $-16\frac{2}{3}$.

Alternate Solution: Chose convenient numbers for this problem since we're looking for the percent change. Let the preannouncement stock price and earnings per share both equal 100. The pre-announce P/E would then be P1 = 100/100 = 1. After the announcement, the earnings per share is 90, and the stock price is 75. The post-announcement P/E is then P2 = 75/90. The percent change in P/E ratio = 100 • (P2 - P1)/P1 = 100(75/90 - 1) = $-16\frac{2}{3}$ percent.

13. Answer B

Let A = the original account value. After the 50% loss, his account is worth .5A. If each succeeding year sees an increase of x percent, then each year's account will have (100 + x)/100 = (1 + x/100) times more than the previous year. So after two years, the account be worth .5A • (1 + x/100)². We are told in the problem that this must equal the original amount, A. Thus, .5A • (1 + x/100)² = A, or simplifying, (1 + x/100) = $\sqrt{2}$. Isolating x, x = ~41.4 percent.

Alternate solution: After the 50% loss, he must double his money in 2 years. In other words, his account will multiply by a factor of 2 over two years. So each year it will multiply by a factor of $\sqrt{2}$ ~ 1.414, a 41.4% increase over the previous year.

105

Percent Calculations · Chapter 4

14. Answer D

In the mixture, the total volume (in cans) is concentrate + water = x + y. Since 15% of the concentrate (x) is HFC, the volume of HFC is .15x. The fraction of HFC to the total is .15x/(x+y), or expressed as a percentage of the total: 15x/(x+y) %.

Alternate Solution: Juice is made by mixing x cans of concentrate with y cans of water. The total volume of juice is v(x + y), where v is the can's volume. Since 15% of the concentrate is HFC, the total volume of HFC in x cans of concentrate is vx·15/100 = .15vx. So this is the volume of HFC. The ratio of HFC volume to the total volume is then .15vx / v(x+y), and, after cancelling the factors of v and converting the ratio to percent, the percentage of HFC in the mixture = 15x/(x+y)%.

15. Answer A

(1) Let T equal the total number of students = number of freshmen + number of sophomores. If the number of sophomores is x, then from the data in the problem, the number of freshmen equals 2x - 100. From (1), T = 2x - 100 + x = 3x - 100. The ratio of sophomores to the total is x/(3x - 100), and the percent of sophomores is 100x/(3x - 100).

Alternate Solution: The total number of students must be 2x - 100 + x = 3x - 100. Thus, that term must be in the denominator of the answer. Only choice (A) includes this term in the denominator.

16. Answer D

Let T equal the total number of students = number of freshmen + number of sophomores. Let F = number of freshmen and S = number of sophomores. We know that F = 300, and we also know that F = 2S - 100. Setting these expressions equal to each other, 300 = 2S - 100, and solving for S, S = 200. The total number of students is F + S = 300 + 200 = 500, and the percentage of sophomores is 200/500·100% = 40%.

17. Answer 3/4 or .75

The total number of students in the school = 300 + 275 = 575. 60% of them attended the club that recent week: 575 · .6 = 345. We can calculate the total number of club members = 250 + 210 = 460. Using these last two numbers in the attendance definition given, the official attendance = 345/460 = .75 = 3/4.

Chapter 5

Ratios, Shares, and Totals

After the kill, share the food.

The concept of a ratio might be older than numbers themselves. Without calculating ratios, our wordless ancestors must have had some sense of being cheated or not – a cerebral, fuzzy guess of what a decent share should be. Animals that hunt in packs will share their prize in ratios based on social rank and contribution to the hunt. They know. Then along came language, leaders, and the need to fairly issue things of value to their people – and advantages assumed by those who wield that fearsome power.

There are three broad areas of hard questions on the SAT involving ratios, shares and totals. One kind of problem sets up scenarios where several people share expenses in complicated ways. A second kind describes the manner in which shares of some total are distributed among people using multiple ratios. Perhaps the most difficult of ratio problems involves two different types of objects with known ratios among them and how these ratios change when objects are subsequently added or removed.

There are 6 archetypes of problems on the SAT involving ratios, shares and totals. The concepts involved, example archetypes, and an additional 13 practice problems that expand on the subject are included below.

Quick Review and Definitions

Converting Between Ratios And Fractions Of A Total

The SAT may have a few problems that require the student to solve problems expressed in terms of ratios, shares, and/or fractions of a total.

For example, if a box contains only red balls and green balls, and the ratio of red balls to green balls is 2:3, then there are two red balls for every *five* balls in the box. The fraction of red balls in the box is therefore $\frac{2}{5}$.

Now assume different proportions of red and green balls in a different box. If we only know the fraction of green balls to the total is $\frac{3}{7}$, then for every 7 balls, 3 balls are green, and therefore 7 - 3 = 4 balls of the 7 must be red. The ratio of red balls to green balls is therefore 4:3.

In general, with only 2 kinds of objects, a ratio of a:b implies that the fraction of a in the total set of objects is a/(a+b).

This can be extended to multiple kinds of objects. Let there be three kinds of objects: A, B, and C. There are a of A, b of B, and c of C. A ratio of a:b:c implies that for every a of kind A, there are b of kind B and c of kind C. The *fraction* of a in this set of objects is a/(a+b+c).

The Total Is Related To The Terms In A Ratio

If a ratio is expressed as a:b, *and the ratio is reduced completely*, then the total number of objects *must be divisible* by a+b. For example, if the ratio of boys to girls is 3:4, then the total number of children must be a multiple of 7.

In this example, if the total number of girls and boys is T, then the fraction of boys is 3/7, and so the number of boys is 3T/7. Likewise, the number of girls will be 4T/7.

Note also that the number of boys must be a multiple of 3, and the number of girls must be a multiple of 4.

Ratios Change When Objects Are Added Or Removed

Consider a box of apples and oranges with 21 pieces of fruit, where the ratio of apples to oranges is 2:1 (note again that the total number of fruit must be divisible by 2+1 = 3). If 5 apples are later eaten, the ratio of apples to oranges will change. There are a couple of SAT archetypes that involve situations like this. In order to calculate the new apples:orange ratio, you will need to first calculate the number of each kind of fruit before the apples were eaten. Since the ratio of apples:oranges was originally 2:1, 2/(2+1) = 2/3 of the fruit in the box were apples. Originally, there were 2/3 • 21 = 14 apples and 21-14 = 7 oranges. After eating 5 apples, there are 9 apples left. Now the apple to orange ratio is 9:7, and the fraction of apples is 9/16.

Notes

Chapter 5 — Ratios, Shares, and Totals

SAT Archetypes

A Ratio Determines the Possible Totals

All the socks in a certain drawer are either white or beige, and the ratio of the number of beige socks to the number of white socks is 3:4. Which of the following could be the total number of pairs of socks in the drawer?

(A) 4
(B) 5
(C) 6
(D) 14

How do I start?

If the ratio of beige to white socks is 3:4, then three *sevenths* of the socks are beige. For every 7 socks, 3 will be beige (and 4 will be white).

Solution

The ratio 3:4 cannot be reduced. For every 3n beige socks, where n is an integer, there must be 4n white socks. The total number of socks must then be 3n + 4n = 7n. The total number of socks must be an integer multiple of 7. Only (D) satisfies this criterion.

Alternate Solution

Hammer this in: you must know this relationship between ratios and fractions: if the ratio of beige to white socks is 3:4, then 3/7 of the socks are beige, 4/7 are white. Since these fractions are fully reduced, the total number of socks *must* be an integer multiple of the denominator, 7. Only (D) satisfies this criterion.

Answer D

The Take-Away

A ratio of a:b implies that the fraction of a in the total set of objects is a/(a+b). After reducing this fraction to its lowest terms, the total must be a multiple of the denominator.

Ratios, Shares, and Totals Chapter 5

Share of Expenses Among Several Persons

Car Rental	10%
Air Travel	50%
Food and Supplies	30%
Gifts	10%

The table above shows the breakdown of Alicia's 5-day camping trip expenses in various categories by percentage of her total expense. The cost of renting the car was shared equally with her 2 companions, but otherwise each person individually paid their own expenses. If Alicia paid a total of $660 for her trip, what was the total cost, to the nearest dollar, for the group to rent the car?

(A) 115
(B) 120
(C) 166
(D) 198

How do I start?

Read this one carefully. The problem asks for the total cost of the rental car, not just Alicia's 1/3 share of that cost. From the data given, we can fairly easily calculate her share. Start with her total expenses.

Solution

Since Alicia spent a total of $660 on the camping trip, and 10% of that expense was her share of the car rental, she spent $66 on car rental. Since the total car rental expense was split equally between three people, the total car rental expense was 3 • $66 = $198.

Answer D

The Take-Away

The cost of one item among many in a percentage breakdown analysis is the total cost multiplied by the fraction of that item (represented by percentage) to the total. If the cost of an item is equally shared, the cost is divided by the number sharing that cost.

Chapter 5　　　　　　　　　　　　　　　　　　　　　　　Ratios, Shares, and Totals

Unknown Ratio, Given Two Combined Sets

The junior class has 360 students with a ratio of girls to boys of 5:4. The senior class has a boy/girl ratio of 4:3. If there are a total of 640 juniors and seniors, what is the ratio of boys to girls for the combined classes?

(A) 9:7
(B) 16:9
(C) 1:1
(D) 3:2

How do I start?

You need to calculate the total number of boys and the total number of girls to get their ratio. You know the number of juniors and its girl/boy ratio, so you can calculate the number of junior girls and boys. You also know the sum of juniors and seniors, which will allow you to calculate the number of seniors. Careful with the wording of the ratios.

Solution

The total number of boys = junior boys + senior boys, and likewise for the girls. There are 360 juniors out of a total (of juniors and seniors) of 640. Thus, there are 640 - 360 = 280 seniors. From the gender ratios given, we can calculate the number of girls and boys in each class. Junior girls:boys is 5:4. So the fraction of juniors who are girls is 5/(5+4) = 5/9, and so there are 5/9 • 360 = 200 junior girls. The rest of the juniors are boys, and so there 360 - 200 = 160 junior boys. Likewise, the fraction of senior boys (*notice the swapped order of boy-girl in that ratio*) is 4/(3+4) = 4/7; there are 4/7 • 280 = 160 senior boys and 280 - 160 = 120 senior girls. The total number of girls is 200 + 120 = 320; the total number of boys is 160 + 160 = 320. So the boy/girl ratio of the combined classes is 1:1.

Alternate Solution: Concentrate on the girls. From the given ratios it is readily seen that 5/9 of juniors and 3/7 of seniors are girls. We know that there are 360 juniors, and by subtraction, there are 280 seniors. Weighing each of the populations by their respective fractions, we can sum them to get the total number of girls: 5/9 • 360 + 3/7 • 280 = 320. This is half of the total number of students, 640, and so the ratio of boys to girls is 1:1.

Answer C

The Take-Away

Difficult ratio problems may involve a combination of two ratios involving two distinct groups. The best way to approach such problems is to first see what information hides behind the data in the problem. In a set of two kinds of objects: a of A and b of B, the objects are present in a ratio of a:b, the total equals a+b, and the fraction of a is a/(a+b).

113

Ratios, Shares, and Totals   Chapter 5

Ratios, When Objects Are Added or Taken Away

A box contains black and white balls in the ratio of 4 black to 3 white balls. After 12 white balls are taken from the box, the ratio of black balls to white balls becomes 2:1. How many balls are left in the box?

(A) 60
(B) 72
(C) 84
(D) 96

How do I start?

There is a mix of black and white balls in the box. The ratio of the number of black balls to the number of white balls is 4:3. We don't know the total number of balls. We are told that after 12 white balls are removed, the ratio of black to white changes from 4:3 to 2:1. But notice: *the number of black balls doesn't change*. The number of black balls can be expressed as both a fraction of the unknown original total *and* as a fraction of the new total after the white balls are removed. Those two expressions must be equal.

Solution

Let T be the original number of balls in the box. The number of black balls doesn't change, so let's concentrate on them. Because there were 4 black balls for every 3 white balls, 4/7 of the original total number of balls, or (1) $4T/7$, were black. After removing 12 white balls, there are a total of $(T-12)$ balls remaining. We are told that after removing the white balls the black-white ratio then becomes 2:1, which means that 2/3 of the remaining $(T-12)$ balls are black, or (2) $2/3 \cdot (T-12)$. Again, the number of black balls did not change, so the number of black balls must be the same before and after removing the white balls. Equating the number of black balls (1) before and (2) after the white balls were removed, $4T/7 = 2/3 \cdot (T-12)$. Solving for T, the original number of balls, $T = 84$. After removing 12 white balls, there are $84 - 12 = 72$ balls remaining in the box.

Answer B

The Take-Away

With changing ratio problems, it may be necessary to express relationships in the problem in terms of some unknown total number of objects. Sometimes the total is constant, but if objects are added or removed, as they were here, the total will change. If the number of one kind of object doesn't change, concentrate on that one.

Chapter 5   Ratios, Shares, and Totals

Exact Total, Given Ratios and the Number of One Kind

Four toddlers are offered jellybeans from a box. The jellybeans come in 6 colors. Camila takes 1/4 of the jellybeans, Jamal takes 1/5, and Denise takes 1/10. If Katlyn gets the remaining 18 jellybeans, how many jellybeans were originally in the box?

(A) 28
(B) 40
(C) 60
(D) 78

How do I start?

Note that *all* of the jellybeans are taken. Express the number each child (except Katlyn) takes in terms of T, the unknown total number of jellybeans in the box. The sum of these expressions involving T (along with Katlyn's 18) is equal to T. The colors are unimportant.

Solution

We need T = the total number of jellybeans in box. Camila takes T/4, Jamal takes T/5, Denise takes T/10, and Katlyn takes 18. The sum of the parts, T = T/4 + T/5 + T/10 + 18. Rearranging, and expressing in a common denominator, T = 5T/20 + 4T/20 + 2T/20 + 18. Simplifying, T = 11T/20 + 18, or 9T/20 = 18. Solving for T, T = 40.

Answer B

The Take-Away

If the fraction or ratios of every kind in a set is known except for one kind, but the *number* of that one kind is known, then the numbers of all kinds (and their total) in the set can be computed. An equation in the form T = f_1·T + f_2·T + ...+ (*known number of one kind*), where f_i is the fraction of objects of type i, may be used to solve for the total, T.

Note that this problem tossed in extraneous information. The solution is independent of the colors of jellybeans that are in the box. You'll have to develop an intuition enabling you to ignore extraneous data. They don't do this often, but students sometimes stumble in confusion at such information, not knowing what to do with such useless data.

Ratios, Shares, and Totals   Chapter 5

Determine Number of Members of Two Combined Sets

The junior class has 180 students, and the ratio of girls to boys is 5:4. The senior class has a boy/girl ratio of 4:3. The ratio of boys to girls for the combined classes is 1:1. How many students make up the combined junior and senior classes?

(A) 320
(B) 325
(C) 330
(D) 346

How do I start?

We have to calculate the number of seniors in order to find the combined total. Using the 5:4 ratio you can calculate the number of junior girls and boys. Using the 4:3 ratio, you can represent the number of senior boys and the number of senior girls in terms of S, the unknown total number of seniors. Then use the 1:1 ratio of boys to girls to solve for the number of seniors. This one is tough.

Solution

From the 1:1 ratio, total # boys = total # girls. The total number of boys = junior boys + senior boys, and the total number of girls = junior girls + senior girls. From the given data, the ratio of junior girls to boys is 5:4, or 5/9 of the juniors are girls and 4/9 of the juniors are boys. The number of junior girls = 5/9 • 180 = 100, and the number of junior boys = 4/9 • 180 = 80. We are not told the number of senior students, but we know that the ratio of senior boys to senior girls is 4:3; so 4/7 of seniors are boys and 3/7 of seniors are girls. Let S be the unknown number of seniors. There are 4S/7 senior boys and 3S/7 senior girls. Now, when the classes are combined, the number of boys equals the number of girls (from the 1:1 ratio). The number of boys is 80 + 4S/7. The number of girls is 100 + 3S/7. Thus, 80 + 4S/7 = 100 + 3S/7. Rearranging to solve for S, 20 = S/7, and so S = 140 = the number of seniors. The combined number of juniors and seniors = 180 + 140 = 320.

Answer A

The Take-Away

Some problems may present two sets (juniors and seniors, here) that are *each* split into two groups (boys and girls here). In this problem we were given a ratio (1:1 boys to girls) that could be expressed in terms an unknown we needed: the number of seniors.

Chapter 5   Ratios, Shares, and Totals

Practice Problems

1.

Car Rental	30%
Air Travel	30%
Food and Supplies	10%
Equipment	30%

The table above shows the percentage breakdown of the total costs incurred during a camping trip on which 4 people went. Jill went on this trip, and all costs were shared equally with her 3 camping companions. If Jill paid $75 for her share of the car rental, how much did she spend on food and supplies?

(A) 14
(B) 15
(C) 24
(D) 25

2.

Car Rental	30%
Air Travel	50%
Gifts	10%
Equipment	10%

The table above shows the percentage breakdown of the total costs incurred during a camping trip on which 4 people went. Mia went on this trip, and the costs were shared equally with her 3 traveling companions except Mia paid for half of all gifts. If Mia paid $275 for her share of the air travel, how much did she spend on gifts?

(A) 110
(B) 120
(C) 125
(D) 130

Ratios, Shares, and Totals　　　　　　　　　　　　　　　　　　　　　　　　　　　　Chapter 5

3. Every outfit in a fashion show is either white or black, and the ratio of the number of black outfits to the number of white outfits is 6-to-7. Which of the following could be the total number of dresses in the show?

   (A) 45
   (B) 72
   (C) 78
   (D) 120

4. The dresses in a small retail shop for women's clothes are red, green, or blue, and they occur in ratios of 2 red to 3 green to 5 blue. If there are 90 dresses, how many green dresses are in the shop?

   (A) 21
   (B) 25
   (C) 27
   (D) 30

5. Blueberry pancake batter is premixed in a restaurant kitchen to have a ratio of 14 cups of plain batter to 3 cups of blueberry paste. If 7 cups of blueberry pancake batter are to be prepared, how many cups of blueberry paste will be needed?

   (A) 1.5
   (B) 2
   (C) 2.25
   (D) $\frac{21}{17}$

6. *CHALLENGE* A graduated cylinder in a lab is initially filled with fluid until the height of the fluid measured from the bottom of the cylinder is 3cm more than the height of air between the top of the fluid and the top of the cylinder. More fluid is then added to the cylinder such that the final fluid level is 4 cm higher than it was initially, and the ratio of fluid height to air height is finally 3:1. How tall is the cylinder from bottom to top?

   (A) 22
   (B) 23
   (C) 25
   (D) 28

7. A club has juniors and seniors in the ratio of 9 seniors to 7 juniors. After 12 seniors quit the club, the ratio of seniors to juniors becomes 5:7. How many students are in the club now?

   (A) 24
   (B) 28
   (C) 32
   (D) 36

8. *CHALLENGE* A club has juniors and seniors in the ratio of 9 seniors to 7 juniors. After 10 seniors quit the club and 10 juniors join, the ratio of seniors to juniors becomes 1:1. How many students are in the club after the change?

   (A) 120
   (B) 135
   (C) 140
   (D) 160

9. A bag contains only red, blue, and white marbles. 1/4 of them are white, and there are 4/3 as many blue marbles as white marbles. If there are 55 red marbles, what is the total number of marbles in the bag?

   SR

10. Four toddlers, Juliana, Helen, Denise, and Katlyn are offered jellybeans from a box containing 400 jellybeans. The jellybeans come in 5 colors. Juliana takes 1/4 of the jellybeans, Helen takes 1/5. The ratio of Denise's jellybeans to Juliana's jellybeans is 3:2. If Katlyn gets the rest, how many does she get?

    (A) 62
    (B) 66
    (C) 70
    (D) 78

Ratios, Shares, and Totals   Chapter 5

11. A 200 kilograms (kg) weight on Earth will only weigh about 33 kg on the Moon. That same 200 kg will weigh about 76 kg on the planet Mercury. How much will an object weighing 100 kg on Mercury weigh on the Moon? Round your answer to the nearest kg.

SR

12. If the ratio of x to y is 6 and the ratio of z to y is 16, what is the ratio of x to z?

SR

13. Weak lemonade is 10% lemon juice by volume. How many liquid ounces of lemon juice must be added to 200 ounces of weak lemonade in order to make strong lemonade, which is 20% lemon juice?

SR

Chapter 5　　　　　　　　　　　　　　　　　　　　　　　Ratios, Shares, and Totals

Practice Problem Hints

1. Several approaches here. You could calculate the total cost of the trip knowing Jill's portion of the car rental was only 1/4 of the total cost of car rental.

2. Calculate the total cost of air travel for all persons, then the total cost of the trip.

3. The ratio 6:7 is fully reduced. If there are 6n black dresses, where n is an integer, there must be 7n white dresses. There must be a total of 13n dresses.

4. 2:3:5 is fully reduced. If there are 2n red dresses, where n is an integer, there must be 3n green dresses and 5n blue dresses. So there are a total of 10n dresses.

5. The given ratio means that if 3 cups of blueberry paste were used to make pancake batter, there would be 14 cups of plain batter used, making a total of 17 cups of blueberry pancake batter.

6. Express the initial heights of fluid and air in terms of the height of the cylinder (which doesn't change). Express the final heights of fluid and air in terms of their initial heights and the height of the cylinder.

7. The number of juniors doesn't change. Represent the number of juniors in two ways: in terms of the total number of students originally in the club *and* in terms of the total number of students after 12 seniors quit.

8. The number of total students didn't change. Represent the number of seniors in terms of the total number of students in the club, using the old *and* the new ratios.

9. There are a couple of approaches here. Develop an expression for the total number of marbles. Solve for the fraction of red marbles.

10. Express the number each child (except Katlyn) takes in terms of the total number of jellybeans in the box, which equals 400. Kaylyn just gets the rest.

11. From Earth-to-Moon and Earth-to-Mercury ratios you'll get the Moon-to-Mercury ratio.

12. Write the ratios in fraction form and look for a way to eliminate y.

13. In the strong lemonade, the new volume of lemon juice will be 20 + x; the new total volume will be 200+x. (You've added x oz. of lemon juice to go from weak to strong).

121

Notes

Chapter 5   Ratios, Shares, and Totals

Practice Problem Solutions

1. Answer D

   Find the total cost of the trip. Jill spent $75 on her portion of the car rental, but she shared the car rental with 3 other friends. So each of the 4 campers spent $75, and the car cost 75•4 = $300 to rent. We are told that this is 30% of the total cost of the trip. If the total cost of the trip is T, then T•30/100 = 300. Isolating T, the total cost of the trip was T = $1000. We are told that food and supplies made up 10% of the total cost, so the total cost of food was $100. Jill's share of this would be $100/4 = $25.

   Alternate Solution: The $75 Jill spent on the car was 30% of her total. Food was 10% of the total, or 1/3 what she spent on car rental. Food was therefore $75/3 = $25.

2. Answer A

   Mia spent $275 on her portion of the air travel, but each traveler spent $275, so the total air travel expenses were 275•4 = $1100. We are told that this was 50% of the total cost of the trip. If the total cost of the trip was T, then T•50/100 = $1100. Isolating T, the total cost of the trip was T = $2200. We are told that gifts made up 10% of the total cost, which means that the total cost of gifts were $220. Since Mia bought half of all gifts, her share of this would have been $220/2 = $110.

   Alternate Solution: Air is 50% of Mia's costs. Gifts are 20% of Mia's costs. Therefore, her gift costs are 20/50 of her air costs: $275 • 20/50 = $110.

3. Answer C

   Given the ratio in the problem, if there are 6n black outfits, where n is an integer, there must be 7n white outfits. This ratio is fully reduced. The total number of outfits must then be 6n + 7n = 13n. So the total number of outfits must be an integer multiple of 13. Only choice (C) satisfies this criterion.

4. Answer C

   Given the ratios in the problem, which are completely reduced, if there are 2n red dresses, where n is an integer, there must be 3n green dresses and 5n blue dresses. The total number of dresses must then be 2n + 3n + 5n = 10n. So the total number of dresses must be an integer multiple of 10. 3 out of every 10 dresses are green. If there are 90 dresses, then there are 90 • 3/10 = 27 green dresses.

Ratios, Shares, and Totals   Chapter 5

5. Answer D

To make blueberry batter, blueberry paste and plain batter must be combined in a ratio of 3 cups of blueberry paste to 14 cups of plain batter. We can then infer that the fraction of blueberry paste in blueberry batter will be 3/(3+14) = 3/17. If 7 cups of blueberry batter are to be made, one must use 3/17 • 7 cups blueberry batter = 21/17 cups of blueberry paste.

Alternate Solution: The 3:14 ratio in the problem means that the fraction of either blueberry paste or plain batter to the whole will be (something)/17. If you are running out of time, your best guess is very likely choice (D).

6. Answer A

Note that the height of the cylinder never changes. Let H = height of cylinder in cm. Let F = <u>initial</u> height of the fluid, A = the <u>initial</u> height of the air above the fluid. Three conditions lead to three simultaneous equations. Thus, (1) H = F+A. Since the initial fluid height was 3 inches more than the air, (2) F = A+3. After pouring in 4 more inches of fluid (and noticing that the air height must then be 4 inches less), and given the ratio of new fluid to air heights: (3) (F+4)/(A-4) = 3. Rearranging this, (3) F = 3A - 16. Equating (3) and (2) we can solve for A: A+3 = 3A - 16, or A = 9.5. From (2) we can now solve for F = 12.5. From (1), H = 9.5 + 12.5 = 22. The cylinder is 22 cm tall.

Alternate Solution: Let H = height of cylinder in cm. Let F = initial height of the fluid, and therefore (H-F) = initial height of the air. From the initial conditions, F = (H-F) + 3, which may be rearranged to give (1) F = (H+3)/2.. After fluid is added, the new fluid height is F+4, the new air height is H - (F+4), and from the stated ratio, (2) (F+4) = 3(H - (F+4)). Substituting the expression for F in (1) into (2) and rearranging, (H+3)/2 + 4 = 3(H - (H+3)/2 -4). Rearranging to isolate H, H = 22.

Alternate Solution II: Let H = height of cylinder in cm. Let F = initial height of the fluid. Initially, the height of the air, A, is F-3. Thus, (1) H = F + F - 3 = 2F - 3. After adding 4 inches to the fluid, the fluid height is F+4. From the ratio given, the height of the air is then equal to 1/3•(F+4). The height of the cylinder is always fluid plus air, which can now be expressed as (2) H = (F+4) + 1/3•(F+4) = 4F/3 + 51/3. The height of the cylinder doesn't change, so equate (1) and (2) for H: 2F - 3 = 4F/3 + 51/3. Now we can use this equation to solve for F. Without showing the algebraic rearrangement, F = 12.5. Thus, A = F - 3 = 9.5. The height of the cylinder is the combined initial heights of the fluid and air: H = 12.5 + 9.5 = 22. Or we could have used (1) to calculate H from F.

Whew. This problem is likely too involved for the SAT, but it demonstrates the type of complicated ratio relationships that may be on the test. It demonstrates how problems can be attacked in multiple ways. It's also good practice for the warrior class.

Chapter 5   Ratios, Shares, and Totals

7. Answer D

Let S and J be the initial number of seniors and juniors. From the problem we can produce two ratios: (1) S/J = 9/7, and (2) (S-12)/J = 5/7. Two equations and two unknowns. Use substitution. From (1) we can solve for S in terms of J: S = 9J/7. This may be substituted in (2) to give (9J/7 - 12)/J = 5/7. Multiplying both sides by J and rearranging, we get 4J/7 = 12, from which we can solve for J = 21. Using this in (1) we can solve for S = 27. Therefore the initial number of juniors and seniors was 21+27 = 48, and the remaining number of students (after 12 leave) is 48 - 12 = 36.

Alternate Solution: Work with the number of juniors, which doesn't change. Let T be the original number of students in the club. Because there were 9 seniors to every 7 juniors, (1) 7T/16 of the students are juniors. After removing 12 seniors, the number of students in the club is T - 12, and the ratio of seniors to juniors becomes 5:7. The fraction of juniors is then 7/12. Therefore, the number of juniors after removing 12 seniors is (2) 7/12 • (T-12). Since the number of juniors didn't change, we can set expressions (1) and (2) equal to one another: 7T/16 = 7/12 • (T-12). Solving for T, the initial number of total students, T = 48. After 12 seniors leave, there are 48 - 12 = 36 students remaining in the club.

Alternate Solution II: Note that the remaining number of students must be a multiple of 5+7 = 12. So only (A) or (D) are possible solutions. If you have to guess, guess smart.

8. Answer D

Okay - clever solution first this time. Because the original ratio of seniors to juniors is 9:7, their respective fractions of the total are 9/16 and 7/16. These fractions being fully reduced means that there must originally have been a multiple of 16 students in the combined classes. But since the total didn't change (10 are lost, but 10 are gained), the final total number of students must be a multiple of 16. Only (D) is a multiple of 16.

Alternate solution: Let T be the original number of students in the club (also the final number of students since 10 are lost and 10 are gained). Because there were originally 9 seniors to every 7 juniors, (1) 9T/16 of the students were seniors before students were removed. After removing 10 seniors and adding 10 juniors, the number of students in the club is unchanged, but the ratio of seniors to juniors becomes 1:1. The number of seniors at this point is (2) T/2. But since 10 seniors were removed, we also know from (1) that the number of seniors is now (3) 9T/16 - 10. Expressions (2) and (3) must be equal to one another. Therefore, T/2 = 9T/16 - 10. Simplifying, T/16 = 10. Isolating T, T = 160.

Alternate solution II: One could have also used the analogous argument and equality for juniors: 7T/16 + 10 = T/2. Solving for T, T = 160.

Ratios, Shares, and Totals																					Chapter 5

Alternate solution III: Let S and J be the original number of seniors and juniors, respectively. So before students are removed, (1) S/J = 9/7. After students are removed, (S-10)/(J+10) = 1, or (2) (S-10) = (J+10). Rearranging (1), we get (3) J = 7S/9. Plugging (3) into (2) gives (S-10) = 7S/9 + 10. Rearranging this last equation gives 2S/9 = 20. Thus, (4) S = 180/2 = 90. From (3) J = 7 • 90/9 = 70, and so the total number of students (which hasn't changed) equals S + J = 90 + 70 = 160.

Of course, using (4) and the fact that 10 seniors were removed, the number of seniors after 10 seniors were removed = 90 - 10 = 80. But at that point, the seniors comprise half of all students (from the 1:1 ratio). Thus there are 80 • 2 = 160 students.

Because a quick, clever solution (the first solution) is available, this problem *might* be within the scope of the SAT. However, it is placed in the *challenge* category because the perplexing paths to an algebraic solution might take it beyond the pale of the SAT.

9. Answer 132

Express the number of blue and white marbles in terms of T, the unknown total number of marbles. From the data given, the number of red marbles = 55, the number of white marbles = T/4, and the number of blue marbles = 4/3 • T/4 = 4T/12. Therefore, the total number of marbles, T = red + white + blue = 55 + T/4 + 4T/12. Expressing this with a common denominator, T = 55 + 7T/12. Isolating T on the left side, we get 5T/12 = 55, or T = 132.

Alternate Solution: The fraction of white marbles is 1/4. From the data given in the problem, the fraction of blue marbles is 4/3 • 1/4 = 1/3. Thus, the fraction of red marbles is 1 - 1/3 - 1/4 = 5/12. Letting T equal the total number of marbles, the number of red marbles equals T • 5/12. But this also equals 55. Thus, T • 5/12 = 55. Solving for T, T = 12 • 55/5 = 132.

10. Answer C

The total number of jellybeans in the box is 400. Juliana takes 1/4 of these, or 100. Helen takes 1/5 of 400 = 80. Since the ratio of Denise's jellybeans to Juliana's jellybeans is 3:2, Denise gets 3/2 • 100 = 150 jellybeans. Katlyn gets the rest. Therefore, Katlyn gets 400 - 100 - 80 - 150 = 70. Note that the colors of the jellybeans are immaterial.

Alternate Solution: Work with the relative fractions. Juliana gets 1/4, Helen gets 1/5, Denise gets 3/2 • 1/4 = 3/8. That leaves Katlyn with a fraction of 1 - 1/4 - 1/5 - 3/8 = 7/40. Since there are 400 total jellybeans, Katlyn gets 400 • 7/40 = 70 jellybeans.

Alternate Solution II: If running out of time, here's a quick guess-y path to the answer. The fractions of the whole of all but the unknown (Katlyn) are 1/4, 1/5, and 3/2•1/4 = 3/8. The common denominator is 40. Because there are 400 total jellybeans, the number of jellybeans left over for Katlyn must be an integer multiple of 400/40 = 10. Only choice (C) is a multiple of 10.

11. Answer 43

The Earth-to-Moon ratio is 200/33. The Earth-to-Mercury ratio is 200/76. Therefore, the Moon-to-Mercury ratio = Moon/Earth • Earth/Mercury = 33/200 • 200/76 = 33 (Moon kg)/76 (Merc kg). So a 100 kg weight on mercury will weigh 100 (Merc kg) • 33 (Moon kg)/76 (Merc kg) = 43.4 kg on the moon.

Alternate Solution: If a rock weighs 76 kg on Mercury and 33 kg on the Moon, then clearly the Moon to Mercury ratio is 33(Moon kg)/76 kg(Merc kg). So a 100 kg object on Mercury will weigh 100 • 33(Moon kg)/76 kg(Merc kg) = 43.4 kg on the moon.

12. Answer 3/8

If the ratio of x to y is 6 and the ratio of z to y is 16, what is the ratio of x to z? Rewritten, (1) x/y = 6 and (2) z/y = 16. We need x/z, i.e., x on the top and z on the bottom. Flip (2) and multiply that by (1): x/z = x/y • y/z = 6 • 1/16 = 3/8. Pretty easy.

13. Answer 25

Weak lemonade is 10% by volume. A 200 liquid ounce container of weak lemonade will contain 20 ounces of lemon juice. We are asked to make strong lemonade, which is 20% (0.2) lemon juice by volume. How many ounces, x, must be added to the original 200 ounces to go from weak to strong? The new volume of lemon juice will be 20 + x, and the new *total* volume of lemonade will be 200 + x. The fraction of lemon juice in this total is (20 + x)/(200 + x). If this is to be a 20% solution of lemon juice, then 0.2 = (20 + x)/(200 + x). Multiplying both sides by the denominator, we can solve for x. Thus, 20 + x = 40 + 0.2x. Rearranging, .8x = 20, or x, the number of ounces added, equals 25.

Notes

Chapter 6

Average, Median, and Mode

This chapter focuses on averages and medians. Modes too. The word *average* derives from an Old French word defined as "sharing the loss of a ship or the goods it carries." The idea is much older than Old French. Early investors would hire a ship to trade for goods at a distant port and hope for profit when the ship returned. If a venture comprising ten Roman merchants agreed to buy 200 jars of fine Greek wine, which later sank, ship and all, while sailing home, the average loss per man was 20 jars. Tough luck, that. In fact, the verb *to venture* originally meant "to risk the loss." But at least that loss was averaged out among those ten. Such enterprises (and their losses) certainly prompted Western law to slowly birth the modern corporation, composed of shares of stock, owned by many, and often hawked with the well-worn adage "nothing ventured, nothing gained."

There are four major categories of questions covering the concepts of average, median, and mode. The first category involves computing a sum from an average. The second category requires students to determine the value of an unknown, given information about the median of the set to which it belongs. The third category, rich in variations, involves combining averages, i.e., the averaging of several groups of several sizes. Calculating the mode in terms of an unknown addition to a set of numbers rounds out the coverage.

There are 7 archetypical problems centering on the subjects of average, median, and mode. Their solutions expose techniques that will be valuable in solving the 20 related problems presented at the end of the chapter.

Don't Show Up Without Knowing...

These Concepts

- Average
- Mean
- Median
- Mode
- Weighted average
- The sum of two numbers is twice their average

How to

- Calculate the average of a set of numbers or expressions
- Determine the median of a set of numbers
- Determine the mode of a set of numbers
- Calculate the total from the average and the number being averaged (TAN)
- Calculate combined, or weighted, averages

Quick Review and Definitions

Average

The average, or arithmetic mean, of n numbers = 1/n • (the sum of all n numbers). For example, the average of 1, 3, and 5 = (1+3+5)/3 = 3. The average of a set of *algebraic expressions* is similarly defined: 1/n • (the sum of all n algebraic expressions). The average of (2x + 4) and 3x is 1/2 • (2x + 4 + 3x) = 1/2 • (5x + 4) = 2.5x + 2.

If numbers in a sequence are arranged in increasing order, the average will be a kind of "balance point." Let Δ_i = the positive difference between number$_i$ and the average. The sum of all Δ_i to the left of the average equals the sum of all Δ_i to the right of the average.

Median

In any ordered sequence of n numbers, half the numbers are to the left of the median and half are to the right. By definition. To find the median, first put the sequence in order.

If n is odd, the median is the middle number. Consider -2, 1, 3, 6, 18. The median is 3.
If n is even, then the median of the sequence is the average of two middle numbers. For example, the median of 1, 3, 6, 18 is the average of 3 and 6 = 4.5.

Average Of An Arithmetic Sequence

An example of an arithmetic sequence is 1, 3, 5, 7, 9. Adjacent numbers in an arithmetic sequence have the same gap between them. The average of an arithmetic sequence *is* its median. (More on sequences in chapter 8). The above sequence has a median and average equal to the middle number, 5.

If an arithmetic sequence has even number of terms, the average will be the average of the two middle terms. The average of 3, 7, 11, 15 is the average of 7 and 11, or 9.

Also - the average of an arithmetic sequence $s_1, \ldots s_n$ = $(s_1+s_n)/2$. The sequence 3, 7, 11, 15 is arithmetic. s_1= 3 and s_n = 15. The average of this sequence is (3+15)/2 = 9.

Mode

The mode is the number occurring *most often* in a set of numbers. If two or more different numbers occur with the highest frequency, then there are multiple modes. E.g., in the set 1,1,2,3,4,4,5,6, there are two modes, 1 and 4. Modes are rarely seen on the SAT.

Average, Median, and Mode   Chapter 6

Finding the Total from the Average: TAN

This concept is often needed on the SAT. The average is defined as the sum total divided by the number of items being totaled. Rearranging, the total is the product of the average times the number of items being averaged (TAN): **Total** = **A**verage • **N**umber.

Perhaps you learned another acronym. For example, if the average points scored by 9 basketball players is 14, then the total number of points scored equals 14 • 9 = 126.

Combined Averages (or Weighted Averages)

Two sets of numbers often have different averages. The combined average will be a *weighted average* of the averages of the individual sets. Let's see how to do that.

For example, consider two school classes, called 1 and 2, which have grade point averages A_1 and A_2, respectively. Let's calculate the grade point average of the combined classes directly. Using TAN, if class 1 has n_1 students, then class 1 will score a total of $n_1 A_1$ points. Likewise, class 2 will score $n_2 A_2$ points. The total number of points of the combined classes is $(n_1 A_1 + n_2 A_2)$, while the total number of students is $(n_1 + n_2)$. Therefore, average of the combined classes is $(n_1 A_1 + n_2 A_2)/(n_1 + n_2)$.

This expression can be decomposed into two terms, each of which represents the relative (weighted) contribution of the original average to the whole:

Combined Average A = $A_1 \cdot n_1/(n_1 + n_2)$. + $A_2 \cdot n_2/(n_1 + n_2)$. <u>Weighted Averages</u>

To calculate the combined average, A, each separate average, A_1 and A_2, is multiplied, or *weighted*, by the fraction of its members contributing to the combined whole. Here, $n_1/(n_1 + n_2)$ is the weight of A_1, and $n_2/(n_1 + n_2)$ is the weight of A_2. Only if $n_1 = n_2$ are the weights equal; only then will the combined average equal the average of the averages.

Another way to think of combining averages A_1 and A_2 is how they would balance on a seesaw with A at the center: $n_1 \cdot |A - A_1| = n_2 \cdot |A - A_2|$. If n_1 is twice n_2, then A_1 must be half the "distance" from A as A_2 is. The skinny kid has to sit further from the center of the seesaw. We'll see a shortcut using this feature.

Finding the Largest or Smallest Number in a Set

If you are looking for the largest possible value that could contribute to an average, force all the other values to be as small as possible. For example, if the average of 4 positive integers is 25, then what is the largest possible value among these 4 numbers? From TAN, we know that their sum equals 25 • 4 = 100. The set containing the largest number of any 4 that sum to 100 is {1, 1, 1, 97}. So the largest possible value will be 97.

Chapter 6 Average, Median, and Mode

SAT Archetypes

Expressing Averages in Terms of Other Averages

The average of x and y is a. Which of the following is the average of x, y, and $\frac{z}{2}$?

(A) $\frac{2a + z}{6}$

(B) $\frac{2a + z}{4}$

(C) $\frac{4a + z}{6}$

(D) $\frac{4a + z}{4}$

How do I start?

In problems involving averages, the TAN concept is frequently employed to convert between sums and averages: total sum = average • (number of items being averaged). From the data in the problem, we can use TAN to conclude that x+y =2a.

Solution

We need the average of x, y, and $\frac{z}{2}$. Algebraically averaging all three terms, the average, A, is (1) A = (x+y+z/2)/3. However, since the average of x and y is a, (x+y)/2 = a. So from TAN, (2) x+y =2a. Substituting (2) into (1) gives A = (2a+z/2)/3. Simplifying this expression by multiplying top and bottom by 2 yields A = (4a+z)/6.

Answer C

The Take-Away

Sums and averages are related via TAN. Complicated problems, like this one involving the average of several algebraic terms, may require the use of TAN on a *subset* of terms to simplify the expression of the average.

Average, Median, and Mode   Chapter 6

Properties of a Sequence, Given the Median

The median of a set of 11 consecutive integers is 31. What is the least of these 11 integers?

SR

How do I start?

The median of an odd number of consecutive integers is always the middle integer. So the middle of this sequence of consecutive integers is 31. There are 11 consecutive numbers.

Solution

Write down 31. There are 11 consecutive numbers: 5 to the left and 5 to the right of 31: 26 27 28 29 30 **31** 32 33 34 36 37. Of these, 26 is the least in value. If you are sure what to do, you could just count backwards from 31 5 places since 2•5 + 1 = 11.

Answer 26

The Take-Away The easiest way of finding the greatest or least member of a small arithmetic sequence (evenly spaced integers) with a known median is to count out from the median toward the extreme. Chapter 8 deals with sequences in detail.

Properties of an Arithmetic Sequence, Given the Average

The average of 34 consecutive even integers is 19. What is the absolute value of the least of these integers?

SR

How do I start?

The average of an arithmetic sequence is also its median. There are an even number of terms (34) in the sequence, so its average is the average of its middle two terms. We are told that the average is 19. Since there are 34 terms here, 17 terms will be less than 19, and 17 terms will be greater than 19. Don't forget, the terms in the sequence are all *even*.

Chapter 6   Average, Median, and Mode

Solution

Starting from the median of the sequence, 19, which is *not* one of the 34 even numbers, we count backward 17 even integers. The first even integer to the left of 19 is 18. The 2nd to the left is 16, the 3rd is 14, the 4th is 12,... and you can infer that the nth even integer to the left of 19 equals 18 - 2(n-1). The least of these even integers corresponds to n = 17. Its value is 18 - 2(16) = -14. The answer is the absolute value of this: 14.

Alternate solution

Knowing the properties of the median and average of an arithmetic sequence, you know there are 17 numbers to the left of the median. You could just count down on your fingers 17 even integers, starting from 19. But what if there were 100 terms in the sequence?

Answer 14

The Take-Away

Just like the median, the average of an arithmetic, i.e., equally-spaced, sequence of integers is the middle of the sequence. Also – it may sometimes be necessary to infer a formula for a sequence or sum, as demonstrated in the original solution.

Median and Average of a Set That Changes

Number of Medals	Number of Soldiers
0	2
1	7
2	1
3	1

A platoon in a multi-player online game currently has 11 soldiers. Soldiers may earn up to 3 medals. The data above details the number of soldiers in this platoon that have earned 0, 1, 2, and 3 medals. Then a new soldier who may already have medals joins the platoon. Thereafter, the average number of medals per soldier equals the median number of medals per soldier. How many medals did the new soldier have?

(A) 0
(B) 1
(C) 3
(D) 4

Average, Median, and Mode   Chapter 6

How do I start?

First, calculate the median and average number of medals of the original set of soldiers. A new soldier comes in and he or she has x medals. Calculate the new average in terms of x. Determine what x must be so that the new average equals the new median.

Solution

Since no soldier can earn more than 3 medals, toss (D). To calculate the initial median number of medals per soldier, list the number of medals in ascending order: 00111111123. The median of this set is 1. Clearly, it will also be 1 no matter the number of medals the new soldier has. So the *new* median will be 1. Therefore, the new average must also equal 1. The original average number of medals per soldier = (7+2+3)/11 = 12/11. The new soldier will bring the total number of soldiers to 12. If the new soldier earns x medals, total number of medals will be 12+x. The new average number of medals will be (12+x)/12. We can see that if the new soldier has zero medals, the average will be 1. No other number of new medals, x, will result in the average equaling the median.

Answer A

The Take-Away

After adding one new number to a set, the new set average will be the new sum of all elements divided by (the original size of the set + 1). This relationship can be used to solve for the value of the new number if it is unknown, but the new average *is* known.

Mode and Average, Given Ratios Among Members

In a high school club, students must attend a certain number of meetings per month. Sophomores must meet 4 times, juniors must meet 3 times, and seniors must meet 1 time. There are half as many juniors as seniors, and half as many sophomores as juniors. What is the mode of the set containing the numbers of meetings in one month these members must attend divided by the average of these values?

SR

How do I start?

Choose some convenient number of seniors allowing even division by 2, twice. Example: there could be 8 seniors, 4 juniors, and 2 sophomores. Assign the number of meetings in 1 month to each of these students; then calculate the mode and average of these values.

Chapter 6 — Average, Median, and Mode

Solution

Assign to each student a "value" according to the number of meetings in 1 month he must attend. If 8 seniors get a value of 1, 4 juniors get a value of 3, and 2 sophomores get a value of 4, the sum of the values = 8•1 + 4•3 + 2•4 = 28. There are 14 students, and the average is then 28/14 = 2. The mode is the mode of 1, 1, 1, 1, 1, 1, 1, 1, 3, 3, 3, 3, 4, 4. The mode is clearly 1. Thus, the mode divided by the average = 1/2, or .5.

Alternate solution

We could solve this one algebraically. Let there be 4n seniors, 2n juniors, and n sophomores: there are 7n students. The sum of all the values given to these students is 4n•1 + 2n•3 + n•4 = 14n. The average = 14n / 7n = 2. The mode is the value most represented in the set of values, that of the seniors, which is 1. The mode divided by the average = 1/2, or .5

Answer .5 or 1/2

The Take-Away

The mode is the value most often occurring in a set of values. Also – in problems involving ratios, you can often choose a convenient number (students in this problem) that fits the problem, or you can solve the problem in general, algebraically. We could have used as well 4 seniors, 2 juniors, and 1 sophomore. Any proportional set of ratios would work.

Combined Averages of Two Different Sets

The average (arithmetic mean) of the test scores of x honors students is 94, and the average of the test scores of y non-honors students is 76. When the scores of both groups of students are combined, the average score is 82. What is the value of y/x?

SR

How do I start?

Using the averages given, express the total number of points of honors and non-honors students in terms of x and y, respectively. The sum of their point totals is the total points earned by all students. This must also be the number of points computed using the combined average of 82.

Average, Median, and Mode — Chapter 6

Solution

Express the total number of points of honors and non-honors students. From TAN, the total number of points of honors students equals 94x, and that of non-honors students is 76y. This must equal the total number of points using the combined average, 82(x+y). Therefore, 94x + 76y = 82(x+y). Rearranging everything to the left side and simplifying, 12x - 6y = 0. Dividing both sides by 6x yields 2 - y/x = 0, and therefore y/x = 2.

Alternate Solution

There are x+y total students. The fraction of honors students is x/(x+y), and the fraction of non-honors students is y/(x+y). The weighted average representation for the combined classes is x/(x+y) • 94 + y/(x+y) • 76 = 82. Multiplying both sides by x+y, one may (with a bit more algebra) solve for y/x as shown above.

Alternate Solution II

y students average 76. x students average 94. Notice that 76 is exactly half the distance from the overall average, 82, as is 94. To balance the "seesaw", y must be twice x.

Answer 2

The Take-Away

We used TAN, weighted averages, and the seesaw concept to solve this problem in three ways. Check out alternate solution II for a savvy shortcut using the seesaw concept.

Extreme Values Possible, Given The Average

Customer service requests that customers rate their service from 1 to 5 points, with 1 being very poor and 5 being very good. On a certain day, 32 clients responded with an average response of 3.5. What is the largest number of clients who could have said that the service was very good?

SR

How do I start?

Use TAN to calculate the total number of points on that day. Try assuming that all callers not rating the service a 5 will rate the service a 1. Find the maximum number of 5-point clients, consistent with a total of 32 clients.

Chapter 6 Average, Median, and Mode

Solution

Trial and error: With 32 customers giving an average of 3.5 points, there were a total of 32•3.5 = 112 rating points given that day. The largest number that said the service was very good, or who gave a rating of 5, would be as many 5's as possible in a total of 112 rating points, constrained by the fact that 32 clients responded. You might step into the trap of thinking the maximum number of "5" ratings would be 22•5 = 110, with 2 giving 1's. But that's only 24 callers, not 32. We need to reduce the number of "5" callers. Next try 21 5's: 21•5 = 105. But this needs 7 leftover 1's to add to 112. But that's 21 + 7 = 28 callers, not 32. Now try 20 clients giving 5's and 12 clients giving 1's: this does result in a total of 112 rating points (and a total of 32 clients).

Alternate Solution

Algebra: Try a set of x clients responding with 5's, and the other 32-x clients each responding with 1's. There are a total of 32•3.5 = 112 rating points given that day. So x•5 + (32-x)•1 = 112. Rearranging, 4x = 80, or x = 20. Thus, 20 clients could respond with a 5, and 32 - 20 = 12 clients respond with a 1. Linear equations only have one solution.

Alternate Solution II

Simultaneous Equations: There are two equations that constrain the number of 5-clients and the number of 1-clients. Let n and m be the number of 5's and 1's. Since there are 32 clients, (1) n + m = 32. Since the total number of points is 32 • 3.5 = 112, (2) 5•n + 1•m = 112. Subtracting (2) from (1) gives 4n = 80, or n = 20. The number of 5-clients equals 20.

Answer 20

The Take-Away

When asked about the greatest number of members of a set having the highest score, try to let all the other members have the lowest score. Variations include greatest number of members with the lowest score, least number of members with the highest score, etc. As in this example, always start your analysis with the extreme possible scores. Also – we can see (Alternate Solution II) that because there are two linear equations constraining the number of 5's and the number of 1's, there is *only one way* for 32 clients to vote with all 5's and all 1's and have an average of 3.5.

However, the situation might have not been so convenient. Here's a counter example that requires more than just 1's and 5's: What if there were 5 clients with an average of 3.6 points? The total number of points would be 5•3.6 = 18. In this case the maximum number of 5's would result from this set of rating points: 5, 5, 5, 2, 1. The lowest scores are not all 1's. In this case, a more brute-force approach would be necessary.

Notes

Practice Problems

1. If the average of x and y is a, which of the following represents the average of x, y, z, and a?

    (A) $(2a + z)/4$

    (B) $(3a + z)/8$

    (C) $(2a + z)/8$

    (D) $(3a + z)/4$

2. If the average of x, y, and $\frac{z}{2}$ equals A, what is the average of x and y in terms of z and A?

    (A) $\dfrac{3A-z}{2}$

    (B) $\dfrac{3A-2z}{4}$

    (C) $\dfrac{3A-4z}{6}$

    (D) $\dfrac{6A-z}{4}$

3. If the average of w and x is y - z and the average of 3y and - z is z, what is the sum of w, x, y, and z?

    (A) 2z

    (B) (2w - z) / 4x

    (C) (2w - z) / (2x - 2y)

    (D) (2w - 2z) / 4x

Average, Median, and Mode   Chapter 6

4. The median of a set of 9 consecutive odd integers is 101. What is the greatest of these 9 integers?

   SR

5. The second greatest of 8 consecutive integers is 48. What is the median of this set of integers?

   SR

6.

Number of Medals	Number of Soldiers
0	3
1	3
2	5
3	1

In a certain platoon (currently with 12 soldiers), soldiers may earn up to 3 medals. The data above details the number of soldiers in this platoon that have earned 0, 1, 2, and 3 medals. After two additional soldiers, Jack and Mala (who may already have medals), join this platoon, the average number of medals per soldier becomes equal to the median number of medals per soldier prior to these new soldiers joining. Which of the following could represent the number of medals Jack and Mala have, respectively?

   (A) 0 and 1
   (B) 1 and 1
   (C) 1 and 2
   (D) 3 and 2

7. The average (arithmetic mean) of the test scores of x honors students is 94, and the average of the test scores of 44 non-honors students is S. When the scores of both groups of students are combined, the average score is 88. If there are 4 times as many non-honors students as honors students, what is the value of S?

   SR

142

Chapter 6   Average, Median, and Mode

8. In a set of 10 different numbers, which of the following <u>cannot</u> affect the value of the median?

    (A) Multiplying every number by 10
    (B) Subtracting every number by 10
    (C) Adding 10 to the largest number
    (D) Adding 10 to the smallest number

9.

Student	Total Game Score
Rhee	1898
James	2302
Audrey	x
Jasona	1991
Clark	2064

The table above shows student scores on a driving simulation game. If every student had a different score and the median score was 1991, what is the greatest possible score of Audrey?

SR

10. If $1/x + 1/y = 10$, $1/xy = 8$, and $xy > 0$, then the average of x and y is

    (A) $\frac{-3}{4}$
    (B) $\frac{-1}{4}$
    (C) $\frac{5}{8}$
    (D) 2

143

11. Kima planted t trees on Saturday, two times this many trees on Sunday as on Saturday, and two more than three times as many trees planted on Monday as on Sunday. What is the average number of trees planted per day on Sunday and Monday?

(A) 4t + 1
(B) 4t + 2
(C) 6t + 1
(D) 6t + 2

12.

Game	Score
1	40
2	39
3	38
4	40
5	44

The table above lists the scores Bob got playing 9-hole games of golf played during the first 5 games days on vacation. If he played a total of 7 such games during his vacation, and the median score for all 7 games was 39, which numbers below could have been the scores in games 6 and 7?

(A) 38, 38
(B) 40, 41
(C) 37, 41
(D) 37, 43

13. The average (arithmetic mean) of two numbers is equal to 3 times the absolute value of the difference between them. The smaller of the two numbers is 10. What is the product of the two numbers?

SR

Chapter 6   Average, Median, and Mode

14. Customer service requests that clients rate their service from 1 to 5 points, with 1 being very poor and 5 being very good. On a certain day clients respond with an average response of 2.5. If the number of clients that reported very good service is 12, what is the maximum number of clients that could have responded to the question?

SR

15. The engineering department at a company has e employees, and the software department has z more than 3 times the number of engineers. If the average employee years of service in engineering is x, and the average employee years of service in software is y, what is the average years of service for both departments?

(A) $\dfrac{ex + (3e + z) \cdot y}{4e + z}$

(B) $\dfrac{ex + (3e + z) \cdot y}{4e}$

(C) $\dfrac{ex + (3e + 2z) \cdot y}{4e}$

(D) $\dfrac{2ex + (3e + 2z) \cdot y}{4e + z}$

16. A college calculus class consists of freshmen and sophomores. The average grade of freshmen at the end of the semester was 72 and that of sophomores was 86. If the class average was 82, what fraction of students in the class were freshmen?

(A) $\dfrac{2}{7}$

(B) $\dfrac{1}{3}$

(C) $\dfrac{3}{8}$

(D) $\dfrac{3}{7}$

Average, Median, and Mode   Chapter 6

17. Two men and two women (including the pilot) must fly in a small plane that weighs 1680 pounds when empty. The average weight of persons in the plane is 140 pounds. If the average weight of the men is 50 percent more than the average weight of the women, what percent of the occupied weight of the plane do the women represent?

   (A) 10
   (B) 12.5
   (C) $14\frac{2}{3}$
   (D) 15

18. Five positive integers are chosen at random. If the average (arithmetic mean) of these integers is 20, what is the greatest possible integer of the five chosen?

   SR

19. The variable a is the average of n and 3, b is the average of 2n and 15, and c is the average of 3n and 18. What is the average of a, b, and c in terms of n?

   (A) n + 6
   (B) n + 12
   (C) 2n + 2
   (D) 2n + 8

20. The average of 4 different positive integers is 4. What is the smallest possible product of all 4 numbers?

Practice Problem Hints

1. Simplify by using (x+y)/2 = a.

2. x+y = twice the average of x and y. Use this in the expression for A.

3. w+x = 2(y-z), and likewise, 3y - z = 2z.

4. The median of an odd number of terms in an arithmetic sequence is always the middle integer.

5. So the *greatest* integer must be 49. The median of an even number of terms in an arithmetic sequence is always the average of the two middle integers.

6. First, calculate the median and average number of medals of the original soldiers. Then form an expression of the new average in terms of the original number of medals plus unknown number of new medals and the number of new soldiers.

7. Express the total number of points of honors and non-honors students from the combined average and in terms of S.

8. The problem asks for the choice that cannot affect the median. If unsure, choose a smaller set of numbers, arrange in numerical order, and test each possibility.

9. List the scores in numerical order and place the maximum value of x such that the median is 1991.

10. Express the first equation using a common denominator, xy. Then 1/xy becomes useful.

11. Express the number of trees on each day in terms of t. The problem asks for the average number of trees planted only on Sunday and Monday.

12. First, order the scores of the first 5 games in increasing numerical value.

13. Translate the first sentence into an equation. The absolute value can be replaced by the difference since we know one of them, 10, is the smaller number.

14. Express the total number of points on that day as a function of n, the number of clients. 12 clients gave 5 points each. Maybe all the rest responded with 1 point?

Average, Median, and Mode Chapter 6

15. As with many problems involving averages, find the total of the units being averaged, in this case years of service, and divide by the total number of things being averaged, in this case, number of employees.

16. Express the total points in terms of the unknown number of freshmen and the unknown number of sophomores using the averages given. Then express the total points in terms of the unknown total number of total students and their combined average.

17. Calculate the total weight of all four passengers, the total occupied weight of the plane, and then use the ratio of men's weight to women's weight to calculate the total weight of the women.

18. 5 numbers averaging 20 will sum to 100. You're looking for one big number and all the rest 1's.

19. The sum of two numbers is twice their average

20. The sum of all four numbers must be 4 • 4 = 16. And they must all be different from one another.

Chapter 6   Average, Median, and Mode

Practice Problem Solutions

1. Answer D

   The average, A, of all four values is (1) A = (x+y+z+a)/4. However, since (x+y)/2 = a, it must be true that (2) x+y =2a. Substituting (2) into (1), A = (2a+z+a)/4 = (3a+z)/4.

2. Answer D

   The average, A, of all three values is A = (x+y+z/2)/3, or (1) 3A = x+y+z/2. However, the average of x and y is (x+y)/2. Letting a = the average of x and y (this is what you must get an expression for), x+y =2a. Substituting this expression for x+y into (1), 3A = 2a+z/2. Rearranging, 2a = 3A - z/2, or a = (6A - z)/4.

3. Answer A

   The average of w and x is (w+x)/2 = y-z, and thus, (1) w+x = 2y-2z. (1) can be cleverly rearranged into the requested sum: (2) w+x+(y+z) = 2y - 2z + (y+z) = 3y-z. Aha! We are also told that the average of 3y and -z equals z, and using TAN, (3) 3y-z = 2z. Plugging (3) into (2), w+x+y+z = 2z. Step (2) is a hard to intuit algebraic trick - learn it.

   Alternate Solution: The average of w and x involves only y and z. The average of 3y-z involves only z. So w+x+y+z can at most depend on y and z. Only (A) fits this. Think!

4. Answer 109

   The median of an odd number of consecutive odd integers is always the middle integer. There are 9 integers with a median of 101, 4 will be less than 101 and 4 will greater than 101. Write the number 101 and then the four consecutive odd numbers to the *right* of 101: **101** 103 105 107 109. 109 is the largest integer in the set of integers.

5. Answer 45.5

   The median, M, of an even number of consecutive integers is always the average of the two middle integers – find those. If there are 8 integers, 4 will be less than M, and 4 will greater than M. Since 48 is the second greatest integer, 49 must be the greatest. Starting with 49 as the largest, write the 4 largest integers in descending order: 49 48 47 46. So 46 is the middle integer greater than M. The next integer in the sequence, 45, is the middle integer less than M, and thus M = (46+45)/2 = 45.5.

Average, Median, and Mode   Chapter 6

6. Answer D

   To calculate the original median number of medals per soldier, list the number of medals in ascending order: 000111222223. The median of this set is 1.5. The average number of medals per soldier = (3•0+3•1+5•2+1•3)/12 = 16/12. When two new soldiers join the platoon with a combined total of x medals, we are told that the new average will equal the old median, 1.5. The new average number of medals is (16+x)/(12+2) = 1.5. Solving for x, we find that x=5. Only choice (D) shows a situation where the two soldiers earned a total of 5 medals.

7. Answer 86.5

   From the stated ratio, since there are 44 non-honors students, there must be 11 honors students. The total number of honors students' points equals 11•94 = 1034, and the total number of non-honors students points' is 44•S. The sum of these points must equal the total number of points calculated using the combined average, which equals 88(44+11) = 4840. Therefore, 1034 + 44S = 4840. Solving for S, S = 86.5

   Alternate Solution: There are 4 times the number of non-honors students as honors students. These two averages sit on either side of the combined average like on a balanced see-saw. So to balance, the non-honors average must be 4 times *closer* to the combined average as the honors average. The honors average is 94 - 88 = 6 more than the combined average, so the non-honors average must be 6/4 = 1.5 less than the combined average. Thus, the non-honors average is 88 - 1.5 = 86.5

8. Answer C

   The set size shouldn't matter. Examine a smaller set of three numbers. Let the three numbers be 1, 2, and 3. The median is 2. If each is multiplied by 10, then the median would be 20. Subtracting 10 from each number results in a median of -8. Adding 10 to the largest number, 3, will not affect the median: the median of 1, 2, 13 will still be 2. Boom. This reasoning would also be true if there are 10 or 1000 numbers in a set.

9. Answer 1990

   List the scores in numerical order and place the x such that the median is 1991: 1898 x 1991 2064 2302. The x must be between 1898 and 1991, inclusive, if the median is to be 1991. However, the problem states that each student had a different score. Thus, the greatest value of x between these values is 1990.

   The "different score" requirement makes all the difference. Here is another example where the good folks sneak in a critical reading question into a math problem.

Chapter 6   Average, Median, and Mode

10. Answer C

From the first equation, after finding a common denominator, (1) (x+y)/xy = 10. Because we are told that 1/xy = 8, plug this into (1), (x+y)•8 = 10. Therefore, x+y = 5/4. The average of x and y = (x+y)/2 = 5/8. Difficult? Yes. Many steps? No.

11. Answer A

Let t equal the number of trees planted on Saturday. There will therefore be 2t trees planted on Sunday and 3•2t + 2 = 6t + 2 trees planted on Monday. A total of 2t + (6t + 2) = 8t + 2 trees were planted on Sunday and Monday, and therefore the average for the two days = (8t + 2)/2 = 4t +1.

Alternate Solution: Choose a convenient value of t to make the calculation easy (and to differentiate the choices). If t = 1, then 1, 2, and 8 trees are planted on Sat, Sun, and Mon. The avg. of Sun and Mon is (2+8)/2 = 5, and only choice (A) gives that answer when t = 1 is plugged into the choices.

12. Answer A

First, order the five scores by increasing value: 38 39 40 40 44. We can see that if 39 is to be the median score, the two unknown scores must be equal to or lower than 39. There are three possibilities: {x y 38 39 40 40 44}, {x 38 y 39 40 40 44}, and {38 x y 39 40 40 44}. Both x and y have to be less than or equal to 39. The only pair of choices, (x, y), that allows the scores of all 7 games to have a median of 39 is 38, 38.

13. Answer 140

Let the two numbers be a and b, and let b be less than a. We are told that 10 is the smaller number: so b = 10. By the definition of average, and from the data in the problem, (a+b)/2 = 3|a-b| = 3(a-b). Multiplying both sides by 2 and using b = 10 yields (a+10) = 6(a -10). Rearranging, 70 = 5a. Solving for a, a = 14. Therefore, the product of the two numbers, a • b = 14 • 10 = 140.

14. Answer 32

Let the unknown number of clients responding be n. We are looking for the maximum possible value of n. Since the average response is 2.5, the total number of points is 2.5•n. If the number of clients that reported very good service (5 points) is 12 then they supplied 12•5 = 60 points to the total. To maximize the number of clients, the remaining (n-12) clients will have to respond with 1 point. The equation for the total number of points is 2.5•n = 12•5+ (n-12)•1. Thus, 1.5n = 60 - 12 = 48, or n = 32.

Average, Median, and Mode   Chapter 6

15. Answer A

From the data in the problem, there are e engineers, 3e + z employees in software, which means there are 4e + z employees in both departments. The combined years of service in engineering is e•x, and the combined years of service in software is (3e + z)•y. The total years of service for both departments is therefore e•x + (3e + z)•y. Therefore, the average years of service for both departments is $\frac{ex + (3e + z) \cdot y}{4e + z}$.

Alternate Solution: The denominator must include z from software. Toss (B) and (C).

16. Answer A

Let f = number of freshmen and s = number of sophomores in class. From the data in the problem, the total points of the freshmen and sophomore classes are 72f and 86s, respectively. The total number of points for both classes = 72f + 86s. However, the total number of points *also* equals 82(f+s). Setting these two expressions equal to one another, 72f + 86s = 82(f+s). Isolating s, s = 2.5f. The fraction of students that are freshmen = f/(f+s) = f/(f+2.5f) = 1/(3.5) = 2/7.

Alternate solution: let the total number of students equal 100, and let f equal the number of freshmen. There are then 100-f sophomores. Calculate the total number of points earned via TAN from each class: 72•f + (100-f)•86. This must also equal the number of points calculated via the combined class average = 100•82. Therefore, 72•f + (100-f)•86 = 100•82. Solving for f, f = 200/7 (oops – it's not an integer, but that's because we choose 100 students, which turned out to make the math not-integer-y). Nevertheless, the *fraction* of freshmen is then (200/7) / 100 = 2/7.

Alternate Solution II: The average of all students is 82; the average of freshmen is 72 (10 away from the combined average) and the average of sophomores is 86 (4 away from the combined average). Balance the seesaw: there must be 10 sophomores (stacked at 86) for every 4 freshmen (stacked at 72) because 10•4 = 4•10. The freshmen:sophomore ratio is 4:10. So 4 out of every *14* students are freshmen = 2/7.

17. Answer A

We'll need the occupied weight of the plane and the total weight of the women. Since there are 4 people on the plane, and the average weight of a person is 140 pounds, the people weigh a total of 4 • 140 = 560 pounds. The occupied plane will weigh 1680 + 560 = 2240 pounds. Now, since the men weigh an average of 50% more than the women, the combined weight of the men, m = 1.5 • w, where w is the combined weight of women. Since the total weight of men and women is 560 pounds, 560 = w + m = w + 1.5w. Solving for w, w = 224 pounds. The combined weight of the women represent 224/2240 •100 percent = 10 percent of the weight of the occupied plane.

18. Answer 96

5 numbers averaging 20 will sum to 5•20 = 100. Try a set of numbers with one huge number, x, and all the rest 1's. There are 5 numbers, so four of them will be 1's. The 5 integers that include the greatest possible integer summing to 100 are x + 1+ 1+ 1 + 1 = 100. Therefore, x = 96 is the greatest possible integer. An easy one for you.

19. Answer A

Express the separate averages a, b, and c as functions of n. Then calculate the average of a, b, and c. The variable a is the average of n and 3, or a = (n+3)/2. Likewise, b is the average of 2n and 15, or b = (2n+15)/2, and c = (3n+18)/2). We are asked to calculate the average of a, b, and c, which by definition is (a+b+c)/3. This equals:

1/3 • [(n+3)/2 + (2n+15)/2 + (3n+18)/2)]

Pulling a factor of 1/6 outside, this equals

1/6 • [(n+3) + (2n+15)+ (3n+18)] = 1/6 • [6n + 36] = n + 6

Alternate Solution: You know that the sum of two numbers is twice their average. The variable a is the average of n and 3, so (n+3) = 2a. Likewise, (2n+15) = 2b, and (3n+18) = 2c. Now we can add the left and right sides of the three equations above to get 6n + 36 = 2(a+b+c). But the term in parenthesis is 3 times the average of a, b, and c: the answer we seek. Let this be A. So 6n + 36 = 2•(3•A). Solving for A, A = n + 6.

20. Answer 60

The numbers must all be positive and different from one another, and their average must be 4. If their average is 4, from TAN, their sum must be 16. We're looking for the smallest product of four different integers that sum to 16. This is going to a manual hunt. The smallest sequence would be 1, 2, 3, 4, but they don't sum to 16. If we want the smallest product, it's likely that most of the numbers will be small. Let's replace 4 with an unknown, x. So 1+2+3+x = 16. Isolating x, x = 10. The product of 1•2•3•10 = 60. Is that the smallest product possible? Let's try another set that fits the criteria: 1•2•4•9 = 72. Nope. How about 1•3•4•8 = 96? Even worse. It looks like (without any strict proof) that the smallest product is 60. This might be a multiple choice problem on the SAT, making it faster (and safer) to solve.

Notes

Chapter 7

Rates and Dimensional Analysis

You have been dealing with rate problems for years in math and science courses. Of course, the concept of a rate isn't limited to speed. *Any* ratio involving quantities with physical units can be called a rate, such as miles per gallon, exams per semester, Ahabs per whale…

Difficult rate problems often involve multiple rates and multiple physical quantities, and they require careful accounting of the units involved. Dimensional analysis is the method of crafting solutions to problems involving many physical quantities by systematic analysis in light of the units involved.

We will thoroughly explore 7 archetypical rate problems. Dimensional analysis is introduced as a solution method, and 21 additional practice problems are included that help to illustrate how it can be used to simplify complicated relationships involving units.

Don't Show Up Without Knowing…

These Concepts

- Speed
- Distance Formula
- Rate
- Average Rate
- Unit Conversion
- Dimensional Analysis

How To

- Calculate speed, distance, and time for multi-leg trips
- Calculate speed, distance, and time according to the geometry of travel
- Utilize dimensional analysis to solve problems
- Convert from one unit to another of the same kind
- Handle problems involving multiple rates
- Compute an average rate, given several individual rates
- Handle problems involving rates with 3 or more units

Quick Review and Definitions

Rate

The most general definition of a rate is the ratio of two measurements of physical quantities with different units. Examples include miles per hour, dollars per ticket, etc. Speed is always in the units of distance divided by units of time: feet per second, miles per hour, etc. Speed is one common rate used in SAT problems, but the concepts involved in developing solutions to speed problems are generally applicable to other rates.

Rate ratios are not always given in the simplest, reduced values. Instead of being told that a car travels at $60 \frac{\text{miles}}{\text{hour}}$, the problem may state that the car can travel 15 miles in a quarter of an hour. *That* ratio is $\frac{15 \text{ miles}}{.25 \text{ hour}}$, but the numbers can be simplified: $\frac{15}{.25} \frac{\text{miles}}{\text{hour}} = 60 \frac{\text{miles}}{\text{hour}}$. This can be more explicitly understood as a ratio of 60 miles per 1 hour. This is basic stuff at your age, but keeping the units in order matters and can be an important guide to solving complicated problems.

The Inverse Rate Is Also True

Note that if the car is travelling 60 miles per hour, it is also taking 1 hour per 60 miles driven. This *inverted ratio*, or rate, is also true, and the inverted ratio is often useful, even necessary, when solving problems by dimensional analysis.

Speed

Let S = speed, D = total distance, and T = time in motion

S = D/T   Speed = $\frac{\text{distance}}{\text{time in motion}}$

D = S•T   Distance = speed • time in motion

T = D/S   Time in motion = $\frac{\text{distance}}{\text{speed}}$

Rates and Dimensional Analysis — Chapter 7

For example, if distance is measured in miles and speed is measured in miles per hour, then the hours taken to drive a given distance is given by hours $= \frac{\text{miles}}{\frac{\text{miles}}{\text{hour}}} = \cancel{\text{miles}} \cdot \frac{\text{hours}}{\cancel{\text{mile}}}$.

Here, we have eliminated all values and have focused on the units of distance and speed only. In particular, we have crossed out the unit miles, which has been cancelled because it occurs in the numerator and the denominator. Dimensional analysis is important in keeping track of values with units in problems, and it will be discussed in detail below.

Cost

Dollars per ticket $= \frac{\text{dollars spent}}{\text{number of tickets}}$

Dollars spent = dollars per ticket • number of tickets $= = \frac{\text{dollars}}{\cancel{\text{ticket}}} \cdot \cancel{\text{tickets}}$

Number of tickets sold $= \frac{\text{dollars spent}}{\text{dollars a ticket}} =$ dollars spent $/ \frac{\text{dollars}}{\text{ticket}} = \cancel{\text{dollars spent}} \cdot \frac{\text{tickets}}{\cancel{\text{dollars}}}$

Dimensional Analysis

Dimensional analysis (also called unit analysis) is a method of expressly accounting for the units of quantities involved in a problem in order to more easily understand the mathematical relationship between these quantities. Some courses (physics and chemistry) teach dimensional analysis as an aid in developing solutions to problems.

Let's take a simple example using speed to illustrate dimensional analysis and why it's a particularly powerful tool in problem solving. If a car travels at 60 miles per hour, *how many hours* will it take to travel 100 miles? One way to solve this problem is by examining the units involved. We want an answer in units of hours, and we have two data points in units of $\frac{\text{miles}}{\text{hour}}$ and miles. If the ratio of 60 miles per 1 hour is true, then the inverted ratio of 1 hour per 60 miles is also true. We can invert the speed (and its units) and still have the truth expressed in the problem: the car takes 1 hour for every 60 miles driven: $\frac{1 \text{ hour}}{60 \text{ miles}}$. By inverting the speed *we have put the units of hours on top* where we need them in the answer. Now we need to cancel the units of miles in the denominator: this suggests multiplying this ratio by the 100 miles travelled, as stated in problem. The equation for total hours spent travelling becomes:

$$\text{Total hours} = \frac{1 \text{ hour}}{60 \cancel{\text{ miles}}} \cdot 100 \cancel{\text{ miles}} = 1\frac{2}{3} \text{ hours}.$$

In general, when a problem asks for a value expressed in some unit, find a combination of values given in the problem who's units can be chain-multiplied together (and inverted if necessary) to yield a result in the unit required. Find the value in the problem containing the unit needed in the answer. If that unit is part of a ratio of units, make sure that the desired unit is on top, i.e., it is in the numerator. Invert the ratio as we did above, if necessary, to get it on top.

Note that the unit required in the answer might itself be a *ratio* of units, e.g., $\frac{\text{dollars}}{\text{pound}}$, $\frac{\text{students}}{\text{class}}$, etc. In that case, the chain-multiplication of units must result in the desired ratio of units.

On the SAT if the answer must be expressed in some particular unit or units, you will always be able to chain-multiply the values and units given in the problem to produce the answer in the desired units. In fact, if you think you have a solution, but discover a sequence that fails to chain-multiply in a way that gives the correct units of the final answer, you may be certain that you are approaching the problem in the wrong way.

Unit Conversion

Many real-world problems give quantities in one unit, but expect an answer in a similar, but scaled unit. A simple example is the conversion of minutes to hours:

$$x \text{ minutes} = x \cancel{\text{ minutes}} \cdot \frac{1 \text{ hour}}{60 \cancel{\text{ minutes}}} = \frac{x}{60} \text{ hours.}$$

This chain-multiplication of units can extend for several related units, such as

$$x \text{ seconds} = x \cancel{\text{ seconds}} \cdot \frac{1 \cancel{\text{ minute}}}{60 \cancel{\text{ seconds}}} \cdot \frac{1 \text{ hour}}{60 \cancel{\text{ minutes}}} = \frac{x}{3600} \text{ hours.}$$

Notes

Chapter 7   Rates and Dimensional Analysis

SAT Archetypes

Final Distance, Given Two Perpendicular Trajectories

Malik and Aaron are campers deep in wooded, flat terrain. They leave their camp at the same time, but head out separately in different directions. They are about to get lost. They each walk for 2 hours. Aaron walks due north at a rate of 2 miles per hour, and Malik walks due east through a dense thicket of trees and brush at a rate of 1 mile per hour. What is the straight-line distance between them after 2 hours?

(A) 3
(B) $3\sqrt{3}$
(C) $2\sqrt{5}$
(D) $4\frac{1}{2}$

How do I start?

Draw the diagram of distances and directions walked by each boy.

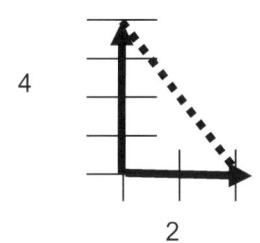

Solution

Aaron will walk 2 miles/hour • 2 hours = 4 miles north, and Malik will instead walk 1 miles/hour • 2 hour = 2 miles east. The distance between them, after two hours, is the length of the dotted-line hypotenuse of the right triangle shown above, which is $\sqrt{4^2 + 2^2}$ = $\sqrt{20}$ = $2\sqrt{5}$.

Answer C

Rates and Dimensional Analysis   Chapter 7

The Take-Away

If two objects are moving at different speeds, their directions, distance, and time traveled must be taken into account. As in this case, if the directions are not collinear, a little geometry will be necessary. North, East, South, and West can form 90° angles from which right triangles can be formed.

Algebraic Expression of Average Speed

The time it took to complete each of 4 consecutive quarter-mile time trials riding a horse was w, x, y, and z seconds, respectively. What was the speed, in miles per hour, averaged over the total running distance and total running time?

(A) $\dfrac{60}{w+x+y+z}$

(B) $\dfrac{225}{wxyz} \cdot [xyz+wyz+wxz+wxy]$

(C) $\dfrac{3600}{w+x+y+z}$

(D) $\dfrac{900}{wxyz} \cdot [wzx+xyz+ywx+zwy]$

How do I start?

Think of this as a single trip with 4 separate legs, ignoring any downtime between legs. The rate of speed averaged over these 4 legs is the total distance divided by the total time (of only the time trials). It is not the average of the rates for the 4 legs.

Solution

Over the 4 time trials, the total distance traveled was 1 mile. The total time was w + x + y + z seconds = (w+x+y+z) seconds • 1 minute /(60 seconds)• 1 hour /(60 minutes) = (w+x+y+z)/3600 hours. The average speed is the total distance divided by the total time = 1 mile/[(w+x+y+z)/3600 hours] = 3600/(w+x+y+z) miles per hour.

Answer C

The Take-Away

The average speed over several trips or legs is the total distance divided by the total time, *not* the average of the rates for the 4 legs.

Chapter 7 — Rates and Dimensional Analysis

Algebraic Expression of the Average of Speeds

The time it took to complete each of 4 consecutive quarter-mile time trials riding a horse was w, x, y, and z seconds, respectively. What was the average of the speeds for these 4 time trials in miles per hour?

(A) $\dfrac{3600}{w+x+y+z}$

(B) $\dfrac{w+x+y+z}{4}$

(C) $\dfrac{900}{wxyz} \cdot [wzx+xyz+ywx+zwy]$

(D) $\dfrac{225}{wxyz} \cdot [xyz+wyz+wxz+wxy]$

How do I start?

Compare the wording of this problem to the previous problem. Here, they are asking for the average of the four recorded speeds. You'll need to get expressions for the speed of each of the 4 time trials and then average *those*.

Solution

Each time trial is .25 miles. The time for the first trial was w seconds, or w/3600 hours. The speed was .25 miles / (w/3600 hours) = 900/w miles per hour. Likewise, the speeds for the other three runs were 900/x, 900/y, and 900/z. The average of these speeds is their sum divided by 4: 1/4 • [900/w + 900/x + 900/y + 900/z]. This equals 225 • [1/w + 1/x + 1/y + 1/z] = 225 • 1/wxyz • [xyz + wyz + wxz + wxy] miles per hour.

Answer D

The Take-Away

If the problem explicitly asks for the average of the speeds, just calculate (or algebraically express) the individual speeds, and then average them.

Rates and Dimensional Analysis   Chapter 7

Rate Calculation Requiring Unit Conversions

Aarnav takes the online final exam for a summer school typing course. He is given a printed report to retype. The report has s sections. Each section has p paragraphs. If each paragraph has 100 words and Aarnav types 50 words per minute, how many hours will it take to complete the report?

(A) $\dfrac{sp}{30}$

(B) $\dfrac{50s}{p}$

(C) $\dfrac{sp}{50}$

(D) $\dfrac{50sp}{30}$

How do I start?

Read carefully. You are given a rate in words per minute, but you need to calculate time in *hours*. We need units of time "on top." Work first in minutes. You could start by inverting the given typing speed to put the minutes unit on top: 1minute/50 words. Chain-multiply the other ratios that describe the paragraphs and sections in such a way that all units are cancelled except minutes. Then convert to hours.

Solution

This is a prime example of a problem where dimensional analysis will be helpful. We need an answer that is in the units of time, and in particular, hours. But let's work in minutes at first. Aarnav takes 1 minute to type 50 words. We need an answer in units of time, so start here. 1 minute/50words • 100words/paragraph • p paragraphs/section • s sections = 2•s•p minutes. All the other units cancel. We now have to convert minutes to hours: the number of hours equals 2sp minutes • 1hour/60minutes = sp/30 hours.

Alternate solution

First, calculate the number of words in the report: # words = s sections • p paragraphs/section • 100 words/paragraph = (1) 100sp words. Since Aarnav types 50 words per minute, flip this ratio to put units of time on top to get (2) 1minute/50words. Multiply (1) and (2): #minutes = 100sp words • 1 minute/(50 words) = 2sp minutes. The number of hours = 2sp minutes • 1 hour / (60 minutes) = sp/30 hours.

Answer A

Chapter 7   Rates and Dimensional Analysis

The Take-Away

Problems involving complex ratio relationships are often best started by finding a ratio that is related to the units of the answer (words per minute above). Invert this if necessary to put the unit we need in the answer on top (via minutes/word above) and chain-multiply the given ratios to cancel all units except those needed (minutes, here). Well, we needed hours, but that is easily converted from minutes.

Round Trip Travel Time At Multiple Speeds

Lowell drove from home to his cabin at an average speed of 75 miles per hour. He drove back home along the same route at an average speed of 45 miles per hour. The roundtrip took a total driving time of 5 hours and 20 minutes. What was the roundtrip distance?

(A) 200 miles
(B) 220 miles
(C) 250 miles
(D) 300 miles

How do I start?

Remember, we can always use a speed ratio in miles per hour, or its inverse in units of hours per mile. The two one-way distances composing the round trip are equal. We don't know the one-way distance driven, so call it D. Because they are driven at different speeds, the time it takes for each leg of the trip is different. Express the two leg times in terms of D. Their sum must equal $5\frac{1}{3}$ hours. Another way of solving this problem is to develop two different expressions for D based on the different speeds and equate them.

Solution

Let D represent the distance from home to the cabin, which also equals the distance from cabin to home. The total driving time = $5\frac{1}{3}$ hours. The total time equals the sum of the two driving times. For the first leg, he drives at an inverted rate of 1 hour per 75 miles. The time driving to the cabin is therefore 1hour/75miles • D miles. Likewise, the time driving home is 1hour/45miles • D miles. We are given that the sum of these two driving times is $5\frac{1}{3}$ hours. Therefore, D(1/75 +1/45) = $5\frac{1}{3}$. Isolating D (after a little algebra), D = 150 miles. The total round-trip driving distance is 2D = 300 miles.

Rates and Dimensional Analysis — Chapter 7

Alternate solution

Let D represent the distance between home and cabin. Let t1 represent the time driving from cabin to home (first half trip). The total driving time = $5\frac{1}{3}$ hours, so $5\frac{1}{3}$ - t1 is the driving time for second half. For the first half, (1) D = 75 miles/hour • t1 hours. For the second half, (2) D = 45miles/hour • ($5\frac{1}{3}$ - t1) hours. Since the distance, D, is the same for the first and second half trips, set expressions (1) and (2) equal to each. Therefore, 75 • t1 = 45 • ($5\frac{1}{3}$ - t1). Isolating t1, t1 = 2 hours. From (1), D = 75 miles/hour • 2 hours = 150 miles. The total round-trip driving distance is twice this, 300 miles.

Answer D

The Take-Away

A roundtrip problem, where the speed of the outgoing trip is different from the return speed, can usually be solved by equating the distance of the outgoing leg to the distance of the return. Dead horse: a ratio involving units can always be inverted to put the desired unit in the numerator.

Labor Performed by People Working at Different Rates

Jacob and Elder combine their labors hammering nails while building a backyard deck. If Jacob can hammer 1 nail per minute, Elder can hammer 1.5 nails per minute, and they completed the job in two and a half hours, how many nails were hammered into the deck?

SR

How do I start?

Both men work for 2.5 hours. Calculate the number of nails each man hammers during that time, using their respective rates. Sum those to get the total.

Solution

Their given rates are in minutes. 2.5 hours is 2.5 hours • 60 minutes / hour = 150 minutes. Both men worked 150 minutes, therefore the total number of nails hammered was: 1 nails/minute • 150 minutes + 1.5 nails/minute • 150 minutes = 375 nails.

Chapter 7 Rates and Dimensional Analysis

Alternate solution

Each minute, the men hammer a combined 1 + 1.5 = 2.5 nails; i.e., their combined rate is 2.5 nails per minute. We are told that they work for 2.5 hours = 150 minutes. Therefore, together they hammer 2.5 nails/minute • 150 minutes = 375 nails.

Answer 375

The Take-Away

Problems where two different rates (nails per minute, above) are involved can sometimes be easily solved by just adding the rates. If the units are the same, and the units are additive (similar acts are combined), they may be added.

Project Duration Based on a Compound Rate

A 19th century railroad engineering manager is given the task of planning a project to lay 40 miles of new railroad extension tracks. He knows from experience that it takes, on average, 12 men 4 days to lay 2 miles of railroad. Assuming the rate of laying new track in this project maintains these same ratios, how many men will it take to lay 40 miles of railroad in 12 days?

(A) 60
(B) 80
(C) 85
(D) 100

How do I start?

The multi-unit rate here has *three* units: 2 *miles* are laid by 12 *men* in 4 *days*. These units will combine to form a three-unit ratio. Use common sense to determine which units go on top and which go on bottom. For example, doubling the men will surely double the miles, and doubling the days will also double the miles. Miles is *jointly proportional* to men and days: (1) miles = (constant)•men•days. Men and days will always go together as a compound factor: the man-day. But note that if you divide miles by man-days in (1), you get a *constant*. This constant, whose units is miles/(man•day), defines how these factors govern labor. And you are given data with which to calculate this constant.

Solution

Rates and Dimensional Analysis — Chapter 7

Using dimensional analysis, the number of miles per man-day may be expressed as $2 \text{ miles} \cdot \frac{1}{4 \text{ days}} \cdot \frac{1}{12 \text{ men}} = 1/24 \frac{\text{miles}}{\text{man} \cdot \text{day}}$. The constant 1/24 tells us that one man can lay 1/24 of a mile in one day. We want to use this compound rate to calculate an answer in the units of men. We'll need the dimension of man on top of the expression, therefore we might start by first inverting the above rate expression: inverted rate $= \frac{24 \text{ man} \cdot \text{day}}{\text{miles}}$. To calculate the number of men, we have to multiply by a quantity in units of miles and divide by a quantity in units of days to cancel those units and leave units of men. We are given such quantities in the problem. Doing so, the number of men it takes to lay 40 miles of track in 12 days is:

$$\text{men} = \frac{24 \text{ man} \cdot \text{day}}{\text{miles}} \cdot 40 \text{ miles} \cdot \frac{1}{12 \text{ days}} = 80 \text{ men}$$

Alternate Solution

It is possible to approach this problem piece-wise. The men need to lay 40 miles of railroad, which is 20 times the number of miles given in the original average rate description (2 → 40). With only the original 4 days, it would take 20 times the original 12 men, or 20 • 12 = 240 men to complete 40 miles. However, they are given 12 days (3 times as many as 4 days), so it will only take 1/3 as many men as that: 240/3 = 80 men.

Answer B

The Take-Away

Dimensional analysis! In complex rate problems involving ratios with 3 units, you will always be given quantities in units that can be chain-multiplied together to cancel all units except the units required in the answer. In labor analysis, combining units of person•hour, man•day, etc., is common, and such units always go together. Learn to manipulate the unit quantities and ratios given to produce an answer in the desired units.

Make sure the arrangement of units makes sense. In this problem it only makes sense that the number of miles laid would be proportional to the number of men on the project and also proportional to the number of days worked.

The alternate solution was quick. But – another problem may not be so transparent to common sense analysis. If the units are unfamiliar, it is always best to perform dimensional analysis.

Practice Problems

1. Kyle and Allie leave school together at the same time and walk for 2 hours. Allie walks due north at the average rate of 2 miles per hour and Kyle walks due east. At the end of 2 hours, the straight-line distance between them is $2\sqrt{5}$ miles. How fast did Kyle walk in miles per hour?

    (A) 1
    (B) $\sqrt{3}$
    (C) 2
    (D) $2\frac{1}{2}$

2. An executive flew himself in his private jet to a business meeting. He flew at 750 kilometers per hour on the way there, but had mechanical trouble on the way back causing an engine to overheat, and thus his return trip only averaged 450 kilometers per hour. If the distance travelled was the same on both trips and he flew a total of 5 hours and 20 minutes, how long did it take to fly back?

    (A) 2 hours
    (B) $2\frac{2}{3}$ hours
    (C) $3\frac{1}{3}$ hours
    (D) 4 hours

3. An office assistant applying for a job must copy a report that has 10 sections. Each section has 6 paragraphs. If each paragraph has 100 words, and it takes 1 hour to type the report, how many words per minute does the assistant type?

    (A) 60
    (B) 72
    (C) 100
    (D) 120

Rates and Dimensional Analysis   Chapter 7

4. Jacob and Elder combine their labors hammering nails while building a storage building. If Jacob can hammer 1 nail per minute, Elder can hammer 1.5 nails per minute, and there was a total of 750 nails hammered in, how many hours did it take to build the storage building?

   SR

5. Jacob and Elder each build one storage building, with each building requiring the same number of nails. If Jacob can hammer 1 nail per minute, Elder can hammer 1.5 nails per minute, and the sum of their times spent was 10 hours, how many nails does it take to build one building?

   SR

6. If it costs x euros to fill an L liter tank and the vehicle gets K kilometers per liter while driving, how much does it cost, in euros, to drive 20 kilometers?

   (A) $\dfrac{1}{20xLK}$

   (B) $\dfrac{x}{20LK}$

   (C) $\dfrac{20x}{LK}$

   (D) $\dfrac{20xK}{L}$

7. It takes 12 men 4 days to lay 2 miles of railroad. How many days would it take to 4 men to lay 20 miles of railroad?

   (A) 60
   (B) 80
   (C) 85
   (D) 120

Chapter 7 Rates and Dimensional Analysis

8. A certain car averages 30 miles per gallon over a particular trip. On that trip, it is driven for 12 minutes at 25 miles per hour and then for an hour and 20 minutes at three times that speed. If gasoline costs $3 per gallon, what was the fuel cost for the trip?

   (A) $9.00
   (B) $10.00
   (C) $10.50
   (D) $12.00

9. If Sarah makes d dollars per year and saves b more dollars than she spends, what fraction of her yearly income does she spend in terms of d and b?

   (A) $\dfrac{d}{b}$
   (B) $\dfrac{d-b}{2d}$
   (C) $\dfrac{d-b}{d}$
   (D) $\dfrac{2(d-b)}{d}$

10. At the beginning of a 500-mile car race between cars A and B, car A leaves immediately at the starting light, while car B has engine trouble, resulting in a delay of 15 minutes before it can leave the starting line. If car A averages 125 miles per hour throughout the race, what is the average speed of car B, in miles per hour, that will allow it to exactly catch up with car A and tie the race at the 500-mile finish line?

    (A) 125
    (B) $133\dfrac{1}{3}$
    (C) 140.5
    (D) $145\dfrac{2}{3}$

11. Jan and Elise work together to prepare 500 academy award "swag bags" (gifts for participants). Jan can prep 4 bags per minute and Elise preps 5 more than three-fourths the number Jan can prepare in a minute. If they start together at the same time, how many minutes will it take them to complete their work?

(A) $41\frac{2}{3}$

(B) $52\frac{2}{3}$

(C) 55

(D) $58\frac{1}{3}$

12. Two engineers must travel from their office near Chicago to Tokyo. They hit bad traffic and must drive one and a half hours to the airport at an average speed of 40 miles per hour. They then wait two hours and 40 minutes after arriving for the plane to take off. The plane flies at an average speed of 500 miles per hour. The flight lasts 13 hours. After arriving and spending one hour 30 minutes at the airport in customs, getting luggage, and renting a car, they drive one hour 20 minutes to their hotel in Tokyo at an average of 60 miles per hour. What was their average speed, in miles per hour, from home to hotel for the entire trip, including any time spent not traveling?

(A) 325
(B) 332
(C) 340.5
(D) 365

13. A prepaid phone costs x cents for every y minutes of airtime. If the user prepays d dollars and has used z minutes already, how many minutes remain until more money must be prepaid, in terms of x, y, z, and d?

(A) $\frac{100yd}{x} - z$

(B) $xyd + z$

(C) $\frac{yd}{x} - z$

(D) $\frac{yd}{100x} - z$

14. *Challenge* Hal can lay 140 bricks per hour. He usually works with his friend, Ashby. Hal and Ashby always work 8 hours per day, Monday through Friday, and never work weekends. They each work at a constant rate, laying the same number of bricks per hour. On Monday they start laying bricks together on a project that begins as soon as they arrive. They lay 9600 bricks in 5 full days to complete the project. But then Hal quits. Next Monday, Ashby has to begin an identical project himself. How many days total, including weekends off, from the start of the first project to the end of the second project will these two projects take?

(A) 15
(B) 17
(C) 19
(D) 23

15. A multi-stop trip by air, starting from the home airport, H, involves 3 equidistant legs to 3 different cities: A, B, and C. The first two legs (H→A and A→B) were flown in a propeller plane at 250 miles per hour, while the third leg (B→C) was flown in a jet at 500 miles per hour. For the entire distance flown, and <u>only counting flight time</u>, what is the average speed of all three flights in miles per hour?

(A) $266\frac{2}{3}$
(B) 300
(C) 325
(D) $333\frac{1}{3}$

16. Ali drives from home to his grandparents using the freeway at an average speed of 60 miles per hour. On the trip back home he must take a different route (but with identical distance), at an average speed of only 36 miles per hour. If the entire round-trip travel time was 3 hours, what is the distance from his home to his grandparents, in miles?

(A) 52.5
(B) 55
(C) 67.5
(D) 72

Rates and Dimensional Analysis   Chapter 7

17. A grain truck with a capacity of 18,000 pounds is already one-third full. It drives into a granary to be filled to capacity. The granary flows grain into trucks at a rate of p pounds every minute. Drivers are charged based on the number of minutes grain flowed into their trucks. The granary charges d dollars for every minute that grain flows. After the truck above is full, it was determined that grain flowed for m minutes. In terms of p, m, and d, what will the granary charge, in dollars, for filling the truck?

(A) $12{,}000 \cdot mpd$

(B) $12{,}000 \cdot \dfrac{md}{p}$

(C) $12{,}000 \cdot \dfrac{mp}{d}$

(D) $\dfrac{m}{12{,}000 \cdot dp}$

18. An engineer works w hours per day and spends w/4 hours per day on the Internet. If the engineer works 5 days per week, how many weeks does it take for her to spend 100 hours on the Internet?

(A) $\dfrac{w}{20}$

(B) $\dfrac{w}{4}$

(C) $\dfrac{4}{w}$

(D) $\dfrac{80}{w}$

19. An industrial gasoline storage tank has one input pipe and many output pipes. Each pipe may be turned either on or off independently. The rate of filling the tank with gas by the input pipe (when active) is 1000 gallons per minute. The rate of draining gasoline out of the tank by each of the output pipes (when active) is -100 gallons per minute; note the - sign indicates drainage from the tank. If the input pipe is active (gas is flowing into the tank), how many output pipes must be draining (active) at the same time if the net rate of draining the tank in this fashion is equal to the drainage rate when the input pipe is not active, but with only 1/2 as many output pipes active?

(A) 15
(B) 20
(C) 25
(D) 30

Chapter 7 — Rates and Dimensional Analysis

20. Child labor was a social ill in the United States up until the early 20th century. In the late 19th century, a small button manufacturer located on the banks of the Mississippi river employed a 6-year-old child to sort barrels of clamshells (used to make buttons) prior to subsequent processing. The owner realized that this child was the bottleneck (slowest link in the chain of production) and decided to make an additional hire: a teenager who could sort clamshells at 5 times the rate of the 6-year-old.

It is known from records discovered at the site that together these children were able to sort an entire barrel of clamshells in 4 hours. The only thing else known was a single equation describing their labor written below. No definition of s or any units were found accompanying this equation:

$$1/s + 5/s = 1/4$$

What is the most likely meaning of the value of 1/s?

(A) The fraction of time the 6-year-old takes to sort each barrel
(B) The length of time the 6-year-old takes to sort each barrel by himself
(C) The number of barrels the 6-year-old can sort in one hour
(D) The labor rate, in hours per barrel, of the 6-year-old

21. Three salespersons are hired to sell a novelty item at an electronics fair. The first two can each sell one case of items every 3 hours, while the third salesperson can sell a case of items every 90 minutes. How long, in minutes, will it take all three salespersons working together to sell one case of items?

SR

Notes

Chapter 7   Rates and Dimensional Analysis

Practice Problem Hints

1. Draw the diagram of distances and directions walked by each person. Use Pythagoras or the distance formula.

2. Express the outbound and return times in terms of 750kph and 450kph and the unknown distance, D (which is the same in each direction). The sum of the times equals $5\frac{1}{3}$ hours.

3. The answer will be in units of words/minute. Calculate the total words and divide by the minutes it took to type the report.

4. If it takes t minutes to build the building, Jacob nails t nails and Elder nails 1.5t nails.

5. Both buildings are identical, but the men do not work the same number of hours to build their respective buildings. Express the number of nails each person hammers in terms of the time they spend hammering.

6. It costs x euros per L liters. Chain multiply the given ratios (or their inverted ratios) with their units to yield a product in units of euros.

7. Express the complex labor rate with the units of man•days in the numerator.

8. Calculate the total distance and then use the inverted mileage ratio to calculate the gallons used.

9. d is the total income. Let s = amount spent. Therefore, d - s is the amount saved. From the problem, the amount saved also = b + s. Equate these expressions for the amount saved to develop an expression for s in terms of d and b.

10. Calculate the time car A takes to complete the race. Subtract 15 minutes for car B.

11. Calculate how many bags they prepare together in a minute.

12. Calculate the total distance traveled and then the total time.

Rates and Dimensional Analysis — Chapter 7

13. Invert the given rate to min/cents. Convert d dollars to cents, and then calculate the number of minutes d dollars will buy.

14. Calculate the number of hours to complete the first job. Knowing Hal's rate, you'll have to then solve for Ashby's rate. And be careful with counting the days – include weekends.

15. Choose a convenient distance (a multiple of 500, say) between cities. Calculate the total time in the air. Average speed = total distance / total time.

16. Flip the rates, putting hours on top. Calculate the total driving time in terms of the unknown distance from home to campus.

17. The truck needs 12,000 pounds to be filled to capacity. You want an answer in dollars. Start with the dollar per minute rate and chain multiply by the other values given.

18. In one 5-day week she will spend 5w/4 hours on the Internet.

19. In the rate equations below, m is the number of output pipes opened up

    Scenario$_1$ net rate = 1000gal/min - m100g/m, if the input pipe is active
    Scenario$_2$ net rate = -m/2 • 100gal/min, if the input pipe is inactive

20. You have to infer the units. 1/4 most likely refers to 1 barrel per 4 hours.

21. Express each work rate in units of case per minute. Invert to get minutes/case.

Chapter 7   Rates and Dimensional Analysis

Practice Problem Solutions

1. Answer A

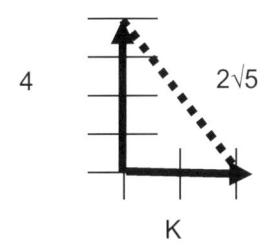

   Allie will walk 2 miles/hour • 2 hours = 4 miles north in two hours. Kyle walks K miles during the same time. The straight line distance then is $2\sqrt{5}$. From Pythagoras, $K = \sqrt{4 \cdot 5 - 16} = 2$. So if Kyle walked 2 miles in 2 hours, he walked 1 mile per hour.

   Alternate Solution: Via distance formula: $(2\sqrt{5})^2 = 4^2 + K^2$. K = 2. So, 1 mile per hour.

2. Answer C

   We need to know the time for the return flight. The outgoing flight is flown at a rate of 750 kilometers/hour, and the return flight is flown at a rate of 450 kilometers/hour. Let D represent the distance flown, *which is the same in both directions*. The total flying time = $5\frac{1}{3}$ hours. The total flying time equals the sum of the two flying times. The time flying there is 1hr/750km • Dkm, and the return time is 1hr/450km • Dkm. The sum of these times is $5\frac{1}{3}$. So D(1/750 +1/450) = $5\frac{1}{3}$. After isolating D, D = 1500km. Since the return flight speed is 450km/hour, we can flip this ratio to put hours on top and multiply by the distance to get the flying time: 1 hour/450km • 1500km = $3\frac{1}{3}$ hours.

   Alternate Solution: If (for example) the return leg were flown at half the speed of the outgoing leg (a return to outgoing speed ratio of 375:750, or 1:2), the ratio of return to outgoing flying *times* would be 2:1. It would take twice as long to return at 375kph as the outgoing speed of at 750kph. Since the return to outgoing flying time ratio is 2:1, the return leg would take 2/(1+2), or 2/3 of the *total* flight time. But in this problem, the return to outgoing speed ratio is 450:750. The return to outgoing flying time ratio is the obverse of this: 750:450. As above, the return leg will take 750/(750+450) = .625 of the total flight time. The total flight time is $5\frac{1}{3}$ hours. The return leg takes .625 • $5\frac{1}{3}$ = $3\frac{1}{3}$ hours. This solution required clever, intuitive savvy, but saved algebra and time.

Rates and Dimensional Analysis   Chapter 7

3. Answer C

   Here is an easy problem that many students manage to miss. We need an answer that is in units of words per minute. From the data, we can determine the number of words typed and the number of minutes. There are 10 sections, which have 6 paragraphs, each of which have 100 words. Thus, there are 10•6•100 = 6000 words. Since it took 1 hour, or 60 minutes to type, the typing speed is 6000 words/60 minutes, or 100 words per minute.

4. Answer 5

   Let t be the number of minutes the job took to complete. During t minutes, Jacob nails 1 nails/~~min~~ • t ~~min~~ = t nails, and Elder nails 1.5 nails/~~min~~ • t ~~min~~ = 1.5t nails. Since the total number of nails used equals 750, 750 = t + 1.5t = 2.5t. Solving for t, t = 300 minutes. The job took 300 min • 1hour / 60 min = 5 hours.

   Alternate Solution: Together Jacob and Elder can hammer 2.5 nails per minute, or inverting the ratio, 1 min / 2.5 nails. To calculate the number of minutes, multiply this ratio by the number of nails: 1 min / 2.5 nails • 750 nails = 300 minutes. Converting, this is 300 minutes / (60 min/hr) = 5 hours.

5. Answer 360

   The men hammer *the same number of nails* into their respective buildings, but at different rates. So derive an equation where the number of Jacob's nails equals the number of Elder's nails. If Jacob works for x minutes, he hammers 1 nail/minute • x minutes = x nails. The sum of the time worked was 10 hours = 600 minutes. Elder worked 600 - x minutes, and so Elder hammers 1.5 nails/minute • (600-x) minutes = 900 - 1.5x nails. Since the number of nails Jacob hammers is the same number of nails Elder hammers, x = 900 - 1.5x. Solving for x, x = 360 nails.

   Alternate Solution: 1min/Nail • xNails + 1min/(1.5Nails) • xNails = 600 min. Solving for x nails, x = 360.

6. Answer C

   This is an excellent problem on which to practice dimensional analysis. The final answer must be in units of euros, so we need to chain multiply the known factors or their inverted forms in the problem to obtain the correct cancellation of units.

Chapter 7 Rates and Dimensional Analysis

Beginning with x euros/(L liters), we can cancel the liters unit by multiplying by 1 liter/(K kilometers). We can cancel the kilometers unit by multiplying by 20 kilometers, finally leaving the answer in units of euros:

x euros/L ~~liters~~ • 1 ~~liter~~/K ~~kilometers~~ • 20 ~~kilometers~~ = 20x/LK euros

Alternate Solution: Starting with 20 kilometers, we see that:
20 ~~kilometers~~ • 1 ~~liter~~/K ~~kilometers~~ • x euros / L ~~liters~~ = 20x/KL euros.

Alternate Solution II: the cost must be proportional to fuel cost (x euros/L liters) *and* inversely proportional to mileage (K kilometers/liter): low mileage → high cost.

7. Answer D

In labor rate problems, units such as person and hour are almost always multiplied. Here, we have man•days. The complete labor rate in this problem can be expressed as 12 men • 4 days / 2 miles, or 24 man-days/mile. Since we want the final units in days, use this ratio as it comes, with days in the numerator. We'll have to multiply this expression by 20 miles and divide by the 4 men to cancel those units:

24 ~~man~~-days/~~mile~~ • 20 ~~miles~~/4 ~~men~~ = 120 days.

Alternate Solution: From the ratio, it would take 12 men <u>40</u> days to lay <u>20</u> miles of track. But there are only 4 men - it will take 3 times longer than that: 3•40 = 120 days.

8. Answer C

First, we must calculate the total number of miles of the trip. 12 minutes = 12/60 hours = .2 hour, so the first part of the trip was $25 \frac{\text{miles}}{\text{hour}}$ • .2 hour = 5 miles. The second part of the trip was driven at 3•25 = 75 miles per hour for one and one third hours. Therefore, the second part of the trip was $75 \frac{\text{miles}}{\text{hour}}$ • $1\frac{1}{3}$ hour = 100 miles. So the total trip was 105 miles. Using the inverted mileage ratio, there were 105 miles • $\frac{1 \text{ gal}}{30 \text{ miles}}$ = 3.5 gallons used on the trip. At $3 per gallon, the trip cost 3.5gal • $\frac{\$3}{\text{gal}}$ = $10.50.

9. Answer B

Yeesh. Let s = amount spent. Thus, d - s is the amount saved. The answer is the ratio of s to d. From the problem, the amount saved also equals b + s. So, b + s = d - s. Isolating s, s = (d-b)/2. The fraction of yearly income spent equals s/d = (d-b)/(2d).

Rates and Dimensional Analysis · Chapter 7

Alternate Solution: The total, spent + saved = d = spent + (spent + b). Isolate spent. Thus, spent = (d-b)/2, and the fraction spent (of the total d) = (d-b)/2d.

Alternate Solution II: d should be in the denominator. If you guess, don't guess (A).

10. Answer B

Car A takes $\frac{1 \text{ hour}}{125 \text{ miles}} \cdot 500$ miles = 4 hours to complete the 500 mile race. Car B must complete the same distance in 4 hours minus 15 minutes, or 3 hours 45 minutes = 3.75 hours. The average speed of car B is therefore $\frac{500 \text{ miles}}{3.75 \text{ hours}} = 133\frac{1}{3}$ mph.

Alternate Solution: 15 minutes is a small fraction of 4 hours, so B doesn't have to go that much faster. But he must go faster, so toss (A). The answer is probably (B).

11. Answer A

Jan preps 4 bags per minute, so Elise preps $\frac{3}{4} \cdot 4 + 5 = 8$ bags per minute. So together they prep 12 bags / minute. We need to calculate how long it takes to prep 500 bags: 500 bags = 12 bags/minute • x minutes. Isolating x, $x = 41\frac{2}{3}$ minutes.

Alternate Solution: 500 bags @ 12 bags/min must be less than 50 minutes. The only choice less than 50 minutes is (A).

12. Answer B

We need distance/time. First determine the total distance of the trip by summing the distances of the trip segments. The formula for each segment will be distance = speed • time. Travel to the airport is $40 \frac{\text{miles}}{\text{hour}} \cdot 1.5$ hours = 60 miles. The plane travels $500 \frac{\text{miles}}{\text{hour}} \cdot 13$ hours = 6500 miles. Travel to the hotel = $60 \frac{\text{miles}}{\text{hour}} \cdot 1\frac{1}{3}$ hours = 80 miles. Therefore, the total distance traveled is 60 + 6500 + 80 = 6640 miles. The total time equals the travel times plus the waiting times = $(1.5 + 2\frac{2}{3} + 13 + 1.5 + 1\frac{1}{3})$ hours = 20 hours. Average speed = distance/time = 6640/20 = 332 miles per hour.

13. Answer A

We want an answer in minutes and have a rate in cents per minute. Invert this rate: (y min)/(x cents). If we multiply by the number of cents prepaid, we'll get the number of minutes prepaid: (y min)/(x ~~cents~~) • (100 ~~cents~~)/(~~dollar~~) • d ~~dollars~~ = 100yd/x minutes.

Since we've use up z minutes, the number of minutes left is 100yd/x - z.

Alternate solution: the number of minutes left *must* be related to the amount of money (d dollars, or 100d cents) that was used to fund the initial minutes. Only (A) includes a term with 100d.

14. Answer D

    Both men work 8•5 = 40 hours together to complete the job of laying 9600 bricks. Hal lays at a rate of 140 bricks/hour. In 40 hours he lays 140 bricks/hour • 40 hour = 5600 bricks. Therefore, Ashby laid 9600 - 5600 = 4000 bricks in 40 hours. Ashby's rate must be 4000 bricks/40hours = 100 bricks/hour. After Hal quits, Ashby has to do an identical 9600 brick job all by himself. How long does this take? Invert his rate and multiply by the number of bricks: 1 hour/(100 bricks) • 9600 bricks = 96 hours = 12 8-hour working days if he works by himself.

    Since Ashby doesn't work weekends, it will take him 5 days on the first week by himself, 2 weekend days off, 5 days on the second week by himself, another 2 weekend days off, and two additional work days on his third week by himself to complete this second job. So Ashby took 7+7+2 = 16 days by himself on the second project (including weekends off). The first job took 5 days, and including the weekend off between projects, a total of 7 days. Both projects took 16+7 = 23 days, from their first day together to the day Ashby completed the second job.

15. Answer B

    We could solve this for some general distance, but since we are calculating the ratio distance / time, we are free to choose convenient distances (the distance between cities are equal, so the average speed will be the same for any chosen distance). If each city is 500 miles apart, the first two trips would each take 2 hours airtime: 1hr/(250miles) • 500 miles = 2 hours. The third trip would clearly take 1 hour, and so the entire trip of 3 • 500 = 1500 miles would take 2 + 2 + 1 = 5 hours. The average speed, over the entire distance, is 1500 miles / 5 hours = 300 miles per hour.

    Alternate Solution: Let the distance between cities be x. The first two trips are flown at 250 mph, and the third is flown at 500 mph. The time for the first trip is 1 hour/ 250 miles • x miles, the time for the second trip is the same, x/250 hours, and the time for the third trip is 1 hour / 500 miles • x miles = x/500 hours. Therefore, the total time in flight is x•(1/250 + 1/250 + 1/500) hours. Simplifying, this equals 5x/500 hours. The total distance is x + x + x = 3x. The average speed is simply equal to total distance / total time = 3x / (5x/500) = 1500/5 = 300 miles per hour.

Rates and Dimensional Analysis   Chapter 7

16. Answer C

Use dimensional analysis. Let d be the unknown distance, in miles, from home to the grandparents. His driving time going there is d miles • 1 hour/60miles = d/60 hours. Driving back home it takes him d miles • 1 hour/36 miles = d/36 hours. We are told that the total drive time was 3 hours. Therefore, 3 = d/60 + d/36. Cross-multiplying denominators to get an easy common denominator, 3 = 36d/2160 + 60d/2160. Collecting terms on the right, 3 = d • (96/2160). Isolating d, d = 67.5.

17. Answer B

Because the truck is 1/3 full, the truck needs an additional 2/3 • 18,000 = 12,000 pounds of grain to be completely filled. The easiest way to handle such problems is by dimensional analysis. Since we want an answer in dollars, start with the ratio that has dollars on top: d dollars /(1 ~~minute~~). Multiply by other data to get an answer in dollars: d dollars /(1 ~~minute~~)• m ~~minutes~~/(p ~~pounds~~) • 12,000 ~~pounds~~ = 12,000 md/p dollars.

Alternate Solution: The answer must have 12,000 on the top, and also be proportional to both the number of minutes, m, and the dollar rate, d. Only choice (B) is consistent with this unit analysis. In a pinch for time, this kind of quick logic can produce a win, or at least reduce the number of possible choices.

18. Answer D

In one 5-day week she spends 5 ~~days~~/week • w/4 hours/~~day~~ = 5w/4 hours/week on the internet. Let n denote the *unknown* number of weeks it takes her to spend 100 hours online. Using the above rate, 100 hours = n ~~weeks~~ • 5w/4 hours/~~week~~. Isolating n, n = 80/w.

Alternate Solution: Pick a convenient number for w and find a matching choice. If w = 4 (she works 4 hours per day - nice!), then she spends 1 hour per day on the Internet. So she'll have to work 100 days to spend 100 hours on the Internet. She works 5 days per week, so she'll have to work 20 weeks to work 100 days. Since w = 4, only choice (D) gives an answer of 80/4 = 20 weeks.

Alternate Solution II: The more hours (w) she works per day, the sooner she'll accumulate 100 hours on the internet. They must be inversely proportional. Only choices (C) and (D) are consistent with this unit analysis.

Chapter 7   Rates and Dimensional Analysis

19. Answer B

In the rate equations below, m is the number of output pipes draining:

The net rate equation in the first scenario, where the input pipe is *active*, as well as m output pipes active, is (1) net rate = 1000gal/min - m•100gal/m. Every minute 1000 gallons flow into the tank, but 100m gallons flow *out* of the tank, and so the outflow term is negative. The second scenario describes draining with no input (input pipe is *inactive*) and only half as many active output pipes (i.e., only m/2 active output pipes), as scenario one. It therefore has a rate equation of (2) net rate = -m/2 • 100gal/min.

We are told that these net rates are the same. If the net rate (1) equals net rate (2), then 1000 - m•100 = -m/2 • 100. Simplifying, 1000 - 100m = -50m, or m = 20.

20. Answer C

The term 1/4 on the right side of the equation is most likely a reference to the fact given to us that 1 *barrel* can be sorted every 4 *hours* by both kids. Both kids together can sort 1/4 barrel per hour. Since the units must be the same for all terms in an equation, both terms on the left side must have units of barrels/hour. Note that the second term, 5/s, is 5 times that of the first term, 1/s, and it most likely represents the how teenager can work 5 times faster than the 6-year-old. So together these terms represent the respective rates at which the 6-year-old and the teenager can sort barrels of clamshells in units of barrels/hour. The SAT sows confusion with the expression 1/s. We don't care what s is. We are asked the meaning of 1/s, not s. So the most likely meaning of 1/s is the number of barrels (clearly less than 1) the 6-year-old can sort in one hour since the right side is the number of barrels per hour. Choices (A) and (B) falsely suggest that the teenager takes longer than the 6-year-old. Choice (C), the number of barrels the 6-year-old can sort in one hour looks correct: it is 5 times less than that of the teenager. Choice (D) *is* a labor rate, but it's in the units of hours/barrel, not barrels/hour, and again the teenager would take longer.

Alternate Solution: Together both kids can sort one barrel every 4 hours. So in one hour they can sort 1/4 barrel. The teenager sorts at 5 times the rate (in barrels/hour) of the 6-year-old. Let r = the rate of the 6-year-old. Thus, (1) r + 5r = 1/4. Solving for r, r = 1/24: the 6-year-old can sort at a rate of 1 barrel/24 hours. But note that (1) is in exactly the same form as the mysterious equation found: 1/s + 5/s = 1/4. Therefore, r = 1/s represents the rate in barrels per hour of the 6-year-old. Choice (C) is correct. Moreover we can solve for s: s = 24, the number of hours the 6-year-old takes to sort one barrel. Of course, we weren't asked to solve this. Anyway, (C) is correct.

Rates and Dimensional Analysis Chapter 7

21. Answer 45

Three hours equals 180 minutes. The first two salespeople can each sell at a rate of 1 case per 180 minutes. The third salesperson sells at a rate of 1 case per 90 minutes. Their combined rate of sales is 1 case/180 min + 1 case/180 min + 1 case/90 min. Combining the all three terms with a common denominator, their combined rate of sales is 4 cases/180 min., or 1 case/45 min. We need only invert this: 45 minutes/case.

Alternate Solution: We can set up an equation using dimensional analysis. We want the time, T, it takes all three people to sell one case of gadgets. Given their known rates of selling, during this unknown time, T, the number of cases the first two salespeople will each sell is 1 case/3 hours • T hours. The third salesperson will sell 1 case/1.5 hours • T hours. Altogether in T hours they sell one case. So, ignoring the units now, 1/3•T + 1/3•T + 1/1.5 • T = 1. Simplifying, T•(2/3+ 2/3) = 1. Solving for T, T = 3/4 of 1 hour, or 45 minutes.

Chapter 8

Sequences

The SAT may have one or more hard questions testing a student's ability to understand and manipulate number sequences. Sequences can have a few terms or an infinite number of terms. Some early Greek philosophers imbued infinite sequences with an almost spiritual quality. However, here we need not gaze into the crystal nor behold the boundless. The SAT does not require any working knowledge of infinite sequences.

We will review non-repeating, repeating, and recursive sequences. There are three basic areas of questions about sequences on the SAT. Students must be able to calculate terms in a sequence, given the formula of the sequence. The formula of a sequence must be inferred, given a few terms in the sequence. Also, students must be able to sum large numbers of terms in an arithmetic sequence, given a formula for doing so.

We present the 11 most common archetypes involving sequences. 26 practice problems at the chapter's end include additional challenges that may be found on the SAT.

Sequences   Chapter 8

Don't Show Up Without Knowing...

These Concepts

    Non-repeating Sequence   Arithmetic Sequence

    Repeating Sequence   Recursive Sequence

    Geometric Sequence   Finite and Infinite Sequences

How To...

- Determine the formula for an arithmetic sequence, given a few terms
- Calculate terms in an arithmetic sequence, given the formula
- Determine the formula for a geometric sequence, given a few terms
- Calculate terms in a geometric sequence, given the formula
- Determine the pattern of a repeating sequence, given a few terms
- Calculate terms in a repetitive sequence, given a few terms
- Calculate terms in a recursive sequence, given the formula
- Re-order sequences based on instructions

Note: it is unnecessary to memorize all the formulas regarding sequences in the following section. But reading the sections is necessary to familiarize you with the concepts. If you *need* a formula for the test it, it will be provided to you. However, some problems that can be solved without a formula could be solved much faster with one. So memorize at will.

Quick Review and Definitions

The First Term is the 1ˢᵗ term

While it is very common in programming languages to assign 0 as the index of the first term in an array or sequence, on the SAT all sequences (unless otherwise instructed) will begin with the first term having an index of 1. A sequence S will have terms S_1, S_2, S_3...

Non-repeating Sequences

A sequence in mathematics is a list of numbers, not necessarily in numerical order. They may include just a few terms 1,4,3,7,11, or infinitely many terms. The terms in an infinite sequence may repeat 1,2,3,1,2,3,..., or never repeat, like the digits of pi.

Arithmetic Sequence

An arithmetic sequence is a sequence of numbers that have a constant difference between consecutive terms. For example, terms in the sequence 4,7,10,13,... have a consecutive difference of 3 between terms. Note that there is also a constant difference between terms that are displaced *any* equal number of intervals from one another. All terms that are 2 intervals away from one another in the above sequence have a difference of 6, and terms 3 intervals away have a difference of 9. In general, the difference between any two terms will always be an integer multiple of the consecutive difference.

For an arithmetic sequence,

nth term = first term + (consecutive difference) • (n-1).

Geometric Sequence

A geometric sequence is a sequence of numbers that has a constant multiplying factor between consecutive terms. For example, in the sequence 3,9,27,81..., each term is 3 times the previous term. There is also a constant factor between terms that are displaced any equal number of intervals from one another in the sequence, and these factors will be the consecutive factor raised to some integer power. For example, in the above sequence, all terms displaced by two terms will have a factor of $3^2 = 9$ between them.

For a geometric sequence:

nth term = (first term) • (consecutive factor)$^{(n-1)}$.

Sequences   Chapter 8

The sum of powers of two has a simple equation: $2^0+2^1+\ldots+2^n = 2^{n+1} - 1$.

In general, if a geometric sequence $s_1, s_2, \ldots s_n$ has a consecutive factor of r between adjacent terms, then the sum of the sequence is given by $S_n = s_1 \cdot (r^n - 1)/(r - 1)$.

Inferring or Determining a Sequence Formula

Given a few terms, you must be able to infer or determine the formula that defines an arithmetic or geometric sequence. For example, in the sequence 2, 5, 8,..., there is a consecutive difference of 3 between terms. The first term is 2, the second term is $2 + 3 \cdot 1$, the third term is $2 + 3 \cdot 2$, and the sequence can be generalized to $s(n) = 2 + 3 \cdot (n-1)$. Or, if given its formula, you must be able to calculate any term in a sequence. Given the formula for the arithmetic sequence $4+3 \cdot (n-1)$, the 101st term (n=101) in this sequence is $4+3 \cdot (100) = 304$. The fifth term in the geometric sequence whose formula is 3^n is $3^5 = 243$.

Repeating Sequences

A repeating sequence is a sequence of numbers that repeats one pattern indefinitely. You will usually be given the first few terms in the sequence (which will include the complete repeated pattern). You'll have to infer the formula, or pattern, of the entire sequence, and be able calculate any term in the sequence.

In the sequence 1,2,3,1,2,3,1,... there are 3 numbers in the pattern "1,2,3." The 101st number in the sequence can be found by dividing 101 by 3. There will be 33 complete patterns, ending at the 99th term. This number must be a 3. The sequence starts over with '1' for the 100th term, and so the 101st term will be a '2.'

Assuming all the terms in a repetitive sequence belong to the pattern, you can determine the nth term of a repeating sequence by first dividing n by the number of terms in the pattern. The remainder of this division will tell you the term number corresponding to the nth term, as shown in the example above.

Properties of Arithmetic Sequences

- The sum of all integers from 1 to n = $n(n+1)/2$.

- In general, the sum of an arithmetic sequence of n terms is $n \cdot (s_1 + s_n)/2$.

- The average of the terms in an arithmetic sequence with an odd number of terms is the middle term, the median of the sequence.

Chapter 8   Sequences

- The average of the terms in an arithmetic sequence with an even number of terms is also the median of the sequence, which is the average of the two middle terms.

- You should be able to look at an arithmetic sequence and immediately pick out (or quickly determine) the median and average of its terms.

- Consider the arithmetic sequence of c consecutive integers starting with s:
  s, s+1, s+2, ... s+c-1. We can subtract s from each of the c terms. Those terms sum to c•s. The sum of all terms can be split thus: c•s + 1+2+...+(c-1).

- All arithmetic sequences can be related to the sequence of consecutive integers. A trivial example would be n, 2n, 3n, ... = n•(1,2,3,...).

- The sum of odd numbers starting with 1 is always a perfect square. E.g., 1+3 = 4, 1+3+5 = 9, 1+3+5+7 = 16, etc. That's odd.

- If the terms in a sequence are anti-symmetric about zero (for every positive term, there is a negative term), then the sum of n terms to the left of zero (all negative) plus n terms to the right of zero equals zero. ...**-6, -4, -2, 0, 2, 4, 6**...

  Symbolically, the sequence -n, -(n-1), ...0, 1, 2, ...,(n-1), n will have a sum of zero. **This is an important tool used in the analysis of sequences.**

- If only some of the terms in a sequence are anti-symmetric, then the sum of *those* terms is zero, and the sum of the whole sequence will be the sum of the remaining terms. For example, the sum of **-3, -1, 1, 3**, 5 is (after zeroing out the anti-symmetric terms) 5.

Recursive Sequences

A recursive sequence is a sequence where the expression for the nth term is a function of the value(s) of one or several previous terms. You must be able to calculate the value of or algebraically express the terms of such sequences.

For example, if the nth term in a sequence equals the square of the sum of the previous two terms, and if the 1st term is 2 and the 2nd term is 1, then the 3rd term will be $(2+1)^2 = 9$. The value of the 4th term is $(1+9)^2$. If you were asked for the value of the 7th term, you would have to also calculate the 5th and 6th terms first.

If you know the formula for the nth term as a function of the (n-1)th term, it may be possible to algebraically express the (n-1)th term as a function of the nth term. This technique is crucial for solving one class of problems in this chapter.

A simple example would be a sequence where the $s_n = 3 \cdot s_{n-1} + 3$. We can generate a formula for s_{n-1} as a function of s_n: $s_{n-1} = (s_n-3)/3$. The formula for the terms of a sequence can be "forward looking" as well as backward.

Operations on Sequences

A new sequence may be formed by operating on each term in the sequence. Each and every term may be operated on by adding to or multiplying by some expression, or raising each term to some power. Sequences may also be added or multiplied together term-by-term. For example (1, 2, 3) + (1, 2, 3) = (2, 4, 6).

Terms in a sequence may also be reordered within the sequence. Sequences may be reordered by operations such as transposing terms, or reversing the order of the adjacent terms. For example, 1,2,3,4 may be transformed into 2,1,3,4, by transposing 1 and 2. 1,2,3,4 may be transformed in like manner twice to form 2,1,4,3.

Sequences may also be reordered by circular rotation. As an example of this, the sequence 1,2,3,4 may be rotated to the left, removing the 1 from the left and placing it to the right of the 4: 2,3,4,1.

The mirror image of 1,2,3,4 is 4,3,2,1.

Moreover, combinations of all the above operations may be applied to a sequence.

On the SAT, such operations would be explicitly defined for you. If problems of this type are on the test (they're pretty rare), you will have to employ the operations carefully, sometimes multiple times, in order to obtain some desired final state.

Chapter 8   Sequences

SAT Archetypes

Sequence Transforms

4 3 2 1

Consider the sequence S = 4,3,2,1 above. Two different types of operations are allowed on this sequence. (1) Any two adjacent terms may be transposed (interchanged). For example, 1,2,3,4 can be transposed into 2,1,3,4. Also, (2) the complete sequence may be circularly rotated one term in either direction. For example, 1,2,3,4 can be rotated to the left to become 2,3,4,1 or rotated to the right to become 4,1,2,3. What is the fewest number of operations that must be performed to transform S into 1,2,3,4?

SR

How do I start?

Use operation (1) to get digits in the correct order except for circular rotation. Then use operation (2) to get the digits in the correct position.

Solution

Transpose 2 and 1: 4,3,1,2. Then transpose 3 and 4: 3,4,1,2. This is in the right order, except it is not in the correct circular position. Rotate the sequence once to the right: 2,3,4,1. Then rotate the sequence once again to the right: 1,2,3,4. Therefore, 4 operations are required.

Alternate solution

One might start with rotating twice to the right to achieve 2,1,4,3, and then transpose 1 and 2, and then 3 and 4. Again, 4 operations.

Answer 4

The Take-Away

If the values of terms in two sequences are the same, but in different positions, the sequences can be transformed into one another by transposition, or circular rotation operations. Other such positional operations may be defined for you, and you will have to apply them as described in the problem.

Arithmetic Sequences: Symmetry About Zero

A sequence of consecutive integers has a sum that is positive and odd. If the least number in the sequence is -3, what is the smallest number of integers that could be in this sequence?

(A) 5
(B) 6
(C) 7
(D) 9

How do I start?

The slow way would have you write the first several terms of the sequence and the sum of all terms up to and including this term. Keep going until you get a positive odd sum. Better yet, you could use symmetry about zero to simplify the process.

Solution

The first term in the sequence is -3. You know that the sum of consecutive integers from -n to n is zero, so the sum of all the terms from -3 to +3 is zero. That accounts for 7 terms. The 8th term is 4, but that is even. However, the sum of the 8th and 9th terms, 4 and 5, sum to 9, which is positive and odd. The smallest number of terms is 9.

Alternate solution

You can solve this problem with brute force. Start with -3 and add with a calculator or in your head. -3, -2, -1, 0. Okay, so far the sum is -6. Continuing: 1, 2, 3. So now, with these seven integers, we're back to a sum of 0. The next term (the 8th) in the sequence, 4, brings the sum positive, but even. We need the sum to be odd. The next term (the 9th), which is 5, does this because 4+5 = 9. Therefore, there are 9 terms in this sequence.

Answer D

The Take-Away

The sum of consecutive integers from -n to n is zero. In general, in *any* arithmetic sequence where each term has a pair-partner with opposite sign, the sum of the first n terms less than zero plus the first n terms greater than zero will be zero. For example, -4 -2 0 2 4. This is a good way to save time when adding terms in an arithmetic sequence.

Chapter 8　　　　　　　　　　　　　　　　　　　　　　　　　　Sequences

In this problem, you could get by with brute force, but what if they'd said the first term was -88? You would have to use the pair-partners of opposite signs relationship to find a timely answer.

Algebraic Relationships Between Sequence Terms

a, b, c, ...

The sequence above is governed by the rule that each number after $\underline{a}$ is two times the sum of the previous number and z. In terms of a and z, what is the average of the first 3 terms in this sequence?

(A) 2a + 3z
(B) 3a + 2z
(C) $\dfrac{7a + 8z}{3}$
(D) 4a + 3z

How do I start?

Use the verbal rule for constructing the sequence to derive algebraic expressions for b and c in terms of a and z. Then perform the requested average.

Solution

By the given rule, b = 2(a+z) = 2a+2z. With this expression for b in terms of a and z, we can get c in terms of a and z. c = 2(b+z) = 2[2a+2z+ z] = 4a + 4z + 2z = 4a + 6z. The sum of the first three terms is a + (2a + 2z) + (4a +6z) = 7a + 8z. The average = (7a + 8z) / 3.

Answer C

The Take-Away

Read a problem very carefully when translating a verbal formula for a sequence. Sometimes, algebraic operations on numeric terms, algebraic terms, or the formula itself will be necessary.

Sequences   Chapter 8

Finding The nth Term in a Repetitive Sequence

-4 6 0 2 4 2 0 -2 -4 -2 0 2 …

The first 11 terms in a repetitive sequence is shown above. Within those 11 terms is a pattern of length m<11, which repeats indefinitely. What is the 101st term?

SR

How do I start?

You'll never brute force your way out of this. The sequence consists of repeated patterns of terms. Determine the number of terms in the *pattern*, and determine the number of whole patterns that exist within a sequence of 101 terms. The last pattern may only be a fragment consisting of the first few terms. You can find the 101st term in the whole sequence by matching positions of this fragment with the first few terms of the pattern.

Solution

Unless you are told otherwise, every term in a repetitive sequence is part of the pattern. Let the sequence pattern begin with -4. The pattern consists of a repeating pattern of 8 terms:-4 6 0 2 4 2 0 -2, where the first three terms, -4 6 0, unambiguously identify the beginning of the pattern that repeats. Each subsequent pattern begins with -4. The 8th, 16th, … terms are all the last terms in their respective patterns, -2. Find the maximum number of 8-term sequences that can fit in 101 terms. Thus, 8•12 = 96. The 96th term of the sequence will equal -2, the 8th number in the 12th pattern. Proceeding 5 more terms into the fragment of the 13th pattern will be the 101st term: -4 6 0 2 **4**. The 101st term is 4.

Alternate Solution

There are 8 terms in the repetitive pattern: -4 6 0 2 4 2 0 -2. We want the 101st term in the sequence. Dividing 101 by 8 gives 12 with a remainder of 5. There 12 patterns of 8 terms with a remainder of 5 terms in an unfinished, 13th pattern. The 5th term in the pattern is 4.

Answer 4

The Take-Away

To find the nth term in a repetitive sequence with m terms in the pattern, find the largest number of *complete* patterns, p, in the sequence, and then count the remaining terms up to n. Thus, compute n/m = p + r, where r is the remainder. If r is 0, the nth term is the last in the pattern. If r>0, the nth term is the rth in the pattern. See alternate solution.

Chapter 8 Sequences

Properties of Sequences, Given Averages

If the average (arithmetic mean) of 12 consecutive integers is 18.5, what is the average of the first 4 integers?

SR

How do I start?

The average of any even number of consecutive integers will equal the average of the two middle integers. For example, the average of 1, 2, 3, 4 is 2.5, which is also the average of 2 and 3. There will be an equal number of terms to the left and right of this average.

Solution

The average of any even number of consecutive integers will equal the average of the two middle integers. Since the average of the terms of this arithmetic sequence is 18.5, the two middle integers must be 18 and 19. Because there are 12 terms in the sequence, there will be 6 numbers less than 18.5. Listing *backwards*, they are 18,17,**16,15,14,13**. The average of the first 4 is 14.5.

Alternate Solution

Of course, the trick of bisecting an arithmetic sequence at the average can be used on the first 4 integers as well. Now listed here in increasing order, the average of 13,14,15,16 is just the average of the two middle integers in this sub-sequence, 14.5.

Answer 14.5

The Take-Away

The average (and also median) of any even number of consecutive integers will equal the average of the two middle integers. In general, the average of an even number of terms in *any* arithmetic sequence (not just consecutive, i.e., difference of one sequences) is the average of the two middle terms. Conversely, if the number of terms in an arithmetic sequence is odd, the average is the middle integer (median) of the sequence. There are always an equal number of terms to the left and the right of the median (and average) in an arithmetic sequence.

Sequences   Chapter 8

Deriving Relationships Between Sequence Terms

1, 1, 2, 3, 5, ...

The sequence above is governed by the rule that the nth number in the sequence is equal to the sum of the preceding two numbers, for $n \geq 3$. Letting $s(n)$ equal the nth number in the sequence, which of the following expressions has the same value as $s(102) - s(100)$?

(A) $s(99) + s(100)$
(B) $s(99) - s(101)$
(C) $s(103) + s(101)$
(D) $s(104)/2$

How do I start?

Forget actually evaluating this. We'll need an algebraic expression for $s(102) - s(100)$ in terms of other members of the sequence. However, the choices (except one) don't involve subtraction. Don't assume the correct choice will. Try rearranging and re-expressing terms according to the formula in various ways if necessary.

Blind Alley

From the rule in the problem, (1) $s(102) = s(100) + s(101)$, and (2) $s(100) = s(98) + s(99)$. Using these expressions directly, $s(102) - s(100) = s(100) + s(100) - s(98) - s(99)$. But this is not one of the choices. Now what?

Solution

Start over. Rearranging (1) above, we can get (3) $s(102) - s(100) = s(101)$. The left side of (3) is exactly what we are looking for, but $s(101)$ is not one of the choices. What does the sequence rule say about $s(101)$? By definition, (4) $s(101) = s(99) + s(100)$, Substituting (4) into the right side of (3), $s(102) - s(100) = s(99) + s(100)$, which is choice (A).

Answer A

The Take-Away

Because a term in a recursive sequence depends on the value of previous terms, and the values of *those* terms depend likewise on more previous terms, one can develop a whole family of relationships between terms. Again, note how (1) was rearranged to arrive at an expression, (3), that we needed. Hard-scrabble algebra. Yes, this was a *really* hard one.

Chapter 8   Sequences

Properties of a Sequence, Given the Formula

Let the function T(n) be defined for positive integers n such that $T(n) = (n-1)(n)(n+1)$. How many values of T are less than 500?

SR

How do I start?

Starting with n = 1, T(n) defines a sequence of terms, all of which have different, monotonically increasing values. We're looking for the number of terms in the sequence whose values are less than 500. Since the product must be less than 500, try a brute-force search for the largest three consecutive integers that multiply to less than 500.

Solution

Guess. Since 10•10•10 = 1000, which is much larger than 500, start with a lower value of n. If n = 8, T(8) = 7•8•9 = 504. That isn't less than 500, but almost. If n = 7, T(7) = 6•7•8 = 336, which *is* less than 500. All terms in the sequence $T(n) = (n-1)(n)(n+1)$ with $1 \le n \le 7$ will be less than 500. There are 7 values of T less than 500.

Alternate solution

One useful approximation technique may be used: note that $(n-1)(n)(n+1)$ is $\sim n^3$. Now this isn't a terribly close approximation. For example, 9•10•11 = 990, whereas 10^3 = 1000. But it's not too far off. Use $(n-1)(n)(n+1) \sim n^3$ as a start for those products less than 500. Thus, if $n^3 \sim 500$, $n \sim (500)^{1/3} \sim 7.9$. From this you can see that 6•7•8 is a good place to start looking. The solution is completed as above.

Answer 7

The Take-Away

Problems that ask how many instances of an expression are less than some value must often be solved by trial-and-error. Also, approximations similar to $(n-1)(n)(n+1) \sim n^3$ can be useful to save time in brute-force situations. Plus - watch out for non-negative vs. positive.

Sequences   Chapter 8

Sums of Arithmetic Sequences

60 can be expressed as the sum of n consecutive positive integers. Which of the following could be a value of n?

    I.   3
    II.   5
    III.   6

(A) I only
(B) II only
(C) III only
(D) I and II only

How do I start?

Use the relationship between the median, average, and sum of n consecutive integers. Two of the choices given are odd and one is even, and these properties may govern the sequence sum.

Solution

Hmmm. The sequence must have n consecutive terms and sum to 60. The first two choices refer to sequences with an odd number of terms. As such, the middle integer, or median, is the average of a consecutive sequence. So the sum of n consecutive integers, where n is odd, is n • the middle integer. Check to see if it is possible for such a product to equal 60. Test (I): 60 = 3•(the median), so 20 = the median. Thus, 19+20+21 = 60, so (I) is possible. Test (II): 60 = 5•(the median), or 12 = the median. As a check, 10+11+12+13+14 = 60, so (II) is also true too. Test (III): if n were 6, which is even, (1) 60 = 6•(the median). Dividing both sides of (1) by 6 produces (2) 10 = the median. But there are *six* consecutive integers. The median of any *even* number of consecutive integers will always be in the form m + 1/2, where m is an integer. The median is the average of the two middle integers. The median of an even number of consecutive integers can never equal *any* integer. Even 10. So (2) is false, and (III) is impossible.

Answer D

The Take-Away

The sum of n consecutive integers is the median•n (also the average•n). You can determine the odd/even and median characteristics of an arithmetic sequence knowing a just few details such as number of terms, value of first term, etc.

Chapter 8　　　　　　　　　　　　　　　　　　　　　　　　　　　　Sequences

Arithmetic Sequences: Find a Term, Given Other Terms

The values of terms in a certain numerical sequence increase from term to term. The difference between any pair of consecutive terms is a constant integer. If the 3rd and 5th terms of the sequence are 21 and 77, respectively, what is the 7th term?

SR

How do I start?

This is the definition of an arithmetic sequence. We aren't given the consecutive difference, but we are given the difference between the 3rd and the 5th terms, which must be *twice* the consecutive difference.

Solution

The difference between the 3rd and 5th terms is 56. Since there is a term between them, there are two intervals, and 56 must be twice the difference between consecutive terms: 56 = 2•28. So consecutive terms will have a difference of 28 between them. The 7th term would then be the 5th term, 77, plus two intervals of 28, or 77 + 56 = 133.

Alternate solution

The sequence is arithmetic, by definition. The numerical difference between *any* pair of terms spaced apart by the same index-difference is a constant. For example, in an arithmetic sequence, $S_9 - S_6 = S_{15} - S_{12}$, where each pair is separated by 3 indices. Moreover, that difference must be an integer multiple of the consecutive difference. Thus, the difference between the 3rd and 5th terms in this problem is the same as the difference between the 5th and 7th terms. The difference between the 3rd and 5th terms is 77 - 21 = 56. So the difference between the 5th and 7th terms will also be 56. The 7th term will be 77 + 56 = 133.

Answer 133

The Take-Away

Knowing *any* two terms in an arithmetic sequence (and their index positions in the sequence) will allow you to determine the sequence's formula. Also, any pair of terms in an arithmetic sequence that are separated by the same index-difference will have the same numerical difference between them: e.g. $S_9 - S_6 = S_{15} - S_{12}$.

Sequences   Chapter 8

Inferring the Formula of a Sequence From a Few Terms

5, 11, 17, 23, ...

Given the sequence above, what is the 211th term?

(A) 1263
(B) 1264
(C) 1265
(D) 1266

How do I start?

Open ended sequences on the SAT are usually arithmetic, geometric, or repeating. Look for a relationship between terms: usually a common difference or ratio. This problem presents an arithmetic sequence: each term is 6 more than the previous term. You need a formula for calculating the nth term in terms of n because you'll never have time to manually count up to the 211th term.

Solution

Each term equals the previous term plus 6. If s(n) is the value of the nth term in the sequence, s(n) = s(n-1) + 6. Analyze the first few terms in the sequence and express each term as a function of the previous term and 6: s(1) = 5, s(2) = 5 + 6•1, s(3) = 5 + 6•2. We can infer that the nth term equals 5 + 6•(n-1). The 211th term equals 5 + 6•210 = 1265.

Alternate Solution

The direct formula for the nth term of an arithmetic sequence is (nth term) = (first term) + (consecutive difference) • (n-1). The 211th term = 5 + 6 • 210 = 1265.

Alternate Solution II

You might instead infer that each term is 6•n - 1. The 211th term = 6 • 211 - 1 = 1265.

Answer C

The Take-Away Given a few terms, you should be able to deduce the formula of arithmetic, geometric, or repeating sequences presented on the SAT. The formula will then allow you to calculate any term in the sequence. In general, for an arithmetic sequence, the nth term = first term + (consecutive difference) • (n-1).

Chapter 8   Sequences

Calculating Terms in a Recursive Sequence

Each term in a sequence of integers is 2 more than 2 times the previous term. The fifth term in this sequence is 174, what is the second term in the sequence?

SR

How do I start?

The problem verbally expresses a formula for this recursive sequence, but only gives us the 5th term, not the 1st. The problem tells how to calculate the nth term when given the $(n-1)^{st}$ term. But we need the 2nd term, going the *other way*. Is this possible? Can we go in the opposite direction, i.e., devise a formula for the (n-1)th term as a function of the nth? You can do this algebraically. The problem gives the 5th term and asks you to calculate the 2nd term. This looks doable with multiple steps, once you have the backward formula. Then work backwards from the 5th term to the 2nd term.

Solution

Letting s(n) be the nth term in the sequence, the problem tells us that $s(n) = 2 \cdot s(n-1) + 2$. We can rearrange this to solve for s(n-1) as a function of s(n): (1) $s(n-1) = [s(n) - 2] / 2$. We've just turned the original formula into a formula for the *previous* term as a function of the current term. Using (1) we can work backwards one step by simply subtracting 2 from the current term, s(n), and dividing the result by 2. Let s(n) in (1) be the 5th term: 174. The 4th term is (174 - 2)/2 = 86. The 3rd term is (86 - 2)/2 = 42. The 2nd term is (42 - 2)/2 = 20.

Alternate Solution

Calculate each term in the sequence as a function of s(1). Let s(1) = m (as yet unknown); s(2) = 2m+2; s(3) = 4m+6; s(4) = 8m+14; s(5) = 16m+30. We are told that s(5) = 174. So 16m+30 = 174. Solving for m, m = 9. Thus, s(1) = 9, and thus, s(2) = 2·9+2 = 20. While this is a more direct solution, it may not suffice on some difficult problems. What if you were given the value of s(11) and asked for the value of s(8)? You'd waste a lot of time getting an expression for the 11th term. You should be able, if necessary, to determine the formula of a recursive sequence in the reverse order from which it is defined.

Answer 20

The Take-Away A formula for a sequence in which the value of the nth term is expressed as a function of the $(n-1)^{st}$ term can sometimes be algebraically rearranged to give a formula for the $(n-1)^{st}$ term as a function of the nth term. Knowing a recursive formula may allow you to calculate terms in the sequence in either direction.

Sequences   Chapter 8

Odd / Even Properties Of Arithmetic Sequences

The sequence $S = S_1, S_2, \ldots S_n$. It is an arithmetic sequence of consecutive integers. If the sum of all the terms is even then:

(A) n must be divisible by 4
(B) n must be odd
(C) S_1 and S_n both must be even
(D) n+1 must be divisible by 4

How do I start?

This is an arithmetic sequence of unknown length, n. We know neither S_1 nor S_n. Use what you know about arithmetic sequence medians and/or sum formulas.

Solution

The formula for the sum of any arithmetic sequence is $n \cdot (S_1 + S_n)/2$. In general, both n and the sum $(S_1 + S_n)$ could be either even or odd. If $(S_1 + S_n)$ is odd we have a problem because we're also dividing it by 2. The only way to ensure that $n \cdot (S_1 + S_n)/2$ is always even is if n is a multiple of 4: Let n = 4m, where m is an integer. The sum of the sequence is then $4m \cdot (S_1 + S_n)/2 = 2(S_1 + S_n)$, which is always even whether $(S_1 + S_n)$ is even or odd.

Alternate Solution

Let e = even and o = odd. Try n = 3. Consecutive integers will be either oeo or eoe. The sum of oeo is even, but the sum of eoe is odd. No good - the sum must be even. So some sequences where n is odd (here: n=3) are not always even. Toss (B). Odd eoe also corresponds to choice (C), so toss (C). Moreover, eoe, which fails the even requirement, has n = 3 terms. Yet n + 1 = 4, which is divisible by 4. Choice (D) would then say eoe is even. The only remaining choice is (A). For example, both eoeo and oeoe are even.

Alternate Solution II

The sum of n terms of the sequence is n•(sequence median). The median is always an integer or (integer + 1/2). The only way n•(integer + 1/2) is always *even* is if n is a multiple of 4, i.e., n = 4m. Thus, 4m•(integer + 1/2) = 4m(integer) + 2m, which is always even.

Answer (A)

Take Away

This was really hard and required an advanced intuition of arithmetic sequence properties.

Chapter 8   Sequences

Practice Problems

1. Let the function T(n) be defined for non-negative integers n such that T(n) = (n-3)(n-2)(n-1). How many values of n result in values of T that are non-negative and less than 10?

   SR

2. A sequence of 33 consecutive odd integers with a median of x has a sum of p. Another sequence of 55 consecutive even integers with a median of y has a sum of q. Which expression below corresponds to q - p?

   (A) $\frac{3}{5}$ (y - x)

   (B) $\frac{33}{88}$ (y - x)

   (C) 11(y-x)
   (D) 11(5y - 3x)

3. The values of terms in a certain numerical sequence increase from term to term. The difference between any pair of consecutive terms is a constant integer. If the 3rd and 6th terms of the sequence are 21 and 105, respectively, what is the absolute value of the 1st term?

   SR

4. A certain sequence, s, has terms $s(n) = \frac{n+2}{n}$, where n is 1, 2, 3, ... What is the product of the first 18 terms?

   SR

205

Sequences Chapter 8

5. 1,1,2,2,2,2,3,3,3,3,3,3...

The sequence s above consists of blocks consisting of identical integers. The block consisting of integer m will have 2m elements (m = 1,2,3,...). The blocks are sequenced in increasing numerical order, as shown. The first term in the sequence having a value of 7 is s(n). What is the value of n?

SR

6. -2, 4, -8, 16, ...

Starting at -2, the sequence of integers above is formed by taking each term and multiplying it by -2 to get the next term. How many of the first 100 terms of this sequence are less than 256?

SR

7.

n, 4n, ...

In the sequence above, the first term is n and each term after this is 4 times the preceding term. If n > 0, and the product of the first 4 terms is 65536, what is the value of n?

SR

8.

4 1 3 2

The sequence above is in the wrong order. Two types of operations are allowed on this sequence: (1) any two adjacent numbers may be interchanged, and (2) the complete sequence may be circularly rotated in either direction: e.g., 1 2 3 4 can be transformed by circularly rotating it into 2 3 4 1, or 4 1 2 3. How many operations, minimum, must be performed to transform 4 1 3 2 into 1 2 3 4?

SR

9. The least integer of a set of consecutive odd integers is -11. If the sum of these integers is 28, how many integers are in the set?

    (A) 13
    (B) 14
    (C) 23
    (D) 25

10. Let x have a domain x>2. It is the first term in a sequence where each term after the first is equal to 2 less than 1/2 of the square of the preceding term. What is the ratio of the first term to the second term?

    (A) $\sqrt{x}-1$
    (B) $2\sqrt{x}-2$
    (C) $\dfrac{2x^2}{(x^2-2)}$
    (D) $\dfrac{2x}{(x+2)(x-2)}$

11.

    5, 13, 21, 29, 37, 45, …

    The first term in the arithmetic sequence above is 5. Each term after the first is calculated by adding 8 to the value of the term preceding it. Which term in this sequence has a value of 13+(23-2)•8?

    (A) 22nd
    (B) 23rd
    (C) 24th
    (D) 25th

Sequences   Chapter 8

12.   1, 2, 3, …x, 1, 2, 3,…x, 1,…

A sequence of consecutive integers from 1 to x is repeated indefinitely, as shown above, where 3<x<11. If the 101st term in the sequence is a 2, what is the value of x?

SR

13. Integers a, b, and c sum to 93. If a, b, and c are consecutive odd integers and c is the largest, which of the following expressions is always true?

(A) c = a + b - 93
(B) c = 30
(C) 3c = 91
(D) c = 33

14.   a, b, c, …

The sequence above is governed by the rule that each number after a is two times the sum of the previous number and 1. If the average of the first three terms is 5, what is a?

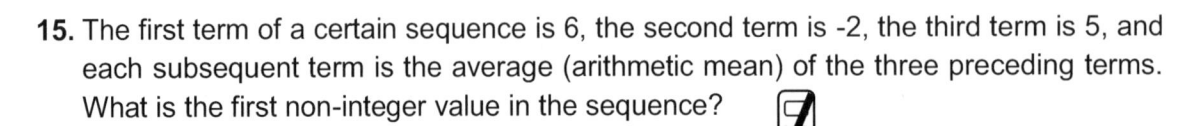

SR

15. The first term of a certain sequence is 6, the second term is -2, the third term is 5, and each subsequent term is the average (arithmetic mean) of the three preceding terms. What is the first non-integer value in the sequence?

SR

16. Let x be the first term in a sequence. Each term after x in the sequence is 1/4 of the previous term plus 2x. If x>0, what is the ratio of the 2nd term to the 3rd term?

(A) $\frac{3}{5}$
(B) $\frac{5}{8}$
(C) 2.25 : 2.5625
(D) 2.25 : 2.75

208

Chapter 8   Sequences

17. If the average (arithmetic mean) of 6 consecutive even integers is 11, what is the average of the first 4 integers?

SR

18. 5, 12, 19, 26, ...

Given the sequence above, what is the 88th term?

(A) 526
(B) 527
(C) 528
(D) 614

19. It can be shown that 1+2+...+n = n(n+1)/2. If a sequence has c consecutive integers and the first term in the sequence is s, what is the sum of the terms in that sequence in terms of s and c?

(A) $\dfrac{c\cdot(2s + c - 1)}{4}$

(B) $\dfrac{(c-s-1)(1-c)}{2}$

(C) $\dfrac{c\cdot(2s + c - 1)}{2}$

(D) $\dfrac{2c\cdot(2s + c - 1)}{2}$

20. A sequence has terms s(1) = 1, s(2) = 3, and thereafter, $s(n) = \dfrac{s(n-2)}{s(n-1)}$. Which of the following terms in the sequence is least?

(A) s(101)
(B) s(102)
(C) s(105)
(D) s(106)

Sequences   Chapter 8

21. The sequence s has the first two terms s(1) = x and s(2) = y. Thereafter, s(n) = the average of s(n-1) and s(n-2). If x and y are chosen such that s(3) = y, what is the value of s(20) - s(19)?

(A) 0
(B) y/2
(C) y
(D) -y

22. In the sequence s, the first two terms are s(1) = x and s(2) = y. Thereafter, s(n) = the average of s(n-1) and s(n-2). If x > y > 0, which of the following expressions is true?

(A) s(102) < s(101)
(B) s(101) - s(100) = 2
(C) s(102) > s(101)
(D) s(101) < s(100)

23. In the sequence s, the first term is -1 and the second term is -4. Thereafter, s(n) is equal to s(n-1)/s(n-2), when n>2. What percent of the first 100 terms are negative?

SR

24. An ancient city under seige devised a plan to make their grain last as long as possible. The first week they divided the grain in half and distributed it to the people. The second week they took a third of the remaining grain and distributed that third. The fourth week they took a fourth of the remaining grain... and so on. After the 9th week's division, how much of the original grain remained?

(A) $\frac{1}{1024}$
(B) $\frac{1}{100}$
(C) $\frac{1}{10}$
(D) $\frac{1}{9}$

Chapter 8   Sequences

25. The sum of n consecutive integers from -8 to n is 30. What is the value of n?

(A) 10
(B) 11
(C) 21
(D) 22

26. *Challenge* The king offers a subject a reward. The subject asks that he be paid 1 cent today, 2 cents, tomorrow, 4 cents the next day, and so on for 30 days. If today is Tuesday, on what day of the week will the subject have accumulated more than a million dollars?

(A) Saturday
(B) Sunday
(C) Monday
(D) Tuesday

Notes

Practice Problem Hints

1. Start with n = 0 and evaluate the function for successively higher values of n.

2. The average of a sequence of consecutive odd or even integers is equal to the median of the sequence. The sum of the sequence = n • average.

3. The difference between the 3rd and 6th terms is three intervals of the difference between consecutive terms.

4. Write the first few terms in the sequence to discover how numerators and denominators in the product cancel one another.

5. Manually (or formulaically) add up the number of 1's, 2's, ... 6's.

6. In the first 100 terms, the number of negative terms = the number of positive terms.

7. Form the product of the first four terms in terms of n.

8. Use operation (1) to get digits into the correct order before rotating, and then use operation (2) to get digits into the correct position.

9. The terms from -11 to 11 will sum to zero.

10. Follow the recipe. Express the second term in terms of x and form the ratio. Then simplify.

11. How many intervals of 8 lie beyond 13? Use the formula for the arithmetic sequence.

12. If the 101st term is a 2, then which term's index is the last x in the sequence before the 101st term?

13. Express the sum in terms of the average of the sequence.

14. If their average is 5, their sum is 15. Caste the sum in terms of a.

15. Perform the averages and calculate subsequent terms to discover the first non-integer value.

16. Get algebraic expressions for the 2nd and 3rd terms; perform the requested ratio.

Sequences   Chapter 8

17. The terms in the sequence are all even. The average of any even number of equally spaced integers will equal the average of the two middle integers.

18. Develop the formula for this arithmetic sequence.

19. Choose convenient values for s and c. Or use the formula for the sum of an arithmetic sequence.

20. Start by calculating the first few terms in the sequence. Try to find a pattern in the sequence.

21. Express the 3rd term in the sequence in terms of x and y, and set it equal to y.

22. Choose an example of x and y and see what patterns emerge.

23. Calculate the first several terms to discover a repetitive pattern.

24. The SAT would never have you calculate all 9 terms in this sequence. Do the first few terms and look for a pattern.

25. The sum from -8 to +8 equals zero.

26. Use your calculator to determine a few powers of 2 (cents) that approach or exceed a million dollars = 10^8 cents.

Chapter 8 Sequences

Practice Problem Solutions

1. Answer 4

   The lowest value of n allowed is n = 0. T(0) = (-3)(-2)(-1) = -6. This is less than zero, and should not be counted. Continuing for higher values of n, T(1) = (-2)(-1)(0) = 0, T(2) = 0, T(3) = 0, T(4) = 6, T(5) = 24. Only T(n), where n = 1, 2, 3, and 4, result in values 0 ≤ T < 10. There are 4 such terms.

2. Answer D

   The average of a sequence of consecutive odd or consecutive even integers is equal to the median of the sequence. So x and y are the averages of these two sequences, respectively. Both sums, p and q, therefore equal = (# terms) • average. Thus, for the first sequence, p = 33x. For the second sequence, q = 55y. Now we can take the requested difference: q - p = 55y - 33x = 11(5y-3x).

3. Answer 35

   The difference between consecutive terms is constant There are three consecutive intervals between the 3rd and 6th terms. The difference between the 3rd and 6th terms is 84, thus the difference between consecutive terms must be 84/3 = 28. The 2nd term = the 3rd term - 28 = 21 - 28 = -7, and the 1st term is the 2nd term - 28 = -7 - 28 = -35. The absolute value of this is 35.

4. Answer 190

   The first 18 terms in the sequence are 3/1, 4/2, 5/3, 6/4, …18/16, 19/17, and 20/18. When forming the product of all these terms, every numerator except 19 and 20 is cancelled by an identical denominator. Likewise, every denominator is cancelled by an identical numerator, except 1 and 2. The product of terms is 19•20 / 1•2 = 190.

5. Answer 43

   Manually add up the number of 1's, 2's, … 6's. The next term in the sequence will be the first 7. The 1's through the 6's will have 2 + 4 + 6 + 8 + 10 + 12 = 42 terms, and thereafter, the 1st 7 will be the 43rd term.

Alternate Solution: The sum of integers 1 through n is n(n+1)/2. However, we need the sum of 2 + 4 + ... 2n = 2(1+2+3+...n) = n(n+1). If n = 6, the last expression is 6•7 = 42, and one more term (the 1st 7) will be the 43rd.

6. Answer 53

The first few terms are -2, 4, -8, 16, -32, 64, -128, 256, -512, 1024... Note that all the even numbered terms are positive, and all the odd numbered terms are negative. *All* the negative terms are less than 256, so the 1st, 3rd, ... 99th terms will be less than 256. There are 50 of these. How many positive terms are less than 256? Only 4, 16, and 64. Therefore, there are 50 + 3 = 53 terms less than 256.

7. Answer 2

This is cookbook math. Form the product of the first four terms in terms of n, and solve for n. $65536 = n(4n)(16n)(64n) = n^4 \cdot (4096) = 65536$. Rearranging, $n^4 = 16$, so n = 2.

8. Answer 2

Use operation (1) to get digits in the correct order, except for rotating: interchanging 3 and 2 gives 4 1 2 3. Then use (2) to get digits in the correct position. Rotating the sequence 4 1 2 3 once to the left gives 1 2 3 4. Two operations are required.

Alternate Solution: You can start by circularly rotating 4 1 3 2 to the left to get 1 3 2 4. Then interchange 2 and 4 to get 1 2 3 4.

9. Answer B

The sequence consists of consecutive *odd* terms. In your mind, start with -11 and run the sequence to +11. From symmetry, the sum of these numbers is zero. The next two numbers are 13 and 15, which sum to 28. Bam! Count the terms. 6 terms less than zero: -11, -9, -7, -5, -3, -1. Plus 6 more that pair with those: 1, 3, 5, 7, 9, 11. The next two terms, 13 and 15, bring the sum to 28. There are a total of 6 + 6 + 2 = 14 terms.

Alternate Solution: Since their sum is even, the number of terms must be even since all the terms are odd. Only (B) is a possible solution. Peruse the choices. Shortcuts!

10. Answer D

The first term is x, and the second term is $x^2/2 - 2$. The ratio of the first term to the second term is $x/(x^2/2 - 2)$. Multiplying top and bottom by 2 gives $2x/(x^2 - 4)$. Factoring the denominator, the ratio becomes $2x / (x+2)(x-2)$.

Chapter 8   Sequences

11. Answer B

   This sequence has a formula of (1) s(n) = 5 + 8•(n-1). We are asked what term in the sequence equals (2) 13 + 8•(23-2). Subtracting 8 from 13 and adding it to the second term, expression (2) then equals 5 + 8•(23-1). Via formula (1), this is the 23rd term.

12. Answer 9

   The long approach would be trial and error. If x = 10, then the repetitive sequence is composed of patterns (1 …10)(1…10)…(1…10). In this case, the 100th term would be a 10, and the 101st term would be a 1. No good. Try a sequence length of 9. (1…9)(1…9)… (1…9). In this case, the 99th term would be a 9, the 100th term would be a 1, and the 101st term would be a 2. That works. But lucky you started with 10.

   Alternate Solution: The sequence consists of a sequence of a repetitive pattern of x terms. Picture the sequence as [1…x] … [1…x][1,2]. If the 101st term is a 2, then the 100th term is a 1 and the 99th term must be an x. I.e., 99 = mx, where m represents the integer number of full patterns [1…x]. So 99/m = x. The only value of x, where 3<x<11, that divides evenly into 99 is 9. Therefore, x = 9.

13. Answer D

   Because a, b, and c are consecutive odd integers, the average of a, b, and c is b. Their sum is 93, so their average is b = 93/3 = 31. Since c is 2 more than b, c = 33.

   Alternate Solution: Express the sum in terms of c. Since the integers are consecutive and odd, they differ from their neighbors by 2. We know a<b<c: a = c-4 and b = c-2. Therefore, c-4 + c-2 + c = 93. Collecting c terms on the left, 3c = 99 , so c = 33.

14. Answer 1

   If the average of three terms is 5, their sum is 15. Using the formula for the sequence, b = 2(a+1) and c = 2(b+1) = 2[2(a+1) + 1] = 4a + 6. The sum of the first three terms is a + (2a + 2) + (4a +6) = 7a + 8. Solving for a, 7a + 8 = 15, or 7a = 7, yielding a = 1.

15. Answer 10/3

   The first triplet of terms, 6 -2 5, has an average of 3. So 3 is the 4th term in the sequence. The second triplet, -2 5 3, has an average of 2. So 2 is the 5th term in the sequence. The third triplet, 5 3 2, has an average of 10/3, which is not an integer.

Sequences   Chapter 8

16. Answer C

The first term in this sequence is x, the second term in the sequence is x/4 + 2x = 2.25x, and the third term in the sequence is 1/4(x/4 + 2x) + 2x = x/16 + x/2 + 2x = 2.5625x. The ratio of the 2nd tem to the 3rd is therefore 2.25 : 2.5625.

17. Answer 9

We have 6 consecutive even integers whose average is 11. The two middle integers must be 10 and 12, in order for the average to equal 11. Write the average and work out toward both ends: 6 8 10 **[11]** 12 14 16. Remember, 11 is not part of the sequence of even integers, just the average. The first 4 integers in the sequence are 6 8 10 12. The average of these terms is 9. Note: you can just average the two middle terms.

18. Answer D

Each term equals the previous term plus 7. In other words, if s(n) is the value of the nth term in the sequence, then (1) s(n) = s(n-1) + 7. This is an arithmetic sequence with a consecutive difference of 7 between terms. With this in mind, express the first few terms of the sequence in intervals of 7: s(1) = 5, s(2) = 5 + 7•1, s(3) = 5 + 7•2. We can infer that the nth term equals 5 + 7•(n-1). So the 88th term equals 5 + 7•87 = 614.

Alternate Solution: You should memorize the formula for an arithmetic sequence: s(n) = s(1) + (n-1)•(consecutive difference). The 88th term is 5 + 87•7 = 614. Easy.

19. Answer C

This may be one of those problems where choosing numbers and testing the answer choices will go faster than producing an algebraic answer. Let's choose s = 1 and c = 2 (although any pair will suffice). The sequence terms are 1 and 2, and their sum is 3. Plug s = 1 and c = 2 into the answer choices and see which choice gives 3. Without showing the work, only choice (D) evaluates to 3.

Alternate Solution: There is a formula for the sum of an arithmetic sequence that does not begin with 1 given in the chapter review: (1) n•(s$_1$ + s$_n$)/2, where n is the number of terms, and s$_1$ and s$_2$ are the beginning and end terms. In this problem, n = c, s$_1$ = s and s$_2$ = s+c-1. Plugging those expressions in (1), the sum is equal to c•(2s+c-1)/2.

Alternate Solution II: subtracting s from each of the c terms leaves a sum of (c-1)•c/2. Adding back the c•s taken away gives c•s + (c-1)•c/2, which is equal to c•(2s+c-1)/2.

Chapter 8   Sequences

20. Answer C

Start by calculating the first few terms in the sequence in order to infer some pattern: 1, 3, 1/3, 9, 1/27, 243, 1/6561, ... Clearly, all the terms are positive. The odd numbered terms (after the first) are less than one, and the even numbered terms are greater than one. Each successive odd numbered term is less than the previous odd term, so the least term in the sequence among the choices would be s(105).

21. Answer A

s(1) = x and s(2) = y. We are told that s(3) = (s(2)+s(1))/2 = (x+y)/2 = y. Therefore, x + y = 2y. So x = y. s(4) = (s(3)+s(2))/2 = (y+y)/2 = y. *All subsequent terms equal y.* s(20) - s(19) =0.

22. Answer A

This is true for <u>all</u> x and y. Choose an example of x and y, where x>y>0, and see what patterns emerges. Pick x and y where at least the first couple of terms will be integers (nice, but not necessary). If x = 4 and y = 2, then the first 6 terms in the sequence are 4, 2, 3, 2.5, 2.75, 2.625, ... From this pattern we see that even numbered terms are less than the previous odd numbered term. The only choice in this pattern is (A).

23. Answer 67

It is necessary to carry this sequence out beyond a few terms to see if a pattern emerges: **-1, -4, 4, -1, -1/4, 1/4** , -1, -4, 4,... and the pattern repeats again with -1, 4. Therefore, the pattern repeats every 6 terms, and 4 out every 6 terms are negative. Because 6 doesn't evenly divide into 100, there will be a first part of the last pattern leftover to get to the 100th term. 100 divided by 6 is 16, with a remainder of 4. The first 16 patterns of 6 will have 96 terms, and they will have 16•4 = 64 negative numbers. There will be the 4 numbers leftover in the final pattern fragment (terms 97, 98, and 99 and 100). Three of these numbers (-1, 4, -4, -1) are negative, and therefore there are a total of 64+3 = 67 negative numbers in the first 100 terms. 67 percent of the numbers will be negative.

Alternate Solution: The sign of a term in this recursive sequence will only depend on the signs of the two previous terms. The signs of the first two terms are -, -. From the formula for the sequence, the sign of the 3rd term is -/- = +. Continuing through to the 4th - 9th terms, the signs are: **-, -, +, -, -, +**. This pattern repeats every 3 terms indefinitely. So, for the first 99 terms (which is divisible by 3), 2/3 of the terms, or 66, will be negative. The 100th term, which is the first term of the next triad of -, -, +, will also be negative. Therefore, 67 out of 100 terms will be negative.

24. Answer C

After the first week's division they have 1/2 left of the original. After the second week's division, they distribute 1/2 • 1/3, so they have leftover 1/2 - 1/2 • 1/3 = 3/6 - 1/6 = 1/3 of the original remaining. After the third week they have 1/3 - 1/3 • 1/4 = 4/12 - 1/12 = 1/4 of the original remaining. It seems that this pattern continues: after the nth week's distribution, there will be 1/(n+1) of the original left. Go for it. After the 9th week's division, there will remain 1/10 the original amount.

Alternate Solution: After the first week 1/2 remains. After the second week, 1 - 1/3 = 2/3 of *that* amount remains, or 1/2 • 2/3 = 1/3. After the third week, 3/4 of that amount remains, or 1/2 • 2/3 • 3/4 = 1/4. So after n weeks, 1/2 • 2/3 • 3/4…n/n+1 = 1/(n+1) remains. After n = 9, the 9th week's division, there will remain 1/10 the original amount.

25. Answer B

We know that the sum of consecutive integers from -8 to 8 equals zero. Therefore, simply start adding consecutive integers beginning with 9 until the sum equals 30: 9+10+11 = 30, and therefore, n equals 11.

26. Answer B

This is a geometric sequence. With Tuesday corresponding to n = 1, on the nth day the subject will be given 2^{n-1} cents. While it may seem necessary to add every term in the sequence to see when the *sum* is greater than one million dollars, the terms grow quickly - let's find the last term less than one million dollars. A million dollars is the same as 10^8 cents. Use your calculator to find that 2^{26} cents is equal to ~ 6.7•10^7 cents. Because the previous term, 2^{25}, equals ~3.4•10^7 cents, the sum of just those two terms exceeds 10^8 cents. So the 2^{26} term *might* be the last term needed to make a million. The exponent is one less than the number of days, so *if* this is the last term, it will take 27 days, including the first Tuesday, for him to become a millionaire.

However, would the sum of only the terms *up to and including* 2^{25} exceed one million dollars? There exists a formula for summing terms in a geometric sequence (see the review in this chapter), but you don't have to remember it. Summing 2^{21} up to 2^{25} amounts to less than 7•10^7. All the terms below 2^{21} are too small to sum up the more than 3•10^7 needed to exceed 10^8 cents. So we do need the 2^{26} term for the sum to *exceed* one million dollars. It will take 27 days. We must go 27 days total, beginning at 2^0, to get to the 2^{26} term, to exceed the sum of a million dollars. The 1st, 8th, 15th, and 22nd days will be Tuesdays. We must go 5 days beyond that Tuesday to get to the 27th day: W Th F Sat Sun, so the subject will be a millionaire on a Sunday.

Alternate Solution: n days: $2^0+2^1+...+2^{n-1} = 2^n - 1$. Solve for n when $2^n - 1$ is greater than 10^{10} cents. Or use logarithm base 2: n ~ $\log_2(10^{10})$. Answer: n ~26.6, or 27 days.

Chapter 9

Inequalities, Absolute Values, and Extreme Values

These seemingly easy problems can be some of the worst dyslexia-inducing, brain-bending challenges many students encounter on the SAT. You can be a wizard at higher math and yet crash ignobly over confusing questions involving inequalities, absolute value expressions, and extreme values. Let us proceed carefully.

There are three broad categories of problems explored in this subject. First, some problems ask students to determine extreme values on a number line that has been confusingly scaled. Second, there are problems that require students to determine relationships among expressions, given complicated, compound inequalities. Third, some problems toss in the above, with the added complexity of algebraic absolute value expressions.

This short and often intimidating chapter includes the five major archetypes found on the SAT and an additional 6 practice problems.

Inequalities and Extreme Values   Chapter 9

Don't Show Up Without Knowing…

These Concepts:

- If x<y<z, then x<z

- If x > y, then - x < -y   the signs are reversed

- If x > y, then 1/x < 1/y   if x and y are either both positive or both negative

- If x > y, then 1/x > 1/y   if x is positive and y is negative

- If x > y, then mx > my   if m is positive

- If x > y, then mx < my   if m is negative

- If x+a < y+b, then x < y+b-a   you can add/subtract to both sides of an inequality

- |n| is *always* ≥ n

- If |x| < n, then x < n *and* x > -n. Thus, -n < x < n   (n is positive)

- If |x| > n, then x > n *and* x < -n   (n is positive)

How To

- Determine and compare mystery values on a number line

- Determine the range of a function, given the domain of the variable

- Rank algebraic expressions, given inequalities governing variables

- Decompose absolute value expressions into inequalities

Chapter 9 — Inequalities and Extreme Values

Quick Review and Definitions

Don't Forget Negative Numbers

The least value of a variable might be the most negative. Students sometimes overlook the negative half of a number line or domain when searching for the least value; instead, they mistakenly pick the number with the least *magnitude*.

Also, some expressions result in the negative of a negative value, which may result in the greatest value within a given range.

The Greatest And Least Values Of A Function

When asked for the greatest or least value of a function of x, quickly characterize the function with head-math first. What does the function do at x=0 and the extremes of the domain of x? Polynomial functions tend toward their largest magnitudes there. Also, what values of x will cause the function to be zero, or make a numerator and/or denominator zero. As a denominator of a function approaches zero, the function will approach plus or minus infinity (unless the numerator is also zero). These are typical characteristic values that will give insight into the behavior of the function over the domain of the independent variable. This kind of quick analysis can give you a kind of mental plot of the function.

There may be other characteristic values. Characteristic values that make one variable or side of an inequality equal to -2, -1/2, 0, 1/2, or +2 often test the behavior of the inequality throughout. Of course, limit these values as necessary when the independent variable has a limited domain, such as x >0.

Greatest & Least Values Involving Absolute Values

- |n| is *always* ≥ n
- If |x| < n, then x < n *and* x > -n. Thus, -n < x < n   (n is positive)
- If |x| > n, then x > n *and* x < -n   (n is positive)

Manipulating Inequalities

Remember that when multiplying or dividing an inequality by a negative number, *you must reverse the direction of the inequality*.

For example, if x > y, then - x < -y. Also, -2x < -2y and -x/2 < -y/2.

In addition you must be careful when multiplying an inequality by a *variable* whose domain includes negative values. Let x > y. Then multiply each side by the variable z whose domain is -2 to +2. Only for positive values of z will z•x > z•y. When z<0, z•x < z•y. This is a property often overlooked by students.

You may invert the left and right sides of an inequality, but you *may* have to reverse the direction of the inequality:

- If x and y are either both (+) or both (-), then reverse the direction of the inequality.
  Examples: 2 < 3, but 1/2 > 1/3   -2 > -3, but -1/2 < -1/3

- If only one of x or y is (-), then <u>do not</u> reverse the direction of the inequality. It is the signs of the terms on either side of the inequality that fix the inequality.
  Examples: -2 < 3, and -1/2 < 1/3   2 > -3, and 1/2 > -1/3

The following rules apply when handling absolute values of algebraic expressions:

- If |x-y| < z, then x-y < z *and* x-y > -z ; another way to express this: - z < x-y < z.

- If |x-y| > z, then x-y > z *and* x-y < -z.

Take a closer look at |x-y| < z ➡ - z < x-y < z. The inequality - z < x-y < z may be rearranged by adding y to all three components. The result is -z+y < x < z+y. In this way, variables within an absolute value function may be isolated.

If you can assume x > y, you can remove the absolute value brackets: |x-y| = x-y.

Chapter 9   Inequalities and Extreme Values

SAT Archetypes

Number Lines With Confusing Scales

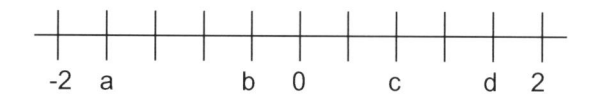

```
+--+--+--+--+--+--+--+--+--+--+
-2  a     b  0     c     d  2
```

Let a, b, c, and d represent numbers on the number line as shown above. Which of the expressions below has the least value?

(A) a+c
(B) d-a
(C) a-c
(D) a+b-1

How do I start?

This number line is divided into equal divisions: there are 5 divisions between 0 and 2. Each division is 2/5 = .4. Use this to get values for a, b, c, and d. The least value may correspond to the most negative value. Test each choice with the values if necessary.

Solution

The least value will *likely* correspond to the most negative value. By eyeballing a graph using head-math, we can often toss choices. Of the listed choices, (C) and (D) appear to be most negative. Test (C) and (D) with the values indicated. Each division is equal to .4. This means a = -1.6, b = -.4, c = .8, and d = 1.6. Plugging in values, (C) gives a - c = -1.6 - .8 = -2.4. (D) gives a + b - 1 = -1.6 - .4 - 1 = -3. Therefore, (D) is most negative.

Answer D

The Take-Away

Number line problems may require careful visual analysis to reduce the graphical information to values needed to solve the problem. Also - sometimes it isn't necessary to assign values to the tick marks on a number line; you may be able to perform calculations in the units of "ticks." That won't work here. Choice (D) subtracts an actual number: 1.

Inequalities and Extreme Values — Chapter 9

Greatest or Least Algebraic Expression

If $-1 < x < 0$, which of the following expressions is always greatest?

(A) $1 + x$
(B) $2 - x$
(C) $\dfrac{(1-x)}{x+3}$
(D) x^4

How do I start?

Use the domain of x to create the ranges of the expressions listed in the choices. Evaluate each expression at the extremes of the domain of x. Because (A) and (B) are linear, the extremes of the domain all that are needed to compute their ranges. Otherwise, check other values of x to map the range, especially if and when a denominator might approach zero. Also - notice they say one expression is *always* greatest.

Solution

Using only the approaching extremes of the domain of x, -1 and 0, we can instantly get the ranges of (A) and (B) because they are linear. $0 < (A) < 1$ and $2 < (B) < 3$. Can the denominator of (C) ever equal zero? No. Test both extremes and one value in the middle of the domain. If $x \sim -1$, (C) ~ 1. If $x \sim 0$, (C) $\sim 1/3$. If $x = -1/2$, (C) $= 0.6$. So $1/3 < (C) < 1$. By inspection, $0 < (D) < 1$. Therefore, choice (B) is always greatest in the domain of x.

Alternate Solution

If one of the choices is *always* greatest within the given domain (here it's $-1 < x < 0$) then you can choose *any* value of x in the domain and test the choices. You could choose a middle value, $x = -1/2$, and calculate that choice (B) is greatest. Even better, you could choose x arbitrarily close to zero and determine that choice (B) is greatest by inspection.

Answer B

The Take-Away

In greatest and least value problems, it is often best to examine values at the extremes of the given domain, or values which would cause a denominator or numerator to approach zero. Also - watch out for expressions using the word "always." In this problem choice (B) represents a range that does not overlap any of the other ranges. At every point within its range, (B) is greater than every point in the other ranges. If the ranges can't overlap, just choose a value of x that makes calculating the expressions trivial. Like $x \sim 0$, here.

Chapter 9　　　　　　　　　　　　　　　　　　　　　　Inequalities and Extreme Values

Ranking Algebraic Expressions, Given Inequalities

Given constants a and b, if 4a < 0 < 3b, which of the following expressions is largest?

(A) a
(B) -4a
(C) 0
(D) 3b - 4a

How do I start?

You don't know the magnitudes of 4a and 3b. However, you do know that 4a is negative and 3b is positive. Therefore, $-\infty < 4a < 0$ and $0 < 3b < \infty$. Thus, a is negative and b is positive.

Solution

We aren't guaranteed that the largest choice is positive, but it's a good bet. Look for choices that must be positive. Since 4a < 0 and 3b > 0, a < 0 and b > 0. Choice (A) is negative, and choice (C) is zero. Note that -4a and 3b are both positive. Choice (B) is positive, but since 3b is positive, choice (D), 3b - 4a, is even larger than (B).

Alternate Solution

Chose values of a and b that are easy to work with. We have already established that a < 0 and b > 0. *Any* pair of values in those domains will test the criterion we seek: which expression among the choices is the largest? If a = -1 and b = 1, then the values of the choices are: (A) = -1, (B) = 4, (C) = 0, (D) = 7. (D) is largest. So the answer is (D).

Answer D

The Take-Away

When testing expressions using a domain interval, carefully consider the positive and negative regions within the interval. Also, compound inequalities (such as 4a < 0 < 3b) might best be split into the component inequalities for greater clarity. Here, $-\infty < 4a < 0$ and $0 < 3b < \infty$. Moreover, if 4a < 0, then a < 0. Likewise if 3b > 0, then b > 0. The alternate solution using concrete values for a and b is probably clearer and quicker for this question. An even easier choice of values for a and b in the alternate solution would be a ~ 0 and b = 1. In that case, every choice is ~ zero but (D). But note that other such questions may not be amenable to the plug and test approach.

227

Inequalities and Extreme Values Chapter 9

Algebraic Inequalities Involving Absolute Values

If $|a - b| < -(c - b)$, which of the following expressions must be true?

(A) $b - c < a < b + c$
(B) $a > c$ and $a < 2b - c$
(C) $a \neq b - c$ and $a \geq b + c$
(D) $a \neq c - b$ and $a \geq b + c$

How do I start?

Simplify the absolute value expression by expanding it into two separate inequalities. First, the inequality is more simply written $|a - b| < b - c$, and this can be written in expanded form as $-(b - c) < (a - b) < (b - c)$.

Solution

But notice: all of the choices isolate a from b and c, so isolate a in the expanded inequality above: $-(b - c) < (a - b) < (b - c)$. Adding b to all sides in this inequality yields $c < a < 2b - c$. This is equivalent to choice (B)

Alternate Solution

Some students are taught to always split up absolute inequalities (or equalities) into two separate relationships. The compound inequality $-(b - c) < (a - b) < (b - c)$ may thereafter be decomposed into (1) $a - b < b - c$ and (2) $a - b > c - b$. Adding b to both sides of both (1) and (2) results in (3) $a < 2b - c$ and (4) $a > c$. But (3) and (4) are identical to choice (B).

Alternate Solution II

By inspection, since b occurs on both sides of $|a - b| < -(c - b)$ with a coefficient of 1, isolating a must result in either 2b or 0b (or both in this case, since it's an inequality involving an absolute value). Only choice (B) includes these terms.

Answer B

The Take-Away

Absolute value expressions involved in an equality or inequality are usually best expanded into their ± pairs. For example, if $|x+y| > z$, then $-z > x+y > z$. And that may be further split up into two inequalities, as exampled in the first alternate solution. Check out alternate solution II. Use of mathematical intuition can sometimes save a lot of time.

Chapter 9   Inequalities and Extreme Values

Real-World Inequalities

Heather decides that she must earn at least $88 in order to buy a pair of headphones. She intends to earn this money by selling homemade lemonade and chocolate bars from a stand on the street in front of her apartment building. A cup of lemonade costs $.14 per cup, but she will sell it for $.75 per cup. Chocolate bars can be purchased in boxes of 50 bars for $12. She intends to sell each bar for 75 cents. If Heather sells L cups of lemonade and C bars of chocolate, which inequality below represents the condition she must satisfy in order to be able to purchase those headphones?

(A) .61L + .51C > 88
(B) .14L + .75C ≥ 88
(C) 61L + 51C ≥ 8800
(D) 14L + .75C ≥ 8800

How do I start?

Determine the costs and then profits for one lemonade and one chocolate bar. Make sure the profits and the headphone cost are in the same units.

Solution

She sells L lemonade cups and C chocolate bars. Let's put all the units in cents. If she needs $88, then she needs 8800 cents. Each lemonade cup costs her 14 cents and is sold for 75 cents, yielding a profit of 75 - 14 = 61 cents. Each box of chocolate bars cost 12•100 = 1200 cents. Since there are 50 bars, each bar cost 1200/50 = 24 cents. The bars are sold for 75 cents, so there is a profit of 75 - 24 = 51 cents per bar. The profit on L cups of lemonade sold is 61L cents, and the profit on C chocolate bars sold is 51C cents. The combined profit of lemonade and chocolate must equal or exceed the cost of the headphones, 8800 cents. Therefore, 61L + 51C ≥ 8800. (C) is correct.

Fair Warning

When formulating an inequality, be especially careful to choose between ≥ and >, for example. Choice (A) is correct except for this difference.

Answer C

The Take-Away

Make sure all the variables in a multivariable problem are in the same units.

Notes

Chapter 9   Inequalities and Extreme Values

Practice Problems

1.

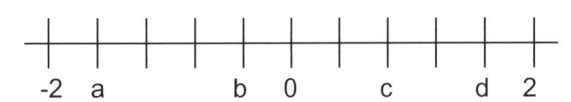

```
+--+--+--+--+--+--+--+--+--+
-2  a      b  0   c   d  2
```

Let a, b, c, and d represent numbers on the real number line shown above. Which of the expressions below has the greatest value?

(A) a+c
(B) d+a
(C) c-a
(D) b+d

2. If $-1 < x < 0$, which of the following expressions can have the greatest value?

(A) 1 - x
(B) (2 - x)/2
(C) $-\dfrac{(1-x)}{x+3}$
(D) $-10x / (100x^2)$

3. If $-4 < 4a < 0 < 3b < 3$, which choice could have the least value?

(A) a
(B) -4a
(C) 3b - 4a
(D) 3b + 4a

231

4. If 3a = 8b = 5c = 6d and each expression is less than zero, which one of the following expressions is true?

   (A) a < b < c < d
   (B) a < c < d < b
   (C) d < c < b < a
   (D) b < d < c < a

5. If $x < 5 < x^{-1}$ then x could be which of the following values?

   (A) -6
   (B) -2
   (C) $\frac{2}{10}$
   (D) $\frac{1}{10}$

6. Which expression below is equivalent to |x-3| < 2?

   (A) x > -2
   (B) -1 < x < 5
   (C) 1 < x < 5
   (D) x > 5

Chapter 9   Inequalities and Extreme Values

Practice Problem Hints

1. While it is possible to eyeball this, keeping the positive and negative values straight while adding and subtracting is difficult. Evaluate a, b, c, and d using the number-line tick marks, and then evaluate the choices. The interval between tick marks is .4.

2. Which choice *can* have the greatest value? In other words, which choice has a range containing the greatest value, given the domain of x? Test each expression at the extremes of the domain of x, and also test the expressions to see if the denominator approaches zero.

3. Test each choice knowing that -4 < 4a < 0 and 0 < 3b < 3.

4. All of the variables, a, b, c, and d, are multiplied by positive coefficients, so a, b, c, and d are all less than zero. Rank the expressions in order of magnitude.

5. You could test each choice carefully by plugging values into the inequality. Better yet, decompose the compound inequality into two inequalities.

6. Expand the absolute inequality into positive and negative domains.

Notes

Chapter 9   Inequalities and Extreme Values

Practice Problem Solutions

1. Answer C

   The greatest value will correspond to the most positive value. Intervals between tick marks are separated by .4. Test each choice with the values indicated by the tick marks: a = -1.6, b = -.4, c = .8, and d = 1.6. Choice (A) is clearly negative. Carefully test the other choices: (B) = 1.6 - 1.6 = 0; (C) = .8 - (-1.6) = 2.4; (D) = -.4 + 1.6 = 1.2. (C) has the greatest value.

   Alternate Solution: All choices refer to sums and differences involving only tick locations on the line. You can simplify the operations listed in the choices by adding and subtracting ticks, essentially assigning a value of 1 to each interval between tick marks. Choice (C) would then be 2 - (-4) = 6, the greatest of the choices calculated using this method.

2. Answer D

   Look at each choice and consider the domain of x (-1< x < 0) to determine that choice's greatest possible value. It's often worthwhile to examine the extremes of a given range, and values where a function's denominator approaches zero. When x ~ -1, (A) ~ 2. When x ~ -1, (B) ~ 3/2. (C) is always negative in the given domain of x. Simplify (D) to -1/10x. (D) is always positive, and as x approaches zero, (D) approaches infinity. Infinity - the greatest!

   Alternate Solution: When asked to identify the least or greatest expression, first examine any denominators in the choices of expressions. If any value in the domain makes the denominator approach or equal zero, focus your attention there first. It should be obvious that choice (D) will blow up toward infinity as x approaches zero.

3. Answer D

   The values of a and b are variable within their defined domains. Test each answer choice knowing that a and b follow these inequalities: -4 < 4a < 0 and 0 < 3b < 3. We're looking for the most negative of the answer choices, given these domains. You can choose any valid pair (a,b). Since 4a is negative, a must negative; likewise 3b is positive, so b is positive. Thus, (B) and (C) are both positive, so toss those choices. We can easily see that -1 < a < 0, and 0 < b < 1. Choosing a ~ -1 and b ~ 0, choice (D) evaluates to ~ -4. Choice (A) has a range between -1/4 and 0. (D) is least.

Inequalities and Extreme Values Chapter 9

4. **Answer B**

   $3a = 8b = 5c = 6d$, and *each expression is less than zero*. All of the variables, a, b, c, and d, are multiplied by positive coefficients, so a, b, c, and d are all negative. Since a is multiplied by the smallest positive coefficient, the *magnitude* of a must be largest. Since a is negative, a is the least. Continue with this reasoning and ranking the equalities in order of the magnitude of the variables: $3a = 5c = 6d = 8b$. Since each of these expressions is less than zero, a must be the most negative. Likewise, c is the next most negative, then d, and finally, b is the least negative. Thus, $a < c < d < b$, which corresponds to choice (B).

   Alternate Solution: All the variables a, b, c, and d, must be negative. Since a is multiplied by the smallest positive coefficient, a must be the most negative. Likewise, because c is multiplied by the next smallest positive coefficient, c is the next least. The ranking must begin with $a < c$. Only choice (B) begins with this ranking.

5. **Answer D**

   $x < 5 < x^{-1}$. Decompose the compound inequality into two inequalities: (1) $x < 5$ and (2) $x^{-1} > 5$. Note that (2) requires that x be positive. Choices (A) and (B) are negative and will never satisfy (2). For positive values of x, (2) may be inverted into (3) $x < 1/5$. The only choice among (C) and (D) satisfying (3) is $x = 1/10$, choice (D).

   Alternate Solution: It might take more time, but plugging in the values of the choices into the compound inequality and test the truth of it is one brute-force solution.

6. **Answer C**

   Let's expand the expression $|x-3| < 2$ into two expressions: (1) $x-3 < 2$ and (2) $x-3 > -2$. (1) can be simplified by isolating x: (3) $x < 5$, and likewise (2) can be rearranged: $x > 1$. This corresponds to choice (C), $1 < x < 5$.

   Alternate Solution: You know enough about absolute values to be able to quickly determine that $|x-3| < 2$ will bound x by some finite range of values. If you're running out of time, in a few seconds you can toss choices (A) and (D) because they describe open ended limits on the value of x.

Chapter 10

Exponents

Difficult problems on the SAT involving exponents usually have fairly straightforward solutions, but often require more than a few algebraic manipulations to complete. By the way, the word *exponent* was first used in English in the mathematical sense you know and love /s. Only later did it evolve into a noun meaning "one who expounds."

There are several twists encountered in exponent problems. The positive & negative, even & odd, and fractional characteristics of exponents are very important and can cause confusion when first reading a problem. Inequalities governing exponents and/or their bases can be difficult to understand. Finally, an equation involving terms with different bases must be recast into one employing a common base prior to delivering a solution.

There are 8 major archetypes of exponent problems on the SAT. We will review the subject and analyze these archetypes as well as the 26 additional problems appended below them.

Exponents   Chapter 10

Don't Show Up Without Knowing…

These Concepts

- $x^0 = 1$
- if $x \geq 0$, then $\sqrt{x^2} = x$
- The radical $\sqrt{}$ sign implies the positive square root
- if $x^2 = c$, then $c = (x)^{1/2} = \pm x$
- if $x^a = x^b$, then $a = b$
- $x^a \cdot x^b = x^{(a+b)}$
- $(x^a)^b = x^{ab}$

- $(x^a)^{1/a} = x$
- $x^{-1} = 1/x$
- $x^{-a} = 1/x^a$
- $(xy)^a = x^a \cdot y^a$
- $(x+y)^a \neq x^a + y^a$ (in general)

Chapter 10 — Exponents

Quick Review and Definitions

Factoring Out The (-) Sign in an Exponential Expression

The negative sign can always be factored out of the base of an exponential expression. For example, $(-x)^a = (-1)^a \cdot (x)^a$. Depending on the values of x and a and their properties (such as ±, even & odd) the final expression may be positive, negative, or complex.

The Effects Of Even And Odd Exponents

If a is even, x^a is non-negative regardless of the sign of x (assuming x is real). For example, $(-2)^4 = 16$. In general, since $(-x)^a = (-1)^a \cdot (x)^a$, then if a is even, $(-1)^a = 1$, and so $(-x)^a = (x)^a$, which is non-negative when a is even, whether x is positive, negative, or zero.

If a is odd, x^a takes whatever the sign of x has. For example, $(-2)^5 = -32$. In general, since $(-x)^a = (-1)^a \cdot (x)^a$. When a is odd, $(-1)^a = -1$, and so $(-x)^a = -(x)^a$.

Putting An Expression In Terms of A Common Base

Problem: If n is an integer greater than zero and (1) $4^n + 4^{n-1} = k$, what is 2^{2n} in terms of k?

We'll have to put all the terms in terms of a common base, 2. (2) $4^n = (2^2)^n = 2^{2n}$, and likewise (3) $4^{n-1} = (2^2)^{n-1} = 2^{2n-2}$. But (3) can be rewritten (4) $4^{n-1} = 2^{2n-2} = 2^{2n}/4$. Using (2) and (4) in (1), $2^{2n} + 2^{2n}/4 = k$. Simplifying, $2^{2n}(1 + 1/4) = k$, or $2^{2n} \cdot 5/4 = k$. Therefore, $2^{2n} = 4k/5$.

In general, if exponential terms in an expression or equation have different bases, it may be necessary to recast all terms in a common base. It will frequently be easier to deal with expressions that involve a common base, and in some problems, conversion to a single base will be the only path to a solution.

Chapter 10   Exponents

SAT Archetypes

Factoring Exponential Expressions

If n is an integer greater than zero and $2^n + 2^{n-1} = k$, what is 2^{n+1} in terms of k?

(A) $\frac{k}{3}$

(B) $\frac{4k}{3}$

(C) $2k$

(D) $\frac{8k}{3}$

How do I start?

We need 2^{n+1}. We have terms involving a common base, 2, but they have different powers of 2. However, note that (1) $2^n = 2^{n+1}/2$ and (2) $2^{n-1} = 2^{n+1}/4$.

Solution

Using equalities (1) and (2) above, $2^n + 2^{n-1} = 2^{n+1}(1/2 + 1/4) = k$. Rearranging, $2^{2+1} = 4k/3$.

Alternate Solution

The original equation for k can be factored in the form $2^{n-1}(2 + 1) = k$. So $2^{n-1} = k/3$. Multiplying both sides by 2^2 yields $2^{n+1} = 2^2 \cdot k/3 = 4k/3$.

Alternate solution II

You could also start by expressing 2^{n-1} as $2^n/2$. Plugging this into the original equation for k, $2^n + 2^n/2 = k$. Factoring, $2^n \cdot (1+1/2) = 3 \cdot 2^n/2 = k$, and so $2^n = 2k/3$. Multiplying both sides by 2, $2^{n+1} = 4k/3$.

Answer B

The Take-Away

Expressions with common bases (2 here) raised to different exponents can almost always be re-expressed in terms of that base raised to a *common* exponent, allowing further simplification. There were many solution paths along this problem.

Exponents   Chapter 10

Evaluating Complicated Exponential Expressions

If $a = 9$ and $b = 1/3$, then what is the value of $(a+\sqrt{a})^r$, where $r = \dfrac{\sqrt{3ab}}{\sqrt{ab^2}}$?

SR

How do I start?

This is a mess. Take it a step at a time. Grab your PEMDAS. Calculate the value inside the parenthesis and the value of the exponent separately.

Solution

Now, $a + \sqrt{a} = 9 + 3 = 12$. Next, evaluate the exponent, r. In the numerator, using the values $a = 9$ and $b = 1/3$, we get $ab = 3$, $3ab = 9$, and so $\sqrt{3ab} = 3$. Likewise, in the denominator, $ab^2 = 9/9 = 1$. The expression for the exponent $r = 3/1 = 3$. Using these values for the exponent and the parenthetical expression, $(a+\sqrt{a})^r$ equals $12^3 = 1728$.

Alternate solution

The expression for the exponent r involves one square root divided by another square root. This is the same as $r = \sqrt{3ab/ab^2} = \sqrt{3/b} = \sqrt{9} = 3$. Since $a + \sqrt{a} = 9 + 3 = 12$, the expression in the problem equals $12^3 = 1728$.

Answer 1728

The Take-Away

Simplify, simplify, simplify! Complicated exponential expressions are often amenable to simplification via PEMDAS. The SAT loves problems that reduce to integers. In fact, the SAT loves problems you can do in your head, with care. Not to suggest *this* was a head-math problem.

Chapter 10　　　　　　　　　　　　　　　　　　　　　　　　　　　　　　　　Exponents

Determining an Exponential Model

The next two questions refer to the following information.

Some scientists believe that the volume of one well-studied Antarctic ice shelf may be disappearing at a rate of .35% per year.

Question 1: If V is the current volume in cubic kilometers (km^3) of the ice shelf, and the formula for its volume y years in the future is V(d)^y, what is the value of d?

SR

How do I start?

The ice shelf is losing .35% = .0035 of its mass each year. How much mass remains from the previous year?

Solution

If .0035 of its mass is lost each year, then 1 - .0035 = .9965 of its mass remains from the previous year. After one year, the mass is V(.9965). After 2 years, the mass is V(.9965)^2. In general, the mass after y years is V(.9965)^y. This is exponential decay.

Answer .996 or .997

Question 2: If the current volume is 2000 km^3, what will be the volume in 100 years?

Solution

So V = 2000 km^3, and thus the volume after 100 years = 2000(.9965)^{100} = 1408.51. You would enter 1408 or 1409.

Answer 1408 or 1409

The Take-Away

The ice shelf will lose .0035 of its mass each year, leaving .9965 of its mass for further reduction in subsequent years. It is this last number that is the base of the exponential function describing the behavior of ice reduction over time. On the test you may see this (1 - one-interval-loss)^n form in descriptions of what is also known as exponential decay.

Exponents   Chapter 10

Signs In Exponential Expressions

If a and b are integers and a never equals zero, which expressions below are always true?

   I. $a^{4b} > 0$

   II. $a^{2b} \cdot b^{2a} > 0$

   III. $(ab)^{ab} \geq 0$

(A) I only
(B) II only
(C) I and II only
(D) I and III only

How do I start?

We don't know the value of integers a and b, except that a ≠ 0. Since a and b are integers, we can ignore any issue that would otherwise arise with fractional exponents, for example ± roots. Also – any real number raised to an even power is always greater than or equal to zero, and several of the terms involve even powers.

Solution

Test (I): $a^{4b} = (a^4)^b$, and a ≠ 0, so a^4 is always positive. Since b is an integer, a^{4b} is always positive. So (I) is always true. Test (II): Rewritten, $(a^b)^2 \cdot (b^a)^2 > 0$. Since a ≠ 0, the first factor is always positive, *but b could be zero*, which means the product in (II) could be zero. So, (II) is <u>not</u> always true. Test (III): If a•b is odd *and* negative, then $(ab)^{ab}$ would be negative. There is nothing in the definitions of a and b to exclude this. For example, it is allowed that a = 1 and b = -1: (III) gives $(-1)^{-1} = -1$, which proves that (III) may be false.

Answer A

The Take-Away

Any real number raised to an even power is always ≥ 0. This is true even for negative even powers. Notice how (II) employed > instead of ≥ in the inequality. Reading comprehension is tested all the time on the math part of the SAT. Moreover, sometimes it is necessary to hunt for values to test an inequality, as the test for (III) above.

Chapter 10   Exponents

Inequalities Involving Exponential Expressions

$2x^2 < (2x)^2$

For which value of x below is the statement above FALSE?

(A) -2.1
(B) 2.1
(C) 0
(D) $-\dfrac{1}{\sqrt{2.1}}$

How do I start?

This could make your eyes hurt or go for a calculator to test the choices, but look first for an easy solution. Simplify both sides and examine the choices.

Solution

$2x^2 < (2x)^2$ can be simplified. Performing the square on the right side produces $2x^2 < 4x^2$. Dividing both sides by 2, (1) $x^2 < 2x^2$. Careful, we can't blithely divide by x^2, because x might be zero. However, it is evident that inequality (1) is always true except when x = 0.

Alternate Solution: If one were to divide (1) above by x^2, the result is 1 < 2, which is *always* true. But in choice (C), x *can* be zero. Dividing by zero is forbidden. Be careful!

Alternate Solution II

You can plug in and test each of the 5 choices, but that will take a lot of time.

Answer C

The Take-Away

Squaring a real, nonzero number, regardless of its sign or the magnitude, will always result in a positive number. As we have seen, when comparing the values of expressions, examine the even & odd properties of any exponents.

Again, note that we could have continued to simplify $2x^2 < 4x^2$ by dividing both sides by $2x^2$. This gives 1 < 2, which is *always* true. However, if x = 0, we would be dividing the inequality by zero - an act that can (and in this case does) produce spurious results. Stopping the simplification process at $x^2 < 2x^2$ and plugging in x = 0 produces 0 < 0, a statement that is clearly false.

Exponents   Chapter 10

Expressing Equations in a Common Base

If $27^r = 81^{r-1}$, then what is the value of r?

SR

How do I start?

Your best and perhaps only hope on this one is to see that both 27 and 81 are each 3 raised to an integer power.

Solution

$27 = 3^3$, and $81 = 3^4$. So $27^r = 81^{r-1}$ becomes $(3^3)^r = (3^4)^{r-1}$. Simplifying, $3^{3r} = 3^{4(r-1)}$. Since the bases are the same, the exponents must be equal: $3r = 4(r-1)$. Solving for r, r = 4.

Alternate Solution

Factoring out 27 on the left side of the original equation, $27 \cdot 27^{r-1} = 81^{r-1}$. Dividing both sides by 27^{r-1}, the equation becomes (1) $27 = 81^{r-1}/27^{r-1} = (81/27)^{r-1} = 3^{r-1}$. Since $27 = 3^3$, equation (1) becomes $3^3 = 3^{r-1}$. The exponents must be equal, so 3 = r-1, or r = 4.

Alternate Solution II

It's a good bet that r is some small integer. If lost for an algebraic solution, test r = 2, 3, 4… on the calculator and see if one of them works. Yup: $27^4 = 81^3$.

Answer 4

The Take-Away

When necessary, simplify expressions and equations so that terms with exponents are expressed using the same base. In problems on the SAT, different bases are often related to a common base. And the base is usually an integer. Also - if at a loss, some problems may be solved by a brute-force search, as shown in alternate solution II.

Compound Interest

A bank has a particular type of savings account that pays interest compounded quarterly (every 3 months). To compute the amount of money after y years in the account following an initial deposit of D dollars, they use the formula $D(1 + i/400)^{4y}$, where i is the advertised percentage interest rate. Which of the following is the expression for the additional money earned at 2% interest compared to 1% (both compounded quarterly) after 18 months?

(A) $D(1.005)^6 - D(1.0025)^6$
(B) $D(1 + 2/400)^6 - D(1 + 1/400)^3$
(C) $D(1.0025)^{18} + D(1.00125)^{18}$
(D) $D(1 + 2/400)^{18} - D(1 + 1/400)^{18}$

How do I start?

This is just a complicated problem in understanding the data given and formulating the difference between two exponential expressions. 18 months is 1.5 years.

Solution

Just plug in the given parameters into the formula. After 18 months (y = 1.5 years), the money earned at 2% annual interest would be $D(1 + 2/400)^{4 \cdot 1.5}$, or $D(1.005)^6$. Likewise, the money earned at 1% annual interest would be $D(1 + 1/400)^{4 \cdot 1.5}$, or $D(1.0025)^6$. The additional money earned at 2% over 1% would be $D(1.005)^6 - D(1.0025)^6$.

Alternate Solution

18 months = 1.5 years. The answer will be the difference of two terms, *both* with an exponent of 4•1.5 = 6. Only choice (A) does this. Take an extra moment and save time!

Alternate Solution II

Use the formula and a calculator to get the difference in interest. Calculate the choices and compare those with the difference. This is the *long* way. Fortunately, (A) is correct.

Answer A

The Take-Away

A complication sometimes thrown into compound interest problems is compounding intervals other than 1 year, even though the interest rate may be given in annual terms. Be careful to keep the units of time intervals straight in such problems. Also - examine the choices! Sometimes the answer is under your nose, as seen in the first alternate solution.

Exponents   Chapter 10

Identifying a Mathematical Model that Fits Data

An astronomer has been studying an exoplanet (a planet orbiting a distant star) for much of her career. Using several methods of measurement and analysis, she has determined its orbital distance from the star is currently 500,000 km, an extremely small orbital radius for a body orbiting a star. Moreover, the orbital distance seems to be diminishing with time (a fact that has generated much news and controversy among her colleagues). She has calculated that the orbital distance is diminishing at a rate of .04% every one million years. Which of the following formula expresses the orbital distance of the exoplanet in kilometers as a function of t, the number of millions of years from now?

(A) $.5(1 - .0004)^{t/1000000}$
(B) $500,000(1 - .00000004)^t$
(C) $500,000(.9996)^t$
(D) $.5(1 - .0004)^{t/1000000}$

How do I start?

Since the distance is diminishing at a rate of .04% every million years, the distance is governed by an exponential function. Note that t is in units of million years.

Solution

This rate of orbital decay (.04% per million years) may be more conveniently expressed as .0004 per million years. After 1 million years the distance will be reduced by a factor of $(1 - .0004)$. After 2 million years the distance will be reduced by a factor of $(1 - .0004)^2$. After t million years, the distance will have been reduced by a factor of $(1 - .0004)^t$. This is equivalent to $(.9996)^t$. The correct rate expression will multiply this decay factor by the original orbital distance: $500,000(.9996)^t$. This corresponds to choice (C) All other choices use either the wrong units for distance or time or both.

Answer C

The Take-Away

A growth or decay rate expressed as a percent per unit of time will almost always give rise to an exponential function of time. Of course, all our choices here were exponential. You will almost always need to convert a percent rate into a decimal rate, and you may have to convert such terms as $(1 - .0004)^t$ to $(.9996)^t$. Make sure to (1) use the correct units (millions of years in this problem) and (2) use the correct initial condition (500,000 *km*, not .5 *million km*). Units!

Chapter 10   Exponents

Practice Problems

1. Since productizing its new invention, quarterly (every 3 months) revenue of a company is tripling every 2 years. Assuming this trend continues, and letting R equal the current quarterly revenue, which of the following expresses the revenue for next the quarter?

   (A) $(R/2)^{1/3}$
   (B) $R(1 - 1/3)^{2/3}$
   (C) $R(3)^{1/8}$
   (D) $(R/4)(3)^2$

2. If n is a positive integer, then $(9 \cdot 10^{-n}) - (12 \cdot 10^{-(n-1)})$ equals

   (A) Approximately $.877 \cdot 10^{-n}$
   (B) $\dfrac{-109}{10^{n-1}}$
   (C) $\dfrac{-111}{10^{-n}}$
   (D) $\dfrac{-111}{10^{n}}$

3. Let a, b, c, and d be positive numbers. If $c^{-2/3} = a^{-2}$ and $d^{2/3} = b^2$, what is the value of $(cd)^{-1/3}$, in terms of a and b?

   (A) $\dfrac{a}{b}$
   (B) $\dfrac{b}{a}$
   (C) $\dfrac{1}{ab}$
   (D) $\dfrac{4}{ab}$

4. If n is an integer greater than zero and $4^n + 4^{n-1} = k$, what is 2^{2n+1} in terms of k?

   (A) k/5
   (B) 4k/3
   (C) 2k
   (D) 8k/5

249

Exponents   Chapter 10

5. If $x = 4^4$, which of the following expressions equals 4^{15}?

   (A) $128x^2$
   (B) $64x^3$
   (C) $32x^4$
   (D) $128x^4$

6. a and b are integers, and a never equals zero. Which of the inequalities below can <u>never</u> be true?

   I. $a^{5b} \geq 0$
   II. $a^{2b} \cdot b^{2a} < 0$
   III. $(ab)^{ab} \geq 0$

   (A) I only
   (B) II only
   (C) I and II only
   (D) I and III only

7. $(-5x^{-5}y^4)^{-2} =$

   (A) $-\dfrac{y^8}{25x^{10}}$

   (B) $\dfrac{x^{10}}{25y^8}$

   (C) $\dfrac{25y^8}{x^{10}}$

   (D) $\dfrac{25x^8}{y^{10}}$

Chapter 10   Exponents

8. $2x^2 < (x/2)^3$

    For which value of x below is the statement above true?

    (A) 2
    (B) 9
    (C) 15
    (D) 31

9. If a and b are positive integers and $100a^4b^2 = 50a$, what is a^2 in terms of b?

    (A) $2/(b^{3/2})$
    (B) $(2/b)^{2/3}$
    (C) $(1/(2b^2))^{3/2}$
    (D) $(1/(2b^2))^{2/3}$

10. If x and y are positive integers and $(2x^{1/4}y^{3/8})^8 = 110592$, what could be the value of $\frac{x}{y}$?

    (A) $\frac{1}{2}$
    (B) $\frac{2}{3}$
    (C) $\frac{4}{3}$
    (D) $\frac{5}{4}$

11. If $n^x n^8 = n^{32}$ and $(n^4)^y = n^{16}$, what is the value of $\frac{x}{y}$?

    SR

12. If $\frac{4}{3} \cdot (2^x + 2^x + 2^x + 2^x + 2^x + 2^x) = 2^9$, what is the value of x?

    SR

251

Exponents   Chapter 10

13. If $27^r = 243^{r+2}$, then what is the value of -r ?

SR

14. If $y = 4^{1/3}$, which of the following expressions is equal to 2^4?

(A) $\dfrac{y^4}{6}$

(B) $\dfrac{y^4}{3}$

(C) y^5

(D) y^6

15. If $x^{\frac{2}{3}} < 9$, which expression below must be true?

(A) $x < -9$ and $x > 9$
(B) $x < -3$
(C) $-9 < x < 9$
(D) $-27 < x < 27$

16. a and b are positive constants, a^3 is one fourth of a^2, and b^2 is one third of b^3. What is the ratio $\dfrac{a}{b}$?

(A) $\dfrac{1}{25}$

(B) $\dfrac{1}{12}$

(C) $\dfrac{1}{10}$

(D) 12

Chapter 10   Exponents

17. If $8 = b^{-c}$, then $16b =$

(A) $2b^{-c}$
(B) $4b^{1-c}$
(C) $128b^{c+1}$
(D) $2b^{c-1}$

18. If $a^4 > a^2$ and $b^8 < b^2$, which of the following expressions must always be true?

I. $|a| > 1$
II. $a > b$
III. $b^2 > b^4$

(A) I only
(B) II only
(C) I and II only
(D) I and III only

19. If 2^{64} to the power of 2^{16} equals 2 to the power of 2^x, what is the value of x?

SR

20. If $4x - y = 5$, what is the value of $\dfrac{16^x}{2^y}$?

SR

21. If $n^{11} = 144$ and $n^{10} = 24m$, what is the value of 4mn?

SR

22. If $3^x = 27$, then what is the value of 2^{3x}?

SR

23. What is the value of x if $16^{4-x} = 8^{x-3}$?

SR

253

Exponents   Chapter 10

24. If $x = 9^2 \cdot 11^2 \cdot 13^4 \cdot 15^6$, and x is a multiple of 12^n, where n is a non-negative integer, which value below equals $n^{12} + 12^n$?

(A) -12
(B) -11
(C) 1
(D) 12

25. If x is real and $x = \sqrt[5]{-33}$, then which condition below must be true?

(A) $\sqrt{-x} > 2$
(B) $x^3 < -8$
(C) $x > -2$
(D) $x^4 > 32$

26. If $x = \sqrt{10} + \sqrt[3]{9} + \sqrt[4]{8} + \sqrt[5]{7} + \sqrt[6]{6} + \sqrt[7]{5} + \sqrt[8]{4} + \sqrt[9]{3} + \sqrt[12]{2}$, which of the following inequalities is true.

(A) 6<x<8
(B) 8<x<10
(C) 10<x<12
(D) x>12

Chapter 10   Exponents

Practice Problem Hints

1. Revenue is tripling every 2 years. How many quarters in 2 years?

2. Put the second term in terms of 10^{-n}.

3. Isolate c and d, and then form the requested expression.

4. Express all terms as powers of 2.

5. $x^3 = 4^{12}$.

6. Any real number raised to an even power is always ≥ 0.

7. Use $(ab)^c = a^c \cdot b^c$

8. Expand the right-hand expression, simplify, and examine the choices.

9. Simplify step-by-step, first the powers of a, then the coefficients.

10. Take the 8th power of the left side and isolate the numbers on the right. Reorganize the left side so that it includes a perfect square. Remember, these are integers.

11. Use the first expression to calculate x and the second expressions to calculate y.

12. Rewrite the expression in parenthesis as a product. Express all terms with a base of 2.

13. Is there a relationship between 27 and 243? A common base?

14. Cube both sides of the equation.

15. Cube both sides of the inequality.

16. Translate the words in the problem into 2 separate equations, and solve for a and b.

17. Multiply both sides by 16, then factor out 16b from the right side.

18. Test both expressions using a and b = {-2, -1/2, +1/2, and +2}. This is a characteristic spread of values that includes positive and negative values that have magnitudes less than and greater than 1.

Exponents   Chapter 10

19. Oh man. Put each number in the question as a power of 2. Then use the rules governing operations on exponents.

20. Put all the terms in the expression in base 2.

21. $n^{11} = 144 = n \cdot n^{10}$

22. Read carefully and follow the directions. What is x?

23. Find a common base and then simplify the exponents.

24. Note that all the terms in the product are odd. What about 12^n?

25. Ignoring complex roots, odd roots of a negative number must be negative. Estimate the 5th root.

26. You'll have to estimate these terms. Any positive root of a positive integer is > 1.

Practice Problem Solutions

1. **Answer C**

   Since the revenue is *tripling* every 2 years, revenue must be expressed by an exponential function with a base of 3. We are looking for a function of the form $R \cdot 3^x$. Only (C) and (D) satisfy this criterion. If we were asked what the revenue would be in two years the answer would be $R \cdot 3^1$. However, we are asked what next quarter's revenue will be. There are 4 quarters per year, 8 quarters every two years (the interval during which revenue will triple), and so one quarter will be 1/8 of the interval during which revenue triples. Therefore, the expression for next quarter's will be $R \cdot 3^{1/8}$. Is this right? As a check, in two years (8 quarters) the revenue would be $R \cdot (3^{1/8})^8 = 3R$.

2. **Answer D**

   We need to simplify (1) $(9 \cdot 10^{-n}) - (12 \cdot 10^{-(n-1)})$. Put the second term in terms of 10^{-n}. Since $10^{-(n-1)} = 10 \cdot 10^{-n}$, (2) $12 \cdot 10^{-(n-1)} = 120 \cdot 10^{-n}$. Plug (2) into (1): $(9 \cdot 10^{-n}) - 120 \cdot 10^{-n} = 10^{-n} \cdot (9 - 120) = -111 \cdot 10^{-n} = -111 / 10^n$.

3. **Answer C**

   If $c^{-2/3} = a^{-2}$, raising each side to the -3/2 power gives $c = a^3$. If $d^{2/3} = b^2$, raising each side to the 3/2 power gives $d = b^3$. So, $cd = (ab)^3$, and therefore $(cd)^{-1/3} = (ab)^{-1} = 1/ab$.

   Alternate Solution: $(cd)^{-1/3}$ equals the square root of $(cd)^{-2/3}$. Start with $(cd)^{-1/3} = c^{-1/3} \cdot d^{-1/3}$. From the problem, $c^{-1/3} = (a^{-2})^{1/2} = a^{-1}$. Likewise, $d^{-1/3} = (d^{2/3})^{-1/2} = (b^2)^{-1/2} = b^{-1}$. So, $c^{-1/3} \cdot d^{-1/3} = (cd)^{-1/3} = a^{-1} \cdot b^{-1} = 1/(ab)$.

   Alternate Solution II: The exponent of c has the same sign as a, and the exponent of d has the same sign as b. Therefore, $(cd)^{-1/3}$ must give rise to an expression that has both a and b in the denominator. Only choices (C) and (D) fit this analysis. There is no "4" in the problem: (D) is nonsense. The correct choice must be (C).

4. **Answer D**

   Find a common base. $4^n = 2^{2n}$ and $4^{n-1} = 2^{2(n-1)}$. So, $4^n + 4^{n-1} = 2^{2n} + 2^{2(n-1)} = 2^{2n} + 2^{2n-2}$. Now, $2^{2n} = 4 \cdot 2^{2(n-1)}$. Factoring out a factor of 2^{2n-2}, we get $4^n + 4^{n-1} = 2^{2n-2}(4+1) = 5 \cdot 2^{2n-2}$. Therefore, from the equation in the problem, $5 \cdot 2^{2n-2} = k$. Rearranging, $2^{2n-2} = k/5$. Multiply each side by $2^3 = 8$ to get the requested value of $2^{2n+1} = 8k/5$.

Exponents   Chapter 10

Alternate Solution: $4^n + 4^{n-1} = 2^{2n} + 2^{2(n-1)} = 2^{2n} + 2^{2n-2}$. Pulling out a factor of 2^{2n}, this sum = $2^{2n}(1 + 1/4) = \frac{5}{4} \cdot 2^{2n}$. Thus, from the problem, $\frac{5}{4} \cdot 2^{2n} = k$. Rearranging, $2^{2n} = 4k/5$, and multiplying both sides by 2, $2^{2n+1} = 8k/5$.

5. Answer B

Note that $x^3 = (4^4)^3 = 4^{12}$. Multiplying both sides by 4^3, $4^{15} = 4^3 \cdot x^3 = 64x^3$.

6. Answer B

Test (I): Since a can be positive or negative, a^{5b} could be positive or negative, so (I) is sometimes true. Test (II): $a^2 \geq 0$ and $b^2 > 0$, so $a^{2b} \cdot b^{2a}$ is always ≥ 0, and therefore (II) is never true. Test (III): ab could be negative or positive, and as a result, $(ab)^{ab}$ could be negative or positive. (III) may be true.

7. Answer B

Multiply the exponents: $(-5x^{-5}y^4)^{-2} = (-5)^{-2} \cdot x^{10} \cdot y^{-8} = x^{10}/(25y^8)$.

Alternate Solution: We can solve this by only examining the factor $(-5)^{-2} = +1/25$. Only choice (B) displays a positive expression with 25 on the bottom.

Alternate Solution II: Likewise, y must contribute a term of y^{-8} or $1/y^8$. Must be (B).

8. Answer D

$2x^2 < (x/2)^3$. Apply the exponent to the right side expression, simplify, and examine the choices. $2x^2 < x^3/8$. Multiply by 8: $16x^2 < x^3$. Dividing both sides by x^2 (which we can do because $x = 0$ fails the inequality), we get $16 < x$. Only (D) satisfies this condition.

Alternate Solution: If out of time: Since $2x^2 < (x/2)^3$ is true as x approaches ∞, and since it is only true for *one* choice, the answer might be the greatest choice, (D).

Alternate Solution II: Plug choices in and chug. A waste of time, but it'll get you there.

9. Answer D

If $100a^4b^2 = 50a$, what is a^2 in terms of b? Note $a \neq 0$. Simplify powers of a and then the coefficients. Thus, $100a^3b^2 = 50$. Then, $2a^3b^2 = 1$. Isolate a^3: $a^3 = 1/(2b^2)$. Raising each side to the 1/3 power, $a = (1/2b^2)^{1/3}$. Squaring each side, $a^2 = (1/(2b^2))^{2/3}$.

Chapter 10 Exponents

10. Answer C

$(2x^{1/4}y^{3/8})^8 = 110592$; what could be the value of $\frac{x}{y}$, where x and y are *positive integers*? Multiplying the exponents in the parenthetical expression on the left side yields $256x^2y^3 = 110592$. Divide both sides by 256 and factor: (1) $y(x^2y^2) = y(xy)^2 = 432$. Note that *(xy)² is a perfect square*. Rearrange (1) into (2) $(xy)^2 = 432/y$. Look for an integer value of y such that dividing 432 by y will yield a perfect square. Trying y = 2 in (1), we see that 216 is not a perfect square. Try y = 3 in (2): $(xy)^2 = 144$. Yes! The square of both sides yields (3) xy = 12. Using y = 3 in (3), x•3 = 12. So x = 4. Therefore, x/y = 4/3. Hard!

Alternate solution: When you get to $y(xy)^2 = x^2y^3 = 432$, you know that x and y are pretty small. Trial-and-error the values of x and y that might fit. x = 4 and y = 3 work.

Alternate solution II: When you get to (1) $y(xy)^2 = x^2y^3 = 432$, you can try the values of x and y suggested in the fractions among the choices. Of course, those values could be factors of the needed values of x and y, but in this case x = 4 and y = 3 solve (1).

11. Answer 6

If (1) $n^x n^8 = n^{32}$ and (2) $(n^4)^y = n^{16}$, what is the value of $\frac{x}{y}$? These equations are both in the form (3) $n^a = n^b$. Because the base is the same on the left and right sides of (3), the exponents must be equal; therefore a = b. From equation (1), it must be true that x + 8 = 32, which means x = 24. Because the exponents in equation (2) must be equal, 4y = 16, or y = 4. With these values, x/y = 24/4 = 6.

12. Answer 6

(1) $\frac{4}{3}\cdot(2^x+2^x+2^x+2^x+2^x+2^x) = 2^9$. Note that (2) $(2^x+2^x+2^x+2^x+2^x+2^x) = 6\cdot2^x$. Use (2) in (1): the left side of equation (1) becomes $4/3 \cdot 6 \cdot 2^x = 8 \cdot 2^x = 2^3 \cdot 2^x = 2^{3+x}$. Thus, equation (1) becomes $2^{3+x} = 2^9$. Same base, exponents equal: 3 + x = 9, which means x = 6.

13. Answer 5

If $27^r = 243^{r+2}$, then solve for -r. Both of these bases look like multiples of 3. We know $27 = 3^3$. See if 243 is also a power of 3. It is, $243 = 3^5$. We can rewrite the equation in the problem in terms of powers of 3. In that case, $(3^3)^r = (3^5)^{r+2}$. Simplifying the exponents, $3^{3r} = 3^{5r+10}$. Equating the exponents, 3r = 5r + 10, and solving for r, r = -5. So, -r = 5.

Exponents									Chapter 10

14. Answer D

We need 2^4 in terms of y. Since (1) $y = 4^{1/3}$, perform identical operations on both sides of equation (1) to transform $4^{1/3}$ into 2^4 on the right. Cubing both sides of equation (1) yields $y^3 = 4$. Of course, $4 = 2^2$, so $y^3 = 2^2$, and by squaring both sides, $y^6 = 2^4$.

Alternate Solution: $y = 4^{1/3} = (2^2)^{1/3} = 2^{2/3}$. Cubing both sides, $y^3 = 2^2$. Squaring both sides of this last equation yields $y^6 = 2^4$.

15. Answer D

If $x^{2/3} < 9$, what is the domain of x? Note that $x^{2/3}$ is always positive (at least all real values of x will make $x^{2/3}$ positive). So both sides of the inequality are positive, and thus we are allowed to cube both sides and maintain the direction of the inequality. After doing so, $x^2 < 9^3$. Since $9 = 3^2$, $x^2 < 3^6$. Taking the square root of both sides (and taking into account both positive and negative roots), $x < 3^3$ and $x > -3^3$. Of course, $3^3 = 27$, and thus, $-27 < x < 27$. Choice (D) is correct.

Alternate Solution: Taking the positive square root of $x^{2/3} < 9$ gives (1) $x^{1/3} < 3$. However, we must account for the negative root. This will give rise to the same inequality after multiplying both sides by -1, and hence we need to reverse the direction of the inequality: (2) $x^{1/3} > -3$. Cubing both sides in (1) and (2) gives (3) $x < 27$ and (4) $x > -27$. (3) and (4) are equivalent to $-27 < x < 27$. (D) it is.

16. Answer B

a and b are positive constants, a^3 is one fourth of a^2, and b^2 is one third of b^3. What is the $\frac{a}{b}$? The two equations translate into $a^3 = a^2/4$ and $b^2 = b^3/3$. Since $a^3 = a^2/4$ and $a \neq 0$, divide both sides by a^2 to get $a = 1/4$. Since $b^2 = b^3/3$, $3b^2 = b^3$. Since $b \neq 0$, divide both sides by b^2: $3 = b$. With these values, $a/b = (1/4) / (3) = 1/12$.

17. Answer C

If (1) $8 = b^c$, then what is 16b? Multiplying both sides by 16 gives $128 = 16b^c$. Multiplying both sides by b^{c+1} gives (2) $128b^{c+1} = 16b$. This is choice (C).

Note: It is also true from (1), $16 = 2b^c$, and thus (3) $16b = 2b^{1-c}$. However, that is not one of the choices. Is it true, equating (2) and (3), that $128b^{c+1} = 2b^{1-c}$? Simplifying, we get $64 = b^{1-c}/b^{1+c} = b^{1-c-1-c} = b^{-2c}$. Taking the square root of both sides, $8 = b^{-c}$. Ignoring the negative root, this is the initial condition we were given in (1).

18. Answer D

If $a^4 > a^2$ and $b^8 < b^2$, which of the following expressions must always be true?

  I. $|a| > 1$
  II. $a > b$
  III. $b^2 > b^4$

You can test these choices manually using characteristic values such as {-2, -1/2, +1/2, and +2}. Only I and III are true. But it's still only a guess based on a few values.

Alternate Solution: Any real number raised to an even power will be non-negative. Because $a^4 > a^2$ we know $a \neq 0$. Divide both sides by a^2: $a^2 > 1$. This is true only if $a > 1$ or $a < -1$, or in other words, $|a| > 1$. So (I) is true. Condition (II) can only result from a mixed equation. The equations governing a and b are homogeneous: the a's and b's are never mixed. So (II) is not always true. Because $b^8 < b^2$, we know $b \neq 0$. After dividing by b^2, we get (1) $b^6 < 1$. From this, $-1<b<1$. Examine (III): Divide both sides of (III) by b^2 to get (2) $1 > b^2$, so again, $-1<b<1$. If (1) is true then clearly (2) is also true, and therefore (III) is true. Only (I) and (III) must be true.

19. Answer 24

Put each number given in the expressions as a power of 2. Thus, $(2^{64})^{2^{16}} = 2^{2^x}$. This is already confusing. Multiply the exponents on the left side to express both sides with a base of 2: $2^{64 \cdot 2^{16}} = 2^{2^x}$. However, $64 = 2^8$, so the equation becomes (1) $2^{2^8 \cdot 2^{16}} = 2^{2^x}$. Aha! Combine (add) the exponents (in the exponent) on the left side of equation (1) to get (2) $2^{2^8 \cdot 2^{16}} = 2^{2^{24}} = 2^{2^x}$. So x = 24. This one has a license to kill.

20. Answer 32

We are given that $4x - y = 5$. Note that $\dfrac{16^x}{2^y}$ can be recast entirely in base 2: $16^x = (2^4)^x$. Thus, $\dfrac{16^x}{2^y} = (2^4)^x \cdot 2^{-y} = 2^{4x-y}$. Now we see the trick. $4x - y = 5$, and therefore $\dfrac{16^x}{2^y} = 2^{4x-y} = 2^5 = 32$. Missed the trick? You are sunk - and not alone.

21. Answer 24

If $n^{11} = 144$ then (1) $n \cdot n^{10} = 144$. But (2) $n^{10} = 24m$. Substituting (2) into (1), $n \cdot 24m = 144$. Therefore, $mn = 144/24 = 6$, and $4mn = 24$. Deceptively easy.

Exponents　　　　　　　　　　　　　　　　　　　　　　　　　　　　　　　　Chapter 10

22. Answer 512

If $3^x = 27$, then $x = 3$, because $3^3 = 27$. What is the value of 2^{3x}? $3x = 9$, so $2^{3x} = 2^9 = 512$. Clearly easy, yet problems like these can be difficult because they are drafted to trigger the dyslexia everyone has to some extent.

23. Answer 25/7

We're told (1) $16^{4-x} = 8^{x-3}$. The base of each expression can be cast as a power of 2: $16 = 2^4$, and $8 = 2^3$. So equation (1) can now be written as $(2^4)^{4-x} = (2^3)^{x-3}$. Multiplying the exponents out on both sides, $2^{16-4x} = 2^{3x-9}$. The bases are equal, thus the exponents must be equal. So $16 - 4x = 3x - 9$. Isolating x, $25 = 7x$. Thus $x = 25/7$.

24. Answer C

Oh god. N0OoOooh. But notice that in the equation $x = 9^2 \cdot 11^2 \cdot 13^4 \cdot 15^6$, the product on the right is odd•odd•odd•odd, which must be odd. So x, whatever it is, is odd. But we are also told that x is also a multiple of 12^n. Huh? 12^n is even for all non-negative n *except n = 0*: $12^0 = 1$, which *is* odd. So x is just a multiple of 1, and n = 0. We are asked to evaluate $n^{12} + 12^n$, which is now rendered trivial: $0^{12} + 12^0 = 0 + 1 = 1$. Problems like this occasionally get students accepted into Harvard.

25. Answer B

This is awful. Hmm. Ignoring complex roots, an odd root of a negative number must be negative. For example, $\sqrt[3]{-8} = -2$. For a better view we can split the 5th root as follows: $\sqrt[5]{-33} = \sqrt[5]{(-1) \cdot 33} = \sqrt[5]{-1} \cdot \sqrt[5]{33}$. But $-1 \cdot -1 \cdot -1 \cdot -1 \cdot -1 = -1$. The 5th root of -1 is -1. Therefore, $\sqrt[5]{-33} = -\sqrt[5]{33}$. Now $x = \sqrt[5]{-33}$ is clearly not an integer, and this is not a problem that allows a calculator. But note that $\sqrt[5]{-33}$ is just slightly more negative than $\sqrt[5]{-32} = -2$. Let's just crudely estimate (1) $x = \sqrt[5]{-33} \approx -2.1$. This will give us something to compare the choices with. Plug estimate (1) for x into (A) $\sqrt{-x} > 2$. Is $\sqrt{2.1} > 2$? Clearly not, so (A) is false. Doing likewise in (B) gives $(-2.1)^3 < -8$. The left side is a bit more negative than -8. (B) is true. We can stop. But just to check, plugging estimate (1) into (C) $x > -2$ gives $-2.1 > 2$, which is false. Plugging estimate (1) into (D) $x^4 > 32$ gives $(-2.1)^4 > 32$. The left side is just a bit more than 16. So (D) is false, and the answer is (B).

You won't see them often, but the properties of higher roots of negative numbers can obliterate what would otherwise be only a modestly hard problem.

Chapter 10   Exponents

26. Answer D

No calculator? Why? How? So $x = \sqrt{10} + \sqrt[3]{9} + \sqrt[4]{8} + \sqrt[5]{7} + \sqrt[6]{6} + \sqrt[7]{5} + \sqrt[8]{4} + \sqrt[9]{3} + \sqrt[12]{2}$, which is some constant value. Unless you can bend steel in your bare hands, you gotta estimate this. At least the choices are *intervals* of x. One thing to remember: *any positive root (and they all are) of a positive integer is greater than 1*. The last 6 terms are clearly each greater than 1 and less than 2. Even the next term (counting from the left), $\sqrt[4]{8}$, is less than 2, given that $\sqrt[3]{8} = 2$. So the last 7 are each bounded below by 1. These 7 terms *must* sum to greater than 7. Since $\sqrt[3]{8} = 2$, $\sqrt[3]{9}$ must be >2. Now we have the last 8 terms summing greater than 2 + 7 = 9. We know that $\sqrt{10} > 3$. We have come up with lower-bound estimates for all 9 terms: 3, 2, 1, 1, 1, 1, 1, 1, 1. All the terms sum to a number greater than 3 + 2 + 7 = 12. Thus, x > 12. You got this? Have a cookie.

Notes

Chapter 11

Algebra and Real-World Problems

The word *algebra* comes from the Arabic phrase *al jebr*, which translates into English as "reunion of broken parts." Poetic, no? It was first coined in the sense we know today by the Persian mathematician Abu Ja'far Muhammad ibn Musa al-Khwarizmi in the 9th century CE. Our English word *algorithm* derives from his last name.

Algebra is extensively tested throughout the SAT. It is tested in a variety of algebra problems per se, which we cover in this chapter, as well as problems in many other subjects, such as simultaneous equations, geometry, data analysis, and probability.

We review here the techniques necessary to solve linear, quadratic, and higher order equations and inequalities found on the test. Proportionality, joint and exponential variation, and the algebra of absolute value expressions are also covered.

There are 26 representative archetypes. The subject is reviewed, the archetypes are explored, and 51 additional problems that expand the scope of this chapter are included for further practice.

This is a huge chapter – with good reason.

Algebra and Real-World Problems — Chapter 11

Don't Show Up Without Knowing…

These Concepts

    PEMDAS   Coefficient

    FOIL method   Quadratic Equation

    Polynomial   Quadratic Factoring & Vertex Form

    Polynomial Division   Combining Like Terms

                                                           Algebraic GCF

These Relationships

$(x+1)(x-1) = x^2 - 1$ $(x+y)^2 = x^2 + 2xy + y^2$

$(x+y)(x-y) = x^2 - y^2$ $(x-1)(x-1) = x^2 - 2x + 1$

$(x+1)(x+1) = x^2 + 2x + 1$ $(x-y)^2 = x^2 - 2xy + y^2$

How To …

- Factor and gather like terms in an expression or equation
- Reorganize a polynomial equation into standard form
- Solve a quadratic equation using factoring or the quadratic formula
- Recast a quadratic expression into vertex form
- Simplify equations by raising both sides to the same reciprocal power
- Solve proportion equations
- Divide and factor polynomials
- Handle problems with fewer equations than unknowns
- Pick convenient values for one unknown to solve for another unknown
- Handle algebraic inequalities and absolute values
- Use a graphing calculator to calculate the roots of a quadratic polynomial
- Solve some kinds of cubic equations by factoring

Chapter 11	Algebra and Real-World Problems

Quick Review and Definitions

PEMDAS

Operations to simplify arithmetic and algebraic expressions should be performed in the order specified by the pneumonic acronym PEMDAS:

Parentheses and Brackets: Simplify and perform calculations inside parentheses prior to simplifying any exponents.

Exponents: Simplify the exponent of an expression and perform calculations within it before further calculations are performed.

Multiplication: Simplify and perform multiplication before division in an expression from left to right.

Division: Simplify and perform division before addition in an expression from left to right.

Addition: Simplify and perform addition before subtraction in expressions from left to right.

Subtraction: Simplify, if necessary, and perform subtraction last of all operations.

Combining Like Terms

Complicated polynomial expressions involving a single variable often need to be simplified into a standard polynomial form: $ax^2 + bx + c$, where a, b, and c are constants.

1. Multiply out terms involving parentheses and other PEMDAS calculations when necessary. For example, $x(3-2x) = -2x^2 + 3x$

2. FOIL (first, outside, inside, last) method: used for pairwise multiplication of two expressions with two terms.

    For example, $(3+7x)(6+2x) = 18 + 6x + 42x + 14x^2 = 14x^2 + 48x + 18$.

3. Multiplying expressions involving more than 2 terms requires careful pair-wise multiplication and subsequent collection of powers of x. For example:

    $(x+3)(2x^2 +10x +1) = 2x^3 +10x^2 +x + 6x^2 + 30x +3 = 2x^3 +16x^2 +31x +3$.

4. If more than two expressions must be multiplied, perform pair-wise multiplications on the first pair of expressions, then multiply that result with the next expression, etc. For example, **(3+7x)(6+2x)(1+x) = (18 + 48x + 14x^2)(1+x)**. Now multiply these two expressions together.

Simplifying With The Greatest Common Factor (GCF)

As discussed in chapter 1, finding the GCF of a number or expression can be very useful in factoring.

Quick review: find the GCF of (24 and 60). Listing factors of each number in order: (1,2,3,4,6,8,12,24) and (1,2,3,4,5,6,10,12,15,20,30,60). The greatest common factor is 12.

Now, find the GCF of ($14x^2y^4$ and $21x$). In the first term, the factors of 14 are (2,7), the factors of x^2 are (1,x,x^2), and the factors of y^4 are (1,y,y^2,y^3,y^4). In the second term, the factors of 21 and x are (3,7) and (1,x), respectively. The GCF of ($14x^2y^4$ and $21x$) is $7x$ because the greatest factors common to both are 7 and x. The sum $14x^2y^4 + 21x$ thus equals $7x(2xy^4 + 3)$. We have factored out $7x$ from the original expression.

Another example: $3x^3 + 27x^2 + 9x = 3x(x^2 + 9x + 3)$

With practice, extracting the GCF can, in most cases, be done by inspection.

Common Quadratic Factors

1. $(x+1)(x-1) = x^2 - 1$.

2. In general, $(x+y)(x-y) = x^2 - y^2$. For example, $(3x+4)(3x-4) = 9x^2 - 16$.

3. $(x+1)(x+1) = x^2 + 2x + 1$, and in general, $(x+y)^2 = x^2 + 2xy + y^2$.

4. $(x-1)(x-1) = x^2 - 2x + 1$, and in general, $(x-y)^2 = x^2 - 2xy + y^2$.

5. Some problems give the value for, say, $x^2 + y^2$, or $(x - y)$, which is sometimes a clue to use the above quadratic relationships.

6. For example, you can simplify expressions with $(x - y)$ in a denominator by multiplying top and bottom by $(x+y)$ to produce $x^2 - y^2$ in the denominator. Here's one:

$3(x^2 - y^2)/(x-y) = 3(x^2 - y^2)(x+y) / [(x-y)(x+y)] = 3(x^2 - y^2)(x+y) / (x^2 - y^2) = 3(x+y)$.

Chapter 11　　　　　　　　　　　　　　　　　　　　　Algebra and Real-World Problems

Division by Zero

Example: Let x have the domain $0 \leq x \leq 4$. Consider the equation $x^2 = 2x$. Solve for x.

In the physical sciences, when equations involve real-world variables that can only *approach* zero, one can dismiss concerns about dividing by zero. However, in the realm of pure mathematics, variables certainly can equal zero, like x above. Suppose you are tired, take the equation (1) $x^2 = 2x$ and simply *divide both sides by x*: $x = 2$. Yes, that's a solution. But not the only solution! Clearly, $x = 0$ is also a solution to (1). Because x may have the value zero (it' in its domain), you have divided both sides by zero when $x = 0$. The result is undefined. By carelessly dividing by x, you have lost one solution.

But there is an easy, algebraic workaround. Simply separate those instances (values in the domain) where division by zero would occur from those where it would not:

$0 < x \leq 4$　　　dividing $x^2 = 2x$ by x yields　　　　　　　　$x = 2$　　solution 1
$x = 0$　　　　　plug $x = 0$ into $x^2 = 2x$, see what happens　　$0 = 0$　　solution 2

Consider another situation involving division by zero. Given that $-10 < x < 10$, solve for x:

(2) $$\frac{x+2}{x-2} - \frac{1}{x} = \frac{2}{x(x-2)}$$

Multiplying both sides by x(x-2) and simplifying yields $x(x+2) - (x-2) = 2$. Simplifying this further, the equation becomes $x^2 - x = 0$, or

(3) $$x(x+1) = 0$$

One might (too quickly) solve this equation, resulting in two solutions: $x = 0$ and $x = -1$.

I'm sorry if you were tired again, but this is wrong. In equation (2), $x = 0$ is in its domain. Whenever a denominator equals zero, watch out. You're also dividing by zero when $x = 2$. But let's look at $x = 0$ because that solves (3). When $x = 0$, equation (2) becomes:

(4) $$-\frac{1}{2} - \frac{1}{0} = -\frac{2}{0}$$

Both sides of equation (4) contain terms with division by zero. These are undefined and there is no solution when $x = 0$. Therefore, only $x = -1$ is a valid solution to equation (2).

Equation (3) is not equivalent to equation (2) because by multiplying both sides of (2) by x(x-2), we obscured the undefined characteristics of the equation when $x = 0$ and $x = 2$.

269

Algebra and Real-World Problems   Chapter 11

Polynomial Equations

In general, a polynomial equation takes the form:

$$cx^n + dx^{n-1} + \ldots + h = qx^m + rx^{m-1} + \ldots + j$$

In the equation above, c, d, …h, and q, r, …j are constant coefficients of powers of x. The powers of x on either side are denoted n, n-1, … and m, m-1, … etc. Note that some of the constant coefficients of x may be zero; not every power of x may be represented. The solution(s) to a polynomial equation are those value(s) of x that solve the equation.

A polynomial equation in *standard form* (all terms are moved to the left) is defined as:

$$ax^n + bx^{n-1} + \ldots + k = 0,$$

where the order of the equation is defined as the highest power of x, represented by n.

The solution(s) to a polynomial equation in standard form are those value(s) of x that cause the left side of the equation to equal zero. Note: the solutions need not be real.

Reorganize Polynomial Equations Into Standard Form

A polynomial equation can always be put in standard form where the right side of the equation is zero. For example, a 2nd order, or quadratic, equation can be put into the form $ax^2 + bx + c = 0$. The solutions of this equation will be those values of x which force the left side to be zero. An nth order equation will have n solutions. However, some solutions may be complex, and some real solutions may be identical. $y = (x-2)^2$ has two real solutions: both equal 2. If there are no real solutions, y never crosses the x-axis.

Quadratic equations may often be factored to promote a solution. To solve for x, first put a quadratic equation in standard form: $ax^2 + bx + c = 0$. Then use factoring to put this equation in the form $(cx + d)(ex + f) = 0$. The solutions will be $x = -d/c$ and $x = -f/e$. Most quadratics on the SAT have expressions where a = 1, which greatly simplifies factoring. In those cases, c = e = 1. Factoring takes practice. You've probably already had a lot.

The coefficients of the same powers of x on each side of an equation are equal

If a polynomial equation is true for all x, then the coefficients of the same powers of x on each side of an equation are equal. If $ax^2 + (1-a)x + 3b = 4x^2 + (b+2)x + c$ is true for all x, then using the above rule, a = 4, (1-a) = (b+2) and 3b = c. These equations can be used to solve for first a, then b, then c. In this case, a = 4, b = -5, and c = -15.

Chapter 11   Algebra and Real-World Problems

Simplifying Polynomial Equations

Combine like terms

Combine all coefficients of like powers of x on the left side to simplify the equation. For example, $-4 + 2x + x^2 = 6x + 14x^2$ can be simplified by subtracting the right side from both sides of the equation and combining like terms: $-4 + (2x-6x) + (x^2-14x^2) = 0$. After combining like terms, we can arrive at the equation in standard form: $-13x^2 - 4x - 4 = 0$.

Factor by the largest power of x that will divide through all terms

$x^4 + x^3 - 6x^2 = 0$. This can be factored in this manner as $x^2(x^2 + x - 6) = 0$. The expression in parenthesis can also be factored producing $x^2(x+3)(x-2) = 0$. Solutions: 0, 0, -3, and 2.

Radical Equations

Equations involving even roots must be treated with special care. For example, what value(s) of x solve equation (1): $\sqrt{2x-5} = x - 4$? Because x is under the square root radical, both sides of (1) must be squared to produce (2) $2x - 5 = (x-4)^2$. Expanding the quadratic of (2) gives us $2x - 5 = x^2 - 8x + 16$. Bring all terms to the right to put this in standard quadratic form: $0 = x^2 - 10x + 21$. This is easily factored: (3) $0 = (x-7)(x-3)$. The solutions to (3) are $x = 7$ and $x = 3$. Are these both solutions to the original radical equation (1)? Let's check. Remember, $\sqrt{}$ always refers to the principal, or *positive* root. Plugging 7 into (1): $\sqrt{14-5} = 7 - 4$, or $3 = 3$. This is true, so $x = 7$ solves (1). Now check $x = -3$. Plugging 3 into (1): $\sqrt{6-5} = 3 - 4$, or $1 = -1$. This is false, so $x = 3$ does *not* solve (1). The only solution to root equation (1) is $x = 7$.

Consider (2) $x^{5/4} = -32$. Raise each side to the power of 4/5: $x = [\,(-32)^{1/5}\,]^4 = [-2]^4 = 16$. If the numerator of the reciprocal power is an even number, the solution must be checked because this method can introduce extraneous roots. Plug 16 in (2) → (3) $(16)^{5/4} = -32$. Let's break this down as $(16^{1/4})^5$. Now $(16^{1/4}) = 2$ (the principal root), so $(16^{1/4})^5 = 32$. Therefore equation (3) becomes $32 = -32$, which is false. So (2) has no solution.

Proportion Equations

Equations involving proportions are solved by isolating the variable. This may involve inverting each side of the equation. For example,

$2/3 = 10/x$. Inverting both sides, $3/2 = x/10$, and so $30/2 = x = 15$.

$25/x = x/1$. Multiplying both sides by x, $25 = x^2$, which means $x = \pm 5$.

$4x^2 = 15/y$. Inverting both sides and solving for y yields $1/(4x^2) = y/15$, or $15/(4x^2) = y$.

Inverse Proportionality

By definition, if y is inversely proportional to x, then $y = a/x$, where a is the constant of proportionality. For example, if $y = 3/x$, y and x are inversely proportional. Also, note that if two variables are inversely proportional, then $xy = $ a constant. In this example, $xy = 3$.

Joint Variation

A variable z varies jointly with x and y if $z = kxy$, where k is a constant.

Combined Variation

If $z = kx^n y^m$, where k, n, and m are constants, then z is said to vary with x and y in a combined manner. The constants may be positive or negative. Joint variation is just the case of combined variation, where $m = n = 1$. You may have seen combined variation describing chemical rate equations. There is an archetype employing combined variation.

Integer Equations

If an equation has a form $m = ny$, where m and n are integers, then y must be an integer or a rational number. If m is *prime*, then either $n = m$ and $y = 1$, or $n = 1$ and $y = m$.

Problems With Fewer Equations Than Unknowns

In general, you need a system of n simultaneous equations to solve for the unknown values of n variables. But there are exceptions to this. We'll cover simultaneous equations in depth in chapter 12.

Some problems have two unknowns, say x and y, and only one equation. These problems will almost always either ask you to solve for x in terms of y, or to solve for some combination of x and y, such as xy or x/y. For example, if $y = 6x$, one may solve for $y/x = 6$, where $x \neq 0$.

Chapter 11 Algebra and Real-World Problems

Likewise, consider the equation ax = by + cz. You could solve for x in terms of y and z. If you were given two equations involving x, y, and z, you could find expressions for each of the variables in terms of either one of the other variables. However, in general, only with three equations could you determine the values of x, y, and z. Much more of this will be encountered in chapter 12.

Absolute Values In Algebraic Equations

|f(x,y,...)| = z implies that either f(x,y,...) = z, or f(x,y,...) = -z. For example, if | x+4 | = 3, then either x + 4 = 3, or x + 4 = -3. Therefore, x = -1 or x = -7.

Solving Polynomial Equations With Change of Variables

Consider the quadratic equation $(z-3)^2 - 6(z-3) + 9 = 0$. If we let x = z - 3, we can rewrite this equation x^2 - 6x + 9 = 0. This is easily factorable: (x - 3)(x - 3) = 0, which has two identical roots at x = 3. Since z = x + 3, z = 3 + 3 = 6 solves the original equation.

The Quadratic Formula

A quadratic equation in standard form, ax^2 + bx + c = 0, may be solved for the two roots using the coefficients a, b and c:

$$x = \frac{-b \pm \sqrt{b^2 - 4ac}}{2a}$$

Math questions on the SAT may occasionally require the quadratic formula to obtain a solution. But always try factoring first - it's usually much faster.

The sum of the two solutions (x-intercepts) equals -b/a, and their product equals c/a.

The Quadratic Discriminant

The discriminant of a quadratic equation in standard form is D = b^2 - 4ac, the argument of the radical in the quadratic formula above. How is this useful? If D is less than zero, both solutions are complex, and the parabola never touches the x-axis. If D equals zero, the roots are real and identical. If D is greater than zero, there are two real, distinct roots.

Vertex Form

A quadratic equation in standard form, $ax^2 + bx + c = 0$ may be recast into the vertex form. The vertex is the point on the quadratic's parabolic graph crossing its vertical line of symmetry. At the vertex the parabola has its least or greatest value depending on whether the parabola is convex (a>0) or concave (a<0). Without developing the proof,

(1) $y = ax^2 + bx + c \leftrightarrow y = a(x - h)^2 + k$, where $h = -b/2a$ and $k = c - b^2/4a$

The vertex of the quadratic at point (h,k) lies on the vertical line of symmetry, x = h, and the value of the function at the vertex, its vertical distance from the x axis, is k = y(h). Of course, any quadratic equation in standard form can be solved (find its roots) using the quadratic formula. However, by casting a quadratic equation in vertex form, a great deal of the character and shape of the function can be immediately discerned.

Consider the function $y = 2x^2 - 4x + 4$. This is not easily factorable, but this function, recast in vertex form using (1), becomes $y = 2(x - (-4/4))^2 + (4 - 16/8) = 2(x-1)^2 + 2$. This is a convex parabola (facing up) because a is positive, whose line of symmetry at the vertex is x = 1, and whose minimum at the vertex is y = 2. The vertex is at the point (1,2). Because it is convex and the vertex is above the x-axis, we know that the roots are complex.

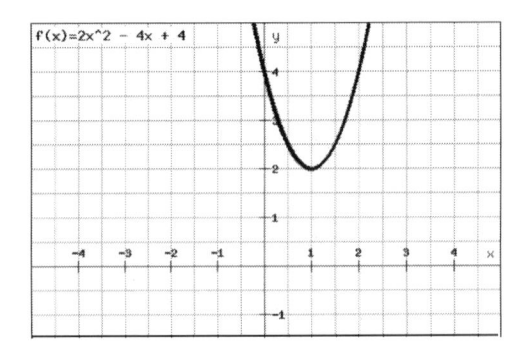

Inequalities

When multiplying inequalities by a negative number, reverse the direction of the inequality: if x > y, then -x < -y.

If |x - y| < z, then x - y < z *and* x - y > -z, or in compact form, –z < x - y < z

If |x - y| > z, then x - y > z *and* x - y < -z

Chapter 11   Algebra and Real-World Problems

Given an expression such as |a - b|, if you know or can assume a > b, you can remove the absolute value brackets: |a - b| = a - b.

Polynomial Factors and Division

If (x-a) is a factor of f(x), then f(x) can be represented (1) f(x) = (x-a)g(x), where g(x) is a lower order polynomial than f(x). If (x-a) is a factor of f(x), f(a) is zero: plug x=a into (1). Alternatively, if f(c) = b, where b is a constant, then f(x) may be separated into parts: (x-c)d(x) + b, where d(x) is a lower order polynomial, and b is a constant remainder.

Polynomial division is performed by the same procedure as arithmetic long division. On the SAT, the divisor will always be a lower order polynomial than the dividend. For example:

$$2x-1 \overline{\smash{\big)}\, -4x^2 + 4x + 5}$$

with quotient $-2x+1$:

$-4x^2 + 2x$

$2x + 5$
$2x - 1$

6

Divide $-4x^2$ by $2x$ and put the $-2x$ on top. Multiply the divisor by $-2x$ and place $-4x^2 + 2x$ on line 3. Subtract line 3 from the dividend and continue just like in long division.

In this example, there is a remainder of 6, meaning that the resulting quotient equals $-2x + 1 + \frac{6}{2x-1}$.

Factoring Cubic Equations

Cubic equations occur occasionally on the SAT - in general, you won't have to solve them. However, certain cubic equations may be factored to facilitate a solution. One particular class of cubic equations occurs when the linear and constant terms together are a factor of the cubic and quadratic terms together. An example will clarify this idea:

$2x^3 - 6x^2 + x - 3 = 0$ may be factored as $2x^2(x-3) + (x-3) = 0$. Both terms in this rendering each have a common factor, (x-3). This is the trick. By isolating this factor and rearranging, $(x-3)(2x^2+1) = 0$. In this form the factors in each parenthesis can be solved

275

(when do they equal zero?) separately. This cubic equation has one real solution from the linear factor, 3, and two imaginary solutions from the quadratic factor: $\pm i/\sqrt{2}$.

Factoring Higher Order Equations

Occasionally on may find equations of orders higher than 3 that may be factored in a way to allow solutions to be developed. For example, if $x^3(x^2 - 5) = -4x$, where $x > 0$, what is one value of x that solves the equation? Rearranging this fifth order equation into standard form, $x^5 - 5x^3 + 4x = 0$. This looks tough, but note the missing even powers of x. We can factor this as $x(x^4 - 5x^2 + 4) = 0$. Okay, x= 0 is a solution, but we need a value of $x > 0$. When does (1) $x^4 - 5x^2 + 4 = 0$? This equation is actually *quadratic in x^2*, and that quadratic equation can be easily factored. Thus, equation (1) becomes $(x^2 - 4)(x^2 - 1) = 0$. See? The solutions to this are clearly $x^2 = 4$ and $x^2 = 1$. So $x = \pm 2$ and $x = \pm 1$. Including x = 0, our 5th order equation has 5 real solutions: 0, ±2, and ±1.

Chapter 11 Algebra and Real-World Problems

SAT Archetypes

Translating Verbal Algebra Into Symbolic Math

When x is multiplied by 5, the product is the same as when 16 is added to x. What is the value of 5x?

(A) 4
(B) 20
(C) 50
(D) 80

How do I start?

Carefully express the verbal expressions involving x as one algebraic equation. "Is the same as" clearly denotes an equality. Note that the answer is the value of 5x, not x.

Solution

From the data given, $5x = 16 + x$. Rearranging to solve for x, $4x = 16$, and therefore, $x = 4$. So $5x = 20$. An easy one, once in a while.

Answer B

The Take-Away

Verbal-math translation problems simply require that you carefully express the components of each expression in the equation into mathematical terms. Again, read all questions carefully (they want 5x, not x, above). Surprisingly, this problem is missed fairly often. But strap in. It's about to get *very* bumpy.

Algebra and Real-World Problems   Chapter 11

Word Problems: Confusing Additions and Subtractions

How many gallons of gasoline were in the tank at the beginning of a trip if x gallons were burned and y gallons were purchased during the trip, and z gallons are currently in the tank?

(A) z - x - y
(B) z + x - y
(C) y - x + z
(D) y - z + x

How do I start?

This problem is straightforward if you read carefully and account for each term correctly. Compose the trip in terms of the current amount of gas. The current amount of gas must be equal to the amount at the beginning of the trip plus the amount purchased during the trip minus the total amount that was burned on the trip.

Solution

(1) Current = Beginning + Purchased - Burned. Substituting the symbols from the problem into this equation, (2) z = Beginning + y - x. Therefore, (3) Beginning = z - y + x.

Answer B

The Take-Away

Some real-world word problems are usually pretty easy once you take the time to understand the underlying situation, or story, of the problem. Often, some answer choices will stand out because the signs seem correct. In the above problem, x, the amount burned, reduces the volume of gas, and it might seem likely that it would have a negative sign in the final expression. However, depending on how the terms in the governing equation (equation (1) above) must be rearranged, a term might end up on "the other side of the equation," and a likely negative candidate may end up with a positive sign in the answer. Like x in equation (3) above. So don't be too quick to whittle the choices down based on a cursory examination of the signs of variables. Had we been asked to develop an expression for the *current* amount of gas based on the other variables, then (as seen in equation (2) in the solution above) x would have provided a negative contribution in the final answer.

Chapter 11 　　　　　　　　　　　　　　　　　　　　Algebra and Real-World Problems

Direct Algebraic Substitution

If $a = 6(c^2 - c + 4)$ and $b = -c + 2$, what is a in terms of b?

(A) $6b^2 - 11b + 24$
(B) $3b^2 - 20b + 24$
(C) $6b^2 - 80b + 24$
(D) $6b^2 - 18b + 36$

How do I start?

The quadratic expression for a in terms of c doesn't seem easily factorable, and in any event we aren't looking for a quadratic solution; we have to put a in terms of b. There may be nothing to do here but brute-force substitution. Using the second equation, express c in terms of b and plug that into the first equation.

Solution

From the second equation, $c = 2 - b$. Plugging this expression into the first equation yields (1) $a = 6[(2-b)^2 - (2-b) + 4]$. Expanding the quadratic in (1), $a = 6(4 - 4b + b^2 - 2 + b + 4) = 24 - 24b + 6b^2 - 12 + 6b + 24 = 6b^2 - 18b + 36$.

Alternate Solution

Notice the 6: if $a = 6(c^2 - c + 4)$, then (after the substitution of $c = 2 - b$ is made) the coefficients of b and b^2 (as well as the constant) must be divisible by 6. Only (D) satisfies this feature. As we have seen, some hard problems have built in shortcuts. Look around the periphery of a problem before launching into a straightforward slash and burn solution.

Answer D

The Take-Away

Most "what is a in terms of b" problems require brute-force substitution. In this problem, the quadratic expression, $c^2 - c + 4$, does not have real roots, and is not easily factorable. In any event, the choices are not factored. Substituting c in terms of b is the only way to get c in terms of b. But check out the alternate solution. Think → Choices → Shortcut!

And just a random reminder - practically every polynomial on the SAT that *can be* easily factored will have factors with integer-valued or other simple (for example, $\sqrt{2}$) coefficients.

Algebra and Real-World Problems   Chapter 11

Brute-Force Algebraic Isolation

If $\dfrac{ab}{a+c} = -1$, where $b \neq -1$, which expression below is a in terms of b and c?

(A) $\dfrac{c+1}{b-1}$

(B) $\dfrac{c-1}{b+1}$

(C) $-\dfrac{c}{b-1}$

(D) $-\dfrac{c}{b+1}$

How do I start?

There is no easy out here. You must isolate a in this equation. Multiply both sides by a+c, and then gather the a terms on the left, in order to solve for a in terms of b and c.

Solution

Note that a+c cannot equal zero. Multiplying both sides by a+c yields ab = -(a+c). Gathering the a terms on the left yields ab + a = -c. Factoring a out of each term on the left, a(b+1) = -c. Now divide each side by (b+1) to isolate a: a = -c/(b+1).

Alternate Solution

If b cannot equal -1, there is a good bet that the answer will have b+1 in the denominator (to avoid division by zero). Eliminate (A) and (C). After multiplying both sides by a+c, you can eliminate (A) and (B) by noting that any expression of a must include a factor or term of -c. The only choice left is (D). But the brute-force solution here is probably the safer path on the test. While such pre-solution analysis can sometimes save significant time, one may easily generate a mistake in that phase since it mostly relies on head-math.

Answer D

The Take-Away

Some straightforward algebra problems are of the type "put x in terms of y and z". They often will require a manual rearrangement in order to isolate one variable (or a combination of variables). Usually the algebra is quickly handled - go for it.

Chapter 11　　　　　　　　　　　　　　　　　　　　Algebra and Real-World Problems

Raising Both Sides by the Inverse Power

If $a > 12$ and $\dfrac{8}{\sqrt{a-12}} = 16$ what is the value of a?

(A) 12.25
(B) 12.5
(C) 13.5
(D) 14

How do I start?

Since the variable of interest, a, is inside a square root, square both sides of the equation, and solve for a.

Solution

Rearrange the equation to put the radical on the right side: (1) $8 = 16\sqrt{a-12}$. Note that it is safe to do this since $a > 12$. Since a is in an expression raised to the power of 1/2, squaring both sides yields $64 = 256(a - 12)$. Dividing by 256, $1/4 = a - 12$. Solving for a gives $a = 12.25$. Because we raised by an even power, we'd better check if 12.25 solves equation (1) above: $8 = 16 \cdot (12.25 - 12)^{1/2} = 16 \cdot (1/4)^{1/2} = 16/2 = 8$. So $8 = 8$. Check. Note that we had to take the principal, or positive square root of $(1/4)^{1/2}$.

Alternate Solution

The value of $\sqrt{a-12}$ must be .5 in order for the equation in the question to hold. As a result, the argument of the radical must be the square of .5, or .25. Therefore, a - 12 = .25, so 12.25.

Answer A

The Take-Away

In algebra problems containing square roots or other exponents, raising each side of the equation to the inverse power can be an effective method of isolating the variable of interest. The square root radical above was eliminated by squaring both sides of the equation. Is the variable of interest raised to the power of a/b? Raising both sides of the equation to the power of b/a may be necessary. However, if b is even, the solution(s) should be checked. And if a is even, ± roots must be included in the solution. See the review above on radical equations for more on this.

Algebra and Real-World Problems　　　　　　　　　　　　　　　　　　Chapter 11

Algebraic Common Denominators

What is the sum of $\frac{1}{x}$, $\frac{2}{3x}$, and $\frac{9}{27x}$?

(A) $\frac{x}{2}$

(B) $\frac{2}{x}$

(C) $x^2 - 27$

(D) $\frac{3x}{25}$

How do I start?

Express all the algebraic fractions using a common denominator and add them together.

Solution

Even though there is a variable in the denominator, find the lowest common denominator, or least common multiple, just like you would arithmetically, and add the fractions. The LCM of the three denominators is 27x. Putting each of the fractional expressions in terms of this common denominator, the sum becomes 27/(27x) + 2·9/(27x) + 9/(27x) = 54/(27x) = 2/x.

Alternate Solution

The last term can be simplified to 1/3x. Therefore, the last two terms sum to 3/3x, or 1/x. When this is added to the first term, the complete sum is 1/x + 1/x = 2/x.

Alternate Solution II

The answer *must* be proportional to 1/x, not x nor x^2. Only choice (B) is proportional to 1/x.

Alternate Solution III

As x approaches zero, the sum must approach infinity. Only choice (B) blows up at zero.

Answer B

The Take-Away

Operations on algebraic expressions that have variables as part of fractions can be simplified (using an LCM common denominator) just like arithmetic fractions. Check out alternate solutions II and III. Think about the behavior of any expressions you are given.

Chapter 11　　　　　　　　　　　　　　　　　　　Algebra and Real-World Problems

Inverse Proportionality

If $f(t)$ is inversely proportional to t and $f(4) = -3$, what is the value of $f(3)$?

(A) -1/3
(B) -4/3
(C) -1
(D) -4

How do I start?

By definition, if $f(t)$ is inversely proportional to t, then $f(t)$ is a constant times $1/t$. They give you the data point $f(4) = -3$, in other words, $f = -3$ when $t = 4$. From this you can calculate the constant of proportionality, which you will need to calculate $f(3)$.

Solution

So, (1) $f(t) = a/t$, where a is the constant of proportionality. When $t = 4$, $f(4) = -3$; using this and (1) we get $f(4) = a/4 = -3$. Solving for a, $a = -12$. Therefore, using this constant of proportionality, the function $f(t)$ is completely described: $f(t) = -12/t$. Thus, $f(3) = -12/3 = -4$.

Alternate Solution

Since $f(t)$ is inversely proportional to t, $f(t) = a/t$. Thus, we see that (2) $f(t) \cdot t = a$. So $f(t) \cdot t$ is a *constant* for *all* values of t. Using (2) when $t = 4$ and $f(4) = -3$, $-3 \cdot 4 = -12 = a$. Now you can infer that $f(3) \cdot 3$ *also* equals -12. Thus, $f(3) \cdot 3 = -12$, and rearranging, $f(3) = -12/3 = -4$.

Alternate Solution II

From their inverse relationship, as t gets closer to zero, $f(t)$ gets further away from zero. Obviously, 3 is closer to zero than 4, so $f(3)$ must be further from zero than $f(4)$. Since $f(4) = -3$, $f(3)$ must be further from zero than -3. Only (D) is further from zero than -3.

Answer D

The Take-Away

When a function $f(x)$ is inversely proportional to the independent variable, it means that $f(x) = a/x$, where a is a constant of proportionality. Knowing any pair of values [x, $f(x)$] will allow you to calculate the constant of proportionality. This can then be used to get *any* value of $f(x)$, given x. Also - look at alternate solution II. Yet another smart shortcut.

Algebra and Real-World Problems   Chapter 11

Direct Proportionality, With Two Unknowns

If s varies directly as t, and if s = -2 when t = x, and if s = 10 when t = x + 4, what is the value of x?

(A) –2/3
(B) -1/3
(C) 0
(D) 3

How do I start?

From the definition of direct proportionality, s = m•t, true for all t, where m is the constant of proportionality and t is the independent variable. When t = x (note that x is an unknown *constant value* in this problem) we are told that s = m•x = -2. We can rearrange this now to solve for the constant of proportionality: m = -2/x. This expression for m in terms of x can be used in the second set of equations to solve to x.

Solution

We have two implied simultaneous equations: (1) -2 = mx, and (2) 10 = m(x+4), where m is the constant of proportionality. From (1), m = -2/x. Substituting this expression into (2), 10 = -2/x • (x+4) = -2 + -8/x. Therefore, 12 = -8/x. Isolating x, x = -8/12 = -2/3.

Answer A

The Take-Away

When a function f(t) is directly proportion to the independent variable, it means that f(t) = a•t, where a is a constant. Knowing any pairs of values, t, and f(t), will allow you to calculate the constant of proportionality, a. This can then be used to get any value of f(t). In this problem, they threw in an additional unknown constant, x, to force you to use a second equation and another pair of values. Note also that the use of x as a constant is meant to be purposefully confusing. Thanks, SAT. As we've already seen, the SAT occasionally presents math problems that are verbally frustrating.

Chapter 11 | Algebra and Real-World Problems

Dividing One Variable by Another to Solve for the Ratio

If $\dfrac{(2y-6x)}{y} = \dfrac{3}{4}$, what is the value of y/x?

SR

How do I start?

This is one equation with two unknowns. It is underdetermined: you could solve y in terms of x (or vice versa), or the ratio of y/x or x/y. It looks like it might take a lot of steps. However, if you divide both top and bottom by y on the left hand side and solve for x/y, you've already cast the equation in terms of the ratio (its inverse, actually) required.

Solution

The left expression has y in the denominator, so y ≠ 0. And they are asking for the value of y/x, so y ≠ 0. First, divide the left side's top and bottom by y and solve for x/y. This results in 2 - 6x/y = 3/4. This gives x/y = 5/24. Inverting both sides gives y/x = 24/5, or 4.8.

Alternate Solution

Divide top and bottom by x: (1) (2y/x - 6)/(y/x) = 3/4. This puts the equation in terms of y/x, which may be isolated by rearranging (1).

Alternate Solution II

Brute force the equation into the form y = f(x). Multiply both sides by y to give 2y = 3y/4 + 6x. Combining y terms on the left gives 5y/4 = 6x. Isolating y yields y = 24x/5. Dividing both sides by x gives us what we want, y/x = 24/5.

Answer 24/5 or 4.8

The Take-Away

One linear equation with two unknowns in the form y = ax, where a is a constant, can always be solved for the ratio y/x (and x/y), assuming y ≠ 0 and x ≠ 0. Now, the equation given in the question isn't in this form, but multiplying both sides by y we can see that it is a linear equation. Also, generally, you are free to multiply or divide the top and bottom of an expression by any variable or algebraic expression in order to cast the equation in terms of a ratio of variables (as long as you don't multiply or divide by zero).

Algebra and Real-World Problems   Chapter 11

Algebraic Relationships: Simpler Than They Look

If $\dfrac{2}{(x+y)^{\frac{1}{3}}} = 2(x+y)^{\frac{1}{3}}$, where $x + y \neq 0$, which of the following might be true?

(A) $(x + y)^3 = 2$

(B) $x + y = 0$

(C) $(x+y)^{\frac{1}{3}} = 2$

(D) $x = 1 - y$

How do I start?

Forget suicide. Express the denominator of the left-hand side with a negative exponent.

Solution

First, toss (B). They already told you that $x + y \neq 0$. Expressing the denominator of the left hand side with a negative exponent gives $2\cdot(x+y)^{\frac{-1}{3}} = 2\cdot(x+y)^{\frac{1}{3}}$. Dividing both sides by 2, $(x+y)^{\frac{-1}{3}} = (x+y)^{\frac{1}{3}}$. The only values that are the inverse of themselves are ±1, which means $x + y = \pm 1$. Isolating x: (1) $x = \pm 1 - y$. Comparing (1) to (D), we see that (D) is true.

Alternate Solution

Multiplying both sides by $(x+y)^{1/3}$ yields $2 = 2\cdot(x+y)^{2/3}$. Again, x+y must equal ±1.

Alternate solution II

A quick eye might see that if (D) $x = 1 - y$, then the original equation reduces to $2 = 2$.

Answer D

The Take-Away

Always look for shortcuts to complicated algebraic rearrangement problems on the SAT.

Chapter 11 — Algebra and Real-World Problems

Joint Variation

Curtis proposes that the growth rate of a certain fungus is proportional to the temperature multiplied by the humidity (within certain narrow limits of these variables). Ignoring the units, the rate is 120 when the temperature is 90 and the humidity is 3. Assuming the model is correct, what would be the growth rate when the temperature is 60 and the humidity is 6?

SR

How do I start?

Express the relationship mathematically: $R = kTH$, where R is the rate, T is the temperature, H is the humidity, and k is the constant of proportionality. R is said to jointly vary with T and H. In the first set of conditions, you know everything but k. Solve for k first, then solve for the rate in the second set of conditions.

Solution

$R = kTH$. Use the data in the first scenario ($R = 120$, $T = 90$, and $H = 3$) to solve for k: $k = R/TH = 120/(90 \cdot 3) = 4/9$. Knowing constant k, we have a fully defined relationship between all three variables, R, T, and H: $R = 4/9 \cdot TH$. If $T = 60$, and $H = 6$, then the rate, $R = 4/9 \cdot 60 \cdot 6 = 160$.

Alternate Solution

The rate is proportional to both temperature and humidity. If the humidity is changed by a factor of 2, and the temperature is scaled by a factor of $60/90 = 2/3$, then the rate will be scaled by a factor of $2 \cdot 2/3 = 4/3$. So the scaled rate $= 4/3 \cdot$ (original rate) $= 4/3 \cdot 120 = 160$.

Answer 160

The Take-Away

On joint variation problems, you'll likely be given a mathematical equation that describes the joint variation (with an unknown constant of proportionality), or a verbal description of a model, as exampled above, from which you must determine the constant of proportionality. In the alternate solution we used the property of joint variation to vary the temperature and humidity separately. Sometimes such an approach might save a little time, especially if the ratios can be calculated in your head.

Algebra and Real-World Problems   Chapter 11

Combined Variation

If $z = kx^n y^m$, where k, n, and m are constants, what is the value of z when $x = 6$ and $y = 3$, given the following table of values:

z	x	y
5	1	2
10	2	2
5	2	4

SR

How do I start?

The trick to solving combined variation problems is to use the table of values to find pairs of rows where one variable (x or y) changes and the other variable doesn't change. For example, y doesn't change values between the first and second row, but x doubles from 1 to 2. Since $z = kx^n y^m$, look at what happens to z in this case.

Solution

y = 2 in both the first and second rows. We see x double from 1 to 2, and the value of z also doubles from 5 to 10. Since y^m didn't change, and the constant of proportionality, k, never changes, the only way for z to double if x doubles is if the right side varies as x^1, i.e., n = 1. So $z = kx^1 y^m$. Now find a pair of rows where y changes, but x does not. Comparing the 2nd row to the 3rd, when y is doubled from 2 to 4, z is *halved* from 10 to 5. In other words, a factor of two is transformed into a factor of 1/2. Since x^1 and k didn't change, the only way for this to happen is if z is proportional to 1/y, or y^{-1}. Therefore, m = -1. Now you know everything about the function z but k: (1) $z = kx^1 y^{-1}$. Any of the scenarios (rows) can now be used to calculate k. From the 1st row, using $z = k \cdot x/y$, $5 = k \cdot 1/2$. Rearranging to solve for k, k = 10. Using this in (1), z = 10x/y. The function z is now fully defined. If x = 6 and y = 3, then z = 60/3 = 20.

Alternate Solution

After you find two rows where only one variable on the right side changes value, take the "column-by-column ratio" of the two rows. If you divide row 2 by row 1 (you are actually pairwise dividing terms in the general equation), $10/5 = [k \cdot (2)^n \cdot 2^m]/[(k \cdot 1^n \cdot 2^m)]$. Simplifying, $2 = 2^n$, and so n = 1. You can proceed with the other constant m in like fashion.

Answer 20

Chapter 11   Algebra and Real-World Problems

The Take-Away

If you encounter a combined variation problem, you'll likely be given the general formula as in the problem above. You must then select pairs of scenarios, or rows in a table to eliminate changes in all but one variable. Values for variables are almost always in simple ratios, like 2:1. It is then easy to determine the exponents that govern the variation.

Calculating $x^2 - y^2$ from $(x + y)$ and $(x - y)$

Let $x = \dfrac{a+b}{b}$ and $y = \dfrac{a-b}{b}$, where a and b are real and $b \neq 0$. Which of the following expressions equals $x^2 - y^2$?

(A) $-4a$
(B) $-4(a+b)$
(C) $\dfrac{a}{b}$
(D) $\dfrac{4a}{b}$

How do I start?

You can calculate x^2 and y^2 directly and then perform the subtraction, but let's first try the relationship we suspect may be useful: $x^2 - y^2 = (x+y)(x-y)$.

Solution

Plugging in the given expressions for x and y into $(x+y)$ and $(x-y)$ yields $(x+y) = (a+b + a-b)/b = 2a/b$, and $(x-y) = ((a+b) - (a-b))/b = 2b/b = 2$. So $x^2 - y^2 = (x+y)\cdot(x-y) = 2a/b \cdot 2 = 4a/b$.

Alternate Solution

Squaring x directly gives $x^2 = (a^2 + b^2 + 2ab)/b^2$. Squaring y gives $y^2 = (a^2 + b^2 - 2ab)/b^2$. From these expressions (after some algebra), $x^2 - y^2 = 4ab/b^2 = 4a/b$. This direct approach is okay here, but what if the expressions for x and y were more complicated? The equation $x^2 - y^2 = (x+y)(x-y)$ must be at the ready at all times.

Answer D

Algebra and Real-World Problems   Chapter 11

The Take-Away

Whenever you see questions that have (x+y) and (x-y), or $x^2 - y^2$, suspect that the relationships between these terms may be useful. Direct calculation may be possible without them, but using these relationships can sometimes save valuable time. Like here.

Relationship Between $x^2 - y^2$, and the Average of x and y

If $x^2 - y^2 = z$, where x and y are non-negative integers, and if the average of x and y is 2, then what is the value of x - y?

(A) $\frac{z}{4}$
(B) 1
(C) z
(D) 2xy -z

How do I start?

Whenever you see either $x^2 - y^2$ or (x+y)(x-y), you may need our well-known relationship (1) $x^2 - y^2 = (x+y)(x-y)$. You are given the *average* of x and y: (x+y)/2 = 2. From the average of x and y, you can get the value of x+y. Note that x and y non-negative integers.

Solution

If the average of x and y is 2, x + y = 4. Possible (x,y) values could be (0,4), (1,3), (3,1), and (4,0). Not one of these produces a value of x - y in the choices. Using x + y = 4 in equation (1), $x^2 - y^2 = z = (x+y)(x-y) = 4(x-y)$. So 4(x-y) = z. Isolating x - y, x - y = z/4.

Alternate Solution

If $x^2 - y^2 = z = (x+y)(x-y)$, and the average (and thus sum) of x and y is a constant, then x - y must be proportional to only z. The only choice fitting this behavior is (A).

Answer A

The Take-Away

Whenever you see the expression $x^2 - y^2$, you should suspect that factoring this expression into (x+y)(x-y) may be useful. Also, given the average of several terms, you might suspect that their sum may be useful when developing a solution.

Chapter 11　　　　　　　　　　　　　　　　　　　　　Algebra and Real-World Problems

Equating Coefficients of the Same Powers of x

If a and b are constants and $2x^2 + ax - 3$ equals $(2x+1)(x+b)$ for all values of x, which is the correct value of a?

(A) -5
(B) -4
(C) 1
(D) 4

How do I start?

This looks like one equation with two unknowns. Except the equation is true *for all x*, and whenever that is true, coefficients multiplying the same powers of x must be equal on both sides of the equation. So there are actually three equations. Expand the right side to put it in standard polynomial form: $ax^2 + bx + c$.

Solution

Expand the two factors on the right side to form a quadratic expression in standard form: $(2x+1)(x+b) = 2x^2 + x(2b+1) + b$. We are told that this is equivalent to quadratic expression on the left. Thus, (1) $2x^2 + ax - 3 = 2x^2 + x(2b+1) + b$. If these expressions are equal for all x, then the coefficients multiplying the same powers of x must be equal. In (1), the coefficient of x^2 is 2 on both sides. While this is one equation, it has no variables: 2 = 2. Nothing learned here. However, the constant and x^1 terms on either side of (1) provide two equations with the two unknowns, a and b. Equating the constant terms we see that b = -3. If the coefficients of the x^1 terms are equal, then a = 2b+1 = 2•(-3) + 1 = -5.

Answer = A

The Take-Away

In a polynomial equation that is true for all values of x, the coefficients multiplying the same powers of x on the left side must be equal to the coefficients of those same powers on the right side. When working with polynomial equations, it is often necessary to put both polynomials in expanded, standard form, $ax^2 + bx + c$.

By the way, why is this true? Let $ax^2 + bx + c = dx^2 + ex + f$. Bring all terms over to the left side and combine like powers of x: $(a-d)x^2 + (b-e)x + (c-f) = 0$. If this is true for all x, then it must be true that a=d, b=e, and c=f.

Algebra and Real-World Problems   Chapter 11

Quadratic Equations with Change of Variables

$$\frac{1}{(z-3)^2 - 6(z-3) + 9}$$

What value of z will cause the above expression to be undefined?

SR

How do I start?

The expression will be undefined when the denominator equals zero. You could expand the quadratic term in the denominator and then collect like terms, but the form of the denominator suggests a change of variables.

Solution

The denominator, $(z-3)^2 - 6(z-3) + 9$, has a $(z - 3)^2$ term, a $(z - 3)^1$ term, and a constant, 9. This expression is quadratic in (z - 3). If we let (1) x = z - 3, we can rewrite the denominator as x^2 - 6x + 9. This quadratic is easily factorable: $(x - 3)^2$. Therefore, the denominator has two zeroes, both of which are x = 3. From (1), z = x + 3. So the original expression given at the top of the problem will be undefined when x = 3, or z = 3 + 3 = 6.

Alternate Solution

You could keep the original variable z, expand the $(z - 3)^2$ term, and gather like terms in the denominator. Doing so yields the denominator z^2 - 12z + 36, which may be factored into (z - 6)(z - 6). With a bit more time.

Answer 6

The Take-Away

Some quadratic expressions and equations will be drafted in such a way that a change of variables is suggested. Look for it right under your nose.

Chapter 11 Algebra and Real-World Problems

Quadratic Equations Solved with Quadratic Formula

$$3(z-1)^2 - 6(z-1) + 3 = -3$$

Which of the expressions below is a solution to the above equation?

(A) -1 + i
(B) 1 - i
(C) 2 + i
(D) 4 + i

How do I start?

Once again, you could expand the quadratic term $(z - 1)^2$ and then collect like terms, but the form of this expression suggests a change of variables.

Solution

Pulling everything over on the left side: $3(z-1)^2 - 6(z-1) + 6 = 0$. This quadratic has a $(z - 1)^2$ term, a $(z - 1)^1$ term, and a constant, 6. This expression is quadratic in $(z - 1)$. If we let (1) x = z - 1, we can rewrite it in standard form as $3x^2 - 6x + 6 = 0$. We can factor out 3 from each term, yielding $3(x^2 - 2x + 2) = 0$. We can now ignore the factor of 3 and solve the quadratic equation $x^2 - 2x + 2 = 0$. However, this is not easily factorable and we have to use the quadratic formula to find its solutions.

Using the quadratic formula to solve the equation $x^2 - 2x + 2 = 0$, x = $(2 \pm \sqrt{4-8})/2$ = $(2 \pm 2\sqrt{-1})/2$ = 1 ± i. So x = 1 ± i. From the change of variable (1), we know that z = x + 1, and thus the solutions to the quadratic in z are z = 1 ± i + 1 = 2 ± i. (C) works.

Answer C

The Take-Away

Some quadratic equations may require the use of the quadratic formula. And don't expect every solution to be real. And be prepared to employ a change of variables.

Algebra and Real-World Problems · Chapter 11

Polynomial Division (1)

Assume x >1. When -4x² + 4x + 5 is divided by 2x - 1 the answer is -2x + 1 + r/(2x - 1). What must the value of r be?

SR

How do I start?

There are two ways to solve this problem. Perform the long division (probably not too time consuming) or look for a shortcut involving the constant 5, and the remainder, r.

Solution

The long division of two polynomials is performed exactly like the long division of two numbers. If unsure, see the review.

$$
\begin{array}{r}
-2x+1 \\
2x-1 \overline{\smash{)}\,-4x^2+4x+5} \\
-4x^2+2x \\
\hline
2x+5 \\
2x-1 \\
\hline
6
\end{array}
$$

The remainder, r, which is the numerator of the term r/(2x - 1), is 6.

Alternate Solution

The problem involves this equation: (-4x²+4x+5)/(2x-1) = (-2x+1) + r/(2x-1). Multiplying each side of this equation by (2x-1) yields: (1) -4x² + 4x + 5 = (-2x+1)(2x-1) + r. Note that we are safe doing this because x>1 and therefore (2x-1) can never equal zero. The constant term on the left side of (1) is 5. However, the constant term resulting from the product of terms within parentheses on the right side of (1) is -1. Thus, the constant r in (1) must account for the difference: 5 = -1 + r. Therefore, the remainder, r, is 6.

Answer 6

The Take-Away

Be familiar with the procedure of polynomial division, but be on the lookout for such shortcuts as presented in the alternate solution.

Chapter 11   Algebra and Real-World Problems

Polynomial Division (2)

Consider the equation $(16x^2 - 16x + 4)/(kx + 3) = (-4x + 1) + 1/(kx + 3)$. Which of the following values of k will make the equation true for all values of $x \neq -3/k$?

(A) -4
(B) -1/3
(C) 1/3
(D) There is no value of k that will make the equation true

How do I start?

In a polynomial equation, the coefficients of each of the several powers of x must be equal to one another.

Solution

Although this problem presents itself as one involving polynomial division, it is not necessary to perform the explicit steps of such division. The equation may be rewritten by multiplying both sides by the divisor on the left-hand side (which may be done because $x \neq -3/k$. This produces (1): $(16x^2 - 16x + 4) = (kx + 3)(-4x + 1) + 1 = -4kx^2 -(12 - k)x + 4$. If equation (1) is true for all allowed values of x, the corresponding coefficients of same powers of x on either side of the equation must be equal. First, and most easily, equating the coefficients for x^2 forces $16 = -4k$, and thus $k = -4$. Just as a check that this value of k solves the equation, equate the coefficients for x^1: $-16 = -12 + k$, which is true if $k = -4$. The constants add up too: $3 + 1 = 4$.

Answer A

The Take-Away

You must be familiar with polynomial division and the algebraic arithmetic necessary to complete the division longhand. However, as shown in the problem above, polynomial division may be presented in the problem, yet the solution to the problem requires other algebraic means (cross-multiplying by the divisor, in this problem).

Algebra and Real-World Problems　　　　　　　　　　　　　　　　　　Chapter 11

Polynomial Factoring (1)

Two functions s(x) and t(x) are given below:

$$s(x) = 3x^3 - 6x^2 + 3x$$
$$t(x) = x^2 - 2x + 1$$

Which of the following expressions is evenly divisible by (3x - 2)?

(A) s(x)/t(x)
(B) s(x) + t(x)
(C) s(x) - 2t(x)
(D) s(x) + 3t(x)

How do I start?

First, notice that even though the polynomials appear to "line up," they are not of the same order. Polynomial s(x) is cubic (with no constant term) and t(x) is quadratic. Polynomial t(x) is actually a factor of s(x), but you'll have to find out how. Put s(x) in terms of t(x). Then find a combination of s(x) and t(x) in the choices given that would be evenly divisible by (3x - 2) – in other words, one where you can pull (3x - 2) out as a factor.

Solution

Polynomial s(x) is cubic (with no constant term) and t(x) is quadratic. However, note that the coefficients of s(x) are related to the coefficients of t(x). Indeed, s(x) may be factored, pulling out the greatest common factor, 3x, to give s(x) = 3x(x² - 2x + 1). And so we see s(x) = 3x•t(x). Hey, that 3x looks familiar. We are looking for a combination of s(x) and t(x) such that the combination is divisible by (3x - 2). Examining choice (A), s(x)/t(x) = 3x, which is <u>not</u> divisible by (3x - 2). The sum (B), s(x) + t(x) = 3x•t(x) + t(x) = (3x + 1)t(x). Which is <u>not</u> divisible by (3x - 2), but we're onto something. The sum (C) is s(x) - 2t(x) = 3x•t(x) - 2t(x) = (3x - 2)t(x). This expression *is* divisible by (3x - 2). This corresponds to choice (C). Look no further.

Answer C

The Take-Away

Problems that involve multiple polynomial expressions may include polynomials that are factors of one another - to make the problem solvable for those clever enough to see it. This may be one of the hardest algebra problems you would ever see on the SAT.

Chapter 11   Algebra and Real-World Problems

Polynomial Factoring (2)

A polynomial function, $f(x)$ equals 1 when $x = -1$. Also, $f(2) = 3$. Which of the choices below must then be true?

(A) When $f(x)$ is divided by $(x-1)$ the remainder is 1
(B) $(x-2)$ is a factor of $f(x)$
(C) $(x-1)$ is a factor of $f(x+1)$
(D) When $f(x)$ is divided by $(x-2)$ the remainder is 3

How do I start?

If $(x-a)$ is a factor of $f(x)$, then $f(x)$ can be represented $f(x) = (x-a)g(x)$, where $g(x)$ is a lower order polynomial than $f(x)$. If $(x-a)$ is a factor of $f(x)$, $f(a)$ is zero. Alternatively, if $f(a) = b$, where b is a constant, then $f(x)$ may be separated into parts: (1) $f(x) = (x-a)h(x) + b$, where $h(x)$ is a lower order polynomial, and b is a constant. From (1), $f(a) = b$.

Solution

If $(x-a)$ is a factor of $f(x)$, $f(a)$ is zero. If (B) were true, then $f(2)$ would equal zero, which is false: we are told that $f(2) = 3$. Toss (B). The information in the problem says nothing about the function when $x = 1$ (where $(x-1)$ would be a factor), and hence (C) isn't necessarily true. Toss (C). Thus, we are left with either choice (A) or (D).

From (1) above and the data in the first data point, we can write (2) $f(x) = (x+1)g(x) + 1$. From (1) above and the second data point given, we can write (3) $f(x) = (x-2)h(x) + 3$.

Consider (A). $(x-1)$ will divide evenly in neither (2) nor (3). For example, dividing (2) by $(x-1)$ will give rise to this polynomial plus a remainder: $f(x)/(x-1) = (x+1)g(x)/(x-1) + 1/(x-1)$. A mess, not 1. Toss (A).

So by elimination, the answer must be (D). But let's see. Using the same kind of functional partitioning as above we can divide (3) by $(x-2)$: $f(x)/(x-2) = h(x) + 3/(x-2)$. So $f(x)$ *is* divisible by $(x-2)$ with a remainder of 3.

Answer D

The Take-Away

If $f(a) = b$, then $f(x)$ may be separated into parts: $(x-a)g(x) + b$, where $g(x)$ is a lower order polynomial. You may see a simpler version of this problem on the SAT - but the principles necessary to solve the problem would be the same. This is another *very* hard problem.

Algebra and Real-World Problems Chapter 11

Higher Order Polynomials

If $x^3(2x^2 + 4) = 6x$, and x is real and greater than zero, what is x?

SR

How do I start?

First, put this higher order polynomial into standard form and see what kind of factoring can be applied.

Solution

Expanding the left-hand side of the equation, $2x^5 + 4x^3 = 6x$. In standard form this becomes $2x^5 + 4x^3 - 6x = 0$. Each term on the left side has a factor of 2 and a factor of x. Thus, the equation may be factored as $2x(x^4 + 2x^2 - 3) = 0$. Clearly $x = 0$ is a solution, but we are seeking a solution that must be positive (and real). The polynomial in parenthesis is 4th order, but notice that it has only even powers of x. If we substitute $y = x^2$, we get a quadratic polynomial in y: $y^2 + 2y - 3 = 0$. This quadratic may be easily factored and solved. $y^2 + 2y - 3 = (y + 3)(y - 1) = 0$. The solutions to this are $y = -3$ and $y = 1$. Since $y = x^2$, this means $x^2 = -3$ and $x^2 = 1$. Thus, the solutions to the equation are $x = \pm\sqrt{-3}$ and $x = \pm\sqrt{1}$. Clearly, the only real solution greater than zero among these choices is +1.

Alternate Solution

This is a hard one. If you're lost, a brute-force guess strategy might work. Since the answer must be positive, and since the SAT will sometimes design problems with integer answers, you might see if any small integers solve the equation. Indeed, a reasonable first guess to try would be $x = 1$. In that case, $1^3(2 \cdot 1^2 + 4) = 6 \cdot 1$ solves the equation. Lucky.

Alternate Solution II

$x^3 \cdot (2x^2 + 4) = 6x$ suggests perhaps $2x^2 + 4$ equals 6 when $x = 1$. It does! Next! Learn to listen to faint signals in the question and the choices (if any).

Answer 1

The Take-Away

Higher order polynomials may sometimes be factored by greatest common factoring as well as substitution of variables. Both are used in the above example. Also - burn in alternate solution II. The SAT will sometimes design problems with *real* shortcuts.

Chapter 11　　　　　　　　　　　　　　　　　　　　　　Algebra and Real-World Problems

Solving Cubic Equations

What real value of x solves the equation $2x^3 - 6x^2 + x - 3 = 0$?

SR

How do I start?

Group the cubic expression into 3rd and 2nd order terms and then 1st order and constant terms, and see if any common factors may be pulled out.

Solution

The 3rd and 2nd order terms are $2x^3 - 6x^2$, which may be simplified by pulling out the greatest common factor $2x^2$: $2x^2(x-3)$. Aha - the (x-3) term is identical to the 1st order term and constant in the cubic equation. So the entire cubic equation may now be rewritten $2x^2(x-3) + (x-3) = 0$. Since *both* terms now include a factor of (x-3), the equation may rewritten as $(x - 3)(2x^2 + 1) = 0$. *This* is easily solved. From the first factor, x = 3. From the second factor $x = \pm\sqrt{-1/2}$. The only real value of x that solves the equation is x = 3.

Alternate Solution

You could test various integers (the SAT loves integer solutions) of low magnitude to see if one solves the equation. The solution here, x = 3, might not take too much time. But this is an all-else-fails method. What if x were not an integer? Or negative? Better know how to solve cubic equations by the method above.

Answer 3

The Take-Away

Grouping cubic equations into (3rd, 2nd) and (1st, constant) order terms may allow you to see a common factor throughout the equation that might otherwise remain obscure. Of course only a small class of cubic (and even higher order) equations can be solved by this method. But on the SAT many non-trivial high order equations will be in this class. When confronted with a cubic expression or equation, this technique should jump on the front burner as a possible tool.

Algebra and Real-World Problems — Chapter 11

Quadratic Inequalities

If $x^2 - 7x > 18$, which of the following expresses the correct domain of x?

(A) $x < -2$ or $x > 9$
(B) $x < -9$ or $x > 9$
(C) $2 < x < 9$
(D) $-9 < x < 2$

How do I start?

Put the quadratic in standard form, $x^2 - 7x - 18 > 0$, and factor it to see when the expression is > 0.

Solution

The quadratic inequality $x^2 - 7x > 18$ is equivalent to $x^2 - 7x - 18 > 0$, which is easily factored: (1) $(x-9)(x+2) > 0$. The secret to the solution is this: in order for the left side of (1) to be > 0, either both factors must be positive, or both factors must be negative. Think about the parabola here: since the left-hand side of (1) has two different zeroes, 9 and -2, these points divide the value of the quadratic function into different positive and negative zones. Any value of x > 9 will result in both factors being positive, and hence a positive value of quadratic in (1). This allows you to ignore choices (C) and (D). Likewise, any value of x < -2 will result in both factors being negative, and in that case, the quadratic in (1) will again be positive. So values of x > 9 and x < -2 will result in positive values of the quadratic inequality (1), and thus satisfy the original inequality in the question. The answer must be (A).

But what of x values between -2 and 9? The left factor is negative, while the right term is positive; in this interval the quadratic expression in (1) is negative.

The original inequality is true only for x having the values x > 9, or x < -2.

Answer A

The Take-Away

The real, distinct roots of a quadratic expression separate the regions of positive and negative values of the quadratic as a function of the independent variable. On the SAT, quadratic expressions will very often (but not always) be factorable if the roots must be determined.

Alternate Solution:

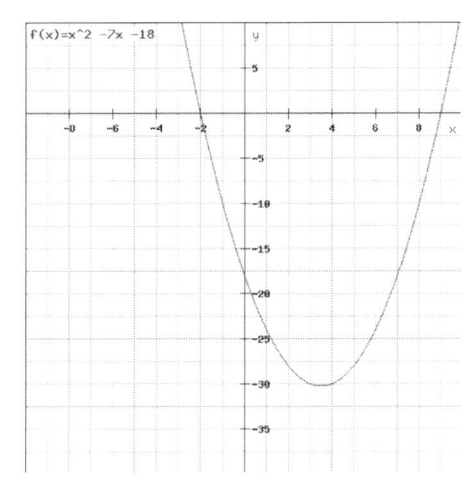

All quadratic expressions can be represented by a parabola.

If this question were instead included in the calculator-allowed section, you could plot the rearranged quadratic inequality (1) in the graphing calculator. If the coefficient of the x^2 term is positive (as in this problem), the parabola opens "up." In this case once the zeroes of the quadratic are found (if any), you can be sure that the only negative values of the quadratic are between the zeros.

On the other hand, if the coefficient of the x^2 term is negative, the parabola opens "down." In that case once the zeros of the quadratic are found (if any), you can be sure that the only positive values of the quadratic are between the zeros.

Of course, a quadratic may have two zeros that are equal to each other, or it might have no real zeros (and two complex zeros). However, the SAT requires only relatively simple complex analysis, so on most problems involving quadratics, any zeros or roots you have to compute, especially on problems like this, will likely be real.

Answer A

The Take-Away

Always consider putting quadratic equations or inequalities in standard form: $f(x) = 0$, $f(x) > 0$, etc. Then find the zeros of the quadratic by factoring (or the quadratic formula if necessary). For inequalities, determine if the parabola opens up or down by the sign of the x^2 term. This will determine the sign of the region between the two zeros (if there are two): (-) for quadratics with positive x^2 terms, and (+) for quadratics with negative x^2 terms.

Algebra and Real-World Problems Chapter 11

Simultaneous Equations with Absolute Values: Unmixed

If $\dfrac{|x-2|}{3} = 2$ and $\dfrac{|y+1|}{2} = 2$, then |x - y| could <u>not</u> be

(A) 1
(B) 2
(C) 5
(D) 7

How do I start?

This is an example of simultaneous equations, which are covered in detail in chapter 12. Because the variables are unmixed (the first equation only involves x, and the second equation only involves y), we can treat each equation separately. Find the values of x that satisfy the first equation and the values of y that satisfy the second equation. An absolute value equation involving linear terms always has two solutions unless the solution is zero.

Solution

Multiplying each equation by their denominators, (1) |x - 2| = 6, and (2) |y + 1| = 4. Solve for x and y separately. From (1), x - 2 = ±6, and so x could be 8 or -4. From (2), y + 1 = ±4, and y could therefore be 3 or -5. The value of x - y could be any of the four combinations possible given these values for x and y: (8 - 3), (8 - (-5)), (-4 - 3), and (-4 - (-5)). So x - y could be 5, 13, -7, or 1. Therefore, |x - y| could only be 5, 13, 7, or 1. Since 2 is not among the possible values of |x - y|, the answer is (B).

Answer B

The Take-Away

When two or more variables are constrained by equalities (or inequalities) involving an absolute value expression, and the equalities (or inequalities) are *unmixed*, independently determine the allowed values of each variable (x and y, here), and then the allowed values of any function of them (|x - y|, here).

Note that polynomials can occur within an absolute value function. In such cases there may be twice the usual number of solutions to the absolute value equation.

Chapter 11 	Algebra and Real-World Problems

Inequalities Involving Absolute Values and Exponents

If $|a| > 1$, which of the following expressions must be true?

    I. $a^4 - 1 > 0$
    II. $a^4 < a^5$
    III. $a^{1/3} > a^{-1}$

(A) I only
(B) II only
(C) III only
(D) I and II only

How do I start?

Decompose the absolute value expression describing the domain first: $a > 1$ or $a < -1$. One of the cases, (I), (II), or (III) must be true for *all* a in its allowable domain. We can toss an incorrect case if it is untrue for any one value. So we can test the cases using characteristic values in the positive and negative domains, depending on the case being tested. Doing so will reduce the chance of error compared with trying to do head-math using only the nature of the domain. Because $|a| > 1$, we can avoid the sometimes confusing behavior of exponentiated fractions. Work with integers whenever you can.

Solution

Given the domain of a: $|a| > 1$, let's test the cases using $a = 2$ and $a = -2$. Test (I): if $a = 2$, (I) becomes $16 > 1$; if $a = -2$, (I) becomes $16 > 1$. Both are true, so (I) is true. Test (II): if $a = 2$, (II) becomes $16 < 32$, which is true. But if $a = -2$, (II) becomes $16 < -32$, which is false. So (II) is not always true. Test (III) by first cube-ing both sides of the inequality. This produces the inequality (1) $a > a^{-3}$. If $a = 2$, then (1) becomes $2 > 1/8$, which is true. But if $a = -2$, equation (1) becomes $-2 > -1/8$, which is false. Therefore, only (I) is always true.

Answer A

The Take-Away

If values can be positive or negative, be careful evaluating these values raised to various powers: even, odd, and negative powers. And remember that when multiplying an inequality by a negative value, reverse the direction of the inequality - not used here, but this is rule often neglected. Also - choose integers as test values whenever you can. Doing so will reduce head-math errors. We were able reduce the domain (for testing purposes) to two values: a negative integer (-2) and a positive integer (2).

Algebra and Real-World Problems   Chapter 11

Checking Radical Equations

If $\sqrt{5 - 4x} = x$, which value(s) of x below solve the equation?

(A) -20 and 1
(B) -5
(C) 1
(D) -5 and 1

How do I start?

Raise both sides to the reciprocal power to get x out from under the radical. In other words, x is under a square root radical (power of 1/2), so each side must be squared. Solve that equation, then check the solutions in the original equation.

Solution

The original equation (1) If $\sqrt{5 - 4x} = x$ contains a term with x under a square root radical. The first step is to get rid of the radical by squaring both sides of (1) to get $5 - 4x = x^2$. Put this in standard form: $0 = x^2 + 4x - 5$. This quadratic is easily factored: (2) $0 = (x+5)(x-1)$. The solutions to (2) are x = -5 and x = 1. But because we raised the original equation by an even power, we must check both solutions; sometimes extraneous solutions are produced by squaring both sides. First, check x = -5 in (1) giving (3) $\sqrt{5 + 20}$ = -5. Now remember the radical symbol always refers to the *positive* root. Thus, (3) becomes 5 = -5, which is false. So x = -5 is *not* a solution. Now try x = 1 in (1): $\sqrt{5 - 4}$ = 1, or 1 = 1. This is true, and thus only x = 1 solves the original equation (1).

Answer C

Take Away

The square root radical above was eliminated by squaring both sides of the equation. Is x raised to the power of a/b? Raising both sides of the equation to the power of b/a may be necessary to isolate x. However, if b is even, the solution(s) should be checked. The only time you are safe *not* checking the solution to an even root radical equation is if it can be put in this form: $\sqrt[n]{a + bx} = c$, where c is a positive constant (and of course, n is even). Otherwise, quickly check that the solutions to the power-raised equation solve the original root equation.

Chapter 11　　　　　　　　　　　　　　　　　　　Algebra and Real-World Problems

Practice Problems

1. If $x^2 - y^2 = z$, where x and y are non-negative integers, and z is a prime number, what is the value of x - y?

    (A) $\frac{z}{2}$
    (B) 1
    (C) z
    (D) x+y

2. If $x^2 - y^2 = z$, where x and y are non-negative integers, and the average of x and y is 2 + y, what is the value of x + y?

    (A) $\frac{z}{4}$
    (B) 1
    (C) z
    (D) 2xy -z

3. The lab has test tubes in two different sizes. The combined volume of 12 test tubes of one type is V liters and the combined volume of 15 of the other size test tube is also V liters. In terms of V, what is the volume, in liters, of each of the smaller test tubes?

    (A) V/12
    (B) (V-3)/12
    (C) 4V/5
    (D) V/15

4. A student who must write an 83 page paper in one week starts on Monday. He plans to work hard Monday, Wednesday, Friday, and Sunday, and ease off a bit on Tuesday, Thursday, and Saturday. On Wednesday, Friday, and Sunday, he plans to double the number of pages written the previous day. On Tuesday, Thursday, and Saturday, he plans to write one-third fewer pages than the previous day. To keep to this plan, how many pages must he write on Tuesday?

    SR

Algebra and Real-World Problems	Chapter 11

5. How many dollars were withdrawn from an account if x dollars were deposited, y dollars were originally in the account, and z dollars are in the account now?

   (A) z - x - y
   (B) y + x - z
   (C) y - x + z
   (D) y - z + 2x

6. If $\dfrac{3x-2y}{2x} = \dfrac{3}{4}$, what is the value of x/y?

   SR

7. If $\dfrac{(x-y)}{(x+y)} = 9$, what is the value of $-\dfrac{x}{y}$?

   SR

8. If ab = c and c = xa, which of the following is equal to x if ac ≠ 0?

   (A) $\dfrac{1}{a}$
   (B) $\dfrac{1}{b}$
   (C) 1
   (D) b

9. Let w, x, y, and z be real numbers not equal to zero. Which of the equations below is not equivalent to the others?

   (A) $\dfrac{w}{y} = \dfrac{z}{x}$
   (B) $\dfrac{1}{y} = \dfrac{x}{zw}$
   (C) $\dfrac{x}{z} = \dfrac{w}{y}$
   (D) $\dfrac{xy}{wz} = 1$

306

Chapter 11	Algebra and Real-World Problems

10. If $a = -2 \cdot (c^2 - c + 4)$ and $b = c + 2$, what is a in terms of b?

(A) $b^2 - 11b + 22$
(B) $2b^2 - 13b - 24$
(C) $-b^2 - 13b + 26$
(D) $-2b^2 + 10b - 20$

11. If $x > 2$ and $\dfrac{4}{\sqrt{x+4}} = \sqrt{x-2}$, what is the value of x?

SR

12. If x is a real number not equal to zero, which of the following expressions could equal zero?

(A) $2x^4 + 50$
(B) $\sqrt{2x^2 + 50}$
(C) $|2x^2 + 50|$
(D) $|27 + x^3|$

13. What is the sum of $\dfrac{1}{2x}$, $\dfrac{2}{3x}$, and $\dfrac{4}{5x}$, multiplied by 30x?

SR

14. If $\dfrac{2ac}{(b-2a)} = 1$, which expression below is a in terms of b and c?

(A) 2b/(c+1)
(B) 2b/(c-1)
(C) b/(2c+2)
(D) 2b/(2c-1)

307

Algebra and Real-World Problems   Chapter 11

15. If $\dfrac{11}{a} - b = 4$, which expression below correctly states a in terms of b?

(A) $\dfrac{11-b}{4}$

(B) $\dfrac{4}{11-b}$

(C) $\dfrac{44}{11-b}$

(D) $\dfrac{11}{4+b}$

16. $(x+5)(x-a) = x^2 + 9ax + b$

a and b are constants in the above quadratic equation. If the equation is true for all values of x, what is the value of -2b?

SR

17. If $x^2 - y^2 = 16$ and $x - y = 2$, what is the value of $x + y$?

SR

18. If $x^2 - y^2 = 8$ and $x + y = 2$ and $xy = 2$, then $x^2y - xy^2 =$

SR

19. If a and b are positive constants, and $2x^2 + ax + 4b^2$ equals $(2x+1)(x+b)$ for all real values of x, which is the correct value of a?

(A) -.25
(B) .25
(C) 1
(D) 1.5

308

Chapter 11　　　　　　　　　　　　　　　　　　Algebra and Real-World Problems

20. If $a = 2x + 4$ and $b = -1 + 4x^2$, what is b in terms of a?

(A) $a^2 - 8a + 15$
(B) $a^2 + 8a + 17$
(C) $a^2 + 36$
(D) $4a^2 - 36$

21. If $y^2 - 2y + (1-a) = 0$, where a is a constant and $(1-a)$ is a solution to the equation, what values may a take?

(A) {-1, 7}
(B) {0, $\sqrt{5}$}
(C) {0, 1}
(D) {-4, 1}

22. If $2x^2 + 4x > 48$, which of the following expressions is true?

(A) $x < -4$ or $x > 6$
(B) $x < -6$ or $x > 4$
(C) $-6 < x < 4$
(D) $-4 < x < 6$

23. If $g(x) = -x^2 + 6x - 2$, which expression below also equals g(x)?

(A) $-(x - 3)^2 - 7$
(B) $-(x - 3)^2 + 7$
(C) $(x + 3)^2 - 7$
(D) $-(x + 3)^2 + 7$

24. In the equation $9x^2 + 24x + 16 = (xy + 4)^2$, if y is a constant and $y - x = 2$, what is the value of $y + x$?

SR

309

Algebra and Real-World Problems   Chapter 11

25. If $x = a - 2$ and $x^2 - y^2 = 2$, which of the following expressions equals y^2?

   (A) $4a$
   (B) $-4(a^2+2)$
   (C) $a^2 - 4$
   (D) $(a-2)^2 - 2$

26. If x (which is less than zero) is multiplied by 6, the product is the same as when 16 is subtracted from x^2. What is the value of -x?

   SR

27. The sum of two numbers, a and b, is S. If $|a - b| = 3$, what, in terms of S, is the value of the <u>larger</u> of the two numbers?

   (A) $2S - 3$
   (B) $\dfrac{(S + 3)}{2}$
   (C) $\dfrac{(S - 3)}{2}$
   (D) $\dfrac{(S + 3)}{6}$

28. A number x is increased by n. The result of that operation is then multiplied by n. The resulting number is subsequently diminished by 5n, and that result is then divided by n. If n = 4, what is the final result, in terms of x?

   (A) $4x$
   (B) $5(x + 4)/4$
   (C) $x - 1$
   (D) $4x - 1$

29. If $\left|\dfrac{x+1}{3}\right| = 1$ and $\left|\dfrac{2}{x-6}\right| = 1/2$, then what is the value of x?

   SR

310

30. Let -1 < a < 1, where a ≠ 0. Which of the following expressions must be true?

   I. $a^2 > 1 - a$
   II. $2a > 2a - 1$
   III. $\dfrac{1}{|a|} > |a|^2$

(A) I only
(B) II only
(C) III only
(D) II and III only

31. Assume x ≠ 0. The following cases present domains of the variable x. For which of the domains will <u>all</u> allowed values of x satisfy the inequality $x^3 \leq x^2$?

   I. $-1 < x < 1$
   II. $-1 < \dfrac{1}{|x|} < 1$
   III. $x \geq -1$

(A) I only
(B) II only
(C) I and II only
(D) I and III only

32. If |a| > 1, which of the following inequalities is always true? Ignore any complex roots, where applicable.

   I. $a^3 - 1 > 0$
   II. $a^4 < |a^5|$
   III. $a^{1/3} > a^{-1}$

(A) I only
(B) II only
(C) III only
(D) I and II only

33. Assume

|x+2| = 2

|y+7| = 11

If x and y are both less than zero, what is the value of y - x, given the equations above?

(A) -14
(B) -9
(C) -1
(D) 1

34. Assume

|x-1| = 2

|y+2x| = 11

If x<0 and y>0, what is the value of y, given the equations above?

(A) -17
(B) -9
(C) 9
(D) 13

35. If f(t) is inversely proportional to 3t, and if f(4) = -1, what is the value of f(3)?

(A) -1/3
(B) -1/2
(C) -1
(D) -4/3

36. If s varies directly as t, and if s = 1 when t = x, and if s = 5 when t = x - 2, what is the value of x?

(A) -2/3
(B) -1/3
(C) -1/2
(D) 3

37. If $|x-1| = 2$ and $|y+7| = x$ and $|y| < 5$, what is the value of $|y|$?

SR

38. If $z = kx^n y^m$, where k, n and m are constants, what is the value of y when x = 3 and z = 9, given the following known table of values:

z	x	y
3	1	3
12	2	3
24	2	6

SR

39.

$|x-1| = 2$

$|y+7| = 11$

If x and y are both less than zero, what is the value of y - x, given the equations above?

(A) -17
(B) -9
(C) -1
(D) 1

Algebra and Real-World Problems   Chapter 11

40. CHALLENGE If $\dfrac{2x}{(x+1)} \cdot \dfrac{3}{x} \cdot \dfrac{x}{2(x-1)} = \dfrac{21}{y}$, where x and y are integers greater than 1,

what is a possible value of y?

SR

41. Consider the polynomial $4x^4 - 3x^2 + x + k$. What value of k will allow this polynomial to be divided by x - 1 with no remainder?

(A) -2
(B) 0
(C) 2
(D) 7

42. The graph of the polynomial $y = ax^2 + bx + c$ passes through the points (0, -2), (1,1), and (2,6). What is the value of a + b?

(A) -2
(B) -1.75
(C) 3
(D) 4.25

43. Old-style city cabs charge $2.50 for the first 1/4 of a mile and then $1.00 for every additional 1/2 mile. Which expression below describes the distance, d, in miles, that a passenger can ride and pay no more than $20?

(A) 2.50 + d ≤ 20
(B) 2.00 + 2d ≤ 20
(C) 2.50 + (2d - 1/2) ≤ 20
(D) 2.75 + d ≤ 20

Chapter 11 Algebra and Real-World Problems

44. Which value of x solves the equation below:

$$\frac{4x}{x+6} + \frac{2x}{2x+12} = \frac{-60}{2(x+6)}$$

(A) There is no solution
(B) -6
(C) 3
(D) 6

45.
$$x^3 - 2x^2 + 2x - 4 = 0$$

The equation above has one real solution. What is it?

46.
$$\frac{2x-4}{x+8}$$

The expression above is equivalent to which expression below?

(A) $2 + \dfrac{4}{2x-4}$
(B) $2 - \dfrac{20}{x+8}$
(C) $2 - \dfrac{x}{x-2}$
(D) $1 + \dfrac{x}{x+8}$

315

Algebra and Real-World Problems   Chapter 11

47.

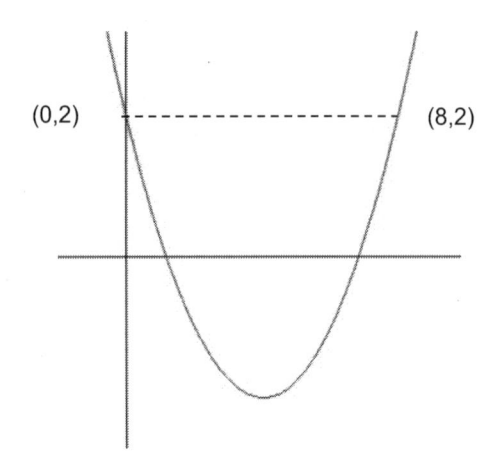

(0,2) .... (8,2)

The parabola shown above has a range of y ≥ -2. When the equation of this function is put in the form $y = ax^2 + bx + c$, what is the value of a?

48. If x - y = z and x + y = r, which expression below represents xy in terms of z and r?

(A) $\dfrac{z}{r+2}$

(B) $\dfrac{r^2-z^2}{4}$

(C) $\dfrac{z}{r+2}$

(D) $\dfrac{r^2-z^2}{2}$

49. If $xy + \dfrac{1}{xy} = 2$, what is the value of $x^2y^2 + \dfrac{1}{x^2y^2}$?

SR

50. What is the value of x if $a = 4\sqrt{4}$ and $4a = \sqrt{4x}$?

SR

51. If $\dfrac{53}{sx-2} - 8x - 3 = \dfrac{24x^2+25x-47}{sx-2}$ for all x, where sx ≠ 2, what is the value of -s?

Chapter 11   Algebra and Real-World Problems

Practice Problem Hints

1. $x^2 - y^2 = (x+y)(x-y)$. A prime number has no factors but itself and 1.

2. $x^2 - y^2 = (x+y)(x-y)$. Use the information about the average of x and y get their sum in terms of y. Then use that equation to solve for (x-y).

3. Express the volume of each type test tube in terms of V. One of these expressions is smaller than the other.

4. One-third fewer pages equals 2/3 times the number pages. Let the number of pages on Monday equal m. Develop the week accordingly.

5. Current = Beginning - Withdrawn + Deposited.

6. Divide top and bottom of the left hand side by x, and solve for y/x.

7. Divide top and bottom of the left-hand side by y.

8. Set ab = xa.

9. Isolate the same variable in each of the choices and compare the results.

10. Express c in terms of b, and plug that into the first equation. Shortcut?

11. Square both sides and solve for x.

12. Inspect each expression to see what value of x^2, x^3, or x^4 might cause the expression to equal zero.

13. Recast all expressions using a common denominator, add them, and then multiply by 30x.

14. Multiply both sides by (b-2a) and gather the a terms on the left. Then factor a out of the left hand expression in order to solve for a in terms of b and c.

15. Multiply both sides by a and gather the a terms together. Then solve for a in terms of b.

16. Expand the quadratic on the left-hand side. The coefficients of same powers of x must be equal.

Algebra and Real-World Problems   Chapter 11

17. $x^2 - y^2 = (x+y)(x-y)$.

18. $x^2 - y^2 = (x+y)(x-y)$, and $x^2y - xy^2 = xy(x-y)$.

19. The coefficients of equal powers of x must be equal.

20. Use the first equation to put x in terms of a. Substitute this into second equation.

21. Since (1-a) is a solution, set y equal to (1-a), and solve for a.

22. Divide the inequality by 2. Put the quadratic in standard form and factor to see when the expression is > 0.

23. The coefficients of equal powers of x must be equal.

24. The coefficients of equal powers of x must be equal. Not as hard as it looks.

25. Substitute x = a - 2 into the expression.

26. Express the two verbal expressions involving x as one quadratic equation.

27. If you assume a > b, you can remove the absolute value brackets and solve for a in terms of S.

28. Carefully translate the verbal expressions of the four algebraic operations into an algebraic expression when n = 4.

29. Each absolute value equation will have two solutions. Find the value of x common to these solutions.

30. Test each inequality at representative points, such as -.5 and .5.

31. Simplify the inequality.

32. The domain is a>1 or a<-1. Test each inequality in the domain.

33. Solve for x and y using the equations given. Each absolute value equation will produce two solutions. Only consider the negative solutions.

34. Solve for x first, given the constraints, and then plug that value into the second equation.

35. f(t) is a constant times 1/(3t). First, solve for the constant.

Chapter 11   Algebra and Real-World Problems

36. From the data, s = m•t, where m is the constant of proportionality. Since 1 = mx, m must equal 1/x. Use this in the second relationship. Note: x is a constant.

37. The absolute value equations, expanded, describe several equations. Solve for the values of x, and use these to solve for the values of y.

38. Choose pairs of rows where one variable is constant and the other variable changes. Determine what happens to z. From this you can determine the fixed exponents. Knowing both exponents you can determine k.

39. While these are simultaneous equations, they are unmixed; each equation only involves a single variable. Solve for x and y from the equations given, and don't forget that x and y are both less than zero when evaluating y - x.

40. $x^2 - 1 = (x+1)(x-1)$. Isolate y and factor the result in the form (integer)•(the other factor).

41. Perform the polynomial division to completion and then determine what value of k will result in no remainder. Another route: x = 1 must be a root of the polynomial.

42. When x = 0, y = -2. Therefore c = -3. Use this value to set up equations for a and b using the other two points given.

43. Develop an expression for the total cost in the format a + b•(distance).

44. Cast each term with a common denominator. Be careful.

45. Find a factor common to these two sums: the first two terms and the last two terms.

46. Recast the numerator in terms of the denominator + another term. Or use polynomial division.

47. Determine the vertex, cast the expression in vertex form, and then use one of the two points given to determine the value of a.

48. The equations can be added to isolate x and subtracted to isolate y.

49. Expand $(xy + \frac{1}{xy})^2$.

50. This is a confusing substitution problem

51. Multiply the equation by the denominator sx-2, and equate coefficients of x^2.

319

Notes

Chapter 11   Algebra and Real-World Problems

Practice Problem Solutions

1. Answer B

   First, factor the quadratic expression: $x^2 - y^2 = (x+y)(x-y) = z$. So z, a prime number, (2, 3, 5,…), is equal to the product of two factors: (x+y) and (x-y). A prime number has only itself and one as factors: one of these factors has to equal z and the other has to equal 1. Note that because x and y are nonnegative, (x+y) must be greater than (x-y). Therefore, x+y must equal z and x-y must equal 1.

2. Answer A

   First, factor the quadratic expression: $x^2 - y^2 = (1)\ (x+y)(x-y) = z$. We need to solve for x + y. We are told that the average of x and y is y + 2. Since the sum of x and y is twice the average of x and y, (2) x + y = 2y + 4. But that's not one of the choices. Now what? Oh - rearranging (2), x - y = 4. That's possibly useful. Plugging that into (1), (x+y)•4 = z. Rearranging, x + y = z/4. Double hard. Blood on the knife. Already.

3. Answer D

   Express the volume of each type in terms of V. The volume of the first type is V/12, and the volume of the other type is V/15. Since V/15 < V/12, it is the smaller tube.

4. Answer 6

   Let m = pages written Monday. So, on Tuesday he reads (1-m/3) = 2m/3 pages, and on Wednesday 4m/3 pages. Continuing his plan, the total number of pages in all seven days must equal 83 = m + 2m/3 + 4m/3 + 8m/9 + 16m/9 + 32m/27 + 64m/27. Expressing this sum with a common denominator, and factoring out m, 83 = m(27+18 +36+24+48+32+64)/27 = 249m/27 = 83. Isolating m, m = 9. On Monday, he writes 9 pages. Therefore, on Tuesday, he writes 2/3 • 9 = 6 pages.

5. Answer B

   This problem is easy if you just read carefully and account for each term correctly. The current dollars must equal the beginning dollars - withdrawn dollars + deposited dollars. Letting w = withdrawn dollars, z = y - w + x. Solving for w, w = y + x - z.

6. Answer 4/3

    Divide top and bottom by x on the left hand side, then solve for y/x. (3 - 2y/x)/2 = 3/4. Rearranging and solving for y/x yields y/x = 3/4. Inverting this gives the requested ratio, x/y = 4/3. Or you could start by dividing top and bottom by y on the left side.

7. Answer 5/4, or 1.25

    Divide top and bottom of the left-hand side by y. This results in the equation (x/y - 1) / (x/y + 1) = 9. Multiplying by the denominator yields x/y - 1 = 9x/y + 9. One may now solve for x/y: -8x/y = 10, or x/y = -5/4. So -x/y = 5/4 or 1.25.

8. Answer D

    You could try isolating x and substituting. But because both ab and xa are equal to c, they are equal to each other: ab = xa. Thus, x = b. Trivial, yet this is a medium-hard problem on the SAT. The variable names and syntax are confusing for many.

9. Answer A

    Rearrange each choice to isolate the same variable. In equation (A), we can rearrange to solve for w, w = zy/x. We can solve for w in the remaining choices and determine which equation gives an expression for w different from the others. In (B), w = yx/z, which is different from (A). Good. Now we only have to solve for w in one remaining choice to rule out (A) or (B). From (C), w = xy/z, which is the same as (B). Therefore, (A) is not an expression equivalent to the others.

10. Answer D

    From the second equation, c = b - 2. Plugging this expression into the first equation yields a = -2($(b-2)^2$ - b + 2 + 4). Now expand $(b-2)^2$: a = -2(4 - 4b + b^2 - b + 2 + 4) = -8 + 8b - $2b^2$ + 2b - 4 - 8 = $-2b^2$ + 10b - 20.

    Alternate Solution: Notice -2 out front? All coefficients must be even. Only (D) fits this.

11. Answer 4

    Squaring both sides yields (1) 16/(x+4) = (x-2). Multiply by (x+4): 16 = (x+4)(x-2). Expanding the right side and subtracting 16 from both sides gives 0 = x^2 + 2x - 24.

Factoring the right side gives 0 = (x+6)(x-4). The solutions to this equation are x = -6 and x = 4. However, because x > 2 in this domain, the only solution is x = 4. Since we raised each side by an even power, we might check x = 4 in (1). 16/8 = (4-2). Yes

12. Answer D

Since x is real and nonzero, x^2 and x^4 are always positive, so (A), (B), and (C) cannot equal zero. By elimination, the answer must be (D). Test (D): how can the argument of $|27 + x^3|$ be zero? Only x^3 = -27 will work. So x = $(-27)^{1/3}$ = -3. Real and non-zero.

13. Answer 59

Find the least common multiple of the denominators. The LCM of 2x, 3x, and 5x is 30x. The sum then becomes $\frac{15}{30x} + \frac{20}{30x} + \frac{24}{30x} = \frac{59}{30x}$. This sum times 30x equals 59.

Alternate Solution: Multiply each fraction separately by 30x and add: 15+20+24 = 59.

14. Answer C

This is a straightforward algebraic rearrangement problem. Multiplying both sides by (b-2a) yields 2ac = (b-2a). Gathering the a terms on the left and factoring out a yields a(2c+2) = b. Rearranging, a = b/(2c+2).

15. Answer D

This is an another exercise in algebraic rearrangement. Multiplying both sides by a yields 11 - ab = 4a. Adding ab to both sides gives 11 = 4a + ab. Factoring a out on the right side yields 11 = a(4+b). Dividing each side by (4+b) gives 11/(4+b) = a.

16. Answer 5

Expand the left-hand side of the given equation: x^2 + (5-a)x - 5a = x^2 + 9ax + b. This equation is true for all x. Thus, coefficients of same powers of x must be equal. It must be true that (1) (5-a) = 9a, and (2) b = -5a. From (1), 5 = 10a, or a = 1/2. Plugging this into the (2) gives b = -5/2. Hence, -2b = 5.

17. Answer 8

$x^2 - y^2$ is factorable and equals (x+y)(x-y), Thus, (1) (x+y)(x-y) = 16. However, (x-y) = 2, and substituting this value into (1) yields (x+y)•2 = 16. Therefore, x + y = 8.

Algebra and Real-World Problems   Chapter 11

18. Answer 8

Whenever you see a form like $x^2 - y^2$, you will often have to factor it. In this problem, $x^2 - y^2 = (1) (x+y)(x-y) = 8$. Since $(x+y) = 2$, substitution into (1) yields $2(x-y) = 8$, so (2) $(x-y) = 4$. We are asked to evaluate $x^2y - xy^2$, which looks bad until we see that this expression can also be factored: $x^2y - xy^2 = xy(x-y)$. Aha. We are told that (3) $xy = 2$. Using (3) and (2), $xy(x-y) = 2 \cdot 4 = 8$.

19. Answer D

Expand the two factors in the second quadratic: $(2x+1)(x+b) = 2x^2 + x \cdot (2b+1) + b$. Thus, $2x^2 + ax + 4b^2 = 2x^2 + x \cdot (2b+1) + b$. If these are the same value for all x, the coefficients of equal powers of x must be equal. Compare the constants: $4b^2 = b$, and solving for b, b = .25. Compare the x^1 terms: $a = (2b+1)$, and using b = .25, a = 1.5.

20. Answer A

We may rearrange the first equation to put x in terms of a: $x = (a-4)/2$. This can be substituted into the second equation: $b = -1 + 4 \cdot [(a-4)^2/4] = -1 + a^2 - 8a + 16$. In standard form, $b = a^2 - 8a + 15$.

21. Answer C

We are told that (1-a) is a solution to the equation. What? OK. If (1-a) is a solution to the equation, then when y = (1-a), the left side equals zero. Plug (1-a) for y into the equation: (1) $(1-a)^2 - 2(1-a) + (1-a) = 0$. Expanding, (1) is $(a^2 - 2a + 1) + (2a-2) + (1-a) = a^2 - a$. This can be factored to give $0 = a(a-1)$. The solutions to this equation are a = 0 and a = 1. An easy one that very few figure out.

Alternate Solution: Since (1-a) is a solution, then y = (1-a) must solve the equation; one can re-express the equation as $y^2 - 2y + y = 0$. Simplifying, (1) $y^2 - y = 0$. Factoring the left side of (1) yields $y(y-1) = 0$. The solutions are y = 0 and 1. Since y = (1-a), a = 1 - y. When y = 0, a = 1, and when y = 1, a = 0. Either way, this problem can burn.

22. Answer B

First, divide the inequality by 2 and then rearrange the inequality into standard quadratic form: $x^2 + 2x - 24 > 0$. The quadratic can be easily factored: $(x+6)(x-4) > 0$. Since the left-hand side has two different zeroes, 4 and -6, these points divide the quadratic into different positive and negative zones. Any value of x > 4 will result in both factors being positive, and hence a positive value of the quadratic. Likewise, any value of x < -6 will result in both factors being negative, and then the quadratic will be positive. But what of x values between -6 and 4? The right factor is negative, while the left term is positive, and so in this interval the quadratic is negative. No good for an answer. The original inequality is true if x > 4, or x < -6.

23. Answer B

$g(x) = -x^2 + 6x - 2$ is not easily factored. The easiest path to finding the correct answer might be to inspect the choices and look to knock some out. Since all the choices are of the form $(x + a)^2 + b$, where a and b are constants, look for a choice that, when expanded, has the same signs and values of coefficients of x^2 and x^1 in the question. The coefficient of x^2 must be negative, eliminating (C). The coefficient of x must be positive, eliminating (D). The constant term must be -2. (A) has a constant term of -9 - 7 = -16, while (B) has a constant term of -9 + 7 = -2. Click. This kind of head-math approach is quicker than expanding all four choices and should always be considered.

24. Answer 4

Expand $(xy + 4)^2 = (1)\ y^2x^2 + 8xy + 16$. This must equal (2) $9x^2 + 24x + 16$. Since y is a constant, the coefficients of equal powers of x in (1) and (2) must be equal. Comparing coefficients of powers of x^1, we see 8xy = 24x, and thus y = 3. Since y - x = 2, x must equal 1. So y + x = 3 + 1 = 4. Note that forcing y - x = 2 forces x to a single value. In general, such quadratic expressions would be valid for any value of x.

25. Answer D

(1) $x^2 - y^2 = 2$. Substitute x = (a-2) in (1): $(a-2)^2 - y^2 = 2$. Rearranging, $y^2 = (a-2)^2 - 2$. This is so trivial, but a lot of students miss this or go on with a full-on substitution.

Alternate Solution: (1) $x^2 - y^2 = 2$. Substitute x = (a-2) in (1): $a^2 - 4a + 4 - y^2 = 2$. Rearranging (1), (2) $a^2 - 4a + 2 = y^2$. The left side of (2) cannot be easily factored. Note however, if we add 2 to both sides of (2), we get (3) $a^2 - 4a + 4 = y^2 + 2$. Now the left side of (3) is $(a-2)^2$. (3) becomes $(a-2)^2 = y^2 + 2$, or $(a-2)^2 - 2 = y^2$. The long way.

26. Answer 2

Translate the verbal information: $6x = x^2 - 16$. Rearranging to put in standard quadratic form, $x^2 - 6x - 16 = 0$. This can be factored to yield (x-8)(x+2) = 0. Solutions to this quadratic are x = 8 and x = -2. Since x must be less than zero, x = -2, making -x = 2.

Algebra and Real-World Problems   Chapter 11

27. Answer B

If we assume that a > b, you can remove the absolute value brackets. So a - b = 3, or (1) b = a - 3. We need a in terms of S. We are told that (2) a + b = S. We may substitute (1) into (2), yielding a + a - 3 = S. Solving for a in terms of S, a = (S+3)/2.

28. Answer C

Substituting n = 4 into the verbiage given in the problem, the result of the first operation is x + 4. The second operation gives 4(x+4) = 4x + 16. The third operation gives 4x + 16 - 5•4 = 4x - 4. The fourth operation results in (4x - 4)/4 = x - 1.

Alternate Solution: Following the directions as above, but keeping n as a variable, the resulting expression is (after some work) x + n - 5. If n = 4, the expression is x - 1.

29. Answer 2

From the first equation, |x+1| = 3. This yields x + 1 = ±3, or (1) x = 2, or -4. From the second equation, 2/(x-6) = ±1/2. Inverting both sides, (x-6)/2 = ±2, or x - 6 = ±4. From this we get (2) x = 10 or 2. The value of x common to (1) and (2) is x = 2.

30. Answer D

Test at a = -.5, and +.5. Test (I): if a = .5, then (I) .25 > 1 - .5 is <u>not</u> true. Test (II): this is true for *any* real value of a; (II) reduces to 0 > -1 and is always true. Test (III): multiplying both sides by |a| (since a ≠ 0), (III) can be reduced to 1 > |a|³. Given the domain -1 < a < 1, (III) is clearly always true. Therefore, (II) and (III) are always true.

31. Answer A

Note that $x^3 \le x^2$ reduces to (1) x ≤ 1 because x ≠ 0 and dividing by x^2 is positive. So only values of x ≤ 1 can be true. If any allowed value in the domains do not satisfy (1), then $x^3 \le x^2$ will not always be true. Test (I): all values in this domain are less than 1, and therefore satisfy the requirement (1). Test (II): split the compound inequality into two inequalities. $-1 < \frac{1}{|x|}$ is always true because |x| is always positive). However, $\frac{1}{|x|} < 1$ becomes |x| > 1 after inversion, which x = 1/2 would fail. So (II) is not always true. Test (III): x could be equal to 2 in (III), but 2 does not satisfy x ≤ 1. As a check, 2^3 is not less than or equal to 2^2. So (III) is not always true. Only (I) is always true.

326

32. Answer B

Note that a>1 or a<-1. (I) is false for all a<-1, so (I) is not always true. For a>1, (II) is true. For a < -1, the absolute value operation also makes (II) true. So (II) is always true. (III) is true (for the real cube root) if a>1, but is *not* true if a < -1. For example, if a = -8, the cube root of -8 equals -2, which is not greater than -1/8. Only (II) is true.

Alternate Solution: Regarding (III): $a^{1/3} > a^{-1}$. One might think to multiply both sides by a to give the inequality (1) $a^{4/3} > 1$. However, this is dependent on the value of a that is used in the multiplication. If a > 0, then the inequality (1) is true as written. But if a < 0, then it is necessary to reverse the sign of the inequality. Thus, for values of a < 0, $a^{4/3} < 1$. Is this always true in the domain of a? No. For example, if a = -8, $a^{1/3}$ = -2, and $a^{4/3}$ = 16. This is not less than 1.

33. Answer A

From the top equation, either x+2 = 2 or x+2= -2. So x can be either 0 or -4. Since x is less than zero, x must equal -4. Likewise, from the bottom equation, y can be either 4 or -18. Since y is less than zero, y must equal -18. y - x = -18 - (-4) = -14.

34. Answer D

From |x-1| =2, either x-1 = 2, or x-1= -2. Thus, x can be either 3 or -1. Since x is less than zero, x must equal -1. Plugging this value of x into |y+2x| = 11, either y - 2 = 11, or y - 2 = -11. From this, y can be either 13 or -9. Since y is greater than zero, y must equal 13.

35. Answer D

From the definition of inverse proportionality, f(t) = a/(3t), where a is some constant. Since f(4) = -1, -1 = a/(3•4) = a/12. Solving for a, a = -12. Therefore, f(3) = -12/(3•3) = -12/9 = -4/3. In fact, you could solve this using f(t) = b/t, where we ignore the "inverse of 3t." The function is inversely proportional to *both* 3t and t.

36. Answer C

To directly vary means directly proportional, and so s(t) = mt, where m is a constant. We have two equations: (1) 1 = mx, and (2) 5 = m(x-2). Note: x is a *constant* here. Thanks, SAT. From (1), m = 1/x. Substituting this expression into (2), 5 = 1/x • (x-2). Multiplying both sides by x, 5x = x-2. Thus, 4x = -2, and isolating x, x = -1/2.

Algebra and Real-World Problems   Chapter 11

37. Answer 4

From |x-1| = 2, x-1 = ±2, or x = 3, and -1. From and |y+7| = x, y+7 = ±x, or (1) y = x - 7 and (2) y = -x - 7. Plug the two values of x into (1) and (2) to arrive at 4 different possibilities. When x = 3, (1) becomes y = 3 - 7 = -4; When x = 3, (2) becomes y = -3 - 7, or y = -10; When x = -1, (1) becomes y = -1 - 7 = -8; and when x = -1, (2) becomes y = 1 - 7 = -6. The only value of y satisfying |y| < 5 is y = -4. Thus, |y| = 4.

Alternate Solution: Note that since |y+7| = x, x must be positive. Don't test x = -1.

38. Answer 1

So, $z = kx^n y^m$, where k, n and m are constants. Note that y doesn't change from the first to the second row. In that case, when x doubles, z quadruples. Thus, n = 2. Likewise, between the second and third rows, x is constant, and y doubles and z doubles. Thus m = 1. So the functional form is $z = kx^2 y^1$. We still don't know k, but we can choose any row to solve for k. Looking at the first row, $3 = k \cdot 1^2 \cdot 3^1$, and thus k = 1. So, $z = x^2 y$, and therefore, $y = z/x^2$. When z = 9 and x = 3, y = 1.

39. Answer A

From |x-1| = 2, either x - 1 = 2, or x - 1 = -2. Therefore, x can be either 3 or -1. Since x is less than zero, x must equal -1. Likewise, from |y+7| = 11, y can be either 4 or -18. Since y is less than zero, y must equal -18. y - x = -18 - (-1) = -17.

Alternate Solution: Since x is less than zero, we know the argument of |x-1| must be negative. Thus x - 1 = -2, or x = -1. Similar reasoning in |y+7| = 11 yields y + 7 = -11, or y = -18. Therefore, y - x = -18 + 1 = -17.

40. Answer 48

Right away you should spot that the combined denominator has (x+1)(x-1) as a factor, which equals $x^2 - 1$. Substituting this on the left, $6x^2 / (2x(x^2 - 1)) = 3x/(x^2 - 1)$. We are told that this equals 21/y. Isolate y by inverting both sides and multiplying by 21 yields $7(x^2-1)/x = y$. We must now search for integer x>1 such that y will also be an integer. The equation can be rewritten as $7/x \cdot (x^2-1) = y$. Since y is an integer, the left-hand side must be an integer. Since $x^2 - 1$ is always an integer, choosing x = 7 will force the left side to be an integer. Therefore, if x = 7, and $y = 7/7 \cdot (7^2-1) = 48$.

Alternate Solution: Start the long road with x = 2 and evaluate y at progressively larger values of x. Ugh. Nope. This problem is designed to save a very clever student time.

Alternate Solution II: Cancelling the factor 2x in the numerator and denominator, one may equate the two numerators 3x = 21, in which case x = 7. Now, this isn't necessarily the only integer value x may take, but it is one possible value. Plugging x = 7 into the remaining denominator, (x+1)(x-1), and equating that to y gives y = 48. An integer! All they wanted was one possible solution. This is one.

41. Answer A

You can get this by algebraic long division. Divide the 4th order polynomial by x - 1.

$$\begin{array}{r} 4x^3 + 4x^2 + x + 2 \\ x-1 \overline{) 4x^4 - 3x^2 + x + k} \end{array}$$

$4x^4 - 4x^3$
_____

$4x^3 - 3x^2 + x + k$
$4x^3 - 4x^2$
_____

$x^2 + x + k$
$x^2 - x$
_____

$2x + k$
$2x - 2$
_____

$k + 2$

If the remainder must be zero, then k must equal -2.

Alternate Solution: If (x-1) divides evenly into the polynomial, then x = 1 is a root of the polynomial. Thus, with x = 1, 4 - 3 + 1 + k = 0. Solving for k, k = -2. *Much* easier.

42. Answer C

If y = ax^2 + bx + c passes through the point (0, -2), then c must equal -2. We can use the remaining two points, (1,1), and (2,6) to solve for a and b. Using the point (1,1), 1 = a + b - 2, or a + b = 3. Well, that's it. However, if you were unlucky enough to have chosen (2,6) as the next point in the process of discovering the constants, you would have to solve for a and b with simultaneous equations before calculating their sum.

43. Answer B

The initial cost of the first 1/4 mile is $2.50. Thereafter each 1/2 mile costs $1, or $2 per mile. Drop the units of $. Expressing the distance, d, in miles, the cost to travel d miles is 2.50 (for the first 1/4 mile) plus (d - 1/4) • 2. The cost of driving d miles is 2.50 + 2d - .50 = 2.00 + 2d. The rider can pay no more than $20: 2.00 + 2d ≤ 20.

Algebra and Real-World Problems   Chapter 11

44. Answer A

$$\frac{4x}{x+6} + \frac{2x}{2x+12} = \frac{-60}{2(x+6)}$$ may be expressed with a common denominator as:

$$\frac{8x}{2x+12} + \frac{2x}{2x+12} = \frac{-60}{2x+12}$$. Since the denominators are all equal, if the equation

can be solved, then 8x + 2x = -60. Solving for x, x = -6. However, this value of x will cause each of the denominators to be zero, the value of their terms will be undefined, and thus there is no solution to this equation. Very tricky, this one.

45. Answer 2

$$x^3 - 2x^2 + 2x - 4 = 0$$

This is a cubic equation, and some cubic equations will have common factors between the higher (cubic and quadratic) pair and lower (linear and constant) pair of terms. The first two terms on the left side can be factored as $x^2(x-2)$. The last two terms can similarly be factored as 2(x-2). Aha - both higher and lower order pairs of terms have a factor of (x-2). This means the entire equation can be rewritten as $(x-2)(x^2+2) = 0$. The (x-2) term produces a solution at x = 2. The (x^2+2) term produces two solutions, $\pm i\sqrt{2}$, but these are both imaginary. So the one real solution to this cubic equation is 2.

Alternate Solution: The SAT will often present equations whose solutions are small integers. If you can't see the algebraic solution, try x = 0, 1, -1, 2, -2...

46. Answer B

The numerator of this expression can be forced to have one term that is a multiple of the denominator: 2x - 4 = 2(x+8) - 20. Therefore the entire expression can be rewritten as $\frac{2(x+8)-20}{x+8} = 2 - \frac{20}{x+8}$. Algebraic manipulations of this kind can sometimes (though not very often) expedite the development of a solution. Cool.

Alternate Solution: When x=0 in the original expression, its value is -1/2. Fortunately, among the choices, only (B) has a value of -1/2 when x=0.

Alternate Solution II: Slog the polynomial division. It won't take that long.

47. Answer 1/4

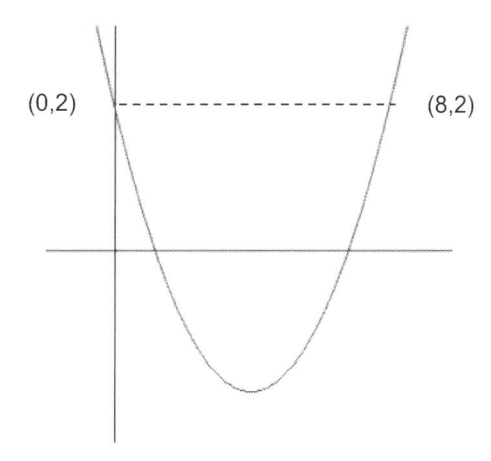

We are given enough information in the graph to determine the vertex, and hence we can put the function in vertex form: $y = a(x-h)^2 + k$. From symmetry, the x value of the vertex is the mid-value between the two points (0,2) and (8,2), i.e., $x = 4$. From the range given, $y \geq -2$, so the y value at the vertex is $y = -2$. Therefore, the vertex form of the function is, by definition, $y = a(x-4)^2 - 2$. The given points *must* solve this equation. To determine a, simply put one of the two points given and solve for a. The simplest point to use is (0,2): $2 = a(0-4)^2 - 2$. Simplifying this, $4 = 16a$, or $a = 1/4$.

Alternate solution: If you forgot to use the vertex form, you can still solve for a using the standard form and plugging in the points given (and the inferred vertex). Plug the point (0,2) into the standard form $y = ax^2 + bx + c$. Thus, $2 = 0 + 0 + c$. So $c = 2$. The other two points are (8,2) and the vertex, which can be determined as above to be (4,-2). Since $c = 2$, we can use these two points to form 2 simultaneous equations:

$2 = 64a + 8b + 2$ using (8,2)
$-2 = 16a + 4b + 2$ using (4,-2)

Multiplying the bottom equation by -2 and adding to the top equation will eliminate terms involving b. The resulting sum is $6 = 32a - 2$, or $8 = 32a$. Thus, $a = 1/4$.

48. Answer B

We need an expression for xy. The two equations, (1) $x - y = z$ and (2) $x + y = r$, can be added to result in (3) $2x = r + z$. Subtracting (1) from (2) gives (4) $2y = r - z$. Multiplying (3) and (4) results in $4xy = (r+z)(r-z) = r^2 - z^2$. Dividing both sides by 4 gives the answer: $xy = (r^2 - z^2)/4$. Difficulty level: *very* high. Number of steps: few.

Alternate Solution: (1) $z^2 = x^2 + y^2 - 2xy$ and (2) $r^2 = x^2 + y^2 + 2xy$,. Subtracting (1) from (2) gives $r^2 - z^2 = 4xy$. Therefore, $xy = (r^2 - z^2)/4$.

Alternate Solution II: Try x=2 and y=1. Thus z=1 and r=3. Only (B) works.

49. Answer 2

If $xy + \frac{1}{xy} = 2$, then (1) $(xy + \frac{1}{xy})^2 = 4$. The left side of (1) can be expanded: $[xy + \frac{1}{xy}]^2 = x^2y^2 + \frac{2xy}{xy} + \frac{1}{x^2y^2} = x^2y^2 + 2 + \frac{1}{x^2y^2}$. From (1), this equals 4. Therefore, $x^2y^2 + \frac{1}{x^2y^2} = 2$.

Alternate Solution: Because x and y occur together everywhere in the question they can be combined into a single variable, m = xy, for easy algebra:

If $m + \frac{1}{m} = 2$, then $(m + \frac{1}{m})^2 = 4$. The expression of the left can be expanded: $[m + \frac{1}{m}]^2 = m^2 + \frac{2m}{m} + \frac{1}{m^2} = m^2 + 2 + \frac{1}{m^2} = 4$. Therefore, $m^2 + \frac{1}{m^2} = 2$, where m = xy.

50. Answer 256

We need the value of x if (1) $a = 4\sqrt{4}$ and (2) $4a = \sqrt{4x}$. This is confusing, but let's carefully use (1) and (2). From (1), we know that $4a = 16\sqrt{4}$. Using this in (2), we see that (3) $16\sqrt{4} = \sqrt{4x}$. We square both sides and get 256•4 = 4x, and so x = 256.

Alternate Solution: From (3) above, we can just bring the 16 inside the radical on the left by squaring it: $\sqrt{256 \cdot 4} = \sqrt{4x}$. From this it is obvious that x must be 256.

Alternate Solution II: Of course, $\sqrt{4} = 2$. Therefore, a = 8. $4a = \sqrt{4x}$ becomes $32 = 2\sqrt{x}$. So $16 = \sqrt{x}$, or $x = 16^2 = 256$.

51. Answer 3

We are given the equation $-\frac{53}{sx-2} - 8x - 3 = \frac{24x^2+25x-47}{sx-2}$ and must solve for s. This looks like a "coefficients of same powers of x must be equal" type question. Multiply each side of the equation by sx - 2 to get rid of the denominators. This results in:

$$-53 - (8x+3)(sx-2) = 24x^2 + 25x - 47.$$

Collect powers of x on the left: (1) $-8sx^2 + (16-3s)x - 47 = 24x^2 + 25x - 47$. Comparing the coefficients of x^2, 24 = -8s, and thus s = -3. The question asked for -s, so -s = 3.

Alternate Solution: You can also compare the coefficients of x^1 in (1) above. In this case, 16 - 3s = 25, again showing that s = -3.

Chapter 12

Simultaneous Equations

A set of simultaneous equations is a set of two or more equations constraining the values of two or more unknowns. The first known description of simultaneous equations can be found in the *Jiuzhang Suanshu* (Nine Chapters of the Mathematical Art), written in China during the second century B.C.E. They've been challenging students ever since. Imagine: simultaneous equations, way back then. Yet, progress here on Earth is often slow and erratic. It took another 2000 years for *Homo sapiens* (Latin: "wise man") to invent the friction match. Let's not get cocky. With just a few changes along the way, our current world might be all sparkly like *Star Trek* – or as muddy as a rugby pitch in rain.

Back to the subject – a set of equations is a set of constraints on the variables involved. Got two equations with two unknowns? Solved (in most cases).

We'll be covering the several broad categories of hard questions on the SAT that are related to simultaneous equations. Among them, the first is the "base constant + rate" type problem. The second category of questions involves one type of object being distributed into sets of two different sizes. A third type involves systems of equations that are *underdetermined*, or have fewer equations than variables. A fourth type of problem involves systems of equations and inequalities.

The subject is reviewed, and 18 Archetypes are fully explored. They should be mastered prior to the test. An additional 27 practice problems support and expand the firmament of archetypes.

Don't Show Up Without Knowing…

How To …

- Translate verbal descriptions into simultaneous equations
- Use direct substitution to solve simultaneous equations
- Add or subtract simultaneous equations to eliminate a variable
- Scale simultaneous equations to allow variable elimination
- Multiply and divide simultaneous equations to effect a solution
- Solve simultaneous equations graphically using the intersection of points
- Recognize simultaneous equations with no solution

Chapter 12					Simultaneous Equations

Quick Review and Definitions

Simultaneous equations are sets of equations (usually two equations on the SAT) involving multiple unknowns. They most often will be linear equations. If the number of unknowns, or variables, is the same as the number of equations, the values of the variables which solve the set of equations can be determined in almost all cases.

Simultaneous equations show up in three basic formats on the SAT: straightforward algebraic math problems, real-world word problems, and problems that are represented by two intersecting lines or other figures. Word problems are often the most difficult because it can be difficult to determine the simultaneous equations that represent the situation in the problem.

Direct Substitution

If there are two equations and two unknowns, say, x and y, you can use one equation to isolate x in terms of y, and then substitute that expression for x in the other equation. That second equation now only involves y. Then you can solve for the value of y. Once the value of y is obtained, it can be used in either of the two original equations to solve for x.

As a trivial example, if

(1) $x = y - 1$
(2) $2x = y + 3$

you can substitute the expression for x in equation (1) into equation (2), creating an equation with one unknown, y. Hence, $2(y-1) = y + 3$, or $2y - 2 = y + 3$. Isolating y, $y = 5$. Now you can substitute $y = 5$ into either equation and solve for $x = 4$.

Adding And Subtracting Simultaneous Equations

Sometimes a much faster way to solve simultaneous equations involves adding or subtracting the equations from each other. Since both equations (1) and (2) above are true, it must also be that the sum or difference of these equations is also true. If the left side of equation (1) is subtracted from the left side of equation (2), and the same is done for the right sides, the result is a single equation where all instances of y have been cancelled: $2x - x = y + 3 - (y-1)$, or $x = 4$. Now $x = 4$ can be plugged into either (1) or (2) to solve for y. Again, $y = 5$.

Scaling Simultaneous Equations Before Addition

Since equation (1) above is true, then after multiplying both sides by a factor of 2, the relationship still holds. Doing so produces a new, scaled equation, (3) $2x = 2y - 2$. So, another way around our original problem is to notice that (3) may be subtracted from (2) to yield $2x - 2x = 0 = y - 2y + 3 - (-2)$, or $0 = -y + 5$, which may be solved with $y = 5$.

So scaling one (or both) simultaneous equations by a constant (or even a variable) prior to subtracting or adding them together may the fastest route to solving simultaneous equations.

Multiplying Simultaneous Equations

Considering the following system of equations, what is the value of xy?

(1) $\frac{y}{z} - 3 = 1$

(2) $3xz + 2 = 6$

This looks beastly. But there's a trick. These equations may be rearranged, moving the constants to the right side:

(1) $\frac{y}{z} = 4$

(2) $4xz = 4$

Multiplying the left side of (1) by the left side of (2), and doing the same to the right sides, we arrive at a single equation, $4xy = 16$. Therefore, $xy = 4$. We had two equations and three unknowns, but were able to eliminate z and come up with a value for the product xy.

Dividing Simultaneous Equations

For example, if

(1) $2yz + 5 = 21$, and
(2) $xz - 2 = 14$,

what is the value of y/x? These equations may be reorganized:

(1) $2yz = 16$
(2) $xz = 16$

Dividing (1) by (2), (notice neither x nor z can be zero) we get $2y/x = 1$, or $y/x = 1/2$.

Linear Simultaneous Equations: Intersecting Lines

A line is represented by a linear equation in standard form: y = ax + b. A system of two linear simultaneous equations may be thought of as two lines. The solution to the system of simultaneous equations is the pair of values, x and y, that solve both equations. In terms of the lines these equations represent, the solution represents the point (x,y) where the lines intersect. The lines have one point in common.

For example, the simultaneous equations

(1) y = x
(2) y = 1 - x

can be represented by their respective lines shown in the graph below.

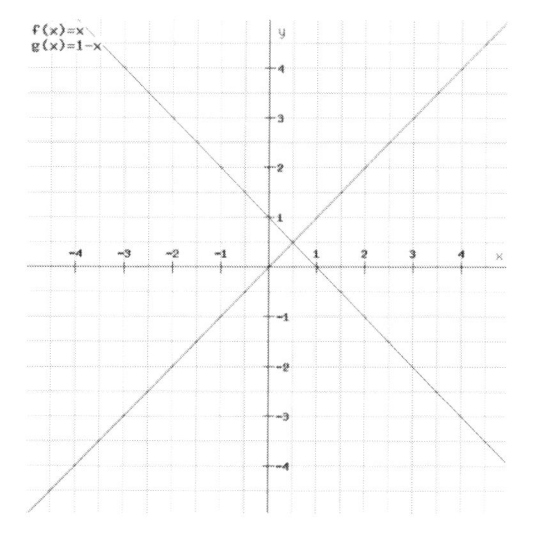

Adding equations (1) and (2) above, we get 2y = 1. The solution to this system of equations is y = 1/2, x = 1/2. You can see that this corresponds to the point of intersection of the two lines in the graph.

Linear Simultaneous Equations: How Many Solutions?

If two different lines are parallel (but not collinear), then there is no point of intersection. So a system of linear equations will have no solution if the lines that the equations represent are parallel to each other (have the same slope). For example,

$$2x - 3y = 4$$
$$4x - 6y = -1$$

has no solution because the lines have the same slopes: x:y → 2:(-3) = 4:(-6).

Simultaneous Equations   Chapter 12

In general if the two simultaneous linear equations are:

$$a_1x + b_1y = c_1$$
$$a_2x + b_2y = c_2$$

Then if $a_1/a_2 \neq b_1/b_2$ the lines intersect and there is one solution
             $a_1/a_2 = b_1/b_2 \neq c_1/c_2$ the lines are parallel and there is no solution
             $a_1/a_2 = b_1/b_2 = c_1/c_2$ the lines are *collinear* → infinitely many solutions

Nonlinear Simultaneous Equations

You can also use substitution when simultaneous equations involve higher powers of unknowns. Consider solving for y, given the following equations:

(1) $y = x + 1$
(2) $2y = -x^2 + 5$

Here is a case of a line (1) and a parabola (2) possibly intersecting each other. From (1), (3) $x = y - 1$. Substitute (3) in (2), yielding a quadratic equation in y: $2y = -(y^2 - 2y + 1) + 5$. In standard form, $y^2 - 4 = 0$. This equation can be factored as $(y+2)(y-2) = 0$. So $y = \pm 2$. These two values for y can then each be substituted into (1) to solve for x. When $y = 2$, $x = 1$ and when $y = -2$, $x = -3$. So the line and the parabola intersect at two points: (2, 1) and (-2, -3). In general, a line and a parabola could intersect at two, one, or zero points.

When There Are Fewer Equations than Unknowns

Two equations and three unknowns cannot in general be solved for all three unknowns independently. Such systems of equations are called *underdetermined*. However, you can often solve for one unknown in terms of one of the other unknowns.

Consider the following set of equations:

(1) $x = 2y + 1$
(2) $x = 2/z + 1$

If $z \neq 0$, what is z in terms of y? Notice that (1), which puts x in terms of y, may substitute for x on the left side of (2) to enable us to solve for z in terms of y. Alternatively, we may subtract (2) from (1) to give one equation in terms of y and z: $0 = 2y - 2/z$. Rearranging, $2/z = 2y$. Inverting both sides and cancelling the 2, $z = 1/y$.

Notice also that you may rearrange this solution to solve for the *value* of $yz = 1$. Asking for the value of yz is a curveball the SAT could throw to make this problem seem harder.

Simultaneous Equations Involving One Inequality

A system of equations may include one or more inequalities. Consider for example,

(1) 12y = x + 4
(2) y > -x + 12

Equation (1) ensures that any solution must lie along the line 12y = x + 4. Inequality (2) limits any solutions to points *above* the line (3) y = -x + 12. Solutions lie above line (3) because for each value of x, *every* value of y *greater than* (above) -x + 12 will solve the system of equations. First, use (1) to put x in terms of y: x = 12y - 4. This expression for x can now be substituted into inequality (2) to yield y > -12y + 4 + 12. So 13y > 16, or y > 16/13. Only points along line (1) with y > 16/13 are solutions.

Simultaneous Equations Involving Two Inequalities

Consider the following system of two inequalities:

(1) y < x
(2) y > 2 - x

What region in the x-y plane do solutions to this system of inequalities exist?

First, sketch the lines y = x and y = 2 - x.

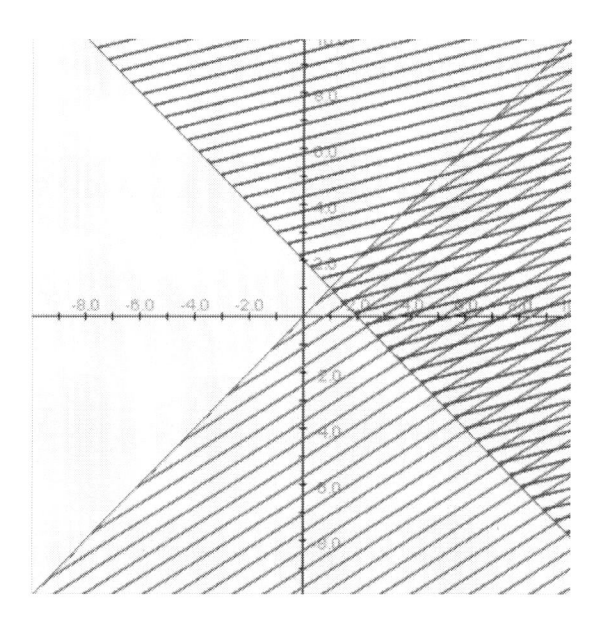

Those points that satisfy both inequalities will occur in the double-hashed region in the sketch above. They correspond to points below the line y = x and above the line y = 2 - x.

On the SAT you might have to identify a figure corresponding to the region where solutions to such a system fall, identify the quadrants in which solutions will fall, or identify which of several points would solve the system of inequalities. Solutions to the above set of simultaneous inequalities are only found in quadrants I and IV (within the double-hashed region). For example, the points (4,2) and (8,-5) are solutions.

Chapter 12 — Simultaneous Equations

SAT Archetypes

Direct Substitution

If $a = 2x + 4$ and $b = 6 + 4x^2$, what is b in terms of a?

(A) $a^2 - 8a + 15$
(B) $a^2 - 8a + 22$
(C) $a^2 + 36$
(D) $4a^2 - 36$

How do I start?

Use the first equation to put x in terms of a. Substitute this into second equation to produce an equation for b in terms of a.

Solution

We may rearrange the first equation to put x in terms of a: $x = (a-4)/2$. This can be substituted into the second equation. Hence, $b = 6 + 4 \cdot [(a-4)^2/4] = 6 + a^2 - 8a + 16$. Simplifying, $b = a^2 - 8a + 22$.

Answer B

The Take-Away

Here we have two equations and three unknowns, a, b, and x. As a result you can (with rare exceptions) only solve for one of the unknowns in terms of either one of the other two unknowns. There is an example of an exception to this rule later in the archetypes.

Simultaneous Equations   Chapter 12

Interpreting Verbal Simultaneous Equations

The square of y is equal to 9 times the square of x. If y is 3 less than 3x, what is the value of -2y?

SR

How do I Start?

Carefully translate each sentence into equations.

Solution

From the first verbal equation, (1) $y^2 = 9x^2$. The second verbal equation corresponds to (2) $y = 3x - 3$, from which we can express x in terms of y: $x = (y+3)/3$. Substituting this expression into (1) gives (3) $y^2 = 9(y+3)^2/9 = y^2 + 6y + 9$. Canceling the y^2 terms on either side of (3) gives $0 = 6y + 9$. Solving for y, $y = -3/2$. Therefore, $-2y = 3$.

Alternate Solution

One can solve equation (1) for y in terms of x by taking the square root: $y = \pm 3x$. Substitute both expressions for y(x) in (2) above: (a) $3x = 3x - 3$ and (b) $-3x = 3x - 3$. Equation (a) simplifies to $0 = -3$; it has no solutions. Equation (b) gives $-6x = -3$, or $x = 1/2$. Using this value in equation (2) gives us $y = 3/2 - 3$, or $y = -3/2$, thus $-2y = 3$.

Alternate Solution II

Squaring (2) above gives $y^2 = 9x^2 - 18x + 9$. We can equate this equation for y^2 to the equation for y^2 given in equation (1) above. Thus, $9x^2 - 18x + 9 = 9x^2$. Cancelling $9x^2$ on both sides, this may be solved for x: $-18x + 9 = 0$, or $x = 1/2$. Using this value in equation (2) gives $y = 3/2 - 3$, or $y = -3/2$, and thus $-2y = 3$.

Answer 3

The Take-Away

Okay, but what was that? Equation (1) $y^2 = 9x^2$ is quadratic in x *and* y, and after taking the square root of both sides yields (4) $y = \pm 3x$. This defines *two* lines with slopes 3 and -3. Equation (2) above, $y = 3x - 3$, is a line with a slope of 3. One of the lines from (4), $y = 3x$, is parallel to the line in (2), and hence those two lines will not intersect and will not produce a solution. This gave rise to the $0 = -3$ equation in the Alternate Solution.

Chapter 12   Simultaneous Equations

Real World Simultaneous Equations

Alva and Jude keep tropical fish in tanks. Alva keeps two fish in each of his tanks, and Jude keeps 4 fish in each of his tanks. If Jude has 5 fewer tanks than Alva, and together they have a total of 100 fish, how many fish does Jude have?

SR

How do I Start?

We are told that the total number of fish equals 100. For each person, the number of fish = the number of fish per tank • the number of tanks. Therefore, the total number of fish = 100 = 2•number of Alva's tanks + 4•number of Jude's tanks.

Solution

Let A = the number of tanks Alva has, and let J = the number of tanks Jude has. We know from the data in the problem that (1) J = A - 5. The total number of fish may be represented by the equation (2) 2A+ 4J = 100. Rearranging (1), A = J + 5, and using this expression of A in terms of J in (2), 2(J+5) + 4J = 100. Rearranging, and solving for J, 6J = 90, and so J = 15. Jude has 15 tanks, and therefore Jude has 4•15 = 60 fish.

Alternate Solution

Of course, (2) can give A in terms of J, which could be plugged into (1) to solve for J.

Alternate Solution II

The problem can be guided by dimensional analysis. There are a total of 100 fish kept by both. Let A and J equal the number of tanks Alva and Jude have, respectively. The number of fish Alva has equals 2 fish/~~tank~~ • A ~~tanks~~ = 2•A fish. Likewise, Jude will have 4 fish/tank • J tanks = 4•J fish. The total number of fish is the sum 2•A + 4•J = 100. We also know that J = A - 5. Substituting that into our expression for the total fish, 2•A + 4•(A-5) = 100. We can rearrange this to get A = 20, then get the number fish Alva has = 2•20 = 40. Since the total number of fish = 100, Jude has 100 - 40 = 60 fish.

Answer 60

The Take-Away

It is imperative that the problem be translated correctly into simultaneous algebraic equations. In particular, begin by assigning variables to corresponding nouns in the problem. Once simultaneous equations are set up, there can be several pathways involving substitution and/or other methods we've reviewed to develop a solution.

Simultaneous Equations Chapter 12

Base Cost And Rate From Two Data Points

A car rental company rents convertibles using the following method:

1. A base cost to rent the car, regardless of miles driven, and
2. An additional charge for every 10 miles driven.

The cost of renting a convertible and driving it 100 miles is $300. If it costs $400 to rent and drive one 200 miles, what is the cost of renting a convertible and driving it 450 miles?

SR

How do I Start?

Cost is a function with a constant term plus a term proportional to every 10 miles driven. This is a linear function: $y = b + m \cdot (\#miles/10)$, where y is the total cost, b is the constant base cost, m is the cost for every 10 miles driven, and #miles is the total miles driven. Note that we have to divide #miles by 10. There are two driving scenarios given, each with different miles and costs. Convert these scenarios into simultaneous equations.

Solution

We are given two scenarios in the problem from which we can form simultaneous equations. Dropping the $ units, (1) $300 = b + m \cdot (100/10)$, and (2) $400 = b + m \cdot (200/10)$. Subtracting (1) from (2), we can eliminate b: $100 = 10m$, which means $m = 10$. Substituting this value into (1), $300 = b + 100$, and so $b = 200$, the base cost. Now we know the values of m and b. The cost of driving 450 miles $= 200 + 10 \cdot (450/10) = 650$.

Alternate Solution

Use (1) to solve for b in terms of m, then substitute that in (2) to solve for m and then b.

Alternate Solution II

Why every 10 miles? Set this up as an additional charge for every *1 mile*: $y = b + r \cdot miles$. (3) $300 = b + 100r$, and (4) $400 = b + 200r$. Subtracting (3) from (4): $100 = 100r$, or $r = 1$. Using this in either (3) or (4), $b = 200$. The cost of driving 450 miles $= 200 + 450 \cdot 1 = 650$.

Alternate Solution III

It costs an extra $100 to go an extra 100 miles – they charge $1 per mile above the base cost. The base cost must be $b = 300 - 100 = 200$. So 450 miles costs $460 + 200 = 650$.

Chapter 12   Simultaneous Equations

Answer 650

The Take-Away

Base cost plus rate problems always express the cost of things or a service in four variables, or potential unknowns: Total cost = fixed cost + cost per unit • number of units.

Purchase of Two Types With Different Unit Costs (1)

The university chemistry supply department spends $1500 on two chemicals: 400 liters of carbon tetrachloride and an unspecified amount of benzene. If carbon tetrachloride costs $2.20 per liter and benzene costs $1.24 per liter, how many liters of benzene were purchased?

(A) 450
(B) 500
(C) 550
(D) 650

How do I start?

The total cost is $1500 = cost of carbon tetrachloride + cost of benzene. From the data, we can calculate the cost of carbon tetrachloride = $2.20/liter • 400 liters = $880.

Solution

Let b equal the unknown liters of benzene. The total cost, $1500, must equal the costs of carbon tetrachloride plus benzene. $1500 = $2.20/liter • 400 liters + $1.24/liter • b liters. Dropping the units, 1500 = 880 + 1.24 • b. Simplifying, 620 = 1.24 • b. Trivial from here to solve for b = 500 liters.

Answer B

The Take-Away

This archetype is often found on the SAT. The general equation for this scenario is: total cost = number of units$_1$ • cost per unit$_1$ + number of units$_2$ • cost per unit$_2$. There are 5 potential unknowns. You'll typically solve for one of the variables and be given values for the other 4 (or at least be given a way to calculate those values).

Simultaneous Equations   Chapter 12

Purchase of Two Types With Different Unit Costs (2)

A recent order for 15,000 items of building supplies was composed of bolts and nails. Nails cost 5 cents each. The entire order arrived at an expense of $1500. If there were 2500 bolts, what is the cost of each bolt?

SR

How do I start?

Let n equal the number of nails and b equal the number of bolts. Let Cn = the cost of each nail and Cb = the cost of each bolt, in dollars. There are two constraints in the problem that will allow us to construct two simultaneous equations that govern this purchase order:

15,000 = n + b
1500   = n•Cn + b•Cb

Solution

The first equation says that the total number of items (15,000) equals the number of nails plus the number of bolts. The second equation says that the total cost (1500) equals the cost of all nails (n•Cn) plus the cost of all bolts (b•Cb). In addition to knowing the left sides of these equations, we also know the number of bolts, b = 2500, and the cost of each nail, Cn = $.05. So there are two unknowns left in this system of 2 equations: n and Cb. Putting in all known values (and ignoring the units), these equations become

15,000 = n + 2500
1500   = n•.05 + 2500•Cb

We can use the first equation to solve for n: n= 12,500. We can use that value in the second equation to solve for Cb, the cost of each bolt. 1500 = 12,500•.05 + 2500•Cb. This equation yields (after isolation) Cb = .35.

Answer .35

The Take-Away

The general form of this system of equations is

Total items = number of type a + number of type b
Total cost = number of type a • unit cost of a + number of type b • unit cost of b

There are 6 potential unknowns, and problems will typically give the value of 4, leaving 2 unknowns that can be solved as a system of simultaneous equations.

Chapter 12   Simultaneous Equations

Subsets With Two Different Sizes

A building houses a company with 20 offices that have either two or three chairs per office. If there are a total of 48 chairs in the company, how many offices have 3 chairs?

(A) 6
(B) 7
(C) 8
(D) 9

How do I start?

Learn to recognize this type of problem - there are many variants, but the relationships between nouns in the problem are the same.

This is a relatively simple simultaneous equation problem. There are a total of 20 offices, which are either two-chair or three-chair types. Let t = the number of two-chair offices, and r = the number of three-chair offices. Note that r + t = 20. Note also that the number of chairs in two-chair offices = 2•t, and the number of chairs in three-chair offices = 3•r.

Solution

First, let's set this up with simultaneous equations. Chairs go into offices of only two types: two-chair or three-chair offices. There are 20 offices total. If t is the number of two-chair offices and r is the number of three-chair offices, then (1) t + r = 20. We are also told that the total number of chairs, which go into either two-chair or three-chair offices, equals 48. The number of chairs in two-chair offices is 2•t, and the number of chairs in three-chair offices is 3•r. So their sum is (2) 2t + 3r = 48. Summarizing:

(1) t + r = 20
(2) 2t + 3r = 48

Rearranging (1), t = 20 - r. Substituting this into (2) gives 2(20-r) + 3r = 48. Solving for r, the number of three-chair offices, r = 8.

Notice a similarity to the fish tank problem we saw earlier in this chapter?

Alternate Solution

Multiplying (1) above by 2 gives (3) 2t + 2r = 40. Subtracting (3) from (2) above eliminates the variable t, immediately giving r = 8. If the equations are amenable to scaling and subtraction (or addition), that is usually quicker than substitution.

Simultaneous Equations   Chapter 12

Alternate Solution II

The total number of offices is 20. Let t = the number of two-chair offices. (4) The number of three-chair offices = (20-t). The number of chairs in two-chair offices is 2t. The number of chairs in three-chair offices is 3(20-t). Since the total number of chairs is 48, 2t + 3(20-t) = 48. Solve for t: t = 12. From (4), the number of three chair offices = (20-t) = (20-12) = 8.

Alternate Solution III

Better still, the number of each kind of office could be expressed in terms of the number of three chair offices. Let r = the number of three chair offices. Then, arguing as above, the number of two-chair offices equals (20-r). The number of chairs in three-chair offices = 3r, and the number of chairs in two-chair offices = 2•(20-r). The total number of chairs (48) is their sum: 48 = 3r + 2•(20-r). Isolating r, 8 = r.

Answer C

The Take-Away

Problems such as this can either be explicitly set up using simultaneous equations and solved by substitution, or scaling, and subtraction. However, one feature of such problems is often obvious (here, the fact that r = 20-t), so that the problem can be easily set up as one equation of a single variable (as in alternate solutions II and III).

Purchase of Two Types With Different Unit Costs (3)

A small country purchased two types of planes for 650 million dollars. A few planes cost 50 million dollars each. Four times that many cost 20 million dollars each. How many planes were purchased in total?

SR

How do I Start?

650 million dollars is the total cost of all 20 million dollar planes and 50 million dollar planes. The total number of planes is the sum of the numbers of 20 million dollar planes and 50 million dollar planes. Let T equal the total number of planes, t equal the number of twenty million dollar planes, and f equal the number of 50 million dollar planes. Therefore, (1) T = t + f. We know that 650 million dollars was the cost of these planes. The amount spent on 20 million dollar planes (in units of million dollars) is 20•t, and the amount spent

on 50 million dollar planes is 50•f. Thus, (2) 650 = 20•t + 50•f. A third constraint is given in the problem: the number of twenty million dollar planes is four times the number of fifty million dollar planes. Thus, (3) t = 4•f. We have a system of three equations and three unknowns: T, t, and f. To recap:

(1) T = t + f

(2) 650 = 20•t + 50•f

(3) t = 4•f

Solution

Ignore (1) for now because it is a single equation with three unknowns. Using (3), substitute t in terms of f into (2): 650 = 20•4•f + 50•f = 130f. Now solve for f: f = 650/130 = 5. Substituting f=5 into (3), t = 4•5 = 20. Now, using (1), the total number of planes = T = 20 + 5 = 25.

Alternate Solution

If we let f be the number of $50 million dollar planes and T be the total number of planes, then the number of $20 million dollar planes would be (T-f). The sum of the costs of both kinds of planes is $650 million dollars. Dropping the units of million dollars, (4) 650 = 50f + 20(T-f). The third sentence in the problem describes a second equation: (5) (T-f) = 4•f. Now we have two equations and two unknowns, T and f. Plugging (T-f) from (5) into (4), 650 = 50•f +20(4•f) = 130•f. Solving for f, the number of $50 million dollar planes, f = 5. The number of 20 million dollar planes = 4•f = 20. Therefore, T, the total number of airplanes, equals f + 4•f = 5 + 20 = 25 airplanes.

Answer 25

The Take-Away

Phrases such as "four times as many..." should lead you to consider an additional constraint on the relationships between variables, leading to an additional equation in the system of simultaneous equations. Identify all unknown variables and the constraints among variables in a problem.

Also - always look for any total that is partitioned into the several types, such as the two types of planes in this problem.

Changing Ratios That Define Simultaneous Equations

So far this semester, Jake has only passed 3 of the daily pass-fail quizzes in anatomy. In order for him to double his current ratio of passes to total quizzes taken, he needs to pass the next 12 quizzes in a row. Thus far, how many quizzes has Jake taken?

(A) 8
(B) 9
(C) 10
(D) 11

How do I Start?

Set up two equations, one for the current (unknown) ratio and another for double this ratio, which occurs after passing all of the next 12 quizzes. We don't know how many quizzes he has taken thus far, so the equations must be in terms of that unknown as well as the unknown original ratio. That's ok - two equations, two unknowns.

Solution

Let r = his current unknown pass/total ratio, and let the total number of quizzes taken thus far equal q. We don't know that either. But we do know that he's only passed 3 exams. Thus, (1) $r = 3/q$. But this ratio will double if he passes all of the next 12 quizzes. After this happens, the number of quizzes taken will be $q+12$, and the number of quizzes he has passed will be $3+12$. Now he has doubled the first ratio: (2) $2r = (3+12)/(q+12) = 15/(q+12)$. We have two equations, (1) and (2), and two unknowns, r and q. To recap:

(1) $r = 3/q$
(2) $2r = 15/(q+12)$

Note that by multiplying (1) by two yields (3) $2r = 6/q$. The left sides of equations (2) and (3) are now equal. Their right sides must be equal to each other: $15/(q+12) = 6/q$. Cross-multiplying denominators and rearranging yields $15q = 6(q+12)$, or $72 = 9q$. Solving for q, the number of quizzes Jake has taken thus far (before the next 12), $q = 8$.

Answer A

The Take-Away

Students may find it difficult to determine just what knowns and unknowns to work with. Also – this is another scenario where an initial ratio changes after some part is changed. We've seen this in chapter 5. It can often be couched in the form original ratio = x/(original total). If items are added, the new ratio is (x + added)/(original total + added).

Chapter 12 — Simultaneous Equations

Two Equations With Three Variables (1)

Assuming $\frac{y}{z} - 3 = 6$ and $3xz + 4 = 8$, then $xy =$

SR

How do I Start?

There are two equations and three unknowns, but we're only asked to solve for the product of x and y. There must be a way to eliminate z to solve for the value of xy. Solve for z in terms of y in the first equation, then substitute into second equation.

Solution

This problem may be solved by rearranging the first equation to solve for z in terms of y and then substituting this expression for z into the second equation. Note from the equations that x, y, and z can never equal zero. Multiplying both sides of the first equation by z yields y - 3z = 6z. Thus, y = 9z, and hence z = y/9. Substituting this result into the second equation yields 3xy/9 + 4 = 8, which yields after rearranging, xy = 4•9/3 = 12.

Alternate Solution

Use the second equation to solve for z in terms of x and substitute that into the first equation. Thus, z = 4/(3x). Plugging this into the first equation, y•(3x/4) - 3 = 6, or 3xy/4 = 9. Isolating xy, xy = 36/3 = 12.

Alternate Solution II

The first equation can be rearranged as (1) y/z = 9. The second equation can be rearranged as (2) 3xz = 4. Multiplying equations (2) and (1), 3xy = 9•4 = 36. So xy = 12.

Answer 12

The Take-Away

Most simultaneous equations can only be solved by substitution. The equations in this problem included terms with products of variables (y/z and xz). It is unlikely that scaling and adding (or subtracting) such equations will work. However, we were able (after rearrangement) to *multiply* the equations together to effect a solution, as shown in alternate solution II. In problems involving two equations and three variables, one can often solve for the value of some function of a two variables (xy, here) or for one variable in terms another.

Two Equations With Three Variables (2)

If $4x + 5y - 6z = 12$ and $x + 2y - 2z = -4$, what is the value of $x - y$?

(A) -2
(B) 0
(C) 16
(D) 24

How do I Start?

Again, we have two equations and three unknowns and are asked to solve for the value of a function of two variables, $x - y$. If you're going to get a value for $x - y$, then you'll have to eliminate z. Substitution is often a mess (but sometimes necessary). However, in this problem, the terms in the equations only include isolated, first-order variables. Add or subtract the equations to eliminate z. You may have to scale one or both of the equations.

Solution

If the second equation is multiplied by -3 and added to the first equation, the result is

$$\begin{array}{r} 4x + 5y - 6z = 12 \\ -3x - 6y + 6z = 12 \\ \hline x - y \phantom{{}+6z} = 24 \end{array}$$

The problem is constructed to not only get rid of z in this way, but to result in the desired expression, $x - y$.

Alternate Solution

Substitution. Use the second equation to solve for z in terms of x and y. Substitute this into the first equation. From the second equation, $z = (x+2y+4)/2$. Plugging this expression into the first equation does indeed result in (after quite a bit of algebra) $x - y = 24$. But, that will grind a whole lot of time compared to adding the scaled equations.

Answer D

The Take-Away

Some simultaneous equation problems are designed to be solved with the time-saving technique of scaling, and adding or subtracting. Always look for this way to solve two simultaneous equations - even problems with more unknowns than equations.

Chapter 12   Simultaneous Equations

Two Equations With Three Variables (3)

If $6x + 3z = y$ and $2x - 2y + z = 10$, what is the value of y?

(A) -15
(B) -6
(C) 0
(D) It cannot be determined from the information given

How do I Start?

There are two equations and three variables. In general, you can't solve for the value of one variable by itself in this situation. Such systems of equations are underdetermined. However, there might be a way to combine the two equations such that both x and z are eliminated. Don't assume that y can't be determined. Try scaling and adding the equations, and if that won't work, try substitution. And if those don't work, pick (D).

Solution

Since there are two equations and three variables, if one can solve for y, there must be a way to combine the two equations such that both x and z are eliminated. Try scaling and adding them. Rearrange each equation in the same format: (1) $6x - y + 3z = 0$, and (2) $2x - 2y + z = 10$. If (2) is multiplied by 3 we get (3) $6x - 6y + 3z = 30$. If (3) is subtracted from (1), the result is $0x + 5y + 0z = -30$, or $5y = -30$. Therefore, $y = -6$.

Alternate Solution

After division by 3, the first equation becomes (3) $2x + z = y/3$. After rearranging the second equation, we obtain (4) $2x + z = 10 + 2y$. Subtracting (4) from (3) allows us to eliminate x and z, thus yielding the equation for y only: $0 = y/3 - 2y - 10$. Collecting terms, $5y/3 = -10$, and so $y = -6$.

Alternate solution II

The second equation can be rearranged to solve for z in terms of x and y: $z = 10 + 2y - 2x$. Plugging this into the first equation, $6x + 3(10 + 2y - 2x) = y$. Multiplying 3 through the second term, this equation becomes $6x + 30 + 6y - 6x = y$, or $30 = -5y$. Therefore, $y = -6$.

Answer = B

The Take-Away

Whenever you encounter a set of simultaneous equations with more unknowns than equations, and you are asked to solve for the *numerical value* of one of the variables, you should remember that it is at least possible that the equations can be solved for that value. Substitution or scaling / addition may possibly give rise to the elimination of all variables except the one in question can be eliminated. But watch out if one of the choices is "It cannot be determined from the information given."

How could we solve for y with too few equations? In effect, the three equations restrict the x-y-z space to the plane y = -6. Within this plane, there are two equations and two (remaining) unknowns, x and z. Plugging y = -6 into the equations in the problem, they become equations for the *same line*: (5) 6x + 3z = -6, and (6) 2x + z = -2. Equation (5) is now just equation (6) multiplied by 3. It would not possible to use these equations together to solve for x and z independently. Any point on this one line is a valid solution pair of x and z. And all points on this line have a y-coordinate of -6. The best you could do is to solve for x in terms of z, or vice versa. You can't independently solve for x, y, and z.

Simultaneous Equations Involving Absolute Values

$|x + y| = 1$

$|x - 2y| = 0$

Given the equations above, which expression below gives the value(s) of y?

(A) 0, -2
(B) 2
(C) 1/3, -1/3
(D) 1/3, -2/3

How do I Start?

Because the equations are mixed (each equation involves two variables), substitution may be the best course to take. And note – if the absolute value of an expression equals zero, then the argument inside the absolute value function must equal zero.

Solution

If the absolute value of an expression equals zero, then the argument is zero. Thus, from the bottom equation, x - 2y = 0, or x = 2y. Substituting this into the top equation, $|x + y| = |2y + y| = |3y| = 1$. Thus, $|y| = 1/3$, or $y = \pm 1/3$.

Alternate Solution

From the top equation, x + y = ±1. So either (1) x = 1 - y, or (2) x = -1 - y. Substituting (1) into the bottom equation in the problem yields |1-y-2y| = |1-3y| = 0. The absolute value argument must be zero, which means that -3y = -1, or y = 1/3. Likewise, substituting (2) into the bottom equation yields y = -1/3. So y = 1/3 *and* y = -1/3 are solutions.

Alternate Solution II

The top equation may be rewritten (3) x + y = ±1, and the bottom equation may be rewritten (because ±0 is just 0) (4) x - 2y = 0. Subtracting (4) from (3) yields 3y = ±1, or y = ±1/3.

Answer C

The Take-Away

First, if the absolute value of an expression equals zero, then the argument (the expression between the two vertical lines | |) of the absolute value operator is zero. Second, simultaneous equations involving absolute values are almost always split into two sets of equations, involving the positive and negative arguments. Dead horse: if |x + y| = 1, then either x + y = 1 or x + y = -1. And notice in alternate solution II, we were able to subtract the equations here, even using the ± symbol to indicate multiple values.

Simultaneous Equations With One Inequality

If x - 5y = -2 and y ≥ -3x + 26, what is the minimum value of y?

SR

How do I start?

We need an inequality y ≥ constant. Use the first equation to put x in terms of y.

Solution

From the first equation, x = 5y - 2. Substituting this expression for x into the second inequality, y ≥ -3(5y - 2) + 26. This gives us y ≥ -15y + 6 + 26. Simplifying and putting all y terms on the left, 16y ≥ 32. Therefore, y ≥ 2.

Answer 2

Simultaneous Equations　　　　　　　　　　　　　　　　　　　　Chapter 12

The Take-Away

Simultaneous equations involving only one inequality may be treated in much the same way as ordinary simultaneous equations. Use the equation to eliminate (via substitution) all but one variable in the inequality. The inequality can then be simplified to define the bounds of the remaining variable.

Simultaneous Equations With Two Inequalities (1)

$$y < 2x + r$$
$$y > -x + s$$

The above system of inequalities is satisfied when variables $y = 0$ and $x = 1$. Which of the following relationships describes how constant r relates to constant s?

(A) $r > s/2$
(B) $r - s > -3$
(C) $r < s/2$
(D) $r + s < 3$

How do I start?

Yeah. This looks really hard. But we know that the point (1,0) satisfies both inequalities. Plug that point into both of them and see what you get. If needed, transform the resulting inequalities to make sure both are either "<," or ">."

Solution

Plugging (1,0) into the top equation gives $0 < 2 + r$, or (1) $-2 < r$. Plugging (1,0) into the bottom equation yields $0 > -1 + s$, or (2) $1 > s$. Now what? Reverse the direction of (2) so that it's also <: (3) $-1 < -s$. Now we can add (1) to (3): $-3 < r - s$. This corresponds to (B).

Answer B

The Take-Away

Simultaneous inequalities may be manipulated (carefully) in many of the ways one may manipulate simultaneous equations. Inequalities must have the same "direction" if they are to be added, etc. Just be careful about changing the direction of the inequality when employing operations such as inversion or multiplying by a negative value. In this problem we had to reverse the direction of inequality (2), and so had to multiply each side by -1.

Chapter 12   Simultaneous Equations

Simultaneous Equations With Two Inequalities (2)

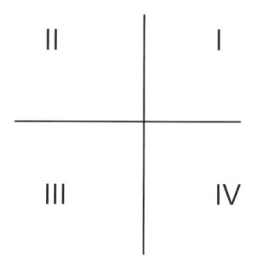

```
        II  |  I
        ----+----
        III |  IV
```

If the system of inequalities given by y > x + 2 and y > x/3 - 3 is graphed in the coordinate system above, which quadrant fails to include solutions to this system of inequalities?

(A) I
(B) II
(C) III
(D) IV

How do I start?

Sketch the lines governing the inequalities and use each inequality to determine its region of solutions. The bold, dotted-lines below represent the baseline equalities of their respective inequalities: (1) y = x + 2 and (2) y = x/3 - 3.

Solution

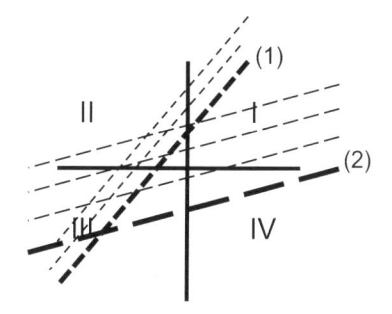

Each inequality has the form y > (linear expression of x). The region of solution to each (greater than) inequality can be thought of as a family of parallel lines shifted up from each bold dotted line. The lines of family (1) are on or above y = x + 2. The lines of family (2) are on or above y = x/3 - 3. Every point where one member of family (1) intersects a member of family (2) is a solution to the simultaneous inequalities. It is apparent by inspection that members of family (2) can have points (solutions) to y > x/3 - 3 in all four quadrants. However, members of family (1) can never have solutions to y > x + 2 in quadrant IV. No positive value of x can result in a negative value of y. There can be no intersection of the families and no solution to the simultaneous inequalities in quadrant IV.

357

Simultaneous Equations   Chapter 12

Alternate Solution

You can solve this with algebra too. Examine the first inequality, y > x + 2. If x > 0 then y > 2: all possible pairs (x,y) where x > 0 are only in quadrant I. Similarly, if x < 0, then y < 2: all possible pairs (x,y) where x < 0 will exist only in quadrants II and III. However, in neither case will points solving y > x + 2 occur in quadrant IV. We lucked out: if we had chosen the second inequality first, all four quadrants would have solutions.

Answer D

The Take-Away

Simultaneous inequalities may be solved graphically by shifting up and down the respective parallel family of graphs of the functions involved, depending on the direction of the inequalities. Also - note the alternative solution. We were able to solve this problem without resort to direct graphical means by analyzing the inequalities themselves.

Simultaneous Equations Involving Quadratics

$$2x + y = -4$$
$$(x+2)^2 + 4(x+2) + 8 = y$$

If y > 4, the above system of equations is solved by what value of y?

SR

How do I start?

Note how the bottom left expression is drafted in such a way that it is quadratic in (x+2).

Solution

Perhaps, given the quadratic on the bottom, there is a substitution of variables that will ease the solution. Letting (1) $z = (x+2)$, the bottom equation becomes (2) $z^2 + 4z + 8 = y$. Rearrange the top equation to isolate y: $y = -4 - 2x = -2(x+2)$. Look there, the gods are kind: $y = -2z$. Plugging this into (2), $z^2 + 4z + 8 = -2z$, or $z^2 + 6z + 8 = 0$. Factoring this equation, $(z + 4)(z + 2) = 0$. So (3) $z = -2$ *and* -4 solve this equation. From equation (1), $x = z - 2$. From (3), $x = -4$ and -6. Plug these values into the top equation and solve for y: $y = 4$ and $y = 8$. We need a value of y > 4, thus the answer is 8. Sometimes substitution of variables is a lot quicker. It wasn't so quick this time, but maybe saved a little effort.

Alternate Solution

From the top equation, (4) y = -4 - 2x. Substituting this expression for y in terms of x into the bottom equation yields (after much algebra) x^2 + 10x + 24 = 0. Factoring gives us (x+6)(x+4) = 0. So x = -6 and -4. Using (4), y = 8 and 4. Only y = 8 is greater than 4.

Answer 8

The Take-Away

Simultaneous equations involving quadratic equations can often be solved through simple substitution or perhaps even graphically. In this case a quirk of the quadratic expression involved enabled us to simplify the work through a substitution of variables.

Simultaneous Equations with No Solution

$$x - 5y = 33 \tfrac{1}{3}$$
$$mx + ny = 100$$

Let r = -n/m. For what value of r might the above system of equations have no solution?

SR

How do I start?

Simultaneous linear equations will never have a solution if the lines represented by the equations never intersect. The lines must be parallel.

Solution

If there is no solution, these lines must be parallel: they will have the same slope. Putting the top equation into slope-intercept form: (1) y = x/5 - 33 $\tfrac{1}{3}$ /5. Likewise, the bottom equation becomes (2) y = -mx/n + 100/n. If these lines are parallel, their slopes are equal. So -m/n in (2) must equal 1/5 from (1) if the lines are to be parallel. Thus, r = -n/m = 5.

Alternate Solution

If there is no solution, then the lines are parallel. If the lines above are parallel, then the y coefficient to x coefficient ratio in each equation must equal that of the other. Thus, -5:1 = n:m. Putting these in fractional representation: -5/1 = n/m. Therefore, r = -n/m = 5.

Answer 5

Simultaneous Equations — Chapter 12

The Take-Away

Linear simultaneous equations may have no solutions. If the lines representing the equations are parallel, then there will be no solutions – with one exception:

It is possible for the simultaneous equations above to have an *infinite* number of solutions. As we have seen, if we force the second equation to have -n/m = 5, then we are assured that the lines representing both equations are parallel. But *if* these parallel lines were also *collinear*, then every point on the top line is identical to a point on the bottom line. We can do this by choosing particular values of n and m. Now thus far we have only constrained the ratio of n/m = -5. If we choose the values n = -15 and m = 3 in the bottom equation, then the bottom equation becomes collinear with the first. Here's why. Putting n = -15 and m = 3 into the bottom equation, we obtain

$$3x - 15y = 100$$

Now, after dividing both sides of this equation by 3 (which doesn't alter the line), we get

$$x - 5y = 33\,^{1}/_{3}$$

which is *identical* to the top equation - the two equations are the same: there is really only one equation; and there are an infinite number of solutions. The simultaneous equations have collapsed into a single, linear equation with two variables. For *any* value of x there is a corresponding value of y that solves the equation, just like any single, linear equation.

So which is it – zero of infinite solutions? It's both, depending on the values of m and n. The ratio of the coefficients must be -5 either way. But *only* if n = -15 and m = 3 will the lines be collinear, resulting in an infinite number of solutions. Otherwise, the lines are parallel, but not collinear, and there will be no solutions.

Chapter 12   Simultaneous Equations

Practice Problems

1. If $a = 3x + 4$ and $b = 9x^2$, what is b in terms of a?

   (A) $a^2 - 8a + 15$
   (B) $a^2 - 8a + 16$
   (C) $a^2 + 36$
   (D) $4a^2 - 36$

2. The square of y is equal to 16 times the square of x. If y is 2 less than 4x, what is the value of x?

   SR

3. Alva and Jude keep tropical fish in tanks. Alva keeps exactly two fish per tank, and Jude keeps exactly four fish per tank. If Jude has twice the number of tanks Alva has, and together they have a total of 60 fish, how many fish does Alva have?

   SR

4. A small country ordered 1.64 billion dollars' worth of planes. Some planes cost x million dollars each, and the rest cost 50 million dollars each. If four times as many x million dollar planes were ordered as 50 million dollar planes, and 20 $50 million dollar planes were ordered, what is x?

   SR

5. A car rental company rents Jeeps using the following method: (1) A base cost to rent the car, regardless of miles driven, and (2) an additional charge for every 10 miles driven. The cost of renting a Jeep and driving it 200 miles is $300. If it costs $400 to rent and drive one 700 miles, what is the cost, in dollars, of renting a jeep and driving it 500 miles?

   SR

Simultaneous Equations   Chapter 12

6. Two gunfighters, Matt and Shorty, stand back-to-back in the middle of the street prior to a duel. They each take 12 steps in opposite directions, stop, turn, and face one another. Matt decides not to duel after all, walks back toward Shorty, who doesn't move, and arrives exactly in front of him in 15 additional steps. If Matt takes steps that do not vary in length and Shorty's steps do not vary in length, what is the ratio of the length of Matt's step to that of Shorty's step?

   SR

7. In an online poll for favorite French actor of all time, 14 million votes were cast, and each vote was for either Alain or Jacque. Jacque received 280,000 more votes than Alain. What Percent of the 14 million votes were cast for Alain?

   SR

8. Jake has only passed n of the 9 pass-fail quizzes in anatomy. In order for him to triple the ratio of passes to total quizzes taken, he needs to pass the next 12 quizzes in a row. How many quizzes has Jake passed thus far?

   SR

9. At one amusement park, customers may purchase tickets that include a park entrance fee as well as the pre-paid cost of a bundle of rides. The ticket price is computed based on the park entrance fee plus an additional charge proportional to the number of rides the ticket buyer is entitled to ride. The price *per ride* is the same for all ride-bundles. If one ticket for 9 rides costs $65 and four entry tickets for 20 rides cost $480, how many dollars would two 15-ride tickets cost?

   (A) 80
   (B) 95
   (C) 120
   (D) 190

10. Alf is currently 4 times the age of his young sister. In 10 years he will be 2 years more than twice her age. How old was Alf when his sister was one-year-old?

    SR

11. If 2x + 5y - 3z = 12 and x + 4y - 3z = -4, what is the value of x + y?

(A) -2
(B) 0
(C) 16
(D) 24

12. In the system of equations below, x and y are variables, and c is a constant.

$$2x + 6y + 5 = 0$$
$$8x + cy - 20 = 0$$

Which value of c will result in a system of equations that cannot be solved for values of x and y?

SR

13. If 2yz + 3 = 21 and 6xz - 2 = 6, then x/y =

SR

14. If $x = 2(3z^2 - z + 6)$ and 4y = -2z + 6, what is x in terms of y?

(A) 36y + 8
(B) $2y^2 - 12y + 12$
(C) $24y^2 - 68y + 60$
(D) $24y^2 + 8y + 24$

15. If $(x+y)^2 = 90$, what is one value of x if $(x-y)^2 = 30$ and 3x = 5y?

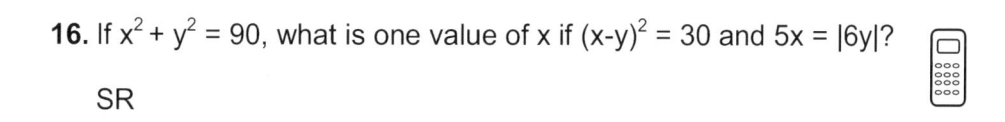

SR

16. If $x^2 + y^2 = 90$, what is one value of x if $(x-y)^2 = 30$ and 5x = |6y|?

SR

17. If 2x - 6y = z - 1 and 8x - z = -20 + 12y, what is the value of y - x?

SR

Simultaneous Equations   Chapter 12

18. Three golfers, Tom, Dick, and Harry, start the game each having T, D, and H golf tees, respectively. During the game, Tom gives Dick 6 tees, and Harry loses 3 tees. After these events, the total number of tees is 4 times the number Tom has. How many tees, in terms of D and H, are in Tom's possession after these events?

(A) $\dfrac{D-H}{4} + 6$

(B) $\dfrac{D+H}{3} + 7$

(C) $\dfrac{D-H}{3} + 3$

(D) $\dfrac{D+H}{3} + 1$

19. In the system of equations below,

$3x - 4y = -8$

$18x + ay = 13$,

where a is a constant, what value of a will result in no solutions for x and y?

(A) -24
(B) -8
(C) -6
(D) 8

20. If $x + 3z = y$ and $2y - 3z = 10 + x$, what is the value of y?

(A) -10
(B) -5
(C) 10
(D) It cannot be determined

21. A pro shop sells golf balls either separately at $3 per ball or in packs of 3 for $7.00. At the end of the week they sold 320 balls at an average price of $2.75. How many single balls did they sell?

(A) 175
(B) 200
(C) 225
(D) 250

22.

$|x + y| = 1$
$|x - y| = 3$
$y > 1$

Given the relations above, which choice below gives the value(s) of y?

(A) 2, 4
(B) 2
(C) 4/5, 5/3
(D) 5/3, 9/3

23. The university chemistry supply department spends $1500 on 800 liters of solvents: carbon tetrachloride and benzene. If carbon tetrachloride costs $2.25 per liter and benzene costs $1.25 per liter, how many liters of carbon tetrachloride were purchased?

(A) 450
(B) 500
(C) 550
(D) 650

24. In a company, each office has either two or three chairs. If 6 offices have three chairs, and there are a total of 118 chairs, how many offices are there?

SR

Simultaneous Equations   Chapter 12

25. The university chemistry supply department spends $3000 on two chemicals: 400 liters of carbon tetrachloride and 500 liters of benzene. If carbon tetrachloride costs $4.40 per liter, how much does benzene cost per liter, in dollars?

SR

26.

y	x
0	-3
2	-2
4	-1
8	1

y	x
-9	-3
-6	-2
-3	-1
0	0

The left and right tables above represent data points of two different linear equations. If these linear equations comprise a set of simultaneous equations, then its solution has what value of y?

SR

27.

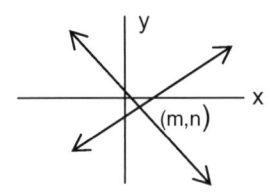

Note: figure not drawn to scale

The lines above represent two simultaneous linear equations of the form y = ax + b whose solution at the point (m,n) is in the 4th quadrant of the x-y coordinate system. If m = -4n, which of the following could be the value of m - n?

(A) -5
(B) -4
(C) -1
(D) 119

28. If $x^2 + 3bx - 4 = (x+2a)(x-b)$, and if b>0, what is a - b?

366

Chapter 12 Simultaneous Equations

Practice Problem Hints

1. Use the first equation to put x in terms of a. Substitute this into second equation.

2. Express the two verbal expressions involving x and y as a system of equations. Use substitution or square root both sides.

3. 2•number of Alva's tanks + 4•number of Jude's tanks = 60.

4. First, compute the number of x million dollar planes.

5. Algebraically express the cost scheme. The two scenarios can be described using two simultaneous equations. You must thereafter solve for the mileage rate and base cost.

6. 12 of Matt's steps + 12 of Shorty's steps equal 15 of Matt's steps.

7. The problem describes simultaneous equations. Let A equal the votes for Alain and J equal the votes for Jacque. A + J = 14,000,000, and A + 280,000 = J.

8. Set up two equations, one for the current ratio and another for triple this ratio after he passes the next 12 quizzes.

9. A 9-ride ticket costs E + 9R, where E is the entrance fee, and R is the cost per ride. Likewise for the 15 and 20 ride tickets. Set up a system of equations.

10. Set up simultaneous equations for Alf's age now and Alf's age in 10 years. Express Alf's age in terms of his sister's age.

11. Look for a way to add/subtract the equations to eliminate z.

12. These two equations each represent lines. If there is no solution to this system of equations, this will correspond to no points of intersection, i.e., two parallel lines.

13. Solve for z in terms of y in the first equation, then substitute into second equation. Or, look for a way to add, multiply, or divide the equations to eliminate z.

14. Solve for z in terms of y in the second equation and substitute.

15. Expand the quadratic expressions.

16. Expand the quadratic in the second equation.

Simultaneous Equations   Chapter 12

17. Look for a way to combine the equations to eliminate z.

18. Develop expressions for the number of tees each golfer has after the losses and exchanges. Then use the "4 times" relationship.

19. Scale the first equation and subtract from the second equation to get rid of x. Or – what value of a (in the x:y ratio) will cause these two lines to be parallel?

20. There are two equations and three variables; however, there might be a way to combine the two equations such that both x and z are eliminated.

21. Calculate the total weekly income from selling balls. Express the total number of balls and income in terms of S, the number of singles, and P, the number of packs.

22. Split each absolute value equation into two equations corresponding to the positive and negative arguments, respectively.

23. Set up simultaneous equations for total liters and total cost.

24. Total chairs = 2(# 2-chair offices) + 3(# 3-chair offices)

25. Find the total cost of carbon tetrachloride first, and then subtract that from the total.

26. Determine the slope-intercept form for each equation given any pair of points in their respective data tables. What is the form of any line running through the origin?

27. You don't have enough information to determine the two simultaneous equations, i.e., the equations of the two lines depicted. But you know which quadrant the solution falls in, and hence, the signs of m and n.

28. This looks like a complicated "coefficients of same powers of x must be equal" type problem.

Chapter 12 Simultaneous Equations

Practice Problem Solutions

1. Answer B

    We may rearrange the first equation to put x in terms of a: $x = (a-4)/3$. This can be substituted into the second equation. Hence, $b = 9 \cdot [(a-4)^2 /9] = a^2 - 8a + 16$.

2. Answer 1/4 or .25

    The first verbal equation is (1) $y^2 = 16x^2$. The second verbal equation is (2) $y = 4x - 2$. From this, we can express x in terms of y, $x = (y+2)/4$. Substituting this expression into the equation (1) gives $y^2 = 16(y+2)^2/16 = y^2 + 4y + 4$. Canceling the y^2 terms on both sides gives $0 = 4y + 4$, and solving for y gives $y = -1$. Plugging this into equation (2) gives $-1 = 4x - 2$, or $x = 1/4$.

    Alternate Solution: Taking the square root of the equation (1) gives $y = \pm 4x$. Using this expression for y in equation (2) yields $\pm 4x = 4x - 2$. This gives two equations, $0 = -2$, and $-8x = -2$. The first of these equations clearly does not represent a solution. From the second equation, $x = 1/4$.

3. Answer 12

    Let A = the number of tanks Alva has, and let J = the number of tanks Jude has. From the data in the problem, we may form two simultaneous equations: (1) $J = 2 \cdot A$ and (2) $2 \cdot A + 4 \cdot J = 60$. Using (1) in (2), $2A + 8A = 10A = 60$. Thus, solving for A, Alva has 6 tanks, and so he has $2 \cdot 6 = 12$ fish.

    Alternate Solution: Rewrite (1) as (3) $J - 2 \cdot A = 0$. Then add (3) and (2): $5 \cdot J = 60$. Therefore, J = 12 = the number of tanks Jude has. Now from (1) we may solve for A: $A = J/2 = 12/2 = 6$, and thus Alva has $6 \cdot 2 = 12$ fish.

4. Answer 8

    There are two types of planes: the 'x million dollar' planes and the 50 million dollar planes. Let the number of x million dollar planes be N_x and the number of 50 million dollar planes be N_f. We can express the total cost of 1.64 billion dollars as 1640 million dollars. Dropping the units of million dollars, the total cost equals the sum of the costs of both types of planes: (1) $1640 = N_x \cdot x + N_f \cdot 50$. We are also told in the problem that

Simultaneous Equations   Chapter 12

$N_f = 20$ and that $N_x = 4 \cdot N_f = 80$. Substituting these expressions for N_f and N_x into (1) gives $1640 = 80 \cdot x + 20 \cdot 50$. Solving for x, x = 8. That plane costs 8 million dollars.

Alternate Solution: Since there are four times as many x million dollar planes as the 20 $50 million dollar planes, there must be 80 x million dollar planes. The total cost is the sum of all these planes. Converting billions to millions, 1640 = 80x + 20·50, or 640 = 80x, or x = 8. Each of those other planes cost 8 million dollars.

5. Answer 360

Letting c equal the total rental cost in dollars, b equal base cost in dollars, and a equal the dollars per 10 miles driven, c = b + m miles • a/(10 miles), where m is the number of miles driven. We are given two constraints from which we can form simultaneous equations. Driving 200 miles it costs: (1) 300 = b + 200·a/10. Driving 700 miles it costs (2) 400 = b + 700·a/10. Subtracting (1) from (2), 100 = 50a, making a = 2. Substituting this value of a into (1), 300 = b + 40, and therefore, b = 260. The general equation of cost is c = 260 + 2m/10. So, the cost of driving 500 miles is 260 + 500·2/10 = 360.

6. Answer 4

Let the length of Matt's step equal m and that of shorty's equals s.

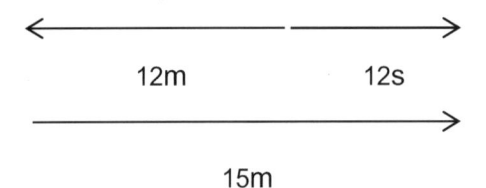

```
        ←—————————  ——————————→
           12m              12s
        ——————————————————————→
                   15m
```

The distance between them when they turn and face one another is 12m + 12s = 12(m+s). However, this distance also equals the distance Matt walks 15 steps back to meet Shorty, 15m. Therefore, 12m + 12s = 15m. So 12s = 3m, and therefore m/s = 4.

7. Answer 49

Set up simultaneous equations using the constraints given in the problem. Let A equal the votes for Alain and J equal the votes for Jacque. Because a total of 14 million votes were cast, (1) A + J = 14,000,000. Because Jacque had 280,000 more than Alain, (2) J = A + 280,000. Substituting (2) into (1), A + A + 280,000 = 14,000,000. Solving for A, A = 6,860,000. The fraction of voters voting for Alain was 6,860,000/14,000,000 = .49, or 49 percent.

Chapter 12   Simultaneous Equations

8. **Answer 2**

    His current pass/fail ratio, (1) r = n/9. We are told that this ratio will triple if he passes the next 12 quizzes. If he passes the next 12 quizzes, his pass/fail ratio will then be (2) 3r = (n+12)/(9+12) = (n+12)/21. Multiplying (1) by 3 yields (3) 3r = n/3. Equating (2) and (3), (n+12)/21 = n/3. Multiply both sides by 21: (n+12) = 7n. So 12 = 6n, or n = 2.

9. **Answer D**

    We are told that entry tickets are priced based on a fixed base cost of admission and an additional, proportional cost per ride. Both costs are unknown. From the information given, one 9 ride ticket costs $65, and *one* 20 ride ticket costs $480/4 = $120. If the entrance fee is E and the cost per ride is R, we can set up a system of equations that describes these scenarios:

    $$E + 9R = 65$$
    $$E + 20R = 120$$

    Subtracting the top equation from the bottom, 11R = 55, or R = 5. Plugging this value into either equation yields E = 20. So, using these values for E and R, one 15 ride ticket would cost 20 + 15•5 = $95. Two such tickets would cost $190.

10. **Answer 19**

    Let a be the age of Alf now and s = age of his sister now. We are told that (1) a = 4s. 10 years from now Alf will be a+10 years old and his sister will be s+10 years old. From the data given, (2) a + 10 = 2(s+10) + 2. This system of equations (1) and (2) can be solved for a and s. Plugging in the expression for a in (1) into (2), 4s + 10 = 2s + 22, or 2s = 12, so s = 6. Since a = 4s, a = 24, Alf's age now. His sister was one year old 6 - 1 = 5 years ago. At that time Alf was 24 - 5 = 19.

    Alternate Solution: Subtract (1) from (2) above to get one equation involving only s.

11. **Answer C**

    Look for a way to scale/add/subtract the equations to eliminate z. If the second equation is multiplied by -1 and added to the first equation, the result is

    $$\begin{array}{r} 2x + 5y - 3z = 12 \\ -x - 4y + 3z = 4 \\ \hline x + y = 16 \end{array}$$

371

Simultaneous Equations   Chapter 12

12. Answer 24

These two equations represent lines. If there is no solution to this system of equations, the lines will not intersect, i.e., the two lines must be parallel. Parallel lines have the same slope. Placing them in slope-intercept form, the equations are: (1) $y = -2x/6 - 5/6$ and (2) $y = -8x/c - 20$. Line (1) has a slope of $-2/6 = -1/3$, and line (2) has a slope of $-8/c$. If (2) is to have the same slope as (1), then $-1/3 = -8/c$, and therefore $c = 24$.

Alternate Solution: Multiply the top equation by 4. Thus, $8x + 24y + 20 = 0$. Subtracting the bottom equation from this scaled top equation yields $0 \cdot x + (24-c) \cdot y + 40 = 0$. Rearranging, $y(24-c) = -40$. One may solve for y for all values of c except for $c = 24$; there will be no value of y where $y \cdot 0 = -40$. There are no solutions if $c = 24$.

Alternate Solution II: From the definition of slope in terms of the coefficients, $2:8 = 6:c$.

13. Answer 4/27

If (1) $2yz + 3 = 21$ and (2) $6xz - 2 = 6$, then $x/y = ?$ This problem may be solved by rearranging equation (1) to solve for z in terms of y. Then, substitute that expression for z into equation (2). From (1), $2yz = 18$. So $z = 9/y$. Substituting this result into equation (2) yields $6x \cdot 9/y - 2 = 6$, which yields, after simplifying, $x/y = 8/54 = 4/27$.

Alternate Solution: The equations may be rearranged as (3) $2yz = 18$ and (4) $6xz = 8$. If equation (4) is divided by equation (3), $3x/y = 8/18$. So $x/y = 8/54 = 4/27$.

14. Answer C

Rearrange the second equation: $-2z = 4y - 6$, $z = 3 - 2y$. Plug this expression for z into the first equation for x: $x = 2[\,3(3-2y)^2 - (3-2y) + 6] = 2[3\{9 - 12y + 4y^2\} - 3 + 2y + 6] = 54 - 72y + 24y^2 - 6 + 4y + 12 = 24y^2 - 68y + 60$.

15. Answer 5

$(x+y)^2$ and $(x-y)^2$ have many terms in common. Expand the quadratic equations: (1) $90 = (x+y)^2 = x^2 + 2xy + y^2$, and (2) $30 = (x-y)^2 = x^2 - 2xy + y^2$. Subtracting (2) from (1), $60 = 4xy$, and so $xy = 15$. From the third equation in the problem, $y = 3x/5$. Substituting this into $xy = 15$, $3x^2/5 = 15$. Isolating x^2, $x^2 = 25$. Thus, $x = \pm 5$, and since you cannot enter negative numbers, the only correct answer is 5.

Alternate Solution: From above, if (1) $xy = 15$, then multiplying by 3, (3) $3xy = 45$. Substituting $3x = 5y$ into (3), $5y \cdot y = 45$, or $y^2 = 9$. So $y = \pm 3$, Substituting these values of y into (1), $x \cdot (\pm 3) = 15$, or $x = \pm 5$.

Chapter 12   Simultaneous Equations

16. Answer 6

Expand the second quadratic equation: (2) $30 = (x-y)^2 = x^2 - 2xy + y^2$. We also know that (1) $90 = x^2 + y^2$. Subtracting (2) from (1), $60 = 2xy$, and so (3) $xy = 30$. From the third (absolute value) equation in the problem, $y = \pm 5x/6$. Substituting this expression for y into (3) yields $\pm 5x^2/6 = 30$. Isolating x^2, $x^2 = \pm 180/5 = \pm 36$. Since you can't enter negative or imaginary numbers, the only possible answer is $x = 6$.

Alternate Solution: Since $xy = 30$, multiply by 6 to get (4) $x(6y) = 180$. From $5x = |6y|$, $6y = \pm 5x$. Substituting this is (4) gives $x(\pm 5x) = \pm 5x^2 = 180$, or $x = \pm 6$.

17. Answer 19/6

Look for a way to combine the equations to eliminate z. Rewrite them for clarity:

$2x - 6y - z = -1$
$8x - 12y - z = -20$

If we multiply the first equation by -1 we get

$-2x + 6y + z = 1$
$8x - 12y - z = -20$,

Adding these equations together yields $6x - 6y = -19$. After rearranging, $6(x-y) = -19$, or $x - y = -19/6$. So $y - x = 19/6$.

18. Answer D

T, D, and H are the number of tees at the <u>start</u> of the game for Tom, Dick, and Harry, respectively. After exchanging and losing tees, Tom then has 6 fewer tees (T-6), Dick has 6 more tees, (D+6), and Harry has lost 3 tees (H-3). Their total number of tees then equals four times Tom's tees. This equation may be written (T-6) + (D+6) + (H-3) = 4(T-6). Rearranging, $D + H + 21 = 3T$. Isolating T, $T = (D+H)/3 + 7$. So the number of tees in Tom's <u>current</u> possession (after giving Dick 6) $= T - 6 = (D+H)/3 + 1$.

Alternate Solution: After exchanging and losing tees, Tom has 6 fewer tees (T-6), which is 1/4 the final total. The total number of tees is now T+D+H-3 (because Harry lost 3). Thus, $4(T-6) = T+D+H-3$. Isolating T, (1) $T = (D+H)/3 +7$, where T is the original number of tees Tom had. Tom now has 6 fewer than (1): $(D+H)/3 + 1$.

This is a tough one. Also, they wanted T - 6, not T, the final number of Tom's tees. Some good students will stop before subtracting 6.

Simultaneous Equations   Chapter 12

19. Answer A

Multiplying the top equation by 6 will allow one to subtract the two equations and eliminate x.

$$18x - 24y = -24$$
$$18x + ay = 13$$

Subtracting the bottom from the top yields 0x - 24y - ay = -37. Rearranging, -y(24+a) = -37. One can solve for y for any value of a except that value of a that will cause (24+a) to equal zero. If a = -24, then the resulting equation is 0 = -37, which is false no matter what the value of y is. So a = -24 results in no solution.

Alternate Solution: The two linear equations each represent a line. There will always be a solution (the point of intersection) between two lines unless the lines are parallel, i.e., they have the same slope. We might put the equations into slope-intercept form and force the slope of the second equation to be the same as the first. The top equation becomes y = 3x/4 +2, and the bottom equation becomes y = -18x/a + 13/a. If the slopes are equal, 3/4 = -18/a. Invert both sides and solve for a. a = -18•4/3 = -24.

Alternate Solution II: In fact this could be seen almost by inspection. Multiplying the bottom equation by 3 yields:

18x - 24y = -24
18x + ay = 13

If a = -24, these are the equations of two parallel lines: the coefficients of x and y are the same and only the constants are different. One line is shifted vertically with respect to the other line by their different constants. Of course, it's only the ratio of the x and y coefficients that determine the slope, but it's easier to see after multiplying by 3 since one of the coefficients is equal in both equations.

Alternate Solution III: If the two lines representing these equations are parallel, then their x-coefficient to y-coefficient ratios must be equal. Thus 3:(-4) = 18:a. Clever solution: the magnitude of a must be greater than 18. Only (A) satisfies this criterion.

20. Answer C

Since there are two equations and three variables, *if* one can solve for y, there must be a way to combine the two equations (or use substitution) such that both x and z are eliminated. Rearranging, (1) x - y + 3z = 0 and (2) -x + 2y - 3z = 10. Adding equations (1) and (2) yields y = 10.

Alternate Solution: From (1) x= y - 3z. Sub into (2): -(y - 3z) + 2y - 3z = 10. So y = 10.

Chapter 12   Simultaneous Equations

21. Answer B

Calculate the total weekly income from selling balls. They sold 320 balls at an average of $2.75, and so the total income from sales is 320•2.75 = $880. Express both the total number of balls and income in terms of S, the number of singles, and P, the number of 3-packs. The total number of balls, 320, equals the number of single balls, S, plus 3 times the number of 3-packs, or (1) 320 = S + 3P. Since a single ball costs $3, the money from selling S single balls is 3S. 3-packs sell for $7: the money from P 3-packs is 7P. From here, drop the $. So, the total money received is (2) 880 = 3S + 7P. Solve for S in terms of P in (1), S = 320 - 3P. Substitute this into (2). (3) $880 = 3(320 -3P) + 7P. We can use (3) to solve for P: 880 = 960 - 2P, or P = 40. Since each 3-pack has 3 balls, a total of 3•40 = 120 balls were sold in 3-packs. Since a total of 320 balls were sold, we can find that S = 320 - 120 = 200 balls were sold singly.

Alternate Solution: From (1) above, P = (320-S)/3. Substituting this into (2) yields 880 = 3S + 7(320-S)/3. Multiplying both sides by 3 gives 2640 = 9S + 2240 - 7S. Solving for S, S = 200.

Alternate Solution II: Multiply (1) above by 3: (4) 960 = 3S + 9P. Subtract (2) from (4): 80 = 2P. Thus, P = 40, and so 3•40 = 120 balls were sold in 3-packs. Therefore, 320 - 120 = 200 balls must have been sold as singles.

22. Answer B

Split each equation into two equations corresponding to the positive and negative arguments, respectively, and solve for x. From the top equation, either x + y = 1 or x + y = -1. From these, either (1) x = 1 - y, or (2) x = -1 - y. Likewise, from the bottom equation, either (3) x = 3 + y, or (4) x = -3 + y. These four equations can be used to create 4 different pairs of simultaneous equations that can be used to solve for all possible values of y. Always pair an equation from the top, (1) or (2), with an equation from the bottom, (3), or (4). Pairing (1) and (3), x = 1 - y and x = 3 + y, is solved by y = -1. Likewise, pairing (1) and (4) yields y = 2. Pairing (2) and (3) yields y = -2. Pairing (2) and (4) yields y = 1. Of these solutions, only y = 2 is greater than 1.

Alternate Solution: The first equation can be rewritten (5) x + y = ±1 and the second equation can be rewritten (6) x - y = ±3. Subtracting (6) from (5) yields (taking into account all possible values on the right sides of the equations) 2y = {-2, 4, -4, 2}. So, y = {-1, 2, -2, 1}. The only value of y greater than 1 is 2.

23. Answer B

We know the total number of dollars, $1500, spent on the total number of liters, 800. There are two types of liters, carbon tetrachloride and benzene, and they cost $2.25

375

Simultaneous Equations　　　　　　　　　　　　　　　　　　　　　　　　　　　Chapter 12

and $1.25 per liter, respectively. Let C = the number of liters of carbon tetrachloride, and B = the number of liters of benzene. The total cost, $1500, equals the cost of carbon tetrachloride plus the cost of benzene. So, (1) 1500 = C•2.25 + B•1.25. Given that C + B = 800, (2) B = 800 - C. Substituting B in terms of C from (2) into (1), 1500 = C•2.25 + (800 - C)•1.25. Thus, 1500 = C + 1000, or C = 500.

24. Answer 56

This is a "multiple sets of two different sizes" problem. There are 6 offices that have three chairs, so these offices have 6•3 = 18 chairs. The remaining 118 - 18 = 100 chairs all belong to two-chair offices. Therefore, there are 100/2 = 50 two-chair offices. The total number of offices = 6 + 50 = 56.

Alternate Solution: Letting the number of two-chair and three-offices equal t and 6, respectively, and the total number of offices equal T,

T = t + 6　　　　　　　　　Equation for # offices

118 = 2•t + 3•6　　　　　　Equation for # chairs

Or recast with variables on the left:

(1) T - t = 6

(2) 2t = 100

These simultaneous equations can be solved for T, which is what we need. Using (2), t = 50. Substituting this value into (1), the total # of offices is T - 50 = 6, or T = 56.

Alternate Solution II: If (1) is multiplied by 2 the result is (3) 2T - 2t = 12. Adding (3) and (2) results in 2T = 112, or T = 56.

25. Answer 2.48

The total cost, $3000, is the cost of carbon tetrachloride plus the cost of 500 liters of benzene. The cost of carbon tetrachloride is $4.40/liter • 400 liters = $1760. Therefore, the cost of benzene is $3000 - $1760= $1240. We must find the cost per liter of benzene. If benzene cost $x per liter, $1240 = ($x/liter) • (500 liters benzene). Solve for x. Thus, x = $2.48 per liter of benzene. This one was pretty easy.

Chapter 12   Simultaneous Equations

26. Answer 18

Notice that the right data table contains the point (0,0). It's line in slope-intercept form must be of the form y = mx. Any point will determine m. The first point, (-3, -9), gives -9 = m(-3). Thus, m = 3, and hence its slope-intercept form is (1) y = 3x. We'll need two points from the left table (which doesn't include the origin) to get their line's equation. First, form the point-slope formula using any two points. Take the top two points: (-3, 0) and (-2, 2). The slope is rise/run = (2-0)/(-2 - (-3)) = 2. The point-slope formula using the top point would then be y - 0 = 2(x - (-3)), or in slope-intercept form, (2) y = 2x + 6. Equating (1) with (2) will allow us to first solve for x and then for y. 3x = 2x + 6, or x = 6. Plugging this into either (1) or (2) gives y = 18.

27. Answer D

We need a possible value of m - n. We don't know and cannot determine the formulas for the lines given in the figure. Moreover, we cannot even trust the scale of the figure. But we are told that the point (m,n) lies in the 4th quadrant. We also are told that (1) m = -4n. We need to use this to select m - n from among the choices. From (1), m - n = -4n - n = -5n. We know (4th quadrant) that m ≥ 0 and n ≤ 0. Because n ≤ 0 and m - n = -5n, m - n must be ≥ 0. The only possible non-negative choice is (D). Note that we could not *solve* for the value of m - n, we had to eliminate all other choices but (D).

Alternate Solution: The point in question, (m,n) is in the 4th quadrant. Every point in the 4th quadrant has a non-negative m and a non-positive n. Thus, m - n is non-negative.

28. Answer 1

We are given that x^2 + 3bx - 4 = (x+2a)(x-b). We are told that b>0, and asked to find the value of a - b. This looks like a complicated "coefficients of same powers of x must be equal" type problem. Expand the right side of the equation to make this easier to see: x^2 + 3bx - 4 = x^2 + (2a-b)x - 2ab. Examine the coefficients of x^1: 3b = 2a - b, or 4b = 2a, which leads to (1) 2b = a. Now look at the coefficients of x^0: -4 = -2ab, which may be simplified, after dividing by -2, as (2) 2 = ab. From (1) we can substitute a = 2b into (2): 2 = 2b•b, or 1 = b^2. Therefore, b = ±1. But we are told that b must be greater than 0, so b = 1. Using this in either (1) or (2), we get a = 2. Therefore a - b = 2 - 1 = 1.

Notes

Chapter 13

Functions

The mathematician Euler used the word function in the mid-1700s as the name for an expression involving variables and constants. Today every high school student is familiar with functions such as $f(x) = x^2 - 5x + 4$. In this chapter we will review the definitions and properties of the many classes of functions that may appear on the SAT except trig functions, which will be treated in a separate chapter in volume 2.

There are 16 archetypical math problems involving functions on the SAT that are explored below. An additional 21 practice problems are included as well.

Functions   Chapter 13

Don't Show Up Without Knowing…

These Concepts

Domain   Odd order ↔ odd symmetry
Range   Symmetry of common functions
Zeros of a function   If-then Functions
Characteristic and Extreme Values   Symbolic functions
Polynomial Order   Functions of functions
Even order ↔ even symmetry

How To

- Determine the vertex of a quadratic function from symmetry or the coefficients
- Put a quadratic function into vertex form
- Determine the range of a function, given the domain
- Recognize the graphs of common functions
- Calculate unknown parameters of a function, given data
- Use algebraic relationships between two different functions
- Decode symbolic functions
- Decompose and manipulate functions of functions

Quick Review and Definitions

Most functions are formed from algebraic expressions of independent variables. Examples of types of functions you've seen before are:

- $f(x) = 3x + 1$
- $f(x) = 2x^2 + x - 9$
- $f(x) = |x + 3|$
- $f(x) = (1-x) \cdot 2^{-4x}$
- $f(x,y) = x - 2y + 2x/y$

Chapter 13 | Functions

Let's Concentrate First on Functions of One Independent Variable

Most concepts of single variable functions may be extended to multi-variable functions.

Transforms

The argument of a function f( ) is the expression inside the parenthesis. It's often just the independent variable, x. It's possible to transform the argument of the function. A trivial example is: if $f(x) = x^2$, then $f(x-a) = (x-a)^2 = x^2 - 2xa + a^2$. Note that in this case we can relate the value of the transformed function to the original easily: $f(x-a) = f(x) - 2xa + a^2$.

Domain

The domain of a function is the set of all argument (input) values allowed for that function. Note that transforming the argument may change the domain. Values in the domain that are not allowed are usually of three types: values that don't make sense, e.g., a negative population or length, values that cause the function to become undefined, e.g., dividing by zero, or values that cause a real function to be imaginary, e.g., $f(x) = \sqrt{x}$, if $x < 0$. If $f(x) = x^{-2}$, then the domain of f(x) can be $-\infty < x < \infty$, $x \neq 0$. Of course, a domain can be arbitrarily restricted. For example, $f(x) = x^{-2}$, where $3 < x < 6$.

Range

The range of a function is the set of all possible output values of the function: the set of all values of the dependent variable (usually y) that results from plugging in all input values from the domain. For example, if $y = f(x) = x^2$, and the domain is $-\infty < x < \infty$, then the range is $y \geq 0$. If the domain of x is restricted to $-1 < x < 6$, then $0 \leq y < 36$.

Zeros

The zeros of a function of x are those values of x where $y = f(x) = 0$. The zeros of a function are not only characteristic of its general behavior, they are the solutions of the equation $f(x) = 0$. Its roots. The function $f(x) = x - 1$ has one zero at $x = 1$.

The zeros of a function may be real or complex. For functions of degree n, there will be n zeros. If a zero is complex, say $a + bi$, then $a - bi$ will also be a zero. A polynomial of degree n with real coefficients will have n, n-2, n-4... *real* zeros; the rest are imaginary. Multiple zeroes may have the same value. $f(x) = (x-2)^2$ has two real zeros, both at $x = 2$.

There is almost no difficult complex math on the SAT, and none covered in this chapter. Complex math is covered chapter 16. However, it is good to know the above pattern of possible real and complex zeros of a polynomial function when analyzing any function.

Characteristic values of the independent variable

It is often useful to find the characteristic values of x where a function does something special or helps to illustrate the behavior of the function. Look at x=0 and those values of x that cause the function to equal zero, or approach ± infinity. Especially of interest may be values of x that cause a denominator, numerator, or other terms in a function to approach zero. Simple values such as -2, -1/2, 1/2, and 2 can also be revealing.

Symmetry

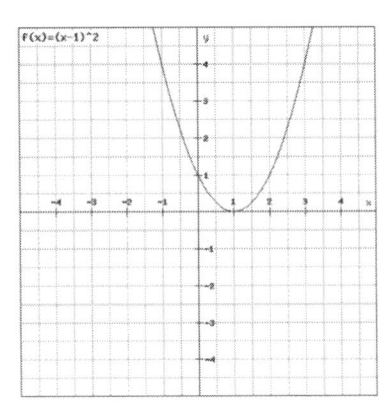

Functions often are symmetric about some axis. The function $f(x) = (x-1)^2$ shown above is symmetric about the vertical line x = 1. The value of the function when x is n units to the left of the line x=1 equals the value of the function when x is n units to the right of the line x=1. For example, we see from the function (and its graph above) that f(0) = f(2). This function will always have paired points of equal value on the other side of the symmetry line. Knowledge of a function's symmetry may be necessary to solve a problem.

Symmetry may be even or odd. The above example has even symmetry — symmetric pairs of points have equal magnitude with the same signs. Odd symmetry will result in symmetric pairs on either side of the symmetry line that have equal magnitude but opposite signs. For example, $f(x) = (x+2)^3$ has odd symmetry about the line x = -2. The value of the function that is n units to the left of the vertical symmetry line x = -2 equals the negative of the value of the function that is n units to the right of the line x = -2. Try it!

Common functions and graphs

The graph of a function can give you some feel for its order, symmetry, and general behavior. And it may allow you to estimate the value of the function at particular points.

Be able to graph functions by hand or your graphing calculator. This can often enable rapid development of a solution. You should be able to draw/plot and recognize the following 10 classes of functions on sight and be familiar with their basic properties.

Chapter 13   Functions

Linear Functions (First Order Functions)

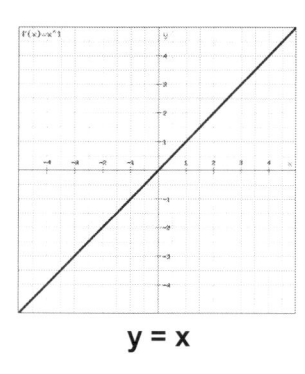

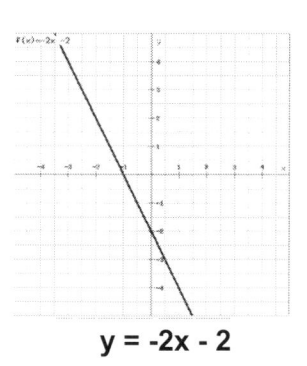

          y = x   y = -2x - 2

- Standard Form: $y = f(x) = ax + b$
- Shape of curve: straight line with slope a
- Symmetry: odd symmetry about $x = -b/a$
- Number of real zeros: 1 at $y = 0$, and hence at $x = -b/a$
- At $x = \pm\infty$ approaches $\pm\infty$ when $a>0$

A linear function, $f(x)$, is any function consisting only of first and zeroth order terms. They can all be simplified to the form $y = f(x) = ax + b$, where a and b are constants. When plotted, they appear as a straight line with slope a. If $f(x) = ax$, the $f(x+y) = f(x) + f(y)$.

Quadratic Functions (Second Order Functions)

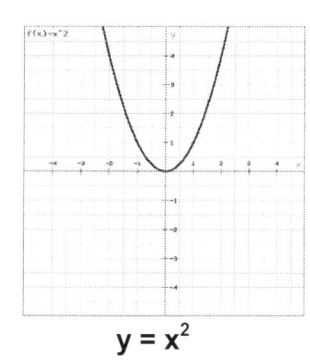

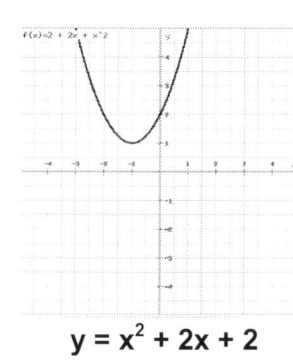

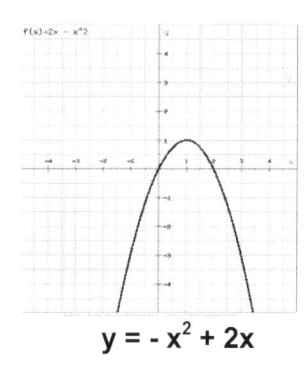

       $y = x^2$ $y = x^2 + 2x + 2$ $y = -x^2 + 2x$

- Standard Form: $y = f(x) = ax^2 + bx + c$
- Number of real zeros: 0, 1 (if the vertex lies on the x-axis), or 2
- Symmetry: even symmetry about the vertex, $x = -b/2a$
- Shape of curve: parabolic
- At $\pm\infty$ both approach $+\infty$ or both $-\infty$

When plotted, all quadratic functions (and not just pure $f(x) = cx^2$) produce parabolas, as exampled above. The parabola opens up if the coefficient of x^2 is positive, and opens down otherwise. If the parabola doesn't cross the x-axis, the function zeros are complex.

All quadratic functions have a minimum or maximum at the vertex. The function has even symmetry about a vertical line through the vertex. The vertex and the symmetry line occur at x = -b/2a. In other words, if the minimum or maximum value of f(x) occurs at x = v, then f(v+a) = f(v-a), where a is a constant. This fact can provide an important shortcut in solving certain classes of problems.

All quadratic functions have a y-intercept (i.e., x = 0) at y = c. There's only one y-intercept.

If $f(x) = ax^2$ (i.e., b = c = 0), then the vertex of the parabola is the origin: f(0) = 0.

Any quadratic function that has the form $y = (ax+b)^2$ has two identical real zeroes (both occur at x = -b/a), and it is symmetric about the line x = -b/a. Its vertex lies on the x-axis.

Any quadratic function that has the form y = (ax+b)(ax-b) will be symmetric about the y-axis. It will have two real zeros (x = -b/a, and x = b/a), that are equidistant from the y-axis.

Third Order Polynomial Functions

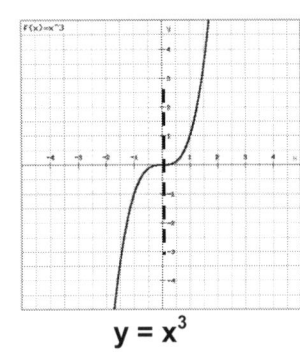

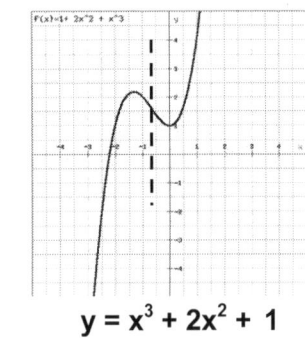

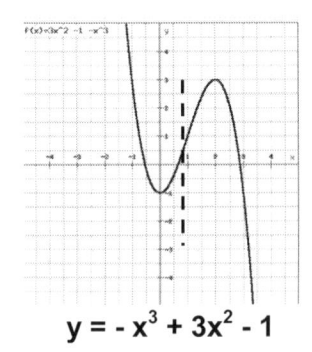

$y = x^3$ $y = x^3 + 2x^2 + 1$ $y = -x^3 + 3x^2 - 1$

- **Standard Form:** $y = f(x) = ax^3 + bx^2 + cx + d$
- **Number of real zeros:** 1 or 3
- **Symmetry:** odd symmetry about the inflection point
- **Shape of curve:** N-shaped
- **At ±∞** approaches ±∞ a>0

When plotted, all third order, or cubic functions (and not just pure $f(x) = ax^3$) produce roughly N-shaped (or backwards N-shaped) curves, as exampled above.

All cubic functions have an inflection point (the point in the middle of the "N-curve"), and the function has odd symmetry about this point. The line of symmetry (dotted lines above) is a vertical line through the inflection point. If the inflection point is *on* the x-axis and this occurs at x = m, then f(m+a) = -f(m-a).

A cubic function must have at least one real zero.

Higher Order Polynomial Functions

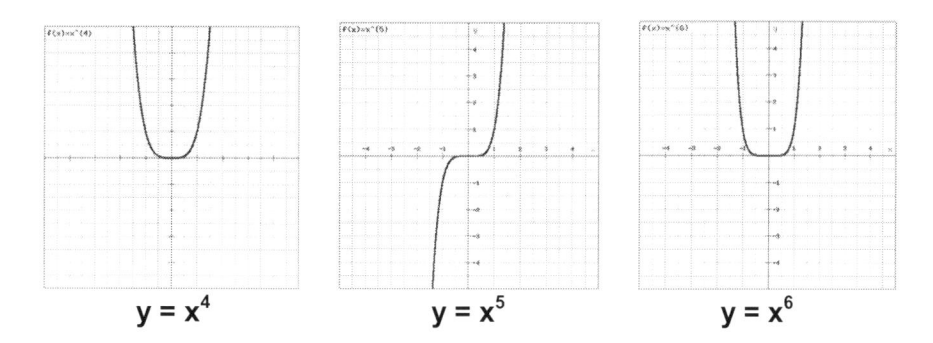

$y = x^4$ $y = x^5$ $y = x^6$

The graphs above show the behavior of several functions of pure, higher-order powers of x. Now in general, a polynomial function can have terms with mixed powers of x, as we have seen in the discussion above. And remember, the number of zeros (real and complex) is always equal to the order of the polynomial. The above graphs depict *pure* higher order functions.

On the SAT, you'll need to be able to evaluate and algebraically manipulate higher order polynomial functions and also know that their symmetry and extreme values follow the same pattern seen in lower order polynomials.

Even powered terms have even symmetry and odd powered terms have odd symmetry. If a polynomial functions consists of many different powers of x, *but all powers are even*, then that function will have even symmetry. If all powers of x are odd, the function will have odd symmetry.

The even & odd characteristics of the largest power of x also controls behavior at $x = \pm\infty$. If the highest power of x is even and that term is positive, say, x^4, then that term will dominate all other terms when x approaches both $\pm\infty$, and the function will approach $+\infty$ when x approaches both $\pm\infty$. If, instead, the highest order term is $-x^4$, then the function will approach $-\infty$ when x is both $\pm\infty$.

Conversely, if the highest power of x is odd and its coefficient is positive, say, x^5, then that term will dominate all others when x approaches both $\pm\infty$, and the function will approach $+\infty$ when x approaches $+\infty$, and $-\infty$ when x approaches $-\infty$. If, instead, the highest order term is negative, such as $-x^5$, then the function will approach $+\infty$ when x approaches $-\infty$ and approach $-\infty$ when x approaches $+\infty$.

Functions Chapter 13

Root Functions

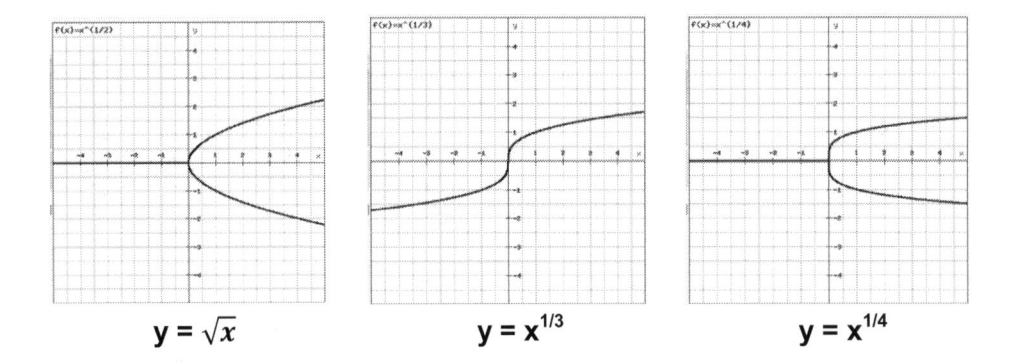

$y = \sqrt{x}$ $y = x^{1/3}$ $y = x^{1/4}$

- **Standard Form:** $y = f(x) = cx^{1/a}$ (the ath root)
- **Domain** $0 \leq x \leq \infty$ (if y is to be real)
- **Number of real zeros:** 1, always at x = 0 (pure root functions only)
- **Symmetry:** odd about y axis when power is 1/(odd)
- **Symmetry:** odd about x axis, ± dual-valued when power is 1/(even)
- **Shape of curve:** s-shaped for 1/(odd) powers
- **Shape of curve:** horizontal U for 1/(even) powers
- **At ±∞** approaches ±∞ for 1/(odd) powers
- **At ∞** approaches to ±∞ for 1/(even) powers

Any complex roots are ignored in this description of root functions.

Root functions (pure functions of $x^{1/a}$, where a is an integer), come in two basic flavors:

If a is even, such as a ±square root, then the "function" is dual-valued, having positive and negative real values for each value of x. However, the principal root is always positive, by convention. For example, if $f(x) = x^{1/4}$, then at x = 16, f(x) = +2.

Note that the domain of even roots is $0 \leq x \leq \infty$.

If a is odd, the function is single-valued and has an s-shape, as shown in the example $y = x^{1/3}$ above. Also, the symmetry is odd about the x-axis.

Fractional Powers

In an expression involving a fractional power, such as $x^{a/b}$, a can be thought of as the power and b as the root, and these operations are performed separately. But it really doesn't matter which order. The expression $x^{2/3}$ can be expanded and calculated using FOIL as either $(x^{1/3})^2$ or $(x^2)^{1/3}$. For example, if x is a perfect cube, it would be much easier (without a calculator) to perform the cube root first and then square the result. $[(8)^{1/3}]^2 = 4$.

Absolute Value Function

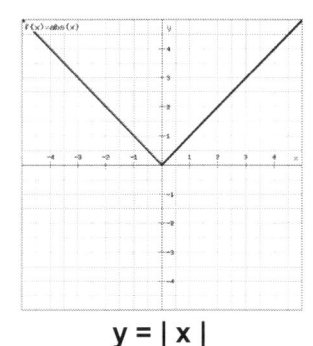

$$y = |x|$$

- **Standard Form:** $y = f(x) = a|x|$
- **Symmetry:** even about x=0
- **Shape of curve:** v-shaped
- **At ±∞** approaches ∞ at both extremes

The SAT likes to get tricky with absolute value functions. Not only are other functions or algebraic expressions sometimes placed inside the absolute value marks, such as | 2x - 4 |, but an absolute value function could be used in an exponent, e.g., $n^{|x+6|}$.

Inverse Proportional Function (1/x)

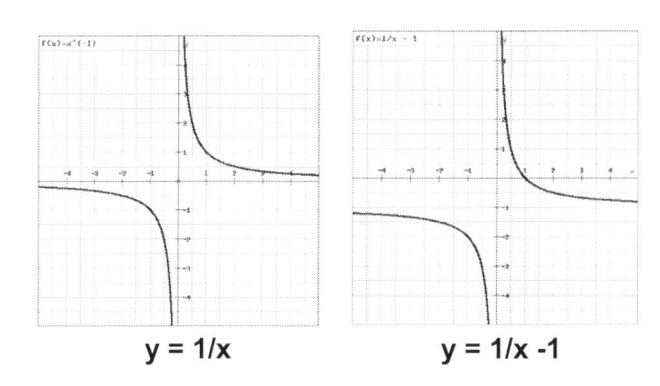

$$y = 1/x \qquad y = 1/x\ -1$$

- **Standard Form:** $y = f(x) = a/x + b$
- **Number of zeros:** 0, 1, depending on value of b
- **Symmetry:** odd about y-axis when b = 0
- **Shape of curve:** opposing anti-symmetric asymptotic curves
- **At ±∞** approaches y = b at x = ±∞
- **At origin** approaches ±∞

Unless b = 0, this is not strictly inverse proportional. Other variations exist too: for example, 1/(2x + 4). This one blows up at x = -2 instead of the origin.

Functions   Chapter 13

Inverse Square Function

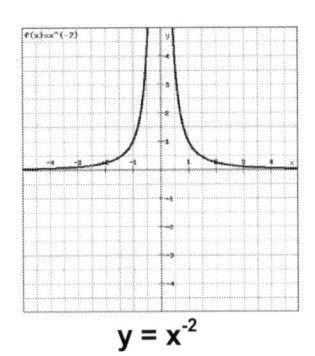

$y = x^{-2}$ 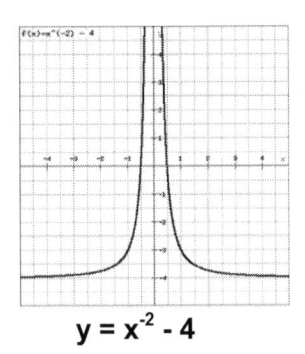 $y = x^{-2} - 4$

- Standard Form: $y = f(x) = a \cdot x^{-2} + b$
- Number of zeros: 0, 2, depending on value of b
- Symmetry: even about the y-axis
- Shape of curve: even symmetric asymptotic curves
- At $\pm\infty$ approaches y = b at $\pm\infty$
- At origin   approaches $+\infty$

The inverse square function is important in physical phenomena, and so the SAT hauls it out sometimes because students will have had some experience with it in math, physics and chemistry. Various transforms of this function are also possible, for example, $1/(x-5)^2$.

Positive Exponential Function with base > 1

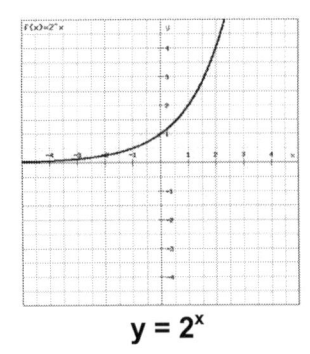

$y = 2^x$

- Standard Form: $y = f(x) = n^x$, where n is a constant > 1, x>0
- Number of zeros: 0, but asymptotic to zero at $-\infty$
- Symmetry: none
- Shape of curve: asymptotic
- At $\pm\infty$ approaches y = 0 at x = $-\infty$ and y = ∞ at x = ∞
- At origin $y = n^0 = 1$

Chapter 13   Functions

Negative Exponential Function with base > 1

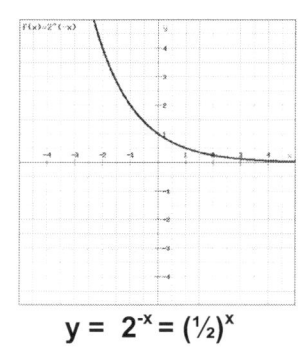

$y = 2^{-x} = (½)^x$

- **Standard Form:** $y = f(x) = n^x$, where n is a constant 0<n<1, x>0
- **Number of zeros:**   0, but asymptotic to zero at $+\infty$
- **Symmetry:**   none
- **Shape of curve:**   asymptotic
- **At $\pm\infty$**   approaches $y = \infty$ at $x = -\infty$ and $y = 0$ at $x = \infty$
- **At origin** $y = n^0 = 1$

A pure negative exponential function is also just the inverse of a positive exponential function: $n^{-x} = 1/n^x$.

Exponential functions (positive and negative) are useful in modeling many physical and economic functions: the exponential growth of bacteria or a bank account, or the exponential decay of radiation from a radioactive source.

Transforms

All of the functions above can be shifted, scaled, and used with and within other functions as well. One important transform you need to get a feel for is $f(x) \to f(x-h)$. The graph of $f(x-h)$ looks exactly like the graph of $f(x)$ except that it is shifted to the right by h units.

Completing the Square

Consider the expression (1) $x^2 + 10x + 28$. This is not easily factored, but it is related to an expression that is: (2) $x^2 + 10x + 25 = (x+5)(x+5)$. Comparing (1) and (2), we see that (1) is 3 more than (2). Therefore (1) can be recast using (2) as $x^2 + 10x + 28 = (x+5)(x+5) + 3$.

In general, we can always cast $ax^2 + bx + c = a(x-h)^2 + k$, where h and k are constants. This is a process called completing the square, which we will not derive here. It has several uses, including putting a quadratic function into vertex form. See below.

Functions   Chapter 13

Putting a Quadratic Function into Vertex Form

A quadratic function of the form (1) $f(x) = ax^2 + bx + c$ is a parabola with a vertex at the point (h,k), where $h = -b/2a$ and $k = f(h) = c - b^2/4a$. So h is tells far to the right (+) or left (-) the parabola will be shifted with respect to the y-axis. k is how far up (+) or down (-) the parabola is shifted with respect to the x-axis. Function (1) above may be rewritten (one can show this by completing the square) in **(2) vertex form: $f(x) = a(x-h)^2 + k$**. The quadratic function written in this form makes it easier to visualize. The vertex is shifted from the axes by the values of h and k, and the shape of the parabola is wide or narrow depending on the value of a. From (2), when x = h (at the vertex), f(h) = k. So k is the value of the function at the vertex. For more on completing the square, see Volume 2.

For example, let $f(x) = 3x^2 - 12x + 5$. In this function, a = 3 and b = -12. Therefore, $h = -(-12)/2 \cdot 3 = 2$, and so $k = f(2) = 12 - 24 + 5 = -7$. Thus, in vertex form, $f(x) = 3(x-2)^2 - 7$.

Functions of Two or More Variables

Functions may also be defined that have two or more independent variables. Some examples are:

$f(x,y) = x^2 + y^2$
$g(x,y) = (x+y)/(1-y)$
$cost(m,n,p) = m - 1/n + (p-1)^2/2$

Most problems on the SAT that involve functions of two or more variables will have you evaluate the function at specific data points, give you data necessary to determine unknown parameters, require variable isolation, or solve simultaneous equations.

Floor Function or Greatest Integer Less Than X

One kind of problem may involve a greatest integer function (sometimes called a floor function). It might be defined something like G(x) = the largest integer less than x. While G is trivially computed for some number x, these problems may require that you calculate the floor function when its argument is an algebraic or functional expression. For example, given a function f and the values of x and y, what is the value of f(G(x) - G(x-y))?

If-Then functions

If-then functions are just what they sound like. Instead of a function being defined by an algebraic expression of the independent variable, it is defined verbally. For example, the function g(x) equals -2 if x is less than -2 and equals 2 if x is greater than 2, and zero otherwise. Like the floor function (which is akin to the if-then function), if-then functions are sometimes presented in confusing combinations with other functions or expressions. They also take part in flowcharts, a subject discussed in volume 2.

Calculating x and y intercepts

The y-intercept of a function f(x) is the value of f(0), i.e., the value of y where f(x) crosses the y-axis at x=0. This can often be determined by inspection or a quick calculation by inserting x = 0 into the expression for f(x). For example, if $f(x) = 2 + 3x^2 + 3^{(x+2)}$, then the y-intercept = $f(0) = 2 + 3 \cdot 0 + 3^{(0+2)} = 2 + 9 = 11$.

The x-intercept(s) of a function are those values of x where f(x) = 0, i.e., the zero(s) of the function, where the graph of the function crosses the x-axis. The x-intercepts may be calculated by setting the expression for f(x) equal to zero and solving for x. For example, if $f(x) = x^2 - 36 = 0$, we may factor the quadratic expression and get $f(x) = (x+6)(x-6) = 0$. Now we can see that the f(x) = 0 at these x-intercepts: x = -6 and x = 6.

Functions That Model Real World Actions

Functions can be used to model real-world behavior. SAT function problems for real-world phenomena often show up in three basic types, (1) matching a graph of data to a choice of functions, (2) determining the value of some constant in a function based on data given in the problem, and (3) developing a functional model of the phenomena from data.

For example, an experiment starts with two rabbits, and these two multiply such that the population of rabbits is governed by the function $p(w) = 2^{a \cdot w}$, where w is the number of weeks since the experiment begins. If the population equals 256 at the end of 72 weeks, what is the value of a? We are told that $256 = 2^{a \cdot 72}$. But since $256 = 2^8$, $2^8 = 2^{a \cdot 72}$. The exponents must be equal: $8 = a \cdot 72$. Therefore a = 8/72, or a = 1/9.

Real-world Word Problem Basics

You've dealt with word problems for years and years. Real-world word problems often use functions to model real-world behavior. However, some problems may be composed of words and concepts with which you are not familiar (or even nonsense verbs and nouns) as a means of making the problem more difficult to analyze and solve.

The most important thing to remember when encountering word problems is to carefully disassemble the problem into its components and their relationships. Then these must be translated into constants, variables, functions, equations, and algebra: mathematical language that can be used to solve the problem.

- Determine what the question is asking.
- Determine what information has been given.
- Translate this information into variables, expressions, functions, and equations.
- Find a mathematical solution path to the answer.

Symbolic Function Definitions

The SAT may designate functions or operators with a symbol to confuse students who aren't reading problems deliberately. You're already familiar with the symbols +, $\sqrt{}$, and !, for example. In fact, any function represented by an algebraic expression of independent variables can be represented symbolically. Really, $f(x,y) = x^2 + 2y^3$ is an example where f is the "symbol." f operates on x and y to produce $x^2 + 2y^3$.

As another simple example, let the symbol & be defined such that a&b = (a+b) - a•b. An easy problem might give values of a and b and ask you to evaluate a&b. If a = 2 and b = 3 above, then a&b = 2&3 = (2+3) - 2•3 = 5 - 6 = -1. A more difficult example could have you evaluate 1&(3&2). In this case, perform the operation in parenthesis first and then "&" that with 1. So 3&2 = 5 - 6 = -1, and finally, 1&(-1) = 1 - 1 - 1•(-1) = 0 + 1 = 1.

The symbolic function is another way the good folks at the CollegeBoard generate confusion within problems that otherwise would not be very difficult. But symbolic functions are nothing more than another way to represent a function or operator: a recipe for calculating the output, given the inputs. Plus: they don't show up on the test too often.

Functions of Functions

You may see a problem that involves a function of another function. Consider two simple functions, $f(x) = x^2 + 2$ and $g(x) = 3x$. Another function, $h(x) = f(g(x))$, may be formed using f(x) and g(x). To express h(x), simply replace x with g(x) everywhere x occurs in the expression for f(x). Hence, $h(x) = f(g(x)) = (g(x))^2 + 2 = (3x)^2 + 2 = 9x^2 + 2$. Likewise, we could flip the order of these two functions: g(f(x)). How are f(g(x)) and g(f(x)) related? Using the same method used to calculate f(g(x)), $g(f(x)) = 3(x^2 + 2) = 3x^2 + 6$. So f(g(x)) and g(f(x)) are not necessarily equal.

One type pair of functions do have the behavior where f(g(x)) = g(f(x)). Both functions are of the type r(x) = ax, where a is a constant of proportionality. Both functions can be represented as lines running through the origin. E.g., f(x) = 2x and g(x) = 3x. Plugging these in both ways, f(g(x)) = 2(3x) = 6x, while g(f(x)) = 3(2x) = 6x.

Chapter 13   Functions

SAT Archetypes

Determining the Vertex of a Quadratic Function

The function f(x) is quadratic and contains the points (1,-3), (3,-3), and (0,0). What is the value of x at which f(x) is minimum?

(A) -3
(B) -$\sqrt{3}$
(C) -2
(D) 2

How do I start?

You are given no information about the quadratic function except the three points that lie on its graph. But note that two of the points have the same y value: -3. A quadratic function is always in the shape of a parabola, and its vertex, or min/max point, is always on the line of symmetry. For every point on the parabola there will be its symmetric pair partner with the same value of y on the other side of the line of symmetry line. The vertex will have a value of x at the midpoint between the two points with y values of -3.

Solution

The function is a parabola, and we can presume it faces upwards since they are asking for a minimum. Because f(1) = -3 and f(3) = -3, we know from symmetry that the bottom of the parabola will occur at the midpoint between x=1 and x=3. Thus, the minimum occurs at x = 2.

Alternate Solution

The long way to solving this problem in general is to use 3 simultaneous equations using the 3 points given. Let f(x) = ax^2 + bx + c. Since (0,0) is a point on the function, f(0) = 0, and thus f(x) = ax^2 + bx; the constant term, c, must be zero. The two other points can be used to set up two simultaneous equations:

   (1) f(1) = -3 = a + b
   (2) f(3) = -3 = 9a + 3b

These simultaneous equations may be solved to give a = 1 and b = -4. Therefore, f(x) = x^2 - 4x. Since the vertex of a quadratic function occurs at x = -b/2a (see the review for more on vertices), the minimum of this function occurs at x = 4/2 = 2.

Answer D

The Take-Away

Use of symmetry in some problems can save *a lot* of time. The SAT really likes hard problems that have clever shortcuts. Also – note that the problem has another built-in shortcut if you choose to solve it using simultaneous equations: the (0,0) point precluded having to solve a system of three simultaneous equations for the more general $f(x) = ax^2 + bx + c$. Note also that if they had asked for the minimum *value* of f(x), it would have been necessary to first get f(x) via the alternate solution.

Putting a Quadratic Function in Vertex Form

$$g(x) = (2x + 2)(x - 2)$$

Which of the functional forms below presents the function above in a form that correctly includes both the function minimum and the value of x at the minimum?

(A) $(2x - 1)(x + 4)$
(B) $2(x + 2)^2 - 12$
(C) $2(x + 1/2)^2 - 4$
(D) $2(x - 1/2)^2 - 4.5$

How do I start?

The problem is asking, in a roundabout way, to put the function g(x) into vertex form.

Solution

The vertex form of a quadratic function is (1) $g(x) = a(x-h)^2 + k$, where h is the value of x at the minimum (or maximum) and k is the value of the function at that point (the vertex). To put g(x) in vertex form, first expand $g(x) = (2x + 2)(x - 2) =$ (2) $2x^2 - 2x - 4$. This is in quadratic standard form ($ax^2 + bx + c$), and its coefficients can be used to put g(x) in vertex form. The vertex occurs at $x = h = -b/2a$; in this case $h = 2/4 = 1/2$. The value of the function at the vertex is $k = g(1/2)$. Using (2) when $x = 1/2$, $k = g(1/2) = 1/2 - 1 - 4 = -4.5$. Comparing (1) and (2), each has the same coefficient multiplying x^2: 2. Therefore, a = 2. Now we can get the vertex form of g(x) via (1): $2(x - 1/2)^2 - 4.5$. Choice (D) shows both the function minimum and value of x at the minimum.

Chapter 13   Functions

Alternate Solution

The quadratic function $g(x) = (2x + 2)(x - 2)$ has two zeros: $x = 2$ and $x = -1$. From parabolic symmetry we know that the x-coordinate of the vertex is at the midpoint of these two zeros (because they have the same y-value). The midpoint is $(x_1 + x_2)/2 = (2 - 1)/2 = x = 1/2$. Only choice (D) indicates a function with a vertex at $x = 1/2$. Shortcuts abound!

Answer (D)

The Take-Away

Some problems involving quadratics will use or require you to put them into vertex form.

Vertex Form in Real World Scenarios

A certain yeast has been studied for almost two hundred years due to its importance in several food manufacturing processes. In order for the yeast to thrive, sucrose must be a part of its nutritional environment. One early experiment involved providing yeast with various initial concentrations of sucrose and then measuring the initial rate of growth of the yeast population as a function of sucrose concentration. The maximum initial rate of growth was 120 GU (growth units) per day, which occurred when the sucrose concentration was 20 CU (concentration units). A best fit curve of the data revealed that the initial growth rate is a 2nd order function of concentration. Above or below 20 CU, the initial rate function is an inverted parabola — the initial rate of growth is ≤ 120 GU. The function g(c) describes the initial growth rate in GU, and the variable c refers to sucrose concentration in CU. One of the functions below could represent g(c). Which one?

(A) $-4c^2 + 160c - 1480$
(B) $-4c^2 + 120c - 1720$
(C) $-4c^2 - 160c + 120$
(D) $-4(c - 120)^2 + 20$

How do I start?

While this question involves how yeast grow, the function g(c) is not a function of time, but rather describes how the *initial* rate of growth (a measurement never described) varies as a function of sucrose concentration, c. You know that the g(c) is 2nd order in the independent variable c (and thus is parabolic in shape). You are given the maximum value of g(c) and the value of c at that maximum. This looks like we need to develop the vertex form of the function since it is composed of exactly these parameters.

Solution

A quadratic function, g(c), with a maximum of 120 occurring at c = 20 will have the form $g(c) = a(c-20)^2 + 120$, where a is the coefficient of the c^2 term. (Note that an entire family of parabolas will have this same maximum point, each member depending on the value of a). There is nothing in the problem that would allow us to determine the value of a, except that *all answer choices have a value of a = -4*. Let a = -4. Therefore, we can assume that (1) $g(x) = -4(c-20)^2 + 120$. We can toss out choice (D): it's a sucker choice in the wrong vertex form. It only remains to expand our vertex form (1) to see which of the remaining choices is correct. Doing so gives $g(x) = -4c^2 + 160c - 1480$, which corresponds to (A).

Answer A

The Take-Away

Functions describing experiments may be quadratic. You have to be able to carefully read the scenario given in the problem to determine how that information corresponds to the quadratic form. Be able to convert between standard and vertex forms of a quadratic. Also - we saw in this problem how a whole family of quadratics fit the data given, but the restricted answer choices allowed us to restrict the value of a = -4. Difficulty rating: %@&!

Greatest Integer Function

The function L(n) is defined over real numbers n such that L(n) is the greatest odd integer less than n. If n lies in the set $3 \leq n < 44$, what is the greatest value of L(6n) - L(4n)?

SR

How do I start?

Note that n doesn't have to be an integer - just a real number in the range $3 \leq n < 44$. We're looking for the greatest value of (1) L(6n) - L(4n). L(6n) is close to 6n and L(4n) is close to 4n. Note that 6n - 4n *increases with increasing n*, so L(6n) - L(4n) will do likewise. Since n < 44, let's choose a value of n as large as possible - extremely close to 44.

Solution

Let n = 43.99. From the first term in (1) above, 6n = 6•43.99 = 263.94 and hence, L(6n) = L(263.94) = 263. For the second term in (1), 4n = 4•43.99 = 175.96, and thus L(4n) = L(175.96) = 175. Therefore, the greatest value of L(6n) - L(4n) = 263 - 175 = 88.

Answer 88

The Take-Away

The feature of L(6n) - L(4n) to notice is that it is monotonic. A *greatest integer less than* function (also known as the floor() or int() function, for those of you versed in software) may be modified in any way. Here, the output of the function here is the greatest *odd* integer less than. It could have been the greatest even integer, the greatest integer less than n-10, etc. Problems such as this are testing how well you can follow directions.

Range of a Function, Given the Domain

If the domain of x is $-\infty < x < \infty$, what is the range of the function $f(x) = 3^{2x+1} + 2$?

(A) $(-\infty, 2)$
(B) $(-\infty, \infty)$
(C) $(2, \infty)$
(D) $(5, \infty)$

How do I Start?

Evaluate the function at the extremes of the domain of x and other characteristic values. For example, in this case, the value of x that makes 2x+1 = 0 *might* be important (but it isn't). Look for those values of x that make f(x) a maximum or minimum, or blow up to $\pm\infty$.

Solution

The 3^{2x+1} term will approach zero when x approaches $-\infty$ and will approach ∞ as x approaches ∞. It can never be less than zero. So this term will range between zero and ∞. But the function adds 2 to this term. Therefore, the range of the function $f(x) = 3^{2x+1} + 2$ is $2 < f(x) < \infty$, or $(2, \infty)$.

Answer C

The Take-Away

If $|a| > 1$, then $a^{-\infty}$ approaches zero and a^{∞} approaches infinity. The ability to determine the range of a function from a given domain will be critical in solving other classes of problems. Characteristic values of the independent variable of a function are $\pm\infty$, 0, and any value of x that causes a term or expression within the function to equal zero (such as 2x+1, here). In addition, values of x that cause a denominator to equal zero (and thus cause the function to approach $\pm\infty$) are possibly of interest. -2, -1/2, +1/2, +2 as well.

Functions   Chapter 13

Exponential Function

Sam bought a houseboat for $100,000. The value of the houseboat decreases by 10 percent each year. The value can be modeled by a function V(y) = 100,000•(9/10)^y, where y is the number of years from the date of purchase. After how many whole years from the date of purchase will the value of the houseboat drop below $60,000?

SR

How do I start?

Each year the price drops by 10%, or a factor of .9, which is expressed as the exponential factor (9/10)^y in the function V(n). Calculate when the value drops below $60,000.

Solution

After the 1st year: 100,000 • .9 = 90,000. 2nd year: 90,000 • .9 = 81,000. 3rd year: 72,900. 4th year: 65,610. 5th year: 59,049. So, after 5 whole years the value drops below $60,000.

Alternate Solution

V(y) = 100,000•(9/10)^y, and we're looking for the year when V(y) is less than $60,000. We can look for the integer value of y that makes (9/10)^y less than .6. This will take fewer keystrokes than the complete calculation. We quickly find that (.9)^5 = ~.59. So 5 years.

Alternate Solution II

How many years (including fractions of a year) will it take to reach 60,000? In equation form, 60,000 = 100,000(.9)^y. Rearranging, .6 = (.9)^y. Taking the log of both sides gives (approximately) -.22 = -.046 • y, or y = about 4.8 years. That's when the boat will be exactly equal to 60,000 dollars (if the value were to decrease continuously). Only after 5 *whole* years will the value be less than 60,000.

Answer 5

The Take-Away

Exponential functions (such as compound interest, etc.) are usually a constant coefficient (100,000 in this problem) multiplied by an exponential factor, such as x^y. Some problems may have you determine successive, or compound, operations of the exponential function to determine some final value. You can often save a little time by concentrating first on the exponential term. Logarithms are not tested on the SAT per se, but may be used if you like.

Chapter 13　　　　　　　　　　　　　　　　　　　　　　　　　　　　　Functions

Algebraic Expressions of Function Values

The function G is defined as G(s) = (s+1)(s-1). Which of the following is equal to G(5) - G(6)?

(A)　G(6) - G(5)
(B)　G(8) - G(3)
(C)　- G(3) - G(2)
(D)　G(3) + G(2)

How do I start?

The function G(s) is quadratic in s. Note that the function G has zeros at s = ±1. Thus, the vertex and symmetry line occurs at s = 0. As a result, G(n) = G(-n). Thus, G(5) - G(6) = G(-5) - G(-6). But this isn't one of the choices. Just evaluate G(5) - G(6), and then compare that value with the values of the choices.

Solution

G(5) - G(6) = 6•4 - 7•5 = 24 - 35 = -11. *So we need a choice that evaluates to -11.* Choice (A) gives G(6) - G(5) = 11 (could have noticed that it is the negative of value in question . (B) gives G(8) - G(3) = 9•7 - 4•2 = don't bother calculating because it's clearly a positive number. (C) gives -G(3) - G(2) = -4•2 - 3•1 = -8 - 3 = -11. All done here boss.

Alternate Solution

We can use the fact the G(s) is positive and monotonic for s>1 to eliminate several choices. Since G(6) must be greater than G(5), G(5) - G(6) must be less than zero. By similar reasoning, choices (A), (B), and (D) must all be positive. By elimination, the only possible choice is (C). Didn't even lift the pencil.

Answer C

The Take-Away

Expressions of functions must sometimes be evaluated explicitly in order to solve a problem. In this problem, there is no general algebraic relationship between G(5) - G(6) and -G(3) - G(2); they are simply numerically equal to each other at these values. Also – sometimes knowing the regions where a function is positive or negative can be used to eliminate answer choices in order to save time, as shown in the alternate solution. Take a couple of seconds before plowing into a brute-force solution. Aim. Then fire.

Functions   Chapter 13

Finding The Zeroes Of A Quadratic Function

The function $g(x) = -2(x+1)^2 + 6$ has two x-intercepts in the xy-plane. What is the distance between these two points?

(A) $\sqrt{3}$
(B) 2
(C) $2\sqrt{3}$
(D) $4\sqrt{2}$

How do I start?

At the x-intercepts, the function g(x) equals zero. Solve for x at those points. Alternatively, notice that when $g(x) = 0$, then $2(x+1)^2$ must equal 6.

Solution

Expanding, (1) $g(x) = -2(x+1)^2 + 6 = -2x^2 - 4x + 4 = -2(x^2 + 2x - 2)$. This is not easily factorable. You can use the quadratic formula and a calculator to solve for its zeros. The zeroes are at $x = -2.7321$ and $x = 0.73205$. The distance between them is ~3.46. Use a calculator to evaluate the choices or just eyeball the choices. (A) < 2. (B) = 2. (D) > 4. By elimination the answer has to be (C). Ugh. Was there a better way?

Alternate Solution

At the x-intercepts, $g(x) = 0$, so using (1), $2(x+1)^2 = 6$, or $(x+1)^2 = 3$. Thus, $x+1 = \pm\sqrt{3}$, and so the zeros occur at $x = \sqrt{3} - 1$, and $-\sqrt{3} - 1$. The distance between these two points on the x-axis is the positive difference between the coordinate values, $2\sqrt{3}$. Shortcut. Exhale.

Answer C

The Take-Away

The x-intercepts are the zeros, or roots, of a function. Problems that ask for x-intercepts often boil down to an algebraic equation with the function on one side and zero on the other. Many times a quadratic equation can be factored, yielding easy solutions, but sometimes (as we have here in the alternate solution) it may be necessary or preferable to manipulate the terms in order to solve for the zeros. In the alternate solution we took the square root of both sides of the equation in order to isolate x. You could solve this problem without a calculator if you had to. Look before you leap.

Chapter 13   Functions

Determining A Function From Data

The cost of producing n luxury game controllers per day at a company may be modeled by the function $e(n) = \frac{500n - 100}{n} + m$, where m is a constant. If 10 units were produced yesterday for a total cost of $800, what is the value of m?

(A) 310
(B) 320
(C) 128
(D) 2400

How do I start?

Functions are algebraic expressions of independent variables and constants. In this case we are given the value of the independent variable, but the constant term, m, is unknown. We know that when (n = 10) units are produced, the value of the function e(n) = 800. The function then becomes one equation with one unknown, m. This is cookbook stuff.

Solution

Plug n = 10 into the equation and set e(10) = 800. Thus, 800 = (500•10-100)/10 + m. Simplifying, 800 = 490 + m. Isolating m, m = 310.

Answer A

The Take-Away

Function representations can thought of as one equation y = f(x,z,…,a,b,c,…), where x,z,… are independent variables. The a,b,c,… are constants, which are either coefficients or simple constant terms in the function. And y is the dependent variable. Knowing all but one of these variables and constants should allow you to calculate the value(s) for the remaining unknown. In this problem the unknown was not one of the variables, but an unknown constant that can be solved for, knowing both x and y.

Note that if two unknown variables or constants were part of the function given, then we would require two data points in order to solve for them. In that case we would have to solve two simultaneous equations.

For a supposedly hard problem, this one is way easy. Yet – it is often missed.

Functions   Chapter 13

Absolute Value Functions

Let the function $f(x) = |x + a|$, where a is a constant. If the points (2,1) and (4,1) lie on the graph of $y = f(x)$ in the xy-plane, what is the value of $f(-1)$?

(A) 1
(B) 2
(C) 3
(D) 4

How do I start?

In order to determine $f(-1)$, we'll need the value of the unknown constant, a. There are two values of x for every value of $f(x)$, so we'll need both data points in order to solve for a. Using the two pairs of (x,y) given, we can form two equations involving the unknown constant a. Because we're dealing with an absolute value function, each equation can be solved by two values of a. However, only one value of a will solve both equations.

Solution

The point (2,1) gives $y = 1 = |2 + a|$, or $\pm 1 = 2 + a$. Hence a is either -1 or -3. The point (4,1) gives $y = 1 = |4 + a|$, or $\pm 1 = 4 + a$. For this point a is either -3 or -5. Since a must solve the equation using both points, a must equal -3. Therefore, $f(-1) = |-1 - 3| = 4$.

Alternate Solution

This absolute value function has V-shaped, even symmetry about the vertical line $x = -a$. At that value of x, the argument *and* value of the function are both zero. We are given two points *with the same value of y:* (2,1) and (4,1). The line of symmetry is on the midpoint between their x-coordinates: $x = 3$. Thus, $|3 + a| = 0$; so $a = -3$. So, $f(-1) = |-1 - 3| = 4$.

Alternate Solution II

$f(x) = |x + a|$ must have a slope of -1 on the left side of the function. Points (2,1) and (4,1) are opposite pairs (equal y-values). (2,1) is on the left side. Walking from $x = 2$ to $x = -1$, a run of -3, the function must rise by 3. The new y-value, $f(-1)$, will equal $f(2) + 3 = 1 + 3 = 4$.

Answer D

The Take-Away

The absolute value of $|ax + b|$ has even symmetry about the vertical line intersecting x, where $ax + b = 0$. Solving for x, $x = -b/a$. Note the slope argument of alternate solution II.

Chapter 13　　　　　　　　　　　　　　　　　　　　　　　　　　　　　　Functions

Functions of Two Variables: Special Constraints

A function h has the property that $h(x+2y) = h(x) + 2h(y)$ for any x and y. Which of the following expressions must be true when $n = m$?

  I. $h(n+2m) = [h(m)]^2$
  II. $h(n+2m) = 3h(n)$
  III. $h(n) + 2h(m) = h(3m)$

(A) None
(B) I only
(C) I and III only
(D) II and III only

How do I start?

This confusing problem presents an unknown function of two variables that has a particular property defined by the constraint (1) $h(x+2y) = h(x) + 2h(y)$. Because the choices use $x = n$ and $y = m$, perform those substitutions in (1). Then recast both sides using $n = m$. Then do the same with the choices.

Solution

With the above mentioned substitutions (and n=m), x=y=n=m. The left-hand-side of (1) above then becomes $h(n + 2n) = h(3n)$. Using x=y=n=m in the right-hand-side of (1), it becomes $h(n) + 2h(n) = 3h(n)$. Thus, (1) becomes (2) $h(3n) = 3h(n)$. Test (I), (II), and (III) by substituting $n = m$ in them and comparing the resulting equations to equation (2). (I) becomes $h(3n) = [h(n)]^2$, which doesn't look anything like (2), so (I) is false. Testing (II) with $n = m$, $h(3n) = 3h(n)$. This *is* (2), so (II) is true. Testing (III) with $n = m$, its left side becomes $h(n) + 2h(n) = 3h(n)$. The right side of (III) becomes $h(3n)$, so (III) becomes $3h(n) = h(3n)$, which is equivalent to equation (2). Thus, (III) is true. (II) and (III) are true.

Answer D

The Take-Away

Here is another problem that attempts to confuse you, but is really a recipe problem. Substitute variable letters, and then set those two variables equal to each other. If the original functional relationship had been defined in terms of n and m, the problem would have been significantly easier. But this one is dizzy.

Functions   Chapter 13

Equations With Symbolic Functions of Two Variables

Let the function Ψ be defined such that $a\Psi b = (a+b)^3$, where a and b are real. If $a = 2 - b$, then $a\Psi b = 3b\Psi-4$. In this case what is one possible value of b?

(A) $-3\sqrt{3}$
(B) $-2\sqrt{3}$
(C) 2
(D) 4

How do I Start?

Symbolic function problems are usually recipe plug-in type problems. Develop an expression for $a\Psi b$ when $a = 2 - b$. This should result in an expression with <u>a</u> eliminated. Then set this equal to $3b\Psi-4$, from which you can solve for b.

Solution

Since $a = 2 - b$, $a\Psi b = (2 - b + b)^3 = (2)^3 = 8$. So even b was eliminated! Easy going from here. So now we know that 8 equals $3b\Psi-4$, which by definition = $(3b - 4)^3$. So, $8 = (3b - 4)^3$. Taking the cube root of both sides, $2 = 3b - 4$, or $6 = 3b$, and therefore $b = 2$.

Answer C

The Take-Away

A symbolic function is just a shorthand representation of the algebraic expression of a function of one or more variables. Follow the recipe and plug into the function values or other expressions as you are given in the problem. These type problems use to be more common on the SAT. Lately, such problems are seldom seen on the test, but there is nothing in the specifications precluding there use on the test. They may be (and are) easily replicated without resorting to the use of a special character to specify the function. Consider $f(x) = x^2$. f is just the symbol for the function. Either way, the math skills required to solve them is *always* on the test.

Chapter 13 — Functions

Symbolic If-Then Functions

For integers k, m and n, the function $\forall$ is defined such that $k\forall(m:n) = 1$ if $m \leq k < n$ and zero otherwise. If $-5\forall(a:-1)$ equals 1, which of the following could be a possible value of a?

    I. -4
    II. -5
    III. -6

(A) I
(B) I and II
(C) II and III
(D) I, II, and III

How do I Start?

Panic, you must not. The value of the function $\forall$ is either 0 or 1, depending on the values of m, k, and n. The function $\forall$ is defined with parameters k, m, and n, in that order, but the following inequality is written in the order m, k, and n. Thanks for the confusion, SAT. Be deliberate. You are told that $-5\forall(a:-1)$ equals 1, and therefore the inequality $m \leq k < n$ must be satisfied. Looking at the definition of $\forall$ in the problem, you must substitute -5 for k, a for m, and -1 for n in the inequality. Then test each value of <u>a</u> in the cases to see if the inequality holds true. Keep the order of symbols straight.

Solution

So $k\forall(m:n)$ corresponds to $-5\forall(a:-1)$. Thus, k = -5, m = a, and n = -1. If we make likewise substitutions to the inequality $m \leq k < n$, it becomes (1) $a \leq -5 < -1$. Because we are told that $-5\forall(a:-1) = 1$, inequality (1) must be true. So $a \leq -5$, and thus, of the values of <u>a</u> given in the cases, both a = -5 and -6 satisfy inequality (1). Only cases (II) and (III) are true.

Answer C

The Take-Away

If-then functions are often binary, step, or other integer valued functions. Problems on the SAT involving if-then functions are usually the follow-the-directions type, and don't involve advanced math in their solutions. Even so, this is a *very* confusing problem, and many students give up in frustration.

Functions   Chapter 13

Quadratic Missile Trajectory: Simultaneous Equations

At time t=0, a toy gun's bullet was shot straight up from an initial height of 5 feet above the ground. From that moment until the bullet hit the ground, its height in feet at t seconds could be modeled by the function $h(t) = c - (d - 5t)^2$, where c and d are positive constants. If the bullet reached its maximum height at t = 2, and its height at this time was 105 feet, what was the height, in feet, of the bullet at time t =3?

SR

How do I start?

The bullet height is a quadratic function of time, a parabola, and there are therefore two values of time associated with each value of height (except the maximum height). Every height will be achieved twice – once on the way up and once on the way down. There are two unknown constants, c and d. We need those values in order to fully characterize the function and calculate h(3), the height at t=3. Within the problem are two simultaneous equations: h(0) = 5, and h(2) = 105. Use these to solve for c and d.

Solution

(1) $h(t) = c - (d - 5t)^2$. At t = 0, we know h(0) = 5. At t = 2, h(2) = 105. Using these in (1), we can form two simultaneous equations that will enable us to solve for c and d:

(2) $5 = c - d^2$
(3) $105 = c - (d - 10)^2$

We could solve these equations by substitution, but they are ripe for subtraction. Subtracting (2) from (3), $100 = -(d - 10)^2 + d^2$. This becomes: $100 = -d^2 + 20d - 100 + d^2$. Rearranging, we get 200 = 20d, or d = 10. Using d = 10 in (3), 105 = c. Knowing c and d, and plugging these into equation (1) when t = 3, $h(3) = 105 - (10 - 5 \cdot 3)^2 = 105 - 25 = 80$.

Alternate Solution

Note that (1) $h(t) = c - (d - 5t)^2$ is a convex quadratic given in modified vertex form (the 2nd term uses 5t instead of t). The maximum height, h(2) = 105, will occur when the 2nd term in (1) is zero. c must equal 105. This occurs at t = 2 when $(d - 5t)^2 = 0$. So $d - 5 \cdot 2 = 0$. Thus, d = 10. Knowing c and d, we can get h(t) at t = 3: $h(3) = 105 - (10 - 5 \cdot 3)^2 = 105 - 25 = 80$.

Alternate Solution II

From the first alternate solution we know c = 105. At t = 0 we are told that h(0) = 5. Thus, $5 = 105 - d^2$. So $d^2 = 100$, or d = 10. Now, knowing c and d, we plug these into the expression for h(t): at t = 3, $h(3) = 105 - (10 - 5 \cdot 3)^2 = 105 - 25 = 80$.

Answer 80

The Take-Away

An object shot or tossed up will have a height function often described by a quadratic function of time. This would strictly only happen in an environment without air resistance. The first solution involved solving two simultaneous equations to determine all the function's constants. But recognizing the vertex form in the alternate solutions was faster.

Substitution of Variables

Let the function T be defined by $T(s) = s^2 + 75$. If $a > 0$ and $T(3a) = 3T(a)$, what is the value of a?

SR

How do I start?

Develop expressions for T(a) and T(3a): plug s = a and s = 3a into T(s). Then set T(3a) equal to 3T(a) and solve for a.

Solution

By definition, (1) $T(s) = s^2 + 75$. Substitute a for s in (1): $T(a) = a^2 + 75$. From this we can get 3T(a): (2) $3T(a) = 3(a^2 + 75) = 3a^2 + 225$. What is T(3a)? Substitute 3a for s in (1) to get (3) $T(3a) = (3a)^2 + 75 = 9a^2 + 75$. We are told in the last equation in the problem that (3) and (2) equal one another: $3a^2 + 225 = 9a^2 + 75$, or after simplifying, $150 = 6a^2$, or $25 = a^2$. Thus, $a = \pm 5$, and since $a > 0$, $a = 5$.

Answer 5

The Take-Away

T(3a) is a pretty simple example of substituting an algebraic expression for the independent variable. In other words, everywhere in the function you see the independent variable s, substitute <u>a</u> and <u>3a</u>. Of course, they make this more confusing by changing the names of the variables (s → a). Pretty simple, yet problems of this type are frequently missed.

Functions of Functions

The number of dots, d, can be approximated by the function d(s) = (s-1)/(s+1), where s is the number of spots. In turn, the number of spots tends to equal one plus the square of the number of jots, j. Which expression below best expresses the approximate number of dots as a function of the number of jots?

(A) j(j+1)/(j-1)
(B) j^2/(j-1)
(C) j^2/(j^2+2)
(D) j^2/(j^2+1)

How do I start?

We can ignore the modifier "approximate" here because the algebraic relationships between d, s, and j are well defined. We need d(j), the number of dots as a function of jots, j. Let d = the number of spots, j = the number of jots, and s = the number of spots. From the information given in the problem, d(s) = (s-1)/(s+1), and s = 1 + j^2. Substitute this last expression for s in the function d(s) to get d(j).

Solution

Letting s = spots and j = jots, (1) d(s) = (s-1)/(s+1), and (2) s = 1 + j^2. Substitute s as a function of j given in (2) into (1): d(j) = (s-1)/(s+1) = (1+j^2-1)/(1+j^2+1) = j^2 / (j^2+2).

Answer C

The Take-Away

Problems involving functions of functions usually may be recast as a substitution of variables problem, as seen in this example. Just substitute the independent variable in the "outside" function with the algebraic expression for the "inside" function. Dots, spots, and jots? They're trying to keep you off balance. Slow and deliberate, folks.

Chapter 13　　　　　　　　　　　　　　　　　　　　　　　　　　　Functions

Practice Problems

1. Let the function f be defined by $f(x) = 3(x^3 - 3)$. When $f(x) = -90$, what is the value of $3 - 3x$?

    (A) -6
    (B) 0
    (C) 2
    (D) 12

2. Mac was told the cost to maintain his boat will rise by 15% each year. This year he paid $450 in maintenance. A function modeling his yearly cost of maintenance over time is $r(y) = 450a^y$, where y = number of years from now. What is the value of a?

    (A) .15
    (B) .275
    (C) .3
    (D) 1.15

3. $b(d) = m - 10d + d^2/4$

    During the first 75 days of the carnival, the box office receipts (in units of $100) for day d could be modeled by the function b(d) above, where m is a constant. On which day were the box office receipts the same as it was on day number 10?

    (A) 15
    (B) 20
    (C) 30
    (D) 40

Functions   Chapter 13

4. The function f is defined as $f(x) = 21 + x^2/9$. If $f(3c) = 10c$, what is the largest possible value of c?

SR

5. The function y(x) is directly proportional to x^3. If $y = 2$ when $x = \frac{1}{2}$, what is the value of x when $y = 16/27$?

(A) $\frac{1}{3}$

(B) $4\sqrt{3}$

(C) 3

(D) $\frac{32}{27}$

6. Let the function f be defined by $f(x) = \frac{x}{4} - 2$. If $\frac{1}{2} \cdot f(\sqrt{a}) = 31$, what is the value of a?

(A) 8

(B) $\frac{31}{2}$

(C) 62

(D) 65536

7. Let the function J(x,y) equal 0 if x - y is an integer, and 1 otherwise. For which of the following pairs of x,y will J(x,y) equal 1?

I. $\frac{-2}{3}, \frac{4}{3}$

II. $-2\pi, 2.5\pi$

III. $2\sqrt{3}, \sqrt{3}$

(A) I only
(B) II only
(C) III only
(D) II and III only

410

Chapter 13 — Functions

8. Let the operation ^ be defined by a^b = (a+2b)/(a-2b) for all real numbers a and b, where a ≠ 2b. If 1^2 = 2^c, and c ≠ 1, what is the value of c?

(A) -2
(B) -1
(C) $\frac{3}{10}$
(D) 4

9. If -1 ≤ x ≤ 6 and -2 ≤ y ≤ 4, which of the following describes the set of all possible values of f(x,y) = xy?

(A) -12 ≤ xy ≤ 24
(B) 0 ≤ xy ≤ 24
(C) xy < -2 and xy > 6
(D) -1 ≤ xy ≤ 6

10. The function ‡ is defined as ‡(x) = ±$\sqrt{(x+2)}$ for all x ≥ -2. Which of the following could be a value of ‡(47) + ‡(7)?

(A) -$\sqrt{43}$
(B) -4
(C) -$\sqrt{13}$
(D) 3

11. If y(x) = (2x^4 + 11)$^{1/2}$, which of the following values can y(x) not take if -∞<x<∞?

(A) -11.01
(B) -3
(C) 11.01
(D) 13.5

Functions   Chapter 13

12. The function f(x) is quadratic and contains the points (1,-3), (3,-3), and (0,0). What is the minimum value of f(x)?

(A) -12
(B) -9
(C) $-4\frac{1}{4}$
(D) -4

13. The function $f(x) = ax^2 + bx + c$, is a parabola having a vertex at the point (2,2). If a < 0, which of the following cannot be a value of c?

(A) 2
(B) 1
(C) 0
(D) -1

14. Let the operator μ be such that a μ b = a - ab. If a and b are positive integers, which of the following expressions might be equal to zero?

I   b μ (a+b)
II (a-b) μ b
III a μ b

(A) I
(B) II
(C) I and II
(D) II and III

15. A Bond villain launches a missile from his missile silo deep underground. The height above the ground, in miles, of a missile launched from the silo s miles below ground is given by the quadratic equation: $h(t) = -2t^2 + 24t - s$, where t is measured in minutes. At launch a timer starts at t = 0. At t = 7, the missile is already falling down and has a height of H miles. At what time does the missile first achieve H miles in height?

SR

Chapter 13   Functions

16. Let the operations ⌐ and ⌀ be defined for all real numbers a and b such that a⌐b = a + 2b and a⌀b = 2a + b. If 2⌐(3c) = 3⌀(2c), what is the value of c?

SR

17. Let a Ξ b equal the average of ab and a - b. If a Ξ b = 2b, and b ≠ -1, what is a in terms of b?

(A) $\dfrac{5}{b+1}$

(B) $\dfrac{5b}{b+1}$

(C) $\dfrac{5b^2}{b+1}$

(D) $\dfrac{5}{(b+1)^2}$

18. The function ⋈ is defined as follows for positive integers n and m: $n \bowtie m = \dfrac{2^{2n-m}}{2^{n+m}}$, where 2n ≥ m. How many values of n result in a value of n ⋈ 4 less than $\dfrac{1}{16}$?

SR

19. Let x* be defined as x* = x² + 2x. If a* = (a+2)*, what is the value of a?

(A) -2
(B) 0
(C) 2
(D) 3

20. The function f(x) = rx - 4. If f(r-6) = -13, how many real values of r solve the equation?

413

21. If $ax^2 + bx + c = 0$ for all real x, which of the following conditions must be true?

(A) $(b-c) = (a^2-b^2)/2$
(B) $b = 0$
(C) $b^2 - 4ac < 0$
(D) $x = \dfrac{-b \pm \sqrt{b^2 - 4ac}}{2a}$

Chapter 13　　　　　　　　　　　　　　　　　　　　　　　　　　　　　　Functions

Practice Problem Hints

1. Set f(x) = 90 and solve for x.

2. If you are uncertain of the answer from the data given, calculate the cost of repairs for, say, the next three years in terms of the 15 percent to notice the resulting pattern.

3. Test each choice by plugging the value for d into the equation for b(d) and comparing it to the b(10). Or you could use a clever symmetry solution.

4. Plug x = 3c into f(x) and set that equal to 10c.

5. In other words, $y(x) = ax^3$, where a is a constant of proportionality. Use y = 2 when $x = \frac{1}{2}$ to calculate the constant a.

6. $f(\sqrt{a}) = 62$. Plug $\sqrt{a}$ into f(x) and set that equal to 62.

7. Determine which of choices I, II, and III differ by an integer. Careful. J(x,y) = 0 if x - y is an integer

8. First, evaluate 1^2, and then set this equal to 2^c to solve for c.

9. Find the least and greatest value of xy by examining the products of x and y at their respective extreme values.

10. Just plug in the numbers for x = 47 and x = 7. Don't forget negative roots.

11. The term $2x^4$ is always greater than or equal to zero. Don't forget negative roots.

12. Because (0,0) is a point on the function, $f(x) = ax^2 + bx$. Use the other points to find a and b. Then find the vertex of the function and the function's value there.

13. The function f(x) is an inverted parabola whose maximum is at (2,2). When will the function f(x) be equal to the value of c? How does that relate to (2,2)?

14. Expand expressions (I), (II), and (III) and examine them to see which can ever equal zero.

15. This is a quadratic function. We'll need to find a matched pair of values, H, of the function. A quadratic is symmetric about the vertex. Or you could solve for t, explicitly.

Functions Chapter 13

16. Expand the given functions using their definitions, and set the expressions equal to each other.

17. Express a Ξ b as an average of the two terms given. Set this expression equal to 2b.

18. Try successively larger values of integer n that satisfy the criterion $2n \geq 4$.

19. Let x = a, expand the left and right hand sides, and set the two expressions equal to each other.

20. Plug x = (r-6) into the function.

21. *How* many values of x solve the equation?

Chapter 13   Functions

Practice Problem Solutions

1. Answer D

   When $f(x) = -90 = 3(x^3 - 3)$, we can solve for x: $-30 = x^3 - 3$, or $-27 = x^3$, so $x = -3$. Thus, $3 - 3x = 3 + 9 = 12$.

2. Answer D

   A 15% increase equals (100 + 15)/100, or a factor of 1.15. After one year the cost will be 450 • 1.15, after two years the cost will be 450 • 1.15 • 1.15 = 450 • 1.15^2, and after three years the cost will be 450 • 1.15^3. Thus, the general function for the cost at year y will be 450 • 1.15^y. Thus, a = 1.15.

   Alternate Solution: This is a variant of a compound interest problem, and you might be able to immediately see that a 15% increase per year will multiply any current year's cost by a factor of 1.15 to get the next year's cost. Thus, after y years the cost would be (original cost)$(1.15)^y$, and hence a = 1.15.

3. Answer C

   You could simply test each choice by plugging the value for d into the equation for b and comparing it to the b(10). First, b(10) = m - 100 + 25 = m - 75. Testing the choices: (A) b(15) = m - 150 + 56.25 = m - 93.75, (B) b(20) = m - 200 + 100 = m - 100, (C) b(30) = m - 300 + 225 = m - 75. There it is. Thus, b(30) = b(10).

   Alternate Solution: The quadratic equation b(d) = m - 10d + d^2/4 is pretty ugly. However, we're only interested when two days have the same box office. If we multiply this equation by 4 and rearrange we have (1) 4b(d) = d^2 - 40d - 4m. We want to know the day, x, when 4b(x) = 4b(10). Get 4b(10) first. Plugging d = 10 into (1), (2) 4b(10) = $(10)^2$ - 40•10 - 4m = -300 - 4m. But this must be equal to 4b(x). So on day x, using (1), (3) 4b(x) = x^2 - 40x - 4m. Equating (2) to (3): (4) x^2 - 40x - 4m = -300 - 4m. Rearranging (4) in standard form: x^2 - 40x + 300 = 0. This can be factored as (d-10)(d-30) = 0. The solutions are 10 (we knew this already) and 30.

   Alternate Solution II: A quadratic function in standard form, (5) b(d) = ad^2 + bd + c, is symmetric about the vertical line (6) d = -b/2a. Compare (5) to b(d) = m - 10d + d^2/4: b = -10 and a = 1/4. Thus from (6), d = -(-10)/(2/4) = 20. The symmetric pair-partner of d = 10 on the other side of d = 20 is d = 30. The function describing box office receipts will have the same values at d = 10 and d = 30 (each having the same distance from the vertex symmetry line at d = 20). Symmetry: sometimes the smart, fast solution.

Functions
Chapter 13

4. Answer 7

Plug $x = 3c$ into the $f(x)$ and set it equal to $10c$. $f(3c) = 21 + 9c^2/9$. Simplifying and equating to $10c$, $c^2 + 21 = 10c$, or $c^2 - 10c + 21 = 0$. This can be factored as $(c-7)(c-3) = 0$. The solutions are $c = 7$ and $c = 3$, so 7 is largest value of c satisfying the condition.

5. Answer A

Since $y(x)$ is directly proportional to x^3, $y(x) = ax^3$, where a is a constant. Since $2 = a \cdot (1/2)^3 = a/8$, it must be true that $a = 16$. Thus, the problem asks what is the value of x when $y = 16/27$? If $16/27 = 16x^3$, then $x^3 = 1/27$, and hence $x = 1/3$.

6. Answer D

Since $\frac{1}{2} \cdot f(\sqrt{a}) = 31$, (1) $f(\sqrt{a}) = 62$. Now, $f(x) = \frac{x}{4} - 2$. We can simply plug in $x = \sqrt{a}$: (2) $f(\sqrt{a}) = \sqrt{a}/4 - 2$. Equating $f(\sqrt{a})$ in (2) and (1): $\sqrt{a}/4 - 2 = 62$, or $\sqrt{a}/4 = 64$. We can now solve for $\sqrt{a}$: $\sqrt{a} = 4 \cdot 64 = 256$. Thus, $a = 256^2 = 65536$.

7. Answer D

The only pair of numbers in the choices whose difference will equal an integer is (I): $4/3 - (-2/3) = 6/3 = 2$. The other pairs, (II) and (III), have a non-integer difference, and hence $J(x,y)$ is 1 in those cases. Hence the answer is (D). This is another reading comprehension problem in math.

8. Answer D

First, evaluate 1^2 and then set this equal to 2^c to solve for c. Plugging a=1 and b=2 into a^b = (a+2b)/(a-2b) gives 1^2 = (1+4)/(1-4) = -5/3. Since 1^2 = 2^c, we'll need an expression for 2^c: (2+2c)/(2-2c). Thus, -5/3 = (2+2c)/(2-2c). Cross-multiplying both sides by (2-2c) and 3 (note $c \neq 1$), and thereafter isolating c, c = 4.

9. Answer A

Consider the domains of x and y. The least value of xy results from $x = 6$ and $y = -2$, yielding $xy = -12$. The largest value of xy results from $x = 6$ and $y = 4$ yielding $xy = 24$. The domains of x and y are continuous: all values of xy between -12 and 24 are valid.

Chapter 13 Functions

10. Answer B

$\ddagger(x) = \pm\sqrt{(x+2)}$. Just plug in the numbers for x = 47 and x = 7 in the requested sum. The result is $\pm\sqrt{49} + \pm\sqrt{9} = \pm 7 + \pm 3$. There are four possible values: 10, 4, -4, and -10. The only one of these values among the answer choices is -4.

11. Answer B

$y(x) = (2x^4 + 11)^{1/2}$, a square root function, represents both positive and negative square roots. Because $2x^4$ is always non-negative for real x, y(x) must be greater than or equal to $\sqrt{11}$, or less than or equal to $-\sqrt{11}$. The only choice not in this range is -3.

12. Answer D

Let y = f(x). Since f(x) is quadratic, $y = ax^2 + bx + c$. We are given three points: (1,-3), (3,-3), and (0,0). We can see from the last point that when x = 0, y = 0, and the only way this can happen is if c = 0. Thus, (1) $y = ax^2 + bx$. We have two other pairs of coordinates and two unknown coefficients, a and b. So we can develop two equations for these two unknowns. Use the first point, when x = 1, y = -3: plugging these values into (1), we get (2) -3 = a + b. Then use the second point, when x = 3, y = -3: plugging these values into (1), we get (3) -3 = 9a + 3b. Rearranging (2), b = -(a+3). Putting this expression for b into (3), -3 = 9a - 3(a+3). Rearranging, we can solve for a: 6 = 6a, or a = 1. Using this value in (2), b = -4. Plugging these values for a and b into equation (1), (4) $f(x) = x^2 - 4x$. The function f(x) is now fully described.

The minimum of this quadratic, at the vertex, will occur on the vertical line of symmetry of the function. Fortunately, we are given two points on the parabola that have the same values of y. The line of symmetry will occur exactly between these two points. From the data in the problem, f(x) = -3 at both x = 1 and x = 3, and the midpoint between these two values is x = 2. Using the fully defined function in (4), the value of the function at x = 2 is f(2) = 4 - 8 = -4.

Alternate Solution: the vertex of the function can also be calculated directly from $f(x) = x^2 - 4x$. The vertex line occurs at x = -b/2a = -(-4)/2 = 2. The minimum occurs at f(2). Plugging x = 2 into $f(x) = x^2 - 4x$ gives f(2) = -4. You can also use the coefficients of $f(x) = x^2 - 4x$ to directly calculate the *value of the function* at the vertex from the formula: $c - b^2/4a$. This results in 0 - 16/4 = -4.

There's no guarantee that two points given in such a problem would have the same y-value. You can always determine a quadratic function from three points. In general, you may find the vertex from the function coefficients, as shown in the alternate solution.

13. Answer A

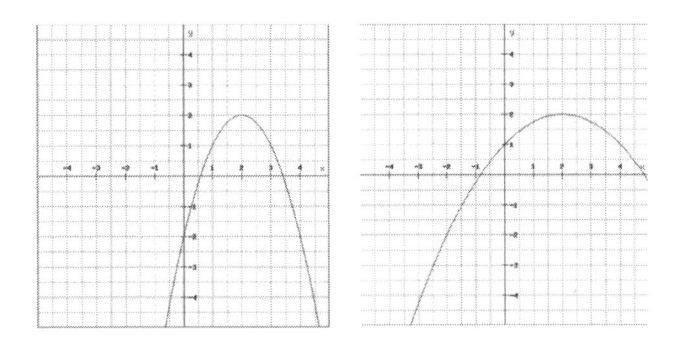

Because a < 0, the parabola is inverted. The vertex is the maximum value that f(x) can equal, which in this case is 2. Shown above are a couple of possibilities for this function. From $f(x) = ax^2 + bx + c$, $f(0) = c$; the value c represents the y-intercept of the graph of this function, at x = 0. Since 2 is the maximum value of y, and this value *only* occurs when x = 2, this maximum value cannot also occur when x = 0. In other words, c cannot equal 2.

14. Answer D

So, a and b are *positive* integers and a μ b = a - ab. Expand (I): bμ(a+b) = b - b(a+b) = b(1 - a - b). Notice that neither b nor (1- a - b) can be zero, so (I) can never be zero. Expand (II): (a-b) μ b = a - b - (a-b)•b = (a-b)(1-b). If b=1 or a=b, then (II) *can* equal zero. From the definition, (III) a μ b equals a - ab = a(1 - b). This equals zero if b = 1.

Alternate Solution: a μ b = a - ab = a(1-b). If a(1-b) = 0, then b *must* equal 1. *Only* if the operand to the right of μ equals 1 will the expression = 0. (I) (a+b) can never equal 1: (I) is false. (II) b can equal 1: (II) is true. (III) b can equal 1: (III) is true.

15. Answer 5

The hard way: (1) $h(t) = -2t^2 + 24t - s$. We can solve for the height at 7 minutes in terms of s: h(7) = -2•49 + 24•7 - s = 70 - s. We must find the time before that, as the missile is going up, when h(t) is also 70 - s. Using (1): $70 - s = -2t^2 + 24t - s$. It's good we can cancel s on both sides. Rearranging gives $-2t^2 + 24t - 70 = 0$. First, factoring -2 outside gives $-2•(t^2 -12t + 35)= 0$. The expression in parenthesis must equal zero. We can factor this from scratch or notice that it can be factored very easily since we already know that t = 7 is a solution. Thus, $t^2 - 12t + 35 = (t - 7)(t - x)$, and so x = 5. The ascending missile reaches the same height at 5 minutes and at 7 minutes.

Alternate Solution: This quadratic function has a vertex at t = -b/2a = -24/(-4) = 6, the time the missile reaches maximum height. Notice that this is independent of s. We want to know when the missile *first* achieved the same height as it did later at t = 7.

Chapter 13 Functions

Because the quadratic function is symmetric about the vertex, we simply reflect the t = 7 value about the vertex t = 6 line: the symmetric pair-partner to t = 7 is t = 5.

16. Answer 1

The first expression, 2⌗(3c), can be expanded using the definition a⌗b = a + 2b, where a = 2 and b = 3c, as (1) 2⌗(3c) = 2 + 6c. Likewise, the second expression can be expanded using its definition, aØb = 2a + b , as (2) 3Ø2c = 6 + 2c. Since we are told that expressions (1) and (2) are equal, 2 + 6c = 6 + 2c, and hence 4c = 4, or c = 1. Just a follow the directions problem.

17. Answer B

The average of ab and a - b equals (ab + a - b)/2. From the data in the problem, (ab + a - b)/2 = 2b. Multiplying both sides by 2, ab + a - b = 4b, and collecting the a terms together on the left side, a(b+1) = 5b. Isolating a, a = 5b/(b+1).

18. Answer 2

$n \bowtie m = \dfrac{2^{2n - m}}{2^{n + m}}$. Here, m = 4, choose successively larger values of n that satisfy the criterion 2n ≥ 4, and compute n ⋈ 4 for each value. We must only count values of n where n ⋈ 4 is less than $\dfrac{1}{16}$. Because 2n ≥ 4, n can take on values 2, 3, 4, … When n = 2, n ⋈ 4 = 2^0 / 2^6 = 1/64. Likewise, when n = 3, n ⋈ 4 = 1/32. When n = 4, n ⋈ 4 = 1/16, which fails the criterion that n ⋈ 4 be *less than* $\dfrac{1}{16}$. All values of n larger than 4 will also result in values of n ⋈ 4 ≥ 1/16. So, only two values of n, n = 2 and n = 3 result in values of n ⋈ 4 < $\dfrac{1}{16}$.

Alternate Solution: Alternatively, one may simplify n ⋈ m = $\dfrac{2^{2n-m}}{2^{n+m}} = \dfrac{2^n}{2^{2m}}$. Here, we restrict m: m = 4, thus n ⋈ 4 = 2^{n-8}. This expression is only < $\dfrac{1}{16}$ for positive integers n = 1, 2, or 3. But n = 1 won't satisfy 2n ≥ 4. Only n = 2 and n = 3 pass the test.

19. Answer A

Let x = a, and set the two expressions equal to each other. From the definitions, (1) a* = a^2 + 2a, which we are told, in this case, equals (2) (a+2)* = $(a+2)^2$ + 2(a+2) = a^2 + 4a + 4 + 2a + 4 = a^2 + 6a + 8. Equating (1) and (2), a^2 + 2a = a^2 + 6a + 8. Cancel a^2 and isolate a to get 4a = -8, and hence a = -2.

Functions																																																																																																																																																																																																																								Chapter 13

Alternate Solution: $a^* = a^2 + 2a$, or (2) $a^* = a(a+2)$. We can use (2) to form $(a+2)^*$ by substituting $(a+2)$ for a in 2). (3) $(a+2)^* = (a+2)(a+4)$. The problems forces us to equate (2) and (3), resulting in (4): $a(a+2) = (a+2)(a+4)$. If we divide both sides by $(a+2)$, we get $a = a+4$. This is nonsense and we might conclude here that there is no solution. But we have to be careful when dividing by a variable term if that term might equal zero. $(a+2)$ *can* be zero if $a = -2$. In the case where $a = -2$, both sides of (4) equal zero: $0 = 0$. True!

Alternate Solution II: plug in the choices and see which value of a works. Lucky us, it's the first one, choice (A).

20. Answer 1

The function in question is $f(x) = rx - 4$. If $f(r-6) = 13$, simply plug $x = (r-6)$ into the function and force it to equal 13: $f(r-6) = r(r-6) - 4 = -13$. Expanding and pulling all the terms to the left, $r^2 - 6r + 9 = 0$. This is a quadratic so there can be either 0, 1, or 2 real solutions. Oh, but this equation is easily factorable: $(r-3)(r-3) = 0$. So there is only 1 value of r, 3, that solves this equation.

Alternate Solution: They only want the number of real values that solves the equation. Because we have an expression quadratic in r, there can be only 0, 1, or 2 real solutions. So even though this question requires a numerical response, if at a loss, you have a good chance to guess.

21. Answer B

If $ax^2 + bx + c = 0$ for all real x... wait a minute. For *all* real x? This is a trick question. A general quadratic equation will have at most 2 solutions, which may or may not be real. That is, at most two different values of x will solve the equation. Here, we are told that all real x solves the equation. The only way this can be true is if all the coefficients, a, b, and c, are equal to zero. So it must be true that $b = 0$. Choices (C) and (D) are for students who know something and read the problem too quickly.

Chapter 14

Transforms and Symmetry

We have already seen functions that are symmetric about an axis. Problems on the SAT are sometimes written so that students who are aware of symmetry properties may use them to save time in developing solutions. But if functions are transformed, their axis of symmetry may change.

How the properties of a function change after a transform has been applied may be tested on the SAT. You must learn to visually recognize how graphs of transformed functions may have been shifted, flipped, scaled, stretched, and squeezed.

These properties and techniques are reviewed below.

There are 8 archetypes in the subjects of transforms and symmetry, and there a further 6 practice problems below that will solidify your experience.

Don't Show Up Without Knowing…

These Concepts

Let c be a constant

- If c > 0, then f(x) + c will shift the graph up c units with respect to the x-axis
- If c > 0, then f(x) - c will shift the graph down c units with respect to the x-axis
- If c > 0, then f(x+c) will shift the graph left c units with respect to the y-axis
- If c > 0, then f(x-c) will shift the graph right c units with respect to the y-axis
- If |c|>1, then c•f(x) will be narrower than f(x) when graphed
- If |c|<1, then c•f(x) will be broader than f(x) when graphed
- If |c|>1, then f(c•x) will be narrower than f(x) when graphed
- If |c|<1, then f(c•x) will be broader than f(x) when graphed
- If c > 0, then -c•f(x) will flip the graph upside down (reflect it about a horizontal line)

Chapter 14   Transformations and Symmetry

Quick Review and Definitions

Transforms of linear functions

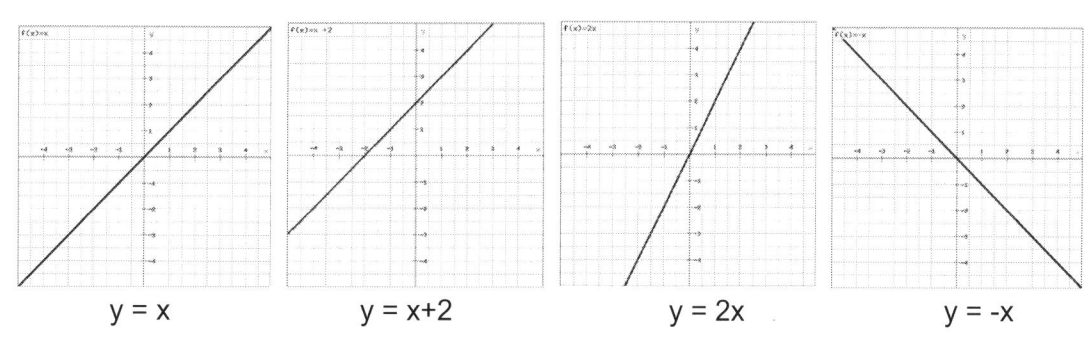

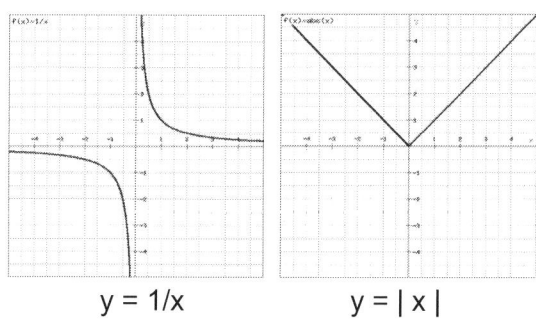

y = x   y = x+2   y = 2x   y = -x

y = 1/x   y = | x |

Transforms of quadratic functions

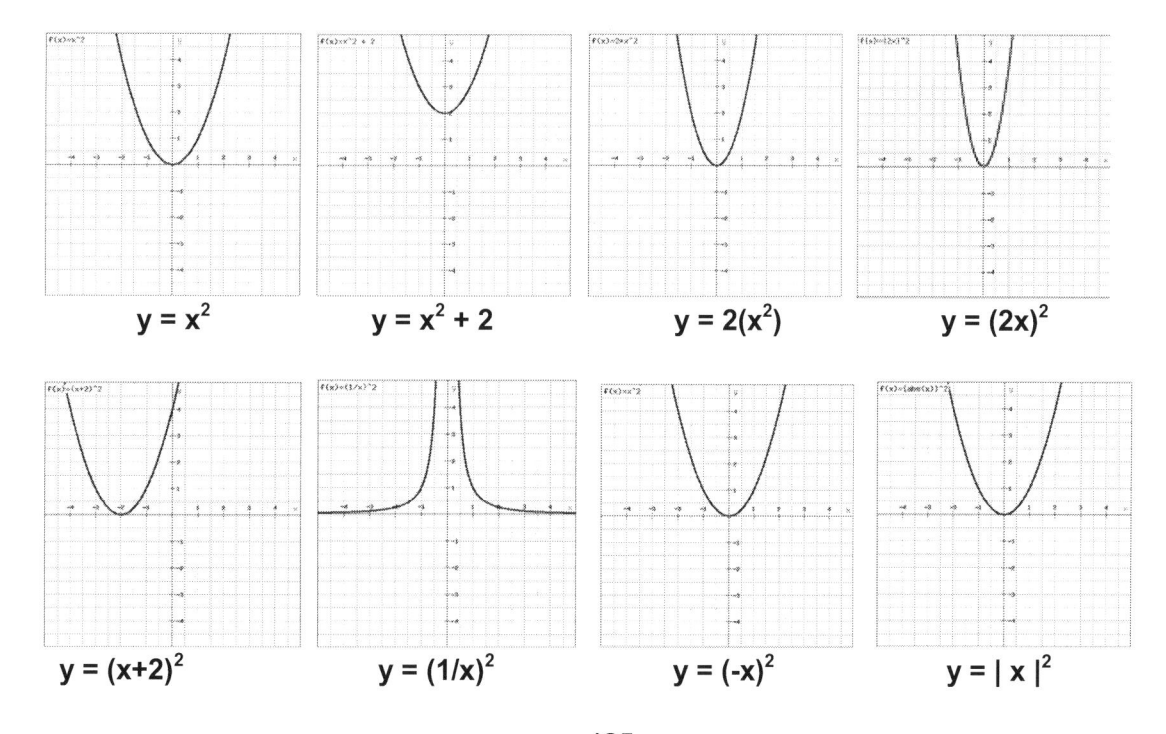

y = x²   y = x² + 2   y = 2(x²)   y = (2x)²

y = (x+2)²   y = (1/x)²   y = (-x)²   y = | x |²

425

Reflection about a line

A point, line, or other figure can be reflected about a line in the xy plane, creating a mirror image of the original figure. This is best illustrated graphically:

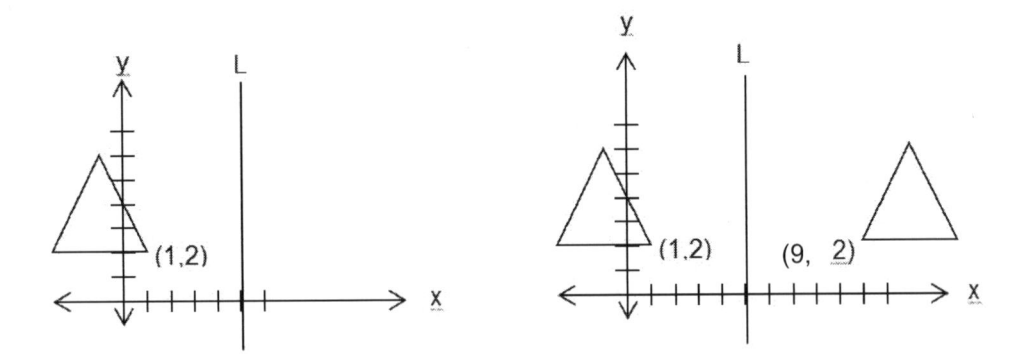

In the above figure, a triangle with one vertex at (1,2) is reflected about vertical line L located at x = 5. Note that vertex (1,2) is 4 units to the left of line L. The reflection of this vertex about L will maintain the same y-coordinate, but the new x-coordinate will be 4 units to the *right* of line L, at (5+4,2) = (9,2). All the other points on the left triangle will have their reflected-triangle analogues, which have been shifted to the right by a similar (but not the same) number of units. The reflected triangle to the right of line L is the mirror image of the original triangle to the left of line L.

Chapter 14   Transformations and Symmetry

SAT Archetypes

Properties of a Function of a Function (1)

```
           y
           ↑
           |
y = f(x)   |8
      \    |
       \   |
    ←———\——|——→
       -10 ↓  x
```

Note: figure not drawn to scale

The figure above depicts a diagonal line representing the function y = f(x) in the xy-coordinate plane as well as its x and y intercepts. If h(x) = -4f(x) + 4, what is the slope of the graph of h(x)?

(A) $-\frac{2}{3}$

(B) $-\frac{5}{3}$

(C) $-\frac{16}{5}$

(D) -4

How do I start?

You need the slope of the line h(x). Since h(x) is a function of f(x), find the formula for f(x) first from the graph. From this you can calculate the formula and slope of h(x).

Solution

We must ignore the apparent slope of the graph for f(x) and instead compute it from the intercepts displayed in the graph. The slope of the line is Δy/Δx = rise/run = 8/10 = 4/5. With a y-intercept of 8, f(x) is a line that has the formula f(x) = 4x/5 + 8. Substitute f(x) for x in h(x) everywhere x occurs. From the definition of h(x), h(x) = -4f(x) + 4 = -4(4x/5 + 8) + 4 = -16x/5 - 32 + 4 = -16x/5 - 28. This is a line with slope -16/5.

Alternate Solution

Using the x and y intercepts of f(x), determine from rise/run that the slope of y = f(x) = 4/5. When the formula for a line is multiplied by a constant, the slope of the resulting line is multiplied by that constant. The rise is multiplied, but the run is not. Thus, the slope of h(x) is -4 times the slope of f(x), or -4 • 4/5 = -16/5. In this problem, just the slope will do.

Answer C

The Take-Away

Some problems force you to take data from a graph or a table in addition to information given directly in the problem. In this problem you had to calculate the slope of f(x) from the graph and then use that and the relationship between h(x) and f(x) to get the slope of h(x). The first solution developed the full-blown function h(x) and then got its slope. But because h(x) is a linear function of f(x), we able to immediately get its slope, as shown in the alternate solution.

Properties of a Function of a Function (2)

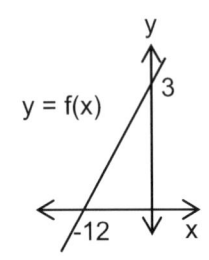

Note: figure not drawn to scale.

The figure above depicts a diagonal line representing the function y = f(x) in the xy-coordinate plane as well as its x and y intercepts. If h(x) = 8f(x) + 4, what is the x-intercept of y = h(x)?

(A) -15
(B) -14
(C) $-\dfrac{16}{5}$
(D) 3

How do I start?

Since h(x) is a function of f(x), you'll first need to determine f(x) from the two intercepts given in the problem. From this you can calculate h(x). Note: h(x) = a • f(x) + b. Since f(x) is a line, h(x) is also a line.

Chapter 14   Transformations and Symmetry

Solution

The slope of f(x) = rise/run = 3/12 = 1/4. Using the slope-intercept formula and the y-intercept of 3, y = f(x) = x/4 + 3. This can be substituted directly into the definition for h(x) = 8f(x) + 4 = 8(x/4 + 3) + 4 = 2x + 24 + 4, or h(x) = 2x + 28. The x-intercept of h(x) occurs when y = 0 = 2x + 28. Solving for x, the x-intercept equals -14.

Answer B

The Take-Away

When handling functions of a function, determine as much as is needed about the first, or interior function. Substitute that functional expression in place of the variable in the expression for the exterior function.

Transformation of Variables: Evaluating Functions

Let the function f be defined by f(x) = 2x + 1. If 2f(a) = 10, what is the value of f(4a)?

SR

How do I start?

If you want f(4a), you'll probably need the value of a first. Calculate f(a) from the second equation, then use the first equation, using x = a, to solve for a. Then calculate f(4a).

Solution

If 2f(a) = 10, then f(a) = 5. Therefore, setting x = a in the first equation, f(a) = 2a + 1 = 5. Solving for a, a = 2. Therefore, f(4a) = f(8) = 2•8 + 1 = 16 + 1 = 17.

Answer 17

The Take-Away

This is a fairly simple example of the use of transformed variables that is, however, medium-hard in difficulty. Not only is the letter of the changed (x->a), but later you are asked to evaluate f(4a). Nevertheless, there is a straightforward sequence of steps, calculating intermediate values on the way to the solution.

Transformations and Symmetry — Chapter 14

Linear Transforms

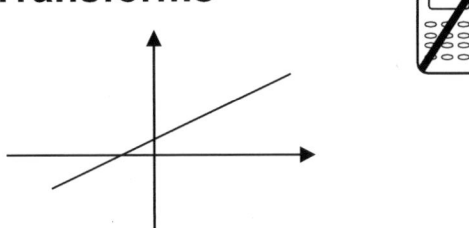

The figure above shows the graph of the line y = mx + b. Which of the following graphs best represents another line defined by $y_2 = -2mx - b$?

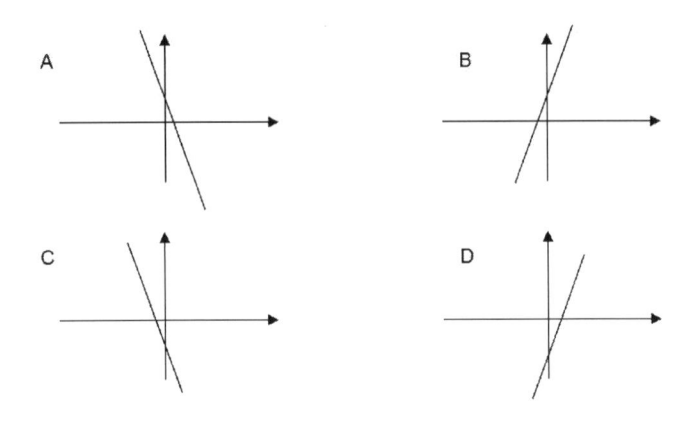

A

B

C

D

How do I start?

You can tell from the original figure that both m (the slope) and b (the y-intercept) are positive. The slope of the line appears to be a bit less than 1. The slope of the transformed function will be -2 times the original slope. The new slope has to be negative and have a higher pitch than the original line. Also, the new transformed function will also be shifted along the y-axis.

Solution

Since the original slope was positive, and the slope of the transformed function is -2 times the original slope, the new slope must be negative and twice as steep. Only (A) and (C) satisfy this constraint. The original line has an x-intercept b>0. Since $y_2(0)$ equals -b in the new function, the y-intercept must be negative, and (C) must be the answer.

Chapter 14   Transformations and Symmetry

Alternate Solution

From its graph we can see that the slope (m) of y = $\underline{m}$x + b is positive. Therefore, the slope of y_2 = $\underline{-2m}$x - b must be negative and twice as steep as y = mx +b. We can thus toss out (B) and (D). The y-intercept of y = mx + b is b, and we can see that b > 0. From y_2 = -2mx - b, you can see that at its y-intercept, which is -b, y_2 has been shifted down along the y-axis by -2b units from b to -b. Graph (C) does this.

Answer C

The Take-Away

Lines will be shifted up or down depending on the value of a constant added to the right side of the equation. If the value of x is scaled, as it is here, the slope of the line will be scaled as well. Negative scaling will result in the slope changing from positive to negative, or vice versa.

Transformation of Variables: Algebraic Expressions

The function g(x) = 4x for all values of x. Which function below is equivalent to g(x-2y)?

(A) $\dfrac{x}{4} - \dfrac{y}{2}$

(B) $\dfrac{y}{2} - \dfrac{x}{4}$

(C) 4x – 8y

(D) 8y

How do I start?

Substitute x - 2y into the function g(x) everywhere x appears and simplify the expression.

Solution

g(x) = 4x. Hence, after substituting x with x-2y, g(x-2y) = 4(x-2y) = 4x - 8y.

Answer C

The Take-Away

Substitution, or transformation, of variables is often a straightforward substitution of an algebraic expression for the independent variable in the functional expression.

Transformations and Symmetry   Chapter 14

Recognizing Transforms: Shifting and Flipping

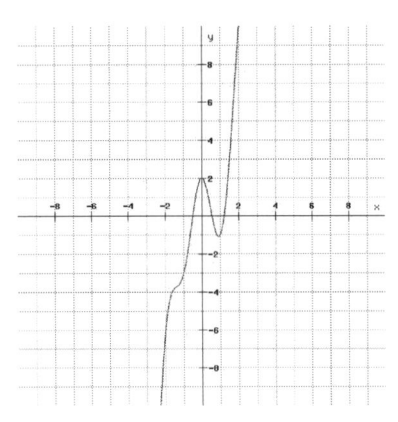

The figure above shows a graph of the function f(x). Which graph below depicts
2 - f(x-2)?

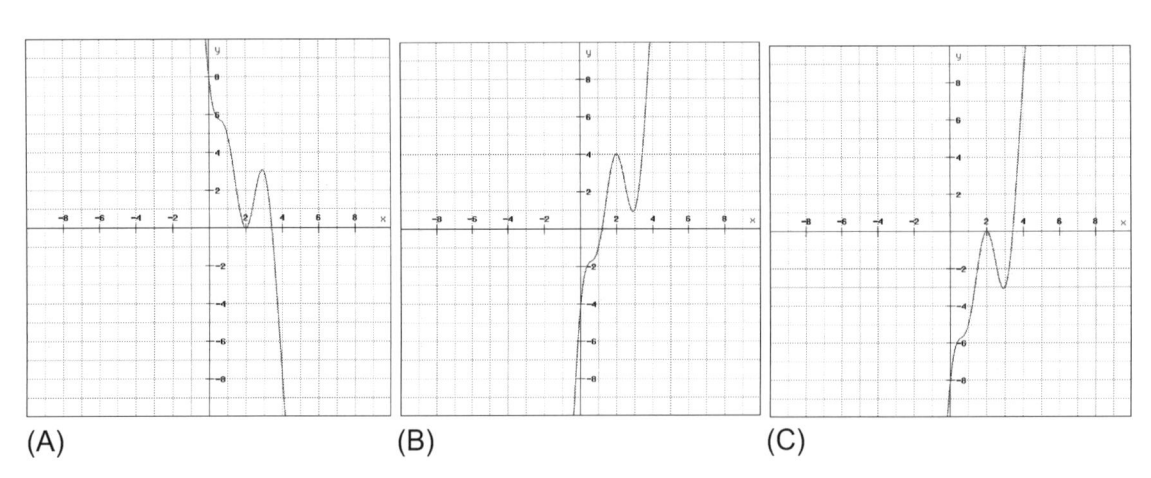

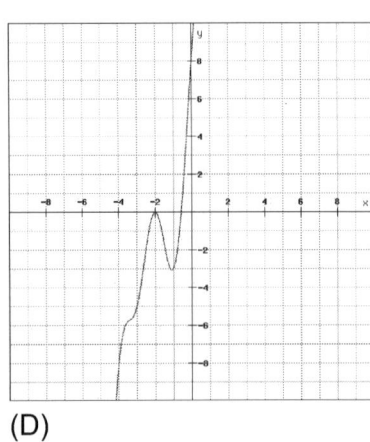

(A)   (B)   (C)

(D)

432

Chapter 14 Transformations and Symmetry

How do I start?

Multiplying a function by -1 flips it around the x-axis. Note how as x approaches ∞, the original function appears to approach ∞. The new function should appear to approach -∞ as x approaches ∞. Also, adding to the argument shifts the function left or right of its original position, depending on the sign of the value added. Adding a constant shifts the graph up or down from its original position depending on the sign of the value added.

Solution

The original function appears to approach ∞ as x approaches ∞. But the new function involves -f(x-2); the figure will be flipped around the x-axis. As x approaches ∞, the new function will approach -∞. This eliminates (B), (C), and (D). The only option left is (A).

Alternate Solution

Since f(0) = 2, f(x-2) will equal 2 at x = 2. Since the function in question involves -f(x-2), the figure will be flipped around the x-axis. Thus, -f(x-2) equals -2 at x = 2. Adding 2 to this will shift the figure up by 2. Hence, 2 - f(x-2) will equal zero at x = 2. Only (A) and (C) have this property. Toss (B) and (D). In order to differentiate between (A) and (C), we must perform the extremity analysis as described in the original solution. (C) shows a function that does not approach -∞ as x approaches ∞. The graph that displays these transforms correctly is (A).

Alternate Solution II

The graph of the original function has a kink in the 3rd quadrant between x = -1 and -2. This feature will be flipped above the horizontal axis (when the function is multiplied by -1) and (after shifting 2 units to the right on the x-axis) should be found in the 1st quadrant in the transformed function. Only choice (A) presents this kink where it should be.

Answer A

The Take-Away

When presented with a function that has been shifted and/or multiplied, individually tease out the effects of the transforms with regard to the function you are given. In this problem, the function is flipped upside down by multiplying the function by -1, shifted right by subtracting 2 from x in the argument of f(x), and then shifted up by adding two to the right side. You can usually eliminate a couple of choices in problems of this type by inspection. Notice that the behavior of the function as x approaches ±∞ was all we really needed to solve this problem.

Transformations and Symmetry — Chapter 14

Recognizing Transforms: Shifting, Flipping, Scaling

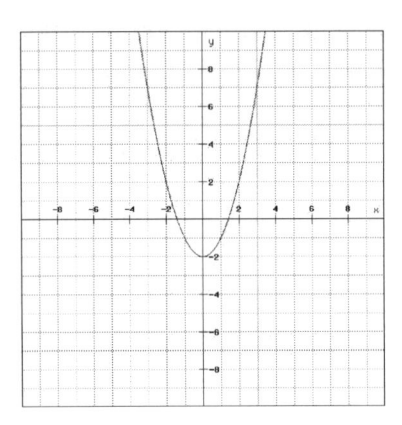

The figure above shows a graph of the function f(x). Which graph below depicts $2 - 2f\left(\frac{x}{2}\right)$?

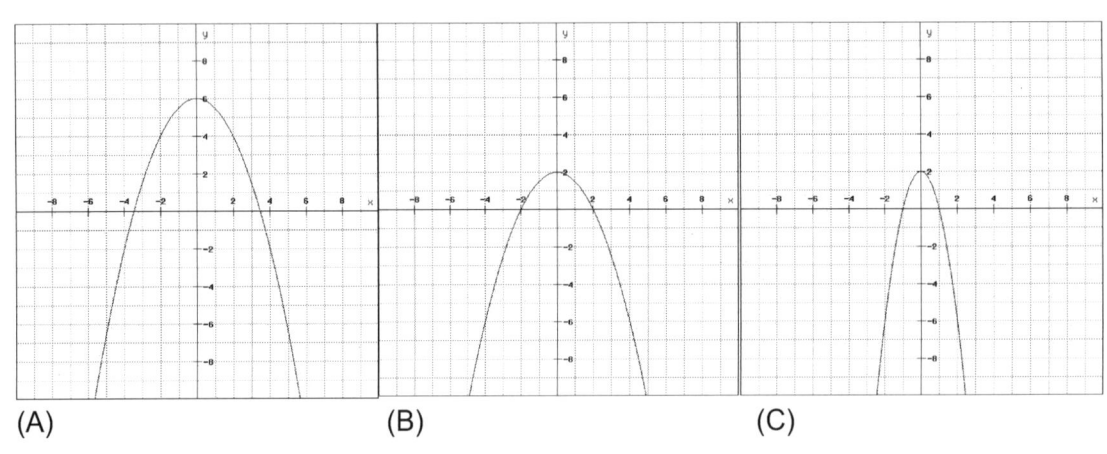

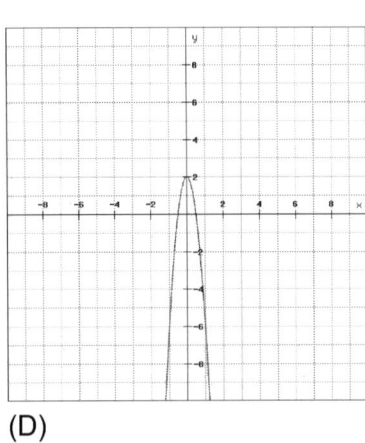

(A)

(B)

(C)

(D)

How do I start?

This looks like a quadratic or higher, even power polynomial function. It looks like the minimum occurs at (0,-2). It might be $y = x^2 - 2$. The transformed function is related to f(x) by scaling the function by the factor of -2 (which results in flipping it down), scaling x by a factor of 1/2 and then shifting y by +2. Take each effect in turn and compare how the original graph would be modified. Look especially at the values of these functions at x = 0.

Solution

Because the new function has a $-2f(\frac{x}{2})$ term, it must be flipped upside down. But all of the choices are flipped. The original function had a y-intercept = -2. Now, -2f(0) by itself would have a y-intercept of y = -2(-2) = 4. However, because the new function has 2 added on the right side, the flipped function will be shifted up on the y-axis by 2 units. It will have a y-intercept of y = 6. This eliminates all choices but (A).

Alternate Solution

The original function is multiplied by -2, which will make the graph appear *narrower* than the original. However, in the argument of $-2f(\frac{x}{2})$, x has been scaled by 1/2. This by itself would make the graph appear *wider* than the original. Even though f(x) isn't linear, near the origin these two features tend to cancel each other: the graph of $2 - 2f(\frac{x}{2})$ should be nearly as broad as f(x). Toss (C) and (D). We can't choose between (C) and (D) without further numerical analysis. But this much would help us guess if time were running out.

Alternate Solution II

One could choose a point other than x = 0 to evaluate. But if you can use a value of the independent variable that will cause terms to collapse to zero, calculating the value of the function at that point is trivial. This will often be x = 0, but a function might include a term like $(x-a)^2$ instead of x^2, and in that case x = a is a natural choice for easy evaluation.

Answer A

The Take-Away

Always attack problems involving graphs of transformed functions one transform at a time. Scaling the independent variable will either stretch or squeeze the graph. If the magnitude of the x-scaling factor is less than one, then the graph will be broadened. If x is scaled by a magnitude greater than one, the graph will be narrowed. If the function is multiplied by a magnitude greater than one it will be narrowed. If less than one, it will be broadened.

Transformations and Symmetry   Chapter 14

Reflection About a line of Symmetry

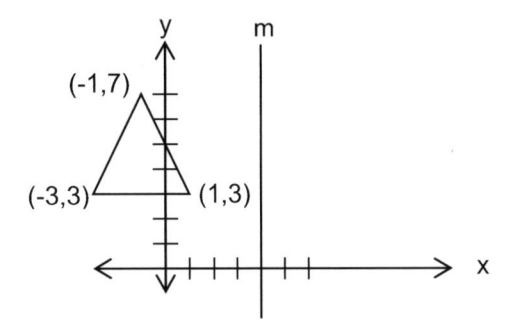

In the diagram above, if the triangle is reflected about line m, what will be the coordinates in the mirror image of the point (-3,3)?

(A) (-3,-3)
(B) (3,3)
(C) (3,11)
(D) (11,3)

How do I start?

It might help to draw the mirror image on the diagram. At least plot the mirror image of the point in question. Manually calculate the distance between the point (-3,3) and vertical line m located at x = 4. The mirror point will be that far from m on the other side. Don't forget to express the new point in terms of the origin.

Solution

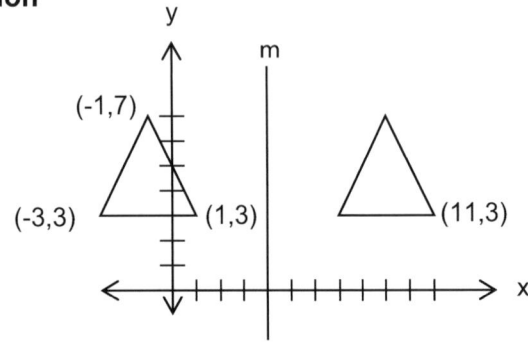

We may toss out (A) and (C) since reflection about a vertical line will never result in a change in the y coordinate. Reflection about the line m will result in a mirror-image triangle on the right. Because the point (-3,3) is 7 units to the left of line m, its reflection will be 7 units to the right of line m. Since line m is x=4, the x coordinate of the reflected point will be 7+4 = 11 and the y coordinate will not change. The reflected point will be (11,3).

Answer D

The Take-Away

Reflection is not the same as shifting the entire figure by a constant. Points that are further from the reflection line on one side will be further from the reflection line on the other side. Just like a mirror. Problems that involve reflection of points or figures about a line of symmetry will almost always reflect about a vertical or horizontal line. It's *possible* such a problem might be constructed using a line of symmetry at, say, a 45 degree angle from the vertical, but you're unlikely to see that on the SAT. But with some triangle geometry, you could kill that off too. And always reference the coordinates of the reflected points with respect to the origin, not the line of reflection.

Notes

Chapter 14   Transformations and Symmetry

Practice Problems

1.

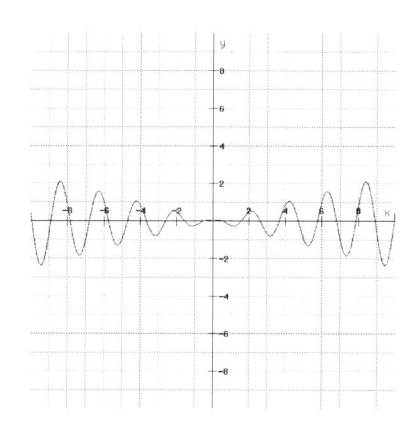

The figure above shows a graph of the function f(x). Which graph below depicts 2 - 2f(x-2)?

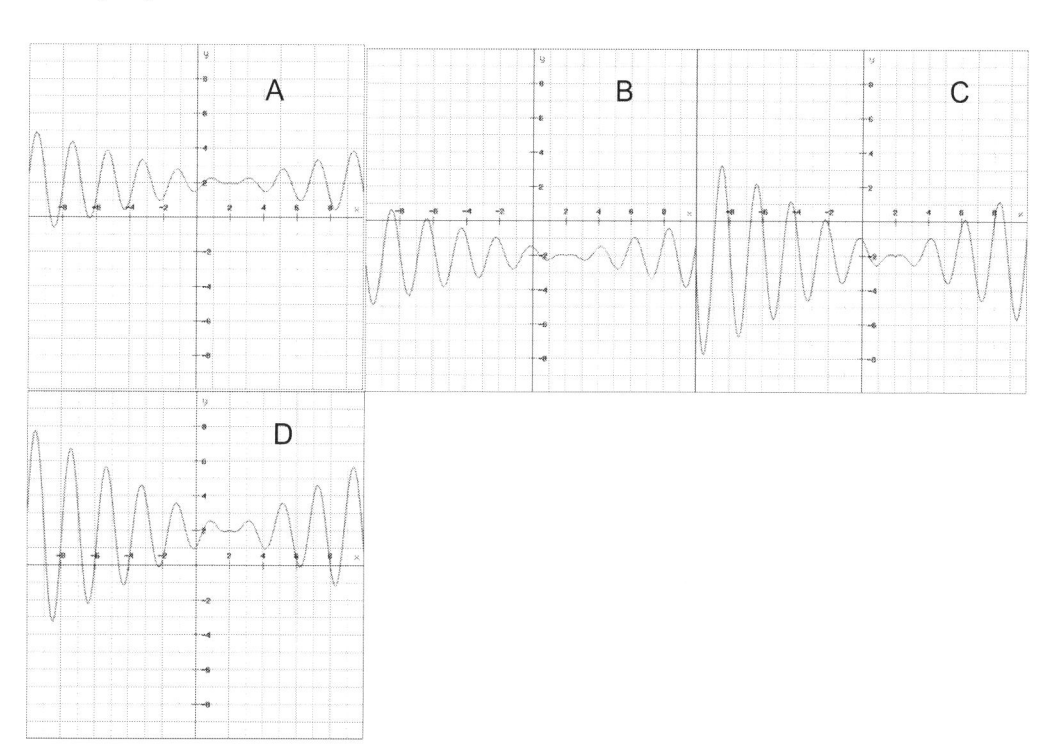

A

B

C

D

439

Transformations and Symmetry   Chapter 14

2. If x is any real number, the function g(x) has a range between -22 and 6, inclusive. If h(x) is defined as h(x) = -4g(x+2) - 10, what is the minimum value of h(x)?

   (A) -34
   (B) -22
   (C) 14
   (D) 16

3. A function g is defined over all x>0 such that $g(x) = \frac{x^2 - 4}{3}$. Assuming g(a) = 15, what is the value of g(2a + 2)?

   (A) 22
   (B) 41
   (C) 84
   (D) 126

4. If f(x) = g(x-3) + 3, and g(1) = 11, what is f(4)?

   SR

5. If $g(x) = x^2 - 2$, and $h(x) = \sqrt{x + 2}$, what is g(h(x))?

   (A) $\frac{x^2}{\sqrt{x + 2}}$
   (B) $\frac{x^2}{\sqrt{x - 2}}$
   (C) x
   (D) $\frac{2x^2}{\sqrt{x - 2}}$

6. Consider the functions below:

   $y(x) = x^2 + 2x$
   $z(x) = x^2 - 2x$

   Which of the following is equivalent to y(a-2), where a is a constant?

   (A) z(a+2)
   (B) z(a) - 2
   (C) z(a)
   (D) y(a)

Practice Problem Hints

1. The argument of the new function is x-2, and hence the function will be shifted to the right by 2 units from the original. The new function also adds 2 to the original, thus shifting up 2 units. What does mean for (B) and (C)? It also scales the function by a factor of 2.

2. The minimum of h(x) occurs at that point in the range of g(x) where g(x) is maximum.

3. From the expression for g(x), set x = a and solve for a, knowing that g(a) equals 15. Then answer the question.

4. When x = 4, x - 3 = 1.

5. Plug the expression for h(x) into the argument for g(x) and simplify.

6. Formulate the expression for y(a-2) and compare to the choices.

Chapter 14 Transformations and Symmetry

Practice Problem Solutions

1. Answer D

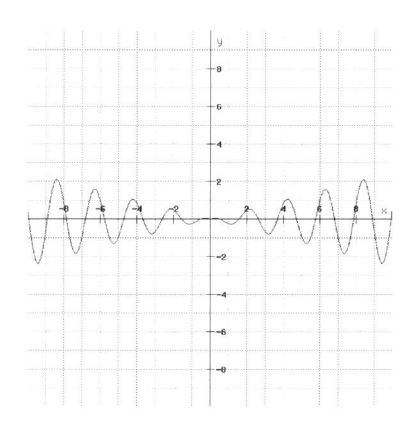

   The figure above shows a graph of the function f(x). Which graph below depicts
   g(x) = 2 - 2f(x-2)?

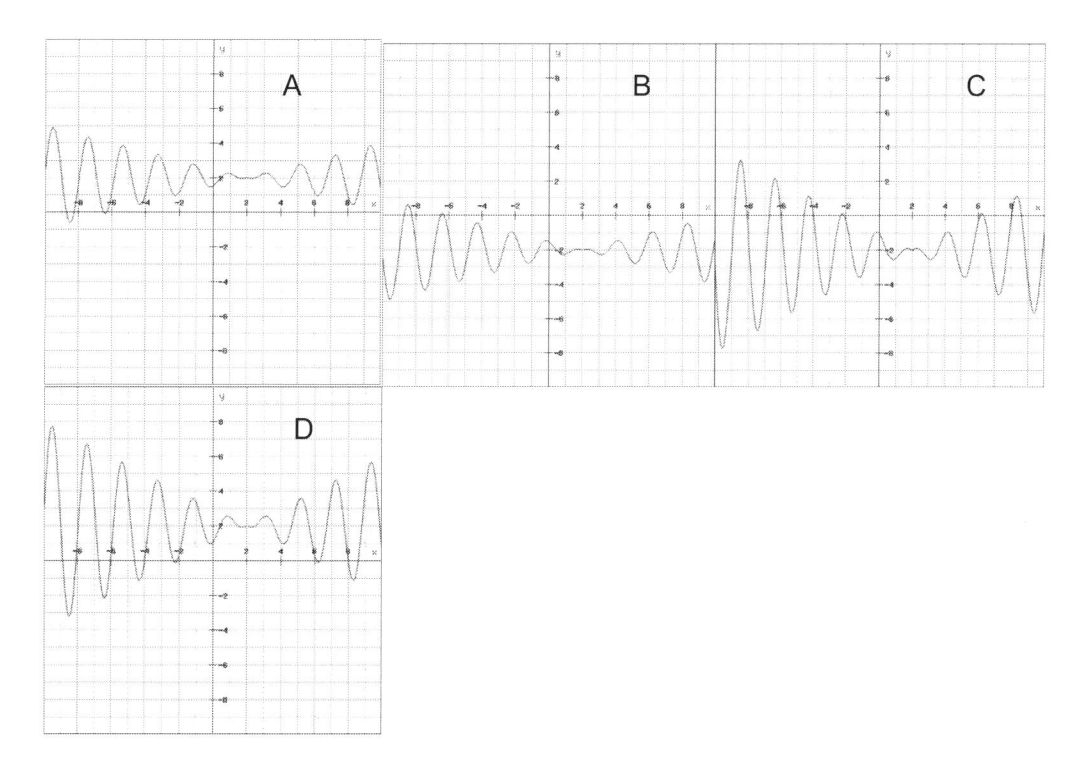

   A

   B

   C

   D

   Since the new function is multiplied by -2, it will be inverted compared to the original, but it's hard to tell inversion from among these choices. This one might be hard to guess from that information alone.

Transformations and Symmetry   Chapter 14

The original function is symmetric about x=0. Because the argument of the transformed function is (x-2) instead of x, the figure will be shifted to the right by 2 units. The new function must have that middle-symmetry line to the right of the y-axis. But all the choices appear to be right-shifted. However, note that f(0) ~ 0. Thus, when x = 2, f(x-2) ~ 0. Moreover, adding 2 in the transform will shift the figure up by 2. Therefore, when x = 2, 2 - 2f(2-2) ~ 2. The graphs that displays this correctly are (A) and (D). But since the transform scales the original function by a factor of -2, resulting in "higher waves," the answer must be (D).

Alternate Solution: Notice that g(x) ~ -2f(x): the "waves" must be twice as high. Only (C) and (D) look like this. Then note its local maximum near x = 0. This feature will be shifted 2 units to the right, but inverted: it must be a local minimum. Only (D) does this.

2. Answer A

The range of a function is the range of values the function takes on over the entire domain. Because h(x) = -4g(x+2) - 10, the least value of h(x) will occur when g(x+2) is a maximum. However, the maximum value of g is already known by knowing its range, regardless of the value of x+2. The maximum value of g(x+2) is 6, and hence the minimum value of h(x) = -4•6 - 10 = -34

3. Answer C

(1) $g(a) = \frac{a^2 - 4}{3}$. Assuming g(a) = 15, what is the value of g(2a + 2)? Multiplying (1) by 3 after setting g(a) = 15, 45 = a^2 - 4, so a^2 = 49, and therefore, a = ±7. Because g(a) is defined for a>0, a = 7. Hence, 2a + 2 = 16, and g(2a+2) = g(16) = (256 - 4)/3 = 84.

4. Answer 14

We need f(4). So x = 4. Plug this into the definition of f(x): f(4) = g(4-3) + 3. Thus, f(4) = g(1) + 3. We are given g(1) = 11! Therefore, f(4) = 11 + 3 = 14. No so obvious.

5. Answer C

Plugging the expression for h(x) into g(x) yields g(h(x)) = $(\sqrt{x+2})^2$ - 2 = x + 2 - 2 = x.

6. Answer C

(1) y(x) = x^2 + 2x and (2) z(x) = x^2 - 2x. To get y(a-2), substitute x with a-1 in (1): y(a-2) = $(a-2)^2$ + 2(a-2) = a^2 - 4a + 4 + 2a - 4 = a^2 - 2a. But from (2), a^2 -2a = z(a).

Chapter 15

Logic and Venn Diagrams

The word *logic* derives from the Ancient Greek word *logos*, meaning speech or reason. We use it here to describe the way that words can be used to represent reasonable statements. The SAT likes to assess the ability of students to use logical reasoning throughout the test. It's one way they have of administering a very challenging test that has a limited academic scope.

If one substitutes symbols for words, those words and the reasoning represented by those words can be expressed using mathematical analogies.

Logical relationships and inferences may be utilized in both math and reading sections of the SAT. The overview given below concentrates on those features of logic that might be encountered in math questions.

Within the math sections of the test, there may be three broad categories of questions involving logic concepts and Venn diagrammatic techniques. While seldom on the test, students must be prepared for them. Most often represented among these are problems where a number of people or objects possess multiple attributes, and the student must determine the distribution of these attributes through algebraic or Venn diagrammatic means. Second, insidious questions may be devised that require the student to recognize the negation of, or the opposite of, a verbal or mathematical statement. Lastly, conditional, or *if-then,* statements must be analyzed to determine their implications.

If the SAT includes a logic problem, it is usually pretty easy. But be prepared for the rare brain-buster. There are 4 archetypes under the subject of logic and Venn diagrams. A review is included, and an additional 6 problems for further practice close out the chapter.

Logic and Venn Diagrams — Chapter 15

Don't Show Up Without Knowing...

How To

- Use a Venn diagram to analyze a shared attribute problem
- Use a Venn diagram with only yes/no information about regions
- Use a Venn diagram to set up simultaneous equations governing the attributes
- Determine the implications of a logical if-then conditional statement
- Determine equivalent statements, ranges, etc. using De Morgan's laws

Quick Review and Definitions

Set Analysis Using Venn Diagrams

You have probably been exposed to Venn diagrams since the 2nd grade (or before). Venn diagrams are useful in analyzing the relationships between intersecting sets. There are virtually no difficult questions on the SAT that refer directly to sets, unions, intersections, etc. However, you may encounter word-problem analogues. In these problems, objects (people, animals, or other objects) have two or more attributes. Venn diagrams can be very useful in visually organizing information, showing the distribution of attributes among these objects and in clarifying algebraic relationships involving this distribution.

Consider T people, each of whom may have any combination of attributes A (for Athletic), B (for Blonde), and/or C (for Cool). A person might be Athletic, Blonde, but <u>not</u> Cool, for example. Or have no attribute at all. There are $2^3 = 8$ combinations of attributes possible. The following Venn diagram organizes the division of these combinations of attributes (and the people possessing them) into eight regions: I through VIII. The diagram will be used to display *the number of people in each region*.

In this representation, each person is assigned to one and only one Roman numeral region inside the box, depending on the combination of attributes possessed. Everyone is in the box. Circles A, B, and C contain all the people possessing attributes A, B, and C,

Chapter 15　　　　　　　　　　　　　　　　　　　　　　　　　　Logic and Venn Diagrams

respectively, (whether or not they also have other attributes). Note that four different regions comprise each circle. Regions I, IV, VII, and VI comprise circle A. The "None" circle (region VIII) represents the people possessing none of attributes A, B, or C. Including region VIII, all regions to which people are assigned are in the box.

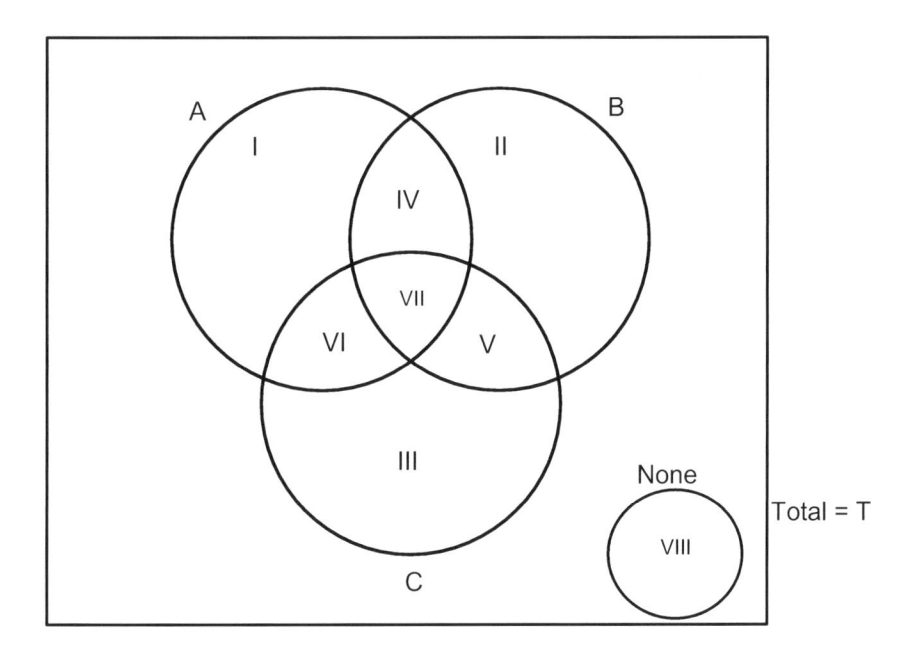

I.   Number of people having only attribute A
II.   Number of people having only attribute B
III. Number of people having only attribute C
IV.   Number of people having attributes A and B only
V.   Number of people having attributes B and C only
VI.   Number of people having attributes C and A only
VII. Number of people having all three (A, B, and C) attributes
VIII. Number of people having no attributes

In some courses, region VIII is not explicitly represented; the number of people with no attributes is, of course, always equal to the total number of people, T, minus the number of people having at least one attribute.

The following examples show relationships among several regions. In the sums below, the region symbols represent the *number of people* in each region:

1. The sum of regions I through VIII = Total = T
2. Number of people with attribute A = I + IV + VI + VII
3. Number of people with attribute B = II + IV + V + VII
4. Number of people with attributes A and B = A∩B = IV + VII
5. Number of people with attributes A or B = A∪B = I + II + IV + V + VI + VII

Such equations (of course, there are many others that we could form) may be used singly or used in a system of simultaneous equations to solve for one or more unknowns (number of people in a region, for example). We'll see how in the problems in this chapter.

It is also possible to use Venn diagrams to represent "some or none" or "yes or no" information regarding the objects in the regions.

De Morgan's Laws

The equivalence of logical statements is occasionally tested on the SAT. In such questions a statement (mathematical or verbal) is given, and students are asked to choose an equivalent statement from among the choices. It can be especially difficult to see the equivalence of statements involving negation, i.e., phrases involving the word *not*. De Morgan's laws give two rules involving negation within compound statements, allowing such statements to be analyzed and equivalent statements to be written or identified.

In general, consider two separate statements, A and B, each of which may or may not be true. The statement A might be "it's raining," and B "it's hailing." The operator *and* in the compound statement (A *and* B) indicates that *both* A and B are true. The operator *or* in the statement (A *or* B) indicates that either A or B (or both) are true. De Morgan's laws regarding negation of these types of compound statements are:

(1) "*not* (A *and* B)" is the same as "(*not* A) *or* (*not* B)"

(2) "*not* (A *or* B)" is the same as "(*not* A) *and* (*not* B)"

An example will clarify. Consider the statement (3) "It never rains while it hails." You can infer that "never" implies negation, or not, and "while" implies the operator *and* in this statement. This statement might be expressed succinctly as: *not* (rains *and* hails). From (1), this is equivalent to: (*not* rain) *or* (*not* hail), or in English, "It either doesn't rain *or* it doesn't hail." Convince yourself that this is indeed an equivalent way of restating the original statement. But in English, double negatives are both frowned at and tend to be confusing.

Note that statement (3) is not equivalent to this: (4) "it either rains or it hails." This would mean that it must either rain or hail: one of those always falls from the sky. Statement (4) is equivalent to (A *or* B) but *not* (A *and* B): the Exclusive OR operator in software logic.

Another example is "Dogs that are either small *or* old are inside. The others are outside." From this, you can infer that "the others" are *not* (small *or* old). From (2), this is equivalent to: "Those dogs that are (*not* small) *and* (*not* old) are outside." With care you can see this is equivalent to the original statement. Translation: only large, young dogs are outside.

Analysis of Conditional Statements: If-Then

Conditional statements use the if-then construction. Consider the conditional statement, "If she wins the lottery, then she will buy an island." Conditional if-then statements may be thought of as a *guarantee*; if she wins the lottery, then she surely will *also* buy an island. One not-so-obvious implication is that "*only if* she buys an island will she *also* have won the lottery." If we know she didn't buy an island, we know she didn't win the lottery. She can't break the guarantee.

There are implications involved in this construction. "If A then C" implies the following:

(1) "Only if C then A" and

(2) "If *not* C then *not* A."

You may have learned the terms "antecedent" and "consequent" in the context of conditional logic. In the conditional statement "If A then C," A is the antecedent, and C is the consequent. A comes before C in the logical analysis (not necessarily involving time). C is a guaranteed consequence of A. A is a *sufficient condition* (but not necessary) to cause C. Note that C could occur without A occurring. First identify the antecedent and the consequent. Then apply the implications (1) and (2) above, as necessary.

In the language of the above general statements, A = "wins the lottery" and C = "buys an island." Winning the lottery (antecedent) is not a *necessary condition* to buy an island (consequent), it is a *sufficient condition*. We know that if she won the lottery, she will buy an island. Notice that she doesn't have to win the lottery to buy an island; maybe islands go on sale, and she can afford to buy one anyway.

One way to depict this relationship is with an Euler diagram, showing the set and subset relationships between antecedent and consequent:

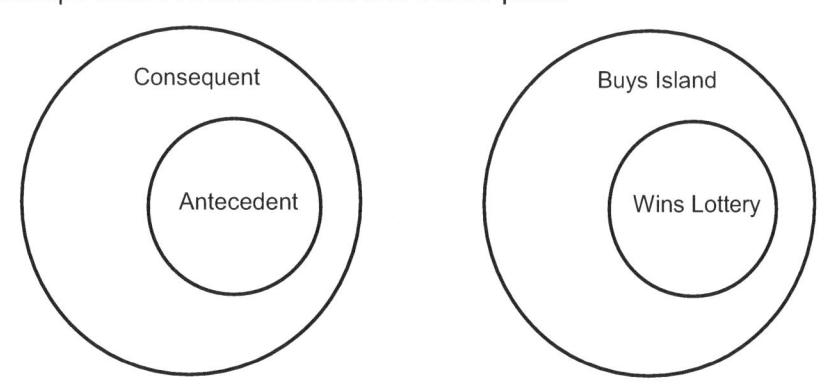

After constructing it, we can clearly see that if she has not bought an island, then she could not have won the lottery. But she could buy an island without winning the lottery.

Another type of if-then conditional statement is the if-and-only-if statement. Altering the example above, consider "If and only if she wins the lottery then she will buy an island." In other words, the only way for her to buy an island is for her to win the lottery, *and vice versa*. The Euler diagram for this condition is instructive.

(Euler diagram: a single circle containing both "Buys Island" and "Wins Lottery")

In this case, we can see that if she wins the lottery, then she will buy an island. But also, if she buys an island, she must have won the lottery. An if-and-only-if conditional statement is equivalent to a *two-way* if-then statement; the antecedent and consequent *always* go together.

What if it is a *necessary* condition that she win the lottery for her to buy an island? In other words, "*Only* if she wins the lottery will she buy an island." This conditional statement can be represented as

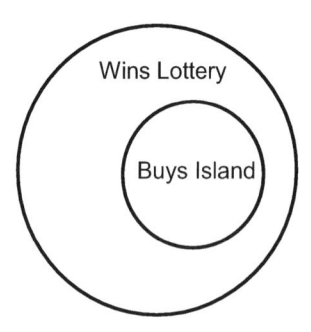

(Euler diagram: a larger circle labeled "Wins Lottery" containing a smaller circle labeled "Buys Island")

In this case we can see, employing implications (1) and (2) above, (1) if she buys an island then she must have won the lottery, and (2) if she doesn't win the lottery, then she can't buy an island. Also, she could win the lottery and *not* buy an island.

Prepending the word "only" to an if-then conditional statement essentially interchanges the antecedent and consequent, as you can see from implication (1), or by comparing the Euler diagram above with its analogue on the last page.

Chapter 15   Logic and Venn Diagrams

SAT Archetypes

Shared Attributes Analysis with Venn Diagrams

An army sergeant gets 26 new recruits. He finds that 14 are thin, 10 are weak, and 5 are tall. Of these, 4 are thin and weak, 3 are thin and tall, and one is weak and tall. If no one is thin, weak, <u>and</u> tall, how many recruits do not exhibit any of these attributes?

SR

How do I start?

There are three attributes that the recruits may possess: thin, weak, and tall. Draw the Venn diagram representing these attributes and determine from the information given how many recruits fall into unknown regions. Total - (sum of all with attributes) = no attributes.

Solution

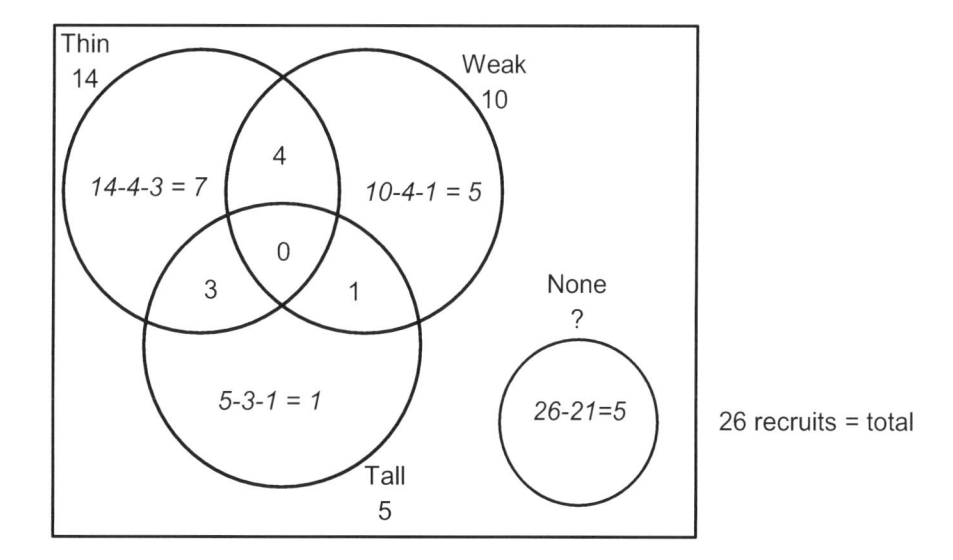

```
Thin
14                        Weak
                          10
              4
14-4-3 = 7        10-4-1 = 5
          0
      3       1              None
                             ?
   5-3-1 = 1         26-21=5      26 recruits = total
      Tall
      5
```

Write down in each of the 8 regions what is known (and unknown). If there are 14 thin recruits and 4 are thin and weak, 3 are thin and tall, and none are thin, weak, and tall, then there are 14 - 4 - 3 - 0 = 7 recruits that are only-thin. By similar reasoning, there are 5 recruits that are only-weak and 1 recruit that is only-tall. Counting the number of recruits that fall into the several regions of the diagram, there are 7 + 5 + 1 = 13 with only one attribute, 4 + 3 + 1 = 8 with two attributes, and zero with all three attributes. This means

Logic and Venn Diagrams   Chapter 15

there are 13 + 8 + 0 = 21 recruits have at least one attribute. Since there are 26 recruits in total, there must be 26 - 21 = 5 recruits with none of these attributes.

Answer 5

The Take-Away

Using the method as outlined in the review section in this chapter, the analysis of attribute distribution problems using Venn diagrams is often straightforward. Such problems will usually present all the information necessary to complete the diagram in every region with values, some/none, or algebraic equations. In this example the equation governing the unknown came from constraint that the sum of the recruits in all regions must equal 26.

Venn Diagrams Filled With Some/None Attributes

At a certain college, some math majors are on the football team, and no members of the football team are juniors. Which of the following must also be true?

(A) Some math majors are juniors.
(B) There are more math majors than footballers.
(C) No math majors are juniors.
(D) Some math majors are not juniors.

How do I start?

There are three attributes students may have: Math, Football, and Junior. In this problem, you are not given specific numbers of students possessing attributes. You are only told whether there are some students or no students possessing attribute combinatons. Draw the Venn diagram for the three attributes, Math, Football, and Juniors, and place an S(ome), N(one), or ? in each region according to the information provided.

Solution

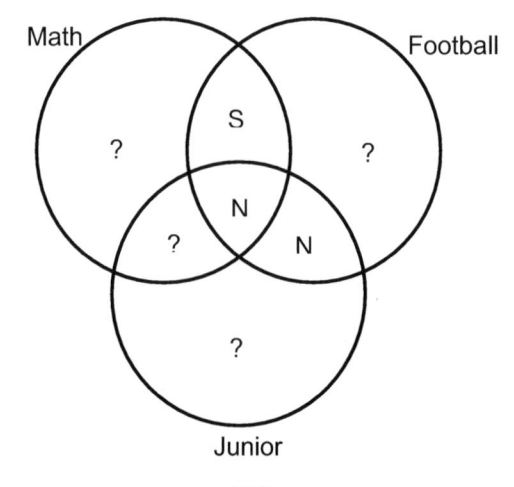

Math, Football, Junior Venn diagram with regions labeled: Math-only: ?, Math∩Football (not Junior): S, Football-only: ?, Math∩Football∩Junior: N, Math∩Junior (not Football): ?, Football∩Junior (not Math): N, Junior-only: ?

452

Chapter 15 Logic and Venn Diagrams

Assume nothing but what you are given in the problem. Since some math majors play football, you could start by putting an S in the region of intersection between math and football that does *not also* include juniors (we are told there are no junior football players). Indicate this by placing an N in *both* regions of intersection between juniors and football.

All other regions are unknown. Put a ? in the unknown regions. The ? could be an S or an N. We know that there must be some math majors and football players because those sets intersect. We don't know for certain whether there are *any* juniors.

Examine the list of choices and compare the statement presented in each with the information contained in the diagram. The statement in the choice *must* be true.

Choice (A) refers to the intersection of Math and Juniors. There are two regions in that intersection: one has a ?, and the other an N. The ? region, revealed, might show (if it were N) that there are no Junior math majors, and therefore choice (A) might not be true. Toss (A). Choice (B) can't be determined – we know that there some math majors and some football players, but we don't know their relative numbers. Toss (B). Choice (C), like choice (A) refers the same N and ? regions – there may be some junior math majors in the ? region – so (C) is wrong. Toss (C). However, (D) is always true. As seen in the diagram, *all* math majors who play football (there are some - in the S region) are not juniors. So those math majors are not juniors.

Answer D

The Take-Away

Venn diagrams can also be used to organized sets of shared attributes where the only information given is whether or not individuals share attributes, or where no information is given about sharing attributes. However, the rules that involve the intersection and union of sets still apply. In effect, the numbers of elements in the several regions are restricted to values of either zero (N) or greater than zero (S) or are explicitly unknown (?). If more than one logical statement is given, it may be possible to determine the value (N, S) of some unknown regions.

Logic and Venn Diagrams   Chapter 15

Logical Negation

x = 1 when a<0, and otherwise x = 0. y = 0 when b<0, and otherwise y = 1. Which expression below indicates the ranges of a and b when x = 1 and y = 1 do <u>not</u> occur together?

(A) a ≥ 0 or b < 0
(B) a ≥ 0 and b < 0
(C) a ≥ 0 or b ≤ 0
(D) a < 0 and b < 0

How do I start?

The statement "x = 1 and y = 1 do not occur together", is the same as, and may be formally recast as, not[(x=1) and (y=1)]. De Morgan's laws of negation may make analysis easier whenever a problem involves a compound statement <u>not</u> occurring.

Solution

The first of De Morgan's Law's states that not(A and B) is the same as (not A) or (not B). Letting A be (x=1) and B be (y=1), we may use the first De Morgan's Law to determine that not [(x=1) and (y=1)] is the same as (1) not(x=1) or not(y=1). Now, not(x=1) is equivalent to x=0, and not(y=1) is equivalent y=0. Using these equivalents, the original logical statement (1) may be recast as (2) (x=0) or (y=0). From the info given, (x=0) occurs when a ≥ 0. Likewise, (y=0) occurs when b < 0. Rewriting (2) using these inequalities involving a and b, (x=0) or (y=0) becomes (a ≥ 0) or (b < 0), which is choice A.

Alternate Solution

You can examine the conditions and logic of this problem without resorting to De Morgan's Law, but doing so increases the chance of error - one mistake and you blow it.

Answer A

The Take-Away

Statements involving negation can be confusing. Sometimes several steps utilizing corresponding relationships must be taken to recast an original statement in terms of other variables or conditions, as seen in this problem. Using the two laws of De Morgan regarding negation are easy to apply. However, applying them correctly and keeping the events, ranges, or statements coordinated throughout the several steps necessary to arrive at a final equivalent statement may be quite difficult. There was no mercy here.

Chapter 15　　　　　　　　　　　　　　　　　　　　　Logic and Venn Diagrams

Confusing If-Then Relationships

Consider the following statement: "If at least one senior is simple, then some juniors are jimple." If the preceding statement is true, which of the following statements must also be true?

(A) If one senior is jimple, then some juniors are simple.
(B) If two seniors are simple, then more juniors are jimple.
(C) If no junior is jimple, then no senior is simple.
(D) If no senior is simple, then no junior is jimple.

How do I start?

This problem presents an if-then conditional statement. It is made especially confusing by the choice of words that alliterate and rhyme. Moreover, "jimple" is a nonsense-adjective. Identify the antecedent and consequent in the statement, and use the rules regarding their relationship to determine the truth of the implications presented in the choices.

Solution

The antecedent is "at least one senior is simple." The consequent is "some juniors are jimple." From the rules regarding antecedents and consequents, it must also be true that:

   (1) Only if some juniors are jimple, will at least one senior be simple.

   (2) If no juniors are jimple, then no seniors are simple.

You can see right away that (2) is the same as choice (C). But let's examine the list of choices to see how such questions may confuse analysis. Choice (A) associates seniors with jimple, and juniors with simple, which is never mentioned in the problem. Toss (A). Choice (B) tosses in the modifier *more*, which is not implied in the problem. Toss (B). Choice (D) is an attractive, but wrong answer. While it reads like a plausible choice, it is not a correct implication from the original conditional statement. The original conditional statement allows for the possibility that there could be some jimple juniors but no simple seniors. There could be *no seniors at all*, but still be some jimple juniors. Toss (D).

Answer C

The Take-Away

It bears repeating: An if-then conditional statement does *not* mean only-if-then. In fact, that will be true in the reverse direction: If (antecedent) then (consequent) implies that *only*-if (consequent) then (antecedent).

Notes

Chapter 15   Logic and Venn Diagrams

Practice Problems

1. In a school of 300 students, 35 students take dance, 125 students are on sports teams, and 25 students participate in both activities. How many students participate in neither sports nor dance?

   SR

2. *CHALLENGE* 22 girls go on spring break together. 12 have light hair (the rest have dark), 6 have short hair (the rest have long), and 13 wear contacts. There is only one girl that has short, light hair and wears contacts. Two of the girls have short light hair, but don't wear contacts. Two of the girls have short dark hair and wear contacts. If all of the girls have at least one of the attributes mentioned in the first sentence, how many girls have long light hair and wear contacts?

   SR

3. *CHALLENGE* An animal shelter has 33 cats. 14 are cute (the rest are ugly), 20 are stupid (the rest are smart), and 17 are kittens (the rest are adults). 6 are stupid kittens, and of these, only 1 is cute. 6 kittens are ugly but smart, and 8 are stupid, ugly adults. How many cats are cute, smart adults?

   SR

4. Let x and y be integers having the following relationship: if $x < 6$, then $y \leq 3$. This relationship also implies which of the following relationships?

   (A) only if $y \leq 3$, then $x \leq 6$
   (B) only if $y \leq 6$, then $x < 2$
   (C) if $x \geq 6$, then $y > 3$
   (D) if $y > 3$, then $x > 5$

457

Logic and Venn Diagrams   Chapter 15

5. *CHALLENGE* Cars on a lot have automatic transmission and/or leather seats. One or more cars have both. If one third of the cars with leather seats are automatics and one seventh of the automatics have leather seats, which of the following could be the number of possible cars on the lot?

   (A) 21
   (B) 27
   (C) 28
   (D) 30

6. The Venn diagram below describes the distribution of students in two majors, engineering and agronomy:

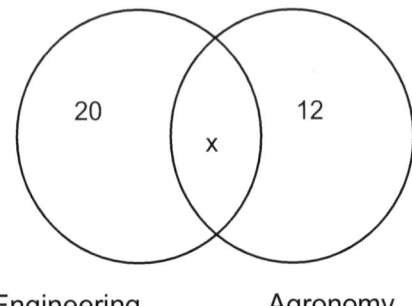

   Engineering   Agronomy

   20   x   12

   Twenty students are majoring only in engineering, twelve are majoring only in agronomy, and x students are majoring in both subjects. How many students, x, are majoring in both subjects if the ratio of the total number of engineering majors to the total number of agronomy majors is 4:3?

   SR

458

Chapter 15 Logic and Venn Diagrams

Practice Problem Hints

1. Fill out a two-attribute Venn diagram and take account of the total number of students in the school.

2. Draw the three-attribute Venn diagram and fill it in. Note that long hair is the equivalent of *not* short hair, and also dark hair is the equivalent of *not* light hair.

3. Draw a Venn diagram with three circles for the three attributes: cute, stupid, kitten. Note that ugly is *not* cute, smart is *not* stupid, and adult is *not* kitten. Some regions will be determined by equations. You will have to solve a system of simultaneous equations to answer the question.

4. An if-then relationship is not an *only if*-then relationship. If A, then B, means that A guarantees B; B *might* occur without A. However, if A occurs, then B *must* occur. What if B didn't occur?

5. The number of automatics must be a multiple of 3. The number of cars with leather seats must be a multiple of 7. And the number of automatics that also have leather must equal the number of leather cars that are automatic.

6. The total number of engineering students = 20 + x.

Notes

Chapter 15　　　　　　　　　　　　　　　　　　　　　　　　　Logic and Venn Diagrams

Practice Problem Solutions

1. Answer 165

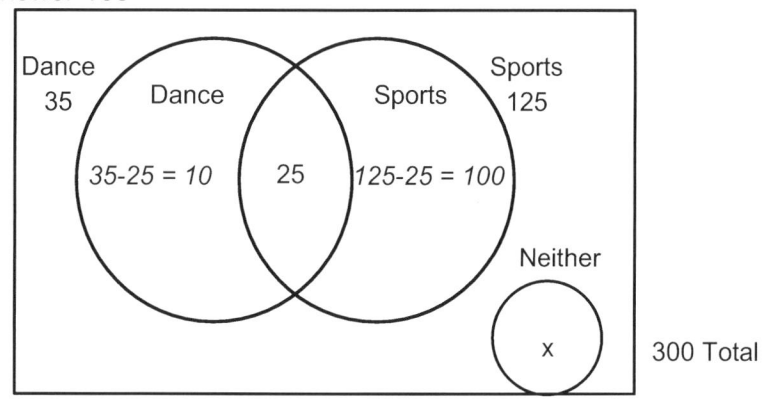

   Dance 35, Dance circle: 35-25 = 10, overlap: 25, Sports circle: 125-25 = 100, Sports 125. Neither: x. 300 Total.

   Because there are 25 students who participate in both activities, there are 35 - 25 = 10 dance-only students, and 125 - 25 = 100 sports-only students. Therefore, there are a combined total of 10+25+100 = 135 students taking at least one activity. So there are x = 300 - 135 = 165 students who take neither sports nor dance. KNOW THIS ONE.

   Alternate Solution: Active students = Dance + Sports - Both = 35 + 125 - 25 = 135. Therefore, the number who take neither sports nor dance = 300 - 135 = 165.

2. Answer 3

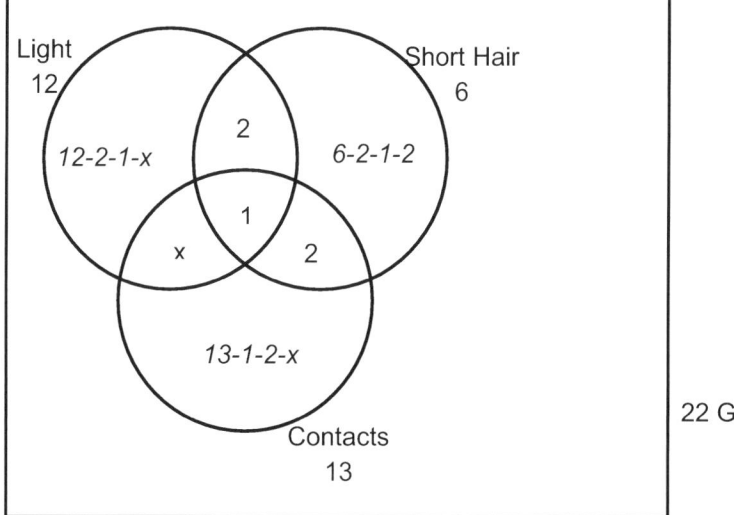

   Light 12, Short Hair 6, Contacts 13. Regions: 12-2-1-x (only light), 2, 6-2-1-2 (only short hair), x, 1, 2, 13-1-2-x (only contacts). 22 Girls Total.

   Using the data in the problem, the diagram can be filled in as shown above. Let x be the desired answer: the number of girls who have light hair, contacts, and long hair. All girls have at least one attribute. The number that are only light is 12 (the total number of light hair girls) minus the number of light hair girls having other attributes as well). So the number of only-light girls is 12-2-1-x. We may calculate the number of only-short-hair girls and only-contacts girls in similar fashion. There are 6-2-1-2

461

only-short-hair girls and 13-1-2-x only-contacts girls. Since there are 22 girls total, it must be true that the sum of each region must equal 22. Therefore, (12-2-1-x) + (6-2-1-2) + (13-1-2-x) + 2 + 1 + 2 + x = 22. Solving for x, x = 3, the number of girls with long light hair who wear contacts. Beastly.

3. Answer 2

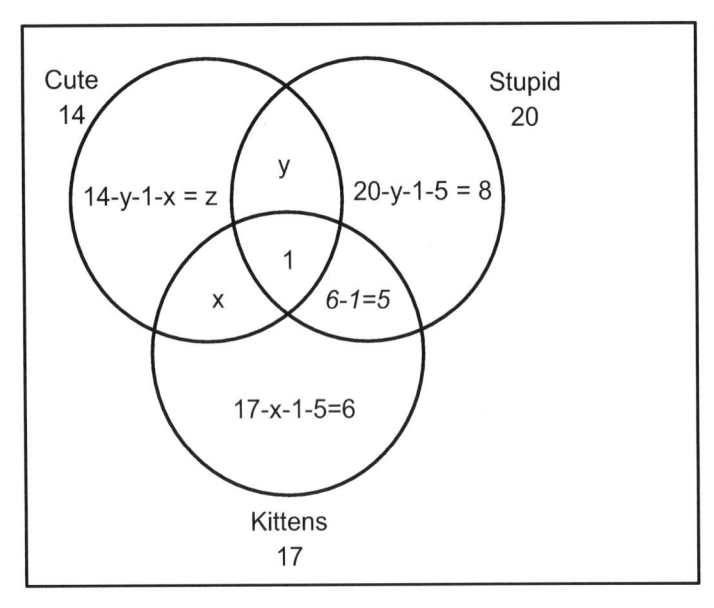

Super-hard. The cute-smart-adults are the z <u>cute-only</u> cats in the diagram. Write 14, 20, and 17 near the Cute, Stupid, and Kittens Venn diagram circles, respectively. If 6 are stupid kittens and one of those is also cute, then the center region (all three attributes) has one representative, and the stupid and kitten-*only* region has 6-1 = 5. The 6 kittens that are ugly but smart are all in the kitten-*only* region, and likewise, the 8 adults (not kittens) that are ugly (not cute) and stupid are stupid-*only*. Let x be the number of cute kittens that are not stupid and y be the number of cute, stupid adults.

There are three simultaneous equations governing the 3 single-only attribute regions. (1) 14-y-1-x = z, where z is the unknown number of cute-only cats. The stupid-only cats are given by (2) 20-y-1-5 = 8. Kittens-only are governed by (3) 17-x-1-5=6. From (3), we can solve for x to get x = 5. From (2) we can solve for y: 20-y-1-5 = 8, or y = 6. Using these in (1) allows us to solve for the number of cute-only cats: 14-6-1-5 = z = 2.

4. Answer D

Rewritten, (1) "If $x < 6$, then $y \leq 3$, assuming both are integers." Using the antecedent-then-consequent rules, statement (1) also implies (1) "only if $y \leq 3$, is $x < 6$," and (2) "if $y > 3$, then $x \geq 6$." However, because x and y are integers, (2) is equivalent to "if $y > 3$ then $x > 5$", or choice (D). Note that choice (C) looks plausible, except that y *could* be ≤ 3, even if $x \geq 6$. It's just that it *must* be ≤ 3 if $x < 6$.

Chapter 15   Logic and Venn Diagrams

5. Answer B

Because 1/7 of automatics also have leather seats, the total number of automatics must be a multiple of 7. Since 1/3 of the cars with leather seats are also automatics, the total number of cars with leather must be a multiple of 3. But notice that the number of dual option cars within each of these two groups must be the same (they are the same cars). The smallest number of cars that might fit this criterion would include a single dual option car: one duel-option car, 7 leather cars, and 3 automatics. This is the only possible set of ratios for one dual-option car. How many cars are there in total? In order to not double count, we have to subtract the one car (in this case) that has both features. So in this case, there are 7 + 3 - 1 = 9 cars. But 9 cars is not a choice. Ugh. Next, examine the scenario with two duel-option cars. Simply multiply the number of cars in each category by 2: 14 leather cars, 6 automatics, and 2 cars with both features: there are 14 + 6 - 2 = 18 cars. Still not one of the choices. Keep going. The next set of cars meeting this criterion is 21 automatics, 9 leather, and 3 cars with both features, and as a result there are 21 + 9 - 3 = 27 cars in total. That is choice (B).

Alternate Solution: The data and relationships given in the question can be represented in a Venn diagram. Let A = the number of automatics and L = the number of leather cars. These sets each include some cars having both features. The number of cars having both features equals both L/3 (via the leather set) and A/7 (via the automatic set). These must be the same number (they represent the same cars).

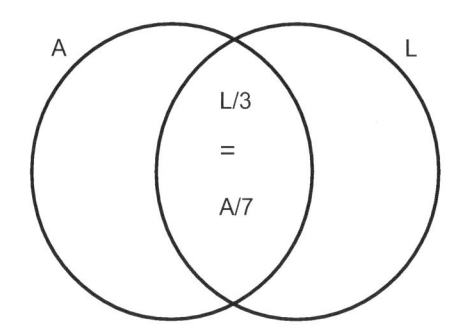

Since L/3 = A/7, just let each equal the same integer value, n. So n = L/3 = A/7. Solve for L and A. Thus, L = 3n and A = 7n. Redraw the Vinn diagram using these equations:

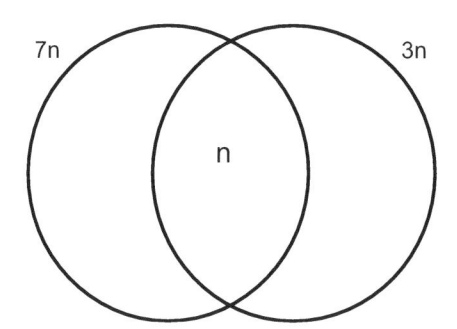

463

Logic and Venn Diagrams   Chapter 15

The total number of cars is equal to 7n + 3n - n = 9n. We had to subtract n cars (those with both features) to avoid double counting. So the total number of cars must be a multiple of 9. Now n can be any positive integer, and there are 9n cars. Only n = 3, which results in 27 total cars, produces one of the answer choices, (B).

6. Answer 12

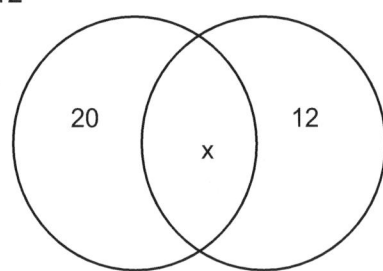

```
        20     12
             x

     Engineering  Agronomy
```

We know that the ratio of the *total number* of engineering majors to the total number of agronomy majors is 4:3. So what is the total number of engineering majors? Clearly it is 20 + x, including the x double majors. Likewise the total number of agronomy majors is 12 + x. Therefore, (total engineering majors) / (total agronomy majors) = (20+x)/(12+x). We are told that this equals 4/3. Thus, (20+x)/(12+x) = 4/3. Cross-multiplying numerators results in 60 + 3x = 48 + 4x. Isolating x, 12 = x, the number of students majoring in both subjects.

Chapter 16

Complex Arithmetic and Algebra

The imaginary number i was discovered as a necessary component in the solutions to certain classes of polynomial equations. But for decades mathematicians argued over the meaning and utility of i. Now many subjects in physics and engineering would be almost impossible to communicate without it.

Mathematics (like most of science) tends to be conservative and slow moving. After all, what could be measured with i? Indeed, even negative numbers, when first introduced, were suspect. As late as 1758, British mathematician Francis Maseres would write that negative numbers "... darken the very whole doctrines of the equations and make dark of the things which are in their nature excessively obvious and simple."

"Make dark of the things which are," he sneered.

Now, sixth-graders use negative numbers without thinking twice.

This chapter will provide a quick review of complex expressions and problems illustrating their arithmetic and algebraic manipulation. The SAT doesn't plumb deeply into the subject of complex math. Most tests will have at most one or two such problems.

In this chapter, you will refresh the concepts of complex arithmetic and algebra, and learn the 5 archetypes. In addition, there are 7 additional practice problems.

Complex Arithmetic and Algebra   Chapter 16

Don't Show Up Without Knowing...

These Concepts

- $i = \sqrt{-1}$

- $i^2 = -1$

- $(-i)^2 = -1$

- A complex expression includes real + imaginary parts: a + ib, where a and b are real numbers.

- The complex conjugate of (a + ib) is (a - ib).

- When a complex expression is multiplied by its conjugate, the result is a real expression (a + ib)(a - ib) = $a^2 + b^2$

- $a^2 + b^2$ = (a + ib)(a - ib) = (b + ia)(b - ia)   (note the equivalence)

These Relationships

Addition of complex numbers

$$(a + ib) + (c + id) = (a + c) + i(b + d)$$

Multiplication of complex conjugates

$$(a + ib)(a - ib) = a^2 + b^2$$

$$(ax + ib)(ax - ib) = a^2x^2 + b^2$$

$$(iax + b)(-iax + b) = a^2x^2 + b^2$$

Chapter 16　　　　　　　　　　　　　　　　　　　Complex Arithmetic and Algebra

How To...

- Add and subtract complex expressions

- Multiply and divide complex expressions

- Factor quadratic expressions into complex factors

Quick Review and Definitions

Complex Addition and Subtraction

A complex expression may always be split into real and imaginary parts: a + bi, where both a and b are real numbers or real algebraic expressions. The rule governing adding and subtracting complex expressions is that real parts must always be added or subtracted to real parts and likewise for imaginary parts. For example,

$$(3 + i4) + (1 - i2) = 4 + 2i.$$

Expressions may also include variables. On the SAT all variables will have real values, but they may be included in complex expressions or functions. E.g., x is real, but

$$f(x) = (3 + i2x) + (-1 - i3x) = 2 - ix \quad \text{is a complex function}$$

Complex Multiplication

Complex expressions are multiplied just like real expressions, however, the relationship $i^2 = -1$ must be used when necessary. For example, using FOIL:

$$(3 + i4)(1 - i2) = 3 + -6i + 4i - i^2 8 = 3 - 2i + 8 = 11 - 2i$$

$$(3 + i2x)(-1 - i3x) = -3 - i9x - i2x - i^2 6x^2 = -3 - i11x + 6x^2$$

Complex Arithmetic and Algebra   Chapter 16

Multiplying Complex Conjugates

The result of multiplying two complex conjugates is the sum of the square of the real coefficient and the square of the imaginary coefficients (including variables, when applicable). For example,

$$(3 + i4)(3 - i4) = 9 + 16$$

$$(3 + i2x)(3 - i2x) = 9 + 4x^2$$

Note that whenever you are presented with a sum of two real, positive, squared terms (like those above), that sum may easily be expressed as the product of their related complex conjugates factors.

Complex Division

Complex division looks formidable:

$$\frac{15 - i5}{(2 - i)}$$

The trick is to multiply numerator and denominator by the complex conjugate of the denominator. Hence,

$$\frac{15 - i5}{(2 - i)} \times \frac{(2 + i)}{(2 + i)} = \frac{30 + 5i + 5}{(4 + 1)} = 6 + i + 1 = 7 + i$$

Complex Factoring

Real polynomial expressions may sometimes be easily be factored using complex factors.

It may sometimes be necessary to factor a real expression into factors of complex conjugates. Consider $4x^2 + 36$. This may first be simplified as (1) $4(x^2 + 9)$. The real expression in parentheses may be factored into a product of complex conjugate factors: $(x^2 + 9) = (x + i3)(x - i3)$. From (1), $4x^2 + 36 = 4(x + i3)(x - i3)$. Note again how $x^2 + 9$ is the sum of two real, positive, squared terms. SAT questions on complex math that involve a sum of two real, positive, squared terms might require such complex conjugate factoring.

In general, $a^2 + b^2 = (a + ib)(a - ib)$. Note that it also equals $(ia + b)(-ia + b)$.

Chapter 16 — Complex Arithmetic and Algebra

SAT Archetypes

Complex Addition

If $f(x) = 3x + 17i$ and $g(x) = -1 + 2xi$, which expression below is the result of $2f(x) - g(x)$?

(A) $(3x - 1) - i(2x - 17)$
(B) $(6x + 1) - i(2x - 34)$
(C) $x(6 + 1) - i(17 - 2x)$
(D) $(2x + 1) + i(3x - 34)$

How do I start?

There's a shortcut you could use to determine the correct choice, but you can slog through the long way by collecting all the like terms and performing the sum.

Solution

We need to segregate the real and imaginary terms (since all the choices do this). First obtain $2f(x) = 6x + 34i$. Then subtract the real part of $g(x) = -1 + 2xi$ from the real part of $2f(x)$ and do likewise with the imaginary parts. Thus (after some complex arithmetic and some rearranging), $2f(x) - g(x) = (6x + 1) - i(2x - 34)$. This corresponds to choice (B).

Alternate Solution

Note that only $f(x)$ has a real x term and that only $g(x)$ has an imaginary, ix term. By calculating in your head, you can see that the real x term of $2f(x) - g(x)$ must equal 6x. We can eliminate (A) and (D) as a result. Also, we can eliminate (C) and (D) because they contain positive ix terms that cannot arise from $-g(x)$. The answer must be (B). If out of time on the test, you can often reduce the set of possible choices using head-math.

Answer B

The Take-Away

The method of complex addition and subtraction (with and without variables) is quite straightforward. The most difficult problems in this category involve linear combinations of complex expressions. Since the real and imaginary parts are separate, a little head-math might allow you to eliminate some or all of the answer choices.

Complex Arithmetic and Algebra   Chapter 16

Complex Multiplication

If $f(x) = (3x + 17i)$ and $g(x) = i(2xi - 1)$, which of the expressions below is $2f(x) \cdot g(x)$?

(A) $(6x + 34i)(i + 2x)$
(B) $(6x - 34i)(i + 2x)$
(C) $-12x^2 - 70xi + 34$
(D) $12x^2 - 74xi + 34$

How do I start?

Clearly, this is will require multiple steps in the multiplication process. Take each step in turn, and of course, keep the real and imaginary parts separated.

Solution

First express $2f(x) = 6x + 34i$. Then multiply i through in $g(x)$: $g(x) = i(2xi - 1) = (-2x - i)$. So $2f(x) \cdot g(x) = (6x + 34i)(-2x - i)$. Use FOIL to multiply out: $2f(x) \cdot g(x) = -12x^2 - 6ix - 64ix + 34 = -12x^2 - 70xi + 34$. This corresponds to (C).

Alternate Solution

Isolate products giving rise to terms in x^2: i.e., the product of the x term from $2f(x)$ and the x term from $g(x)$. $2f(x)$ has $6x$. The function $g(x)$ has a term (after multiplying through by i) of $-2x$. Therefore, the x^2 term of the desired product is $-12x^2$. Only (C) satisfies this criterion. Time saved, if you are *very* careful.

Answer C

The Take-Away

Problems that test the student's skill in complex multiplication are seldom very difficult. Difficulty may be increased when complex multiplication is included as only one step toward the solution. Also - when asked to compare two algebraic expressions, you can often start by comparing either the highest or lowest power of x. On SAT problems, this may allow you to eliminate some choices, as shown in the alternate solution.

Chapter 16   Complex Arithmetic and Algebra

Complex Division

$$\frac{bi-4}{5} + \frac{4}{4+bi} = 0$$

What positive, real integer value of b solves the equation above?

SR

How do I start?

Yeesh. This may be a long, hard one. Maybe start by simplifying the quotient of the second term. The usual first step in complex division is to multiply top and bottom by the complex conjugate of the denominator. Note: b must be an <u>integer</u>. This might enable some clever head-math, or require a brute-force search. Another way?

Solution

The second term can be simplified thus: $\frac{4}{4+bi} \cdot \frac{4-bi}{4-bi} = \frac{16-4bi}{16+b^2}$. Now the denominator is real. Using this in the equation introduced in the problem:

$$(1) \quad \frac{bi-4}{5} + \frac{16-4bi}{16+b^2} = 0$$

They've told you that b is an integer. In this case that might be a big fat hint to just start plugging in integer values of b to see what would work. Oh - but check this out. Note that the <u>numerator of the second term</u> is equal to -4 times <u>the numerator of the first term</u>. All we need is a value of b that makes the denominator of the second term equal to +4 times the denominator of the first term to make the sum to equal zero. A value of b = 2 will make the denominator of the second term equal to 20 (4 times the denominator of the first term). The resulting sum will equal zero. Clever. But involved.

Alternate Solution

Forget division altogether. We just need a value of b that solves the equation. Rearrange the equation in the problem and solve for b. Put the second term on the right side:

$$\frac{bi-4}{5} = \frac{-4}{4+bi}$$

471

Cross multiplying denominators gives:

$$(bi - 4)(4 + bi) = -20$$

Multiplying out the left side yields:

$$4bi - b^2 - 16 - 4bi = -20$$

Combining terms on the left side gives:

$$-b^2 + 4 = 0$$

We are told that b is positive (and real). So only b = 2 solves this last equation. Not bad.

Answer 2

The Take-Away

The mechanics of complex division is, by itself, straightforward. However, difficult problems on the SAT may force the student to see around corners in order to reach a solution. The first solution jumped into the typical "multiply top and bottom by the complex conjugate" step. The alternate solution was a straightforward, mundane solution without resorting to that (often necessary) first step of simplifying complex division.

Complex Factoring

$$-a^2x^2 - b^2$$

Which expression below is a factor of the above expression?

(A) $(axi + b)$
(B) $(ax + b)$
(C) $(axi + bi)$
(D) $(ax - b)$

How do I start?

This will require multiple steps to complete. Factor the quadratic expression into complex conjugate factors as shown in the review. Take each step in turn, and keep the real and imaginary parts separated. But this one requires a magic trick.

Solution

Since $-a^2x^2 - b^2 = -[(ax)^2 + b^2]$, we see that the expression in square brackets is real and is the type that will have complex conjugate factors: the brackets contain two real, positive, squared terms. As shown in the chapter review, such a sum can be factored into complex conjugate factors: (1) $-[(ax)^2 + b^2] = -(ax + bi)(ax - bi)$. However, neither of these factors appears in the list of choices. Now what do we do? Here's the really hard part. The factor of -1 on the outside of the square brackets in (1) may be equated to i•i. The factor of -1 can be replaced by multiplying each factor on the right side of (1) by i: $-(ax + bi)(ax - bi)$ = $i(ax + bi) • i(ax - bi)$. But neither of *these* is listed in the choices. Now multiply each factor through by i: $(axi - b)(axi + b)$. The second factor here corresponds to choice (A). Life in the complex universe: often complex, not always fair.

Answer A

The Take-Away

Problems involving complex factoring will often involve expressions of the form $a^2 + b^2$, which can always be factored as $(a + bi)(a - bi)$. Note that this expression is *also* equal to $(b + ai)(b - ai)$. The feature of the above problem that destroys students is having to factor out the negative sign in the original expression (1) and then to disassemble that (-1) into i•i . On the SAT, this would be a really, *really* hard problem in complex math.

You did well? Step *this* way.

Complex Arithmetic and Algebra   Chapter 16

Complex Simultaneous Equations

$$2x + 5y - 2i = 0$$
$$-6x - 10y + 4i = -40$$

What value of x solves the above system of equations?

SR

How Do I Start?

Scaling the equations will allow you to get rid of everything but terms in x.

Solution

Notice how the last two terms on the left side in the top equation are -1/2 times those same terms in the bottom equation? Multiply the top equation by 2:

$$4x + 10y - 4i = 0$$
$$-6x - 10y + 4i = -40$$

Now the equations can be added together to eliminate all but the x terms. The sum of the two equations is thus

$$-2x = -40$$

And clearly, x = 20.

Answer 20

The Take-Away

Complex simultaneous equations may be solved with exactly the same techniques as real simultaneous equations. Substitution, adding, subtracting, scaling, multiplication and division can all be used. But care must be taken to maintain separation between the real and imaginary components of the equations.

Chapter 16 Complex Arithmetic and Algebra

Practice Problems

1. What is the coefficient of i in the product (1 - i)(2 + 2i)(1 + i)?

    SR

2. The function e^x is defined to be the infinite series (sum): $1 + \frac{x^1}{1!} + \frac{x^2}{2!} + \ldots$. What is the real component of the first three terms of $e^{(1+2i)}$?

    SR

3. What is the real component of $\frac{4-i}{4+i}$?

    SR

4. If $\frac{a+2i}{4+i}$ is real, what is the value of a?

    SR

5. Which expression below is equivalent to $\frac{3-2i}{6+2i}$

    (A) $\frac{3+2i}{40}$
    (B) $\frac{7-9i}{20}$
    (C) $\frac{3+6i}{20}$
    (D) $\frac{22+4i}{40}$

475

Complex Arithmetic and Algebra　　　　　　　　　　　　　　　　　　　　Chapter 16

6. If x and y are real, what is the value of $x + y$ if $3y + ix = 4 + x - i$?

7. If $x = 2$, what is the real coefficient of the complex conjugate of $x - 2i - 2$?

Chapter 16   Complex Arithmetic and Algebra

Practice Problem Hints

1. Two of these factors are complex conjugates of one another.

2. Determine the real component of each of the 1st three terms, then add those together.

3. Multiply the top and bottom of this complex fraction by the complex conjugate of the denominator to eliminate the imaginary component on the bottom.

4. If the given quotient is real, then numerator and denominator are proportional (by a real number) to one another.

5. Multiply top and bottom by the complex conjugate of the denominator.

6. The real part on the left must be equal to the real part on the right. The same is true for the imaginary parts. Use the real and imaginary parts of the complex equation to form simultaneous equations, allowing you to solve for x and y.

7. Plug x = 2 into the expression and take the complex conjugate. This is easy - it only looks confusing.

Notes

Chapter 16　　　　　　　　　　　　　　　　　　　　　　　Complex Arithmetic and Algebra

Practice Problem Solutions

1. Answer 4

    In the product (1 - i)(2 + 2i)(1 + i), perform the product of the first pair of factors first, (1) (1 - i)(2 + 2i) = 2 - 0i + 2 = 4. Therefore, the product of all three terms is 4(1 + i), and the imaginary coefficient is 4. Note that the second factor in (1) is twice the complex conjugate of the first factor, hence their product is real.

    Alternate Solution: Only those terms in the product that have either i^1 or i^3 will contribute to the coefficient of i in the final product. Multiplying bye eye: there are three i^1 terms: -i•2•1 + 1•2i•1 + 1•2•i = 2i. There is only one i^3 term: (-i)•(2i)•(i) = 2i. Therefore the sum of the imaginary terms is 2i + 2i = 4i. The imaginary coefficient is 4.

    Alternate Solution II: the first and third factors are complex conjugates of one another, and their product is 2 by inspection. Therefore, multiplying 2 by the imaginary term in the middle factor gives 4i. The coefficient is i is 4.

2. Answer 1/2

    The first three terms in the series are $1 + \frac{(1+2i)^1}{1!} + \frac{(1+2i)^2}{2!}$. By inspection, the real parts of the first two terms are 1 and 1, respectively. The third term is (1 + 2i)(1 + 2i)/2 = (1 + 4i - 4)/2. The real part of this term = -3/2. So the first three terms have a real component of 1 + 1 - 3/2 = 1/2.

3. Answer 15/17 or .882

    Multiply the top and bottom of $\frac{4-i}{4+i}$ by the complex conjugate of the denominator.

    Thus, $\frac{4-i}{4+i} \cdot \frac{4-i}{4-i} = \frac{16-8i-1}{16+1}$. The real component of this expression is 15/17 ~ .882

4. Answer 8

    If the quotient $\frac{a+2i}{4+i}$ is real, then the imaginary part must be zero. Multiply the top and bottom of $\frac{a+2i}{4+i}$ by the complex conjugate of the denominator. Thus,

479

$\dfrac{a+2i}{4+i} \cdot \dfrac{4-i}{4-i} = \dfrac{4a + i(8-a) + 2}{17}$. If this is real, then 8 - a = 0, or a = 8.

Alternate Solution: If $\dfrac{a+2i}{4+i}$ is real, then numerator and denominator are proportional to one another (by a real number). If this is the case, since the imaginary part of the numerator is twice the imaginary part of the denominator, the real part of the numerator, a, must be twice the real part of the denominator, or a = 4•2 = 8. Easy.

5. Answer B

All answer choices have a real value in the denominator. Multiply the top and bottom of $\dfrac{3-2i}{6+2i}$ by the complex conjugate of its denominator, 6+2i. The result is $\dfrac{3-2i}{6+2i} \cdot \dfrac{6-2i}{6-2i}$

$= \dfrac{18-12i-6i-4}{36+4} = \dfrac{14-18i}{40} = \dfrac{7-9i}{20}$.

6. Answer 0

If x and y are real, the equation 3y + ix = 4 + x - i can be broken into real and imaginary parts, forming simultaneous equations:

(1) 3y = 4 + x
(2) ix = -i

From (2), x = -1. Plugging this into (1), 3y = 4 - 1 = 3. So y = 1, and therefore x + y = 0.

7. Answer 2

This is one of those "this can't be that easy" hard questions. Good students will sometimes stumble on trivial questions. First, it seems odd to ask "what is the real coefficient" of a complex expression. A complex expression has two terms in general. What? Maybe one term (real or imaginary) is equal to zero. We are told that x = 2 and that we need the real coefficient of the expression x - 2i - 2. After plugging in x = 2, the expression becomes purely imaginary: -2i. The complex conjugate of this is 2i, and its real coefficient is 2. Thanks, SAT.

Chapter 17

Science, Engineering, and Business Problems

The SAT includes several questions in the math sections that are practically reading comprehension questions with a little math tossed in. The math involved in solving the question is usually elementary, but the analysis of data presented in the question may be involved.

These questions might include lengthy descriptions of an experiment and the science behind the experiment. Or they may present data describing the performance of a business. The student is then asked to reach a conclusion based on data presented numerically or graphically. Such questions will require a careful analysis of real-world scenarios in order to a reach conclusion.

In this chapter, 12 representative archetypes are included. Note that the math involved in these types of questions is not archetypical. These are math-easy questions. It is rather the type and length of these questions with which you must be familiar. 7 practice problems are also included.

Notes

Chapter 17　　　　　　　　　　　　　　Science, Engineering, and Real World Problems

SAT Archetypes

Kinetic Energy

The translational kinetic energy of an object in motion is $1/2 \cdot m \cdot v^2$, where m is the mass and v is the velocity of the object. In a game of billiards, a cue ball, which is in motion, collides with the number 3 ball, which is at rest, somehow transferring <u>all</u> of its translational kinetic energy to the 3 ball. The mass of the cue ball is .17kg (kilograms), the mass of the 3 ball is .16 kg, and the velocity of the cue ball is v_c = 3 m/s (meters per second). After the cue ball transfers its translational kinetic energy to the 3 ball, what is the velocity of the 3 ball, v_3, immediately after the collision, in units of meters per second?

SR

How do I start?

Calculate the translational kinetic energy of the cue ball and set that equal to the formula for the kinetic energy of the 3 ball. Then solve for the unknown 3 ball velocity.

Solution

The 3 ball (v_3 = 0) has zero initial kinetic energy. The translational kinetic energy of the cue ball is $1/2 \cdot m \cdot v_c^2 = 1/2 \cdot .17 \cdot 3^2$ kg(m/s)^2. This must equal the translational kinetic energy of the 3 ball after the collision = $1/2 \cdot .16 \cdot v_3^2$ kg(m/s)^2. To recap:

$$1/2 \cdot .17 \cdot 3^2 \text{ kg(m/s)}^2 = 1/2 \cdot .16 \cdot v_3^2 \text{ kg(m/s)}^2$$

We can cancel the units on each side of the equation (and the factor of 1/2) and solve for v_3, representing the 3 ball's velocity in units of m/s. Thus, $.17 \cdot 3^2 = .16 \cdot v_3^2$. Rearranging and isolating v_3, $v_3 = \sqrt{\frac{.17 \cdot 9}{.16}} \sim 3.09$. This answer is in units of meters per second.

Answer 3.09

The Take-Away

Even if you haven't seen this equation in a physics or chemistry course, you can follow the science explained in the problem and solve for the desired unknown. Several questions on the SAT may teach some math based science and then require that you use the math-science foundation presented in the problem. Be prepared to read such problems carefully. The math is often elementary, as in the simple algebraic solution above.

The Effects of Thermal Insulation

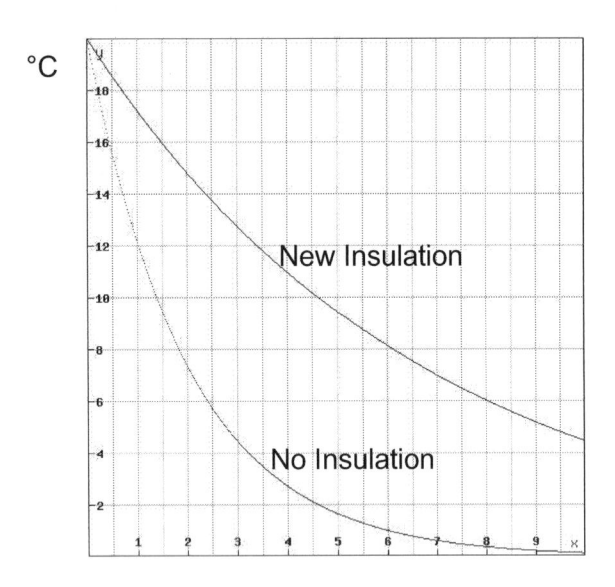

Hours

A company is developing a new type of insulation for a line of storage buildings it manufactures in hopes of improving their energy efficiency compared to the insulation currently used. The graph above shows the temperature inside their smallest storage building over several hours during two separate tests. Each test was performed under the following conditions: the storage building was first heated internally to 20°C while the temperature outside the storage building (conducted during the winter and inside a temperature controlled aircraft hangar) was held at 0°C. At the start of the experiment, the internal heat source was cut off, and the internal temperature of the storage building was allowed to decrease for several hours in a process called equilibration. The lower, dotted curve shows the decrease in temperature over time during the first test, when the building had all insulation removed. Then the new insulation was reinstalled, and a second test was performed in otherwise identical conditions, and the results of that test are shown on the upper, solid curve. Based only on the above experimental results, which of the conclusions below is best supported by the data.

(A) The new insulation is more thermally protective for the line of buildings that the company makes compared to the thermal protection when no insulation is used.
(B) The average rate of change of temperature using new insulation is greater between the 8th and 9th hours than when using current insulation between the 8th and 9th hour.
(C) The cost of heating the smallest storage buildings made by this company is lower with the new insulation compared to the insulation currently used.
(D) The average rate of change of temperature using no insulation is greater between the 2nd and 3rd hours than for the test with new insulation between the 2nd and 3rd hours.

Chapter 17 — Science, Engineering, and Real World Problems

How do I start?

This is another long-read data analysis question. Read the question carefully, and then dissect the meaning of the choices, comparing their meanings to the data in the graph.

Solution

Let's go through the choices. Choice (A) claims that the new insulation is more thermally protective across *the (entire) line of buildings.* But only their small building was tested. While likely true, (A) is an inference not directly supported by data. Very tricky, but probably not (A). Choice (B) compares new insulation with *current* insulation. But they only compared new insulation to *no* insulation: toss (B). Choice (C) likewise compares new insulation with current insulation: toss (C). By elimination the answer must be (D). An inspection of the graph confirms that the average rate of change between the 2nd and 3rd hours with no insulation is ~3°C, whereas that of the new insulation is ~ 2°C.

Answer D

The Take-Away

This is a fairly easy data analysis question that tests the ability of students to interpret a graph. Before launch, read and underline the important data given in the question.

Population Flows

The next two questions refer to the following information.

Biologists often follow the flow of animals into and out of an area. In general, if animals enter a certain area at a rate of s individuals per second and stay within the area for t seconds, then the average number of animals in that area at any one time, A, is A = s•t. This very simple relationship, known as Little's law, was only first established in 1961.

At the Aswa-Lolim Game Reserve in Uganda, a graduate student is studying the drinking habits of local animals at one lake. She has determined that on average 72 ungulates per hour enter the area of the lake during daylight hours and stay for 5 minutes.

Question 1: Assume that Little's Law may be applied to partitions of an area and also to individual species. The grad student divides (in software) the lake into 4 equal-area quadrants: North, South, East, and West, and then observes that, on average, 120 ducks per hour arrive at the North quadrant and stay for 1 minute. On average how many ducks will she expect to observe in both North and East quadrants at any one time?

SR

Science, Engineering, and Real World Problems Chapter 17

How do I start?

This is another long read with relatively easy math. Be careful of the units involved.

Solution

The description of Little's law used units of individuals per second and seconds. But a unit analysis of the equation will reveal that as long as the time units are the same in the first and second factors, it doesn't matter what units are used:

$$A \text{ (individuals)} = \text{(individuals)}/\cancel{\text{(time unit)}} \cdot \cancel{\text{(time unit)}}$$

So there's no need to convert everything to seconds. In this question, the rate of ducks is given as 120 ducks/hour, but they stay 1 minute. Convert hours to minutes: the number of ducks per minute = 120 • 1/60 = 2 ducks per minute. According to Little's law, she will expect 2 ducks/minute • 1 minute = 2 ducks to be in the North quadrant at any one time. Since this should be the same as the (equal area) East quadrant, she expects 2 + 2 = 4 ducks in these two quadrants together at any one time.

Answer 4

Question 2: She has also observed that, on average, 180 lions per 12 hour daylight period approach the area of the lake and stay for 4 minutes. On average, how many more ungulates are expected than lions at any one time during daylight?

SR

How do I start?

Information about ungulates is given in the question background. Use Little's law after converting to the same time units. Calculate the number of ungulates and lions expected.

Solution

From Little's law, the number of ungulates = 72 ungulates/~~hour~~ • 1 ~~hour~~/60 ~~minutes~~ • 5 ~~minutes~~ = 6 ungulates. The number of lions = 180 lions/12 ~~hours~~ • 1 ~~hour~~/60 ~~minutes~~ • 4 ~~minutes~~ = 1 lion. Therefore, there will be 6 - 1 = 5 more ungulates than lions expected at any one time.

The Take-Away

Again, long read, be careful. And always be careful of the units presented in the problem. Read carefully. Underline the data.

Chapter 17　　　　　　　　　　　Science, Engineering, and Real World Problems

Geothermal Gradient

The geothermal gradient is the rate of change of temperature per kilometer of depth within the Earth's interior. At 10 kilometers below the surface of the Earth, the temperature is 240°C, while at 25 kilometers below the surface the temperature is 500°C. Change in temperature is linearly proportional to change in depth from 10 to 100 kilometers beneath the surface. In this range (temperature increase)/(depth increase) is a constant.

Much of the heat within the Earth is a result of the nuclear decay of radioactive isotopes. However, not all rocky planets are thought to be as rich as the Earth in radioactive materials. It is thought that Mars has no such nuclear processes contributing to its internal heat. Some speculate the Martian thermal gradient is half that of Earth's. In other words, the internal temperature of Mars may only increase with depth at half the rate of Earth (between 10 and 100 kilometers). If true, and the internal temperature of Mars is 120°C at 10 kilometers, what is the temperature at 50 kilometers beneath its surface, in °C?

SR

How do I start?

The temperature gradient of Mars is half that of Earth. First, calculate the linear rate of change of temperature in the Earth: (temperature increase)/(depth increase).

Solution

The rate of change of temperature is linear, so we only need two points to calculate the rate. From the data given about Earth, when the depth increases from 10 to 25 kilometers (a change of 15 kilometers), the temperature increases 500 - 240 = 260°C. Therefore, the rate of increase is 260/15 = 17$\frac{1}{3}$ °C/kilometer. Since the rate of increase on Mars is only half this rate, the temperature under the surface of Mars increases at a rate of 8 $\frac{2}{3}$°C/kilometer. We are told to assume that the internal temperature of Mars is 120°C at 10 kilometers. We need to calculate the temperature at 50 kilometers beneath the surface. This is 40 kilometers beyond the 10 kilometer data point. In that 40 kilometers the internal temperature will increase by 40 ~~kilometers~~ • 8 $\frac{2}{3}$ °C/~~kilometer~~ = 346 $\frac{2}{3}$ °C. Thus, at 50 kilometers, the internal temperature is 120 + 346 $\frac{2}{3}$°C = 466 $\frac{2}{3}$ °C.

Answer 466 or 467

The Take-Away

The SAT may present a scientific model of one system, compare that with a model of a different system, and ask questions about the second system.

Science, Engineering, and Real World Problems   Chapter 17

Comparison of Different Cost Plans

The cost of mobile roaming calls in a certain country is Asia using carrier A is $2.50 for any usage less than or equal to 38 minutes and 5 cents per minute thereafter. In that same country the cost of calls using carrier B is 6 cents per minute for the entire duration of the call. If a call with carrier A starts at the same time as a call with carrier B, after how many hours will the calls have the same cost?

SR

How do I start?

Express the two cost schemes algebraically in terms of dollars and minutes, and equate the expressions. Express the final answer in hours.

Solution

We need to solve for the call duration, in minutes, where each call costs the same. Let m be the duration of the calls, in minutes. Carrier A has a fixed cost of $2.50 for calls lasting up to 38 minutes. After 38 minutes they charge $.05 per minute. If m>38, then (1) $cost_A$ = $2.5 + $.05(m-38). Carrier B has a scheme of (2) $cost_B$ = $.06m. We are asked to find the call duration where both schemes cost the same. Let's drop the $ unit. First, how much does Carrier B charge for a 38 minute call? Answer: 38 • .06 = 2.28. So the duration of call that cost the same must be >38 minutes. We need to equate cost schemes (1) and (2). Thus, 2.5 + .05(m-38) = .06m. Simplifying, 2.5 - 1.9 = .01m, and after isolating m, 60 = m minutes. The answer must be in the units of hours. Converting to hours, after one hour the calls cost the same.

Answer 1

The Take-Away

Some costs schemes are structured with two terms: a fixed cost ($2.50 for carrier A) and a per unit cost ($.05 per minute for carrier A). Others have a flat rate per unit ($.06 per minute for carrier B). These may be used separately or together in problems.

One variation of this archetype would give you two plans costing the same for a given call duration, and then have you calculate the value of some unknown parameter in one of the plans, such as an unknown cost per minute for Carrier B. You would use the same equation, but solve for the parameter instead of the duration of the call.

Chapter 17	Science, Engineering, and Real World Problems

Cost Ratio of Ingredients to Final Products

The price of oranges is x dollars for a dozen oranges, and each orange makes y glasses of juice. In terms of x and y, how many dollars does it cost to make 1 glass of juice?

(A) $\dfrac{x}{12y}$

(B) $\dfrac{xy}{12}$

(C) $\dfrac{y}{12x}$

(D) $\dfrac{12x}{y}$

How do I start?

The problem asks for the cost to make one glass of orange juice, or the cost per glass. The answer must be in units of dollars per glass. Use dimensional analysis. There are ratios in the problem that have units of dollars per dozen oranges, and oranges per y glasses. Dollars must be on top and glasses on bottom in the desired ratio expression. These terms look ready to multiply as they are without inverting.

Solution

Start with x dollars/(12 Oranges). We have to get rid of the units of oranges, so multiply it by the 1 orange/y glasses term. Thus, x dollars/(12 oranges) • 1 orange/y glasses = x/12y dollars per glass.

Answer A

The Take-Away

This is a compound rate problem. There are two rates: dollars per dozen oranges and oranges per glass. These problems are usually best solved using dimensional analysis. By knowing the final units needed in the answer, the correct chain-multiplication of terms can be determined.

Alternate Problem: What if they had asked how many glasses will $10 buy? The answer must be in units of glasses. Try this chain multiplication:

y glasses/orange • 12 oranges/x dollars • 10 dollars. So 10 dollars buys y•12•10/x glasses.

Science, Engineering, and Real World Problems   Chapter 17

Splitting Costs Among People

x employees give m dollars each to buy gifts for r fellow employees retiring from their company. If each retiree receives one gift, and all gifts are identical, which expression below correctly states the cost of each gift?

(A) $\dfrac{mr}{x}$

(B) $\dfrac{mx}{r}$

(C) $\dfrac{xr}{m}$

(D) $m(x-r)$

How do I start?

Calculate the total cost of gifts, and divide by the number or retirees. Or use dimensional analysis to obtain the answer in units of dollars per retiree.

Solution

Since x employees each give m dollars, a total of x•m dollars are available to purchase gifts. Since they have to buy r identical gifts for the retirees, each retiree will get a gift of xm/r dollars in value.

Alternate Solution

Use dimensional analysis. The desired expression must be in the units of dollars per retiree. Thus, m dollars/~~employee~~ • x ~~employees~~ / r retirees = mx/r dollars per retiree.

Alternate Solution II

Cost per gift = total cost / r retirees. The answer must be proportional to 1/r. Only (B) fits.

Answer B

The Take-Away

Splitting costs, or cost per person, is a fairly common theme in real-world word problems on the SAT. These problems are sometimes best approached using dimensional analysis. But again and often, shortcuts may be ready to pluck, as shown in alternate solution II.

Chapter 17   Science, Engineering, and Real World Problems

Changing Cost Per Person With More People

e employees of a company agree to equally share the fixed expense of d dollars to host a party for a fellow employee who's leaving. If a additional employees decide to attend and share that expense, how much less will each of the original e employees have to spend?

(A) $\dfrac{d}{e} - \dfrac{a}{d}$

(B) $\dfrac{d}{(e+a)}$

(C) $\dfrac{2d}{(e+a)}$

(D) $\dfrac{da}{e(e+a)}$

How do I start?

Note that this problem is asking how much *less* each of the original e employees has to spend. So, we need to obtain expressions for (1) the original expense per employee and (2) the final expense per employee after a addition employees contribute to the total fixed cost of d dollars.

Solution

The original expense per employee was d dollars/(e employees) = d/e. When a additional employees decide to share the expense, the new expense per employee will be d/(e+a). Therefore, the difference in expense per employee = d/e - d/(e+a). This isn't one of the choices. But we can simplify this expression by forming a common denominator. After cross-multiplying denominators, this equals (d(e+a) - de) /[e(e+a)] = da/[e(e+a)].

Answer D

The Take-Away

When the number of persons sharing a fixed cost changes, the cost per person changes. A problem may ask for the new value or formula representing the cost per person, or, as in this case, the change in the cost per person. The wording is easy to mistake and is one reason why this moderately easy type of problem is frequently blown on the SAT.

Science, Engineering, and Real World Problems

Translating Limits into Absolute Value Expressions

A company makes a small, motorized model airplane kit for customers to assemble. The kit comes with main spars that are 8 inches long. Spars that are longer than $8\frac{1}{32}$ inches or shorter than $7\frac{31}{32}$ inches are unusable and must be discarded. If L is the length of a spar, which expression below represents the allowable spar lengths?

(A) $8\frac{1}{32} < L < 7\frac{31}{32}$

(B) $L < 7\frac{31}{32}$ and $L > 8\frac{1}{32}$

(C) $|L-8| < \frac{1}{32}$

(D) $|L-8| \leq \frac{1}{32}$

How do I start?

Apart with manipulating inequalities, this is foremost a reading comprehension question. Read carefully! Express the range of allowable spar lengths as simple inequalities. Re-express this range using absolute values, if necessary, to match one of the choices.

Solution

The *allowable* range may be expressed as (1) $L \leq 8\frac{1}{32}$ and $L \geq 7\frac{31}{32}$. These may be combined as: (2) $7\frac{31}{32} \leq L \leq 8\frac{1}{32}$. (1) and (2) are neither (A) nor (B) (which are actually the same). (A) and (B) express the lengths *outside* the allowable range of L. Toss (A) and (B). Rearrange the allowable range (2) by subtracting 8 from all sides: $-\frac{1}{32} \leq L-8 \leq \frac{1}{32}$. This is not among the choices either, but it is equivalent to the expression $|L-8| \leq \frac{1}{32}$ in (D).

Answer D

The Take-Away

In this problem, it is necessary to see the equivalence between the inequalities $7\frac{31}{32} \leq L \leq 8\frac{1}{32}$, $-\frac{1}{32} \leq L-8 \leq \frac{1}{32}$, and $|L-8| \leq \frac{1}{32}$. And to carefully distinguish < from ≤.

Chapter 17 Science, Engineering, and Real World Problems

Duration of Travel, Given Change of Time Zones

When it is 8 AM pacific standard time (PST) in LA, it is 11 a.m. eastern standard time (EST) in Boston and New York City. A plane took off from Boston at noon EST and later arrived non-stop in Los Angeles (LA) at 4 p.m. (PST). If a second plane left LA at noon (PST) and took exactly the same amount of time as the Boston-LA trip, what was the plane's arrival time (EST) in New York City (NYC)?

(A) 4
(B) 7
(C) 8
(D) 10

How do I start?

Note that Boston and New York are both in the (EST) time zone. First, calculate the duration of the Boston-LA flight, taking into account the time zone difference. That would also be the same duration of the LA to New York City (NYC) flight. Don't forget the time zone difference when calculating the arrival time for that flight.

Solution

The first sentence of the question tells us that there is a 3 hour difference between (EST) and (PST). When the plane leaves Boston at noon (EST), it is 12 - 3 = 9 a.m. (PST) in LA. The plane arrives in LA at 4 p.m (PST). The duration of the flight is thus 3 hours (9am EST to noon EST) plus 4 hours (noon EST to 4pm EST), or 7 hours. The second plane leaves LA at noon (PST), which is 3 p.m. (EST), and also has a flight duration of 7 hours. Thus, the second plane arrives in NYC at 3pm (EST) + 7 hours = 10 p.m. (EST).

Answer D

The Take-Away

Time zone problems are only difficult because several steps may be required to account for durations and time zone differences. Bridging a.m. and p.m. must be done with care. Pull the problem apart and apply the given information methodically. They tried to make this problem more confusing: one flight went from Boston to LA, while the other went from LA to NYC. This change is immaterial. The pertinent information is that the flight times and the time zones were the same for both flights.

Science, Engineering, and Real World Problems   Chapter 17

Exponential Behavior

It takes 3 hours for all of the active ingredients in a pill to enter the blood. After one additional hour the liver begins to filter out these ingredients by halving their concentration in the blood every 4 hours. 24 hours after swallowing the pill, what fraction of the active ingredient is still in the blood?

(A) $\dfrac{1}{64}$

(B) $\dfrac{1}{32}$

(C) $\left(\dfrac{1}{2}\right)^{\frac{21}{4}}$

(D) $\dfrac{1}{12}$

How do I start?

The active ingredients are halved every 4 hours by the liver, so every four hours the concentration is multiplied by 1/2. However, note that the liver does not begin filtering until 3 + 1 = 4 hours after the pill was ingested.

Solution

All of the active ingredients finally entered the bloodstream 3 hours after it was swallowed. But it takes one additional hour before the liver starts filtering them out. The liver begins filtering the drug 3 + 1 = 4 hours after the pill is ingested. Therefore, 24 hours after ingestion, the liver would have only been filtering for 20 hours. There are 5 4-hour periods in this 20-hour interval, and thus there would be 5 reductions by one half in this interval. There would be $(1/2)^5$ = 1/32 of the active ingredient remaining in the blood.

Answer B

The Take-Away

This is a word problem that implicitly models the reduction in drug concentration in the blood as an exponential function: "halves." Where most good students fail here is not correctly taking into account the 3 + 1 hour unfiltered interval.

Chapter 17　　　　　　　　　　Science, Engineering, and Real World Problems

The Leaky Fluid Pump

A truck has a fuel tank with a capacity of x gallons. Normally, the truck can drive m miles on y gallons of fuel. However, the fuel line between the tank and the engine has developed a leak that results in only a fraction, z, of every gallon pumped out of the tank getting to the engine, thus reducing the truck's driving distance. If the tank is half-filled, how many miles can the truck drive in terms of x, y, z, and m?

(A) $\dfrac{ym}{2zx}$

(B) $\dfrac{2ym}{zx}$

(C) $\dfrac{mzx}{2y}$

(D) $\dfrac{2mzx}{y}$

How do I start?

Dimensional analysis will really help you keep a correct account of the various factors. Since the fuel line leaks, for each gallon of fuel in the tank, only a fraction of a gallon, z, gets to the engine. First, calculate the total gallons of fuel available to the engine.

Solution

If the truck is half filled, there are x/2 gallons in the tank, so only a fraction, zx/2 gallons, gets to the engine. The mileage of the truck is (m miles)/(y gallons to the engine). If we multiply this by the corrected number of gallons *to the engine*, zx/2, we'll have the miles the truck can drive. The number of miles the truck can go if zx/2 gallons get to the engine is: (m miles)/(y ~~gallons to the engine~~) • (zx/2 ~~gallons to the eng~~ine) = mzx/2y miles.

Alternate Solution

The number of miles *must* be proportional to x/2, the number of gallons in the tank (even though it leaks). Only (C) is proportional to x/2. How many of you saw this?

Answer C

The Take-Away

The main rate, miles/gallon, is modified because only a fraction of the tank's fuel gets to the engine. However, the ratio still holds as long as you keep clear just what "per gallon" means: per gallon to the engine (after any leaking). Don't miss the alternate shortcut.

Notes

Chapter 17　　　　　　　　　　Science, Engineering, and Real World Problems

Practice Problems

1. The cost of buying one case of imported olive oil is d dollars. A second case may be purchased at a cost of x dollars less than the first case, and additional cases may be purchased at a cost of y dollars less than the second case. Which of the following represents the customer's cost, in dollars, to purchase c cases?

   (A) dc - x(1-c) - y(2-c)
   (B) dc - x(1-c) + y(2-c)
   (C) dc + x(1-c) + y(2-c)
   (D) d(c-2) - x(1-c) + y(2-c)

2. The owner of a startup company, Aiza!, needs 3 pieces of ribbon, each 2 feet long, to wrap each present she intends to give to each of her employees at the company holiday party. She took two new 200 ft. rolls of ribbon out of the supply cabinet. She uses as much of the first roll as possible and only uses the second roll if necessary. Without wasting any ribbon, which of the following expressions is the total number of feet of ribbon left on the <u>partially</u> used roll after she wraps x presents?

   (A) if x<34 : 200 - 6x; if x>33: 200 - 6x

   (B) 200 - 6x

   (C) if x<34 : 200 - 6x; if x>33: 202 - 6(x-33)

   (D) 400 - 24x + 4

3. Ann, a professional wildlife photographer, lives far from town. The printing company she uses is 20 miles from her house. It allows customers to upload image files to its server for subsequent printing, but charges 5 cents per megabyte of data for this service. Including gas, oil, insurance, car payments, etc., it costs Ann 50 cents per mile to drive. What size data, in megabytes, will result in an uploading charge equal to the cost of driving back and forth to the printer?

   SR

4. The ski team has t members and plans to go to an out-of-town competition where the fixed cost of the trip to the team is d dollars. The team members share the cost of the trip equally. However, f team members later decide not to go, thus making the trip more expensive for the members who will go. Which expression below is the extra cost that must be borne by each team member that goes on the trip?

(A) $\dfrac{d}{(t-f)}$

(B) $\dfrac{d}{t}$

(C) $\dfrac{df}{(t-f)}$

(D) $\dfrac{df}{t(t-f)}$

5. A football team must purchase jerseys to sell in a fundraiser. Each jersey costs the team x dollars, and they are then sold for 3x dollars each. How many jerseys must they sell to raise $15,000?

(A) 5000x
(B) 7500x
(C) 15000/(x-2)
(D) $\dfrac{7500}{x}$

6. The football team has a + 2c players and the basketball team has b + 4c players. If 3c players are members of both teams, which expression below, in terms of a, b, and c is the number of players that are on one team but not both?

(A) b + c - a
(B) a + b
(C) a + b + 3c
(D) 2a + b + c

7. It takes 3 hours for all of the active ingredients in a pill to enter the blood. After another hour the liver begins to filter it out by halving the concentration in the blood every 4 hours. How many hours after swallowing the pill does it take the liver to reduce the concentration of ingredients to 1/16 of their original concentration?

(A) 6
(B) $6^{4/3}$
(C) 16
(D) 20

Practice Problem Hints

1. The cost of c cases is the cost of the first two cases plus the cost of the next c-2 cases. Collect common d, x, and y terms (because the answer choices are expressed in these terms).

2. Calculate the number of presents the first roll can wrap. Use any left-over ribbon on the first roll to wrap more presents if necessary.

3. Calculate the cost of driving back and forth first.

4. The original cost per member was d/t. Note: the problem asks what the *extra* cost is, not the total cost.

5. The profit on each jersey is 2x dollars. Use dimensional analysis to multiply the terms to get the answer in units of dollars.

6. First, calculate the total number of players. This is a "don't over-count" problem. Use a Venn diagram if necessary.

7. How many 4 hour periods will reduce the ingredient by a factor of 1/16? Don't forget the initial 4 hour period during which no filtering takes place.

Chapter 17　　　　　　　　　　　　Science, Engineering, and Real World Problems

Practice Problem Solutions

1. Answer C

The cost of c cases is the cost of the first two cases plus the cost of the next c-2 cases. The cost of the first case is d dollars. The cost of the second case is d-x dollars. The cost of each of the c-2 subsequent cases is d-x-y dollars. The total cost is therefore d + (d-x) + (c-2)(d-x-y). Collecting d, x, and y terms, this expression is the same as the expression d(1+1+c-2) - x(1+c-2) - y(c-2) = dc +x(1-c) +y(2-c).

Alternate Solution: The 2nd and 3rd terms in (A) are positive. Yet because of the discount, the cost must be less than dc. So you can toss choice (A) if you're guessing.

2. Answer C

Each present uses a total of 6 ft. of ribbon. If she wraps x presents, it will take 6•x ft. of ribbon. Wrapping 1 present will leave 200 - 6 ft. on the first roll. Wrapping two presents will leave 200 - 12 ft., etc. She can wrap 200/6 = 33 1/3 presents with the first roll, or 33 presents with 1/3 • 6 = 2 feet left over. I.e., there will be one 2 ft. ribbon left over on the first roll after wrapping 33 presents. Good! She can use that 2 ft. of ribbon on the 34th present if there is one. Thus, (1) with x representing a range of 1 to 33 presents, there will be 200 - 6x ft. left over. If she wraps more than 33 presents, she has to use the second roll (and the 2 unused feet left over from the first roll). There will be 200 - 6 + 2 feet left on the second roll after 34 presents (using the 2 feet left over from the first roll). There will be 200 - 6•2 + 2 left after 35 presents, and in general, (2) if x is >33, there will be 202 - 6 • (x-33) feet left over on the second roll. Choice (C) correctly describes the number of feet left over as a function of x, the number of presents.

3. Answer 400

The roundtrip is 40 miles. The cost to drive back and forth is $.5 x 40 miles = $20. How many megabytes uploaded will $20 buy? $20 = $.05/1megabyte • n megabytes. Solving for n, n = 20/.05 = 400 megabytes. Some students are too fast and use 20 miles instead of 40 miles in their cost analysis.

4. Answer D

The original cost per member was d/t. When f members can't go, the cost per person increases to d/(t-f). The difference between these two costs is d/(t-f) - d/t. Expressed with a common denominator, the extra cost is (dt - dt + df)/(t(t-f)) = df/(t(t-f)).

5. Answer D

The total to be raised equals 15,000 dollars. The profit on each jersey equals 3x - x = 2x dollars per jersey. Let J = number jerseys they need to sell. Dimensional analysis: 15,000 dollars = 2x dollars/jersey • J jerseys. Thus, 15,000 = 2xJ, so J = 15,000/2x, or J = 7500/x.

Alternate Solution: The profit per jersey is $2x. The larger x is, the fewer jerseys must be sold to get $15,000. The number of jerseys should be inversely proportional to x. Only choice (D) displays a function with this behavior.

6. Answer B

The total number of football members is a + 2c. The number of basketball members is b + 4c. To calculate the total number of players, take the sum of the above, a + b + 6c, and subtract the 3c members who belong to both teams, *to avoid counting those twice*. Thus, there are a total of a + b + 6c - 3c = a + b + 3c players. However, we need to calculate the number of players not playing both sports. Hence, we have to once more subtract the 3c players who play both: the number of players that are on one team but not both equals a + b + 3c - 3c = a + b.

Alternate Solution: A Venn diagram can be used to analyze the situation

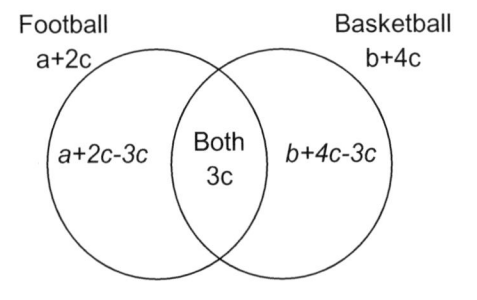

```
      Football              Basketball
      a+2c                  b+4c
         _____
        /      \   /      \
       /        \ /        \
      | a+2c-3c | Both | b+4c-3c |
       \        / \        /
        _____/   _____/
                 3c
```

Given the initial data and using the diagram, it's easy to see that the players who play football-only number a+2c-3c, and the players who play basketball-only number b+4c-3c. Thus, the players who only play one sport = (a+2c-3c) + (b+4c-3c) = a + b.

7. **Answer D**

The liver does not begin filtering until after an initial 3+1 = 4 hours. *Thereafter*, each 4 hour period reduces the amount by a factor of 1/2. If x is the number of 4 hour periods after the initial 4 hours, the concentration will be $(1/2)^x$ of the original concentration. We need to solve for x in the equation $1/16 = (1/2)^x$. This is head-math: x must be 4. There are 4 4-hour periods = 16 hours of filtering. Including the 4-hour initial delay before the liver begins filtering, it will take 4 + 16 = 20 hours for the liver to reduce the ingredients by a factor of 1/16.

Notes

WORKSPACE

Notes

Notes

Notes

Notes

Notes

Notes

Notes

Notes

Notes

Notes